East African Expressions
of Christianity

Edited by
THOMAS SPEAR
&
ISARIA N. KIMAMBO

James Currey
OXFORD

Mkuki na Nyota
DAR ES SALAAM

EAEP
NAIROBI

Ohio University Press
ATHENS

James Currey Ltd
73 Botley Road
Oxford
OX2 0BS

Mkuki na Nyota
PO Box 4205, Dar es Salaam

East African Educational Publishers
Kijabe Street, PO Box 45314
Nairobi, Kenya

Ohio University Press
Scott Quadrangle
Athens, Ohio 45701, USA

1 2 3 4 5 03 02 01 00 99

British Library Cataloguing in Publication Data
East African expressions of Christianity. - (East African
    studies)
    1. Christianity - Africa, East   2. Church history - 19th
    century   3. Church history - 20th century   4. Africa, East -
    Church history
    I. Spear, Thomas   II. Kimambo, Isaria N. (Isaria Ndelahiyosa)
    276.7'6'08
        ISBN 0-85255-757-4 (James Currey Cloth)
        ISBN 0-85255-758-2 (James Currey Paper)

**Library of Congress Cataloging-in-Publication Data is
available from the Library of Congress**

    ISBN 0-8214-1273-6 (Ohio University Press Cloth)
    ISBN 0-8214-1274-4 (Ohio University Press Paper)

Typeset in 10/11pt Baskerville
by Long House Publishing Services, Cumbria, UK
Printed in Great Britain
by Villiers Publications, London N3

East African Expressions
of Christianity

Eastern African Studies

Revealing Prophets
Prophecy in Eastern
African History
Edited by DAVID M.
ANDERSON & DOUGLAS H.
JOHNSON

Religion & Politics in East Africa
The Period Since
Independence
Edited by HOLGER BERNT
HANSEN & MICHAEL
TWADDLE

Swahili Origins
Swahili Culture & the
Shungwaya Phenomenon
JAMES DE VERE ALLEN

Being Maasai
Ethnicity & Identity in
East Africa
Edited by THOMAS SPEAR
& RICHARD WALLER

*A History of Modern Ethiopia
1855–1974*
BAHRU ZEWDE

*Ethnicity & Conflict
in the Horn of Africa*
Edited by KATSUYOSHI
FUKUI & JOHN MARKAKIS

*Conflict, Age & Power
in North East Africa*
Age Systems in Transition
Edited by EISEI KURIMOTO
& SIMON SIMONSE

Jua Kali Kenya
Change & Development
in an Informal Economy
1970–95
KENNETH KING

*Control & Crisis in
Colonial Kenya*
The Dialectic of Domination
BRUCE BERMAN

Unhappy Valley
Book One: State & Class
Book Two: Violence &
Ethnicity
BRUCE BERMAN
& JOHN LONSDALE

Mau Mau from Below
GREET KERSHAW

*The Mau Mau War in
Perspective*
FRANK FUREDI

*Squatters & the Roots
of Mau Mau 1905–63*
TABITHA KANOGO

*Economic & Social Origins
of Mau Mau 1945–53*
DAVID W. THROUP

Multi-Party Politics in Kenya
The Kenyatta & Moi
States & the Triumph of
the System in the 1992
Election
DAVID W. THROUP
& CHARLES HORNSBY

*Decolonization & Independence
in Kenya 1940–93*
Edited by B.A. OGOT
& WILLIAM R. OCHIENG'

*Penetration & Protest in
Tanzania*
The Impact of the World
Economy on the Pare
1860–1960
ISARIA N. KIMAMBO

Custodians of the Land
Ecology & Culture
in the History of Tanzania
Edited by GREGORY
MADDOX, JAMES L. GIBLIN
& ISARIA N. KIMAMBO

*Education in the Development
of Tanzania 1919–1990*
LENE BUCHERT

*The Second Economy
in Tanzania*
T.L. MALIYAMKONO
& M.S.D. BAGACHWA

*Ecology Control &
Economic Development in
East African History*
The Case of Tanganyika
1850–1950
HELGE KJEKSHUS

Siaya
The Historical
Anthropology of an
African Landscape
DAVID WILLIAM COHEN
& E.S. ATIENO ODHIAMBO

*Uganda Now
Changing Uganda
Developing Uganda
From Chaos to Order*
Edited by HOLGER BERNT
HANSEN & MICHAEL
TWADDLE

*Kakungulu & the Creation
of Uganda 1868–1928*
MICHAEL TWADDLE

Controlling Anger
The Anthropology of Gisu
Violence
SUZETTE HEALD

Kampala Women Getting By
Wellbeing in the
Time of AIDS
SANDRA WALLMAN

*Slaves, Spices & Ivory
in Zanzibar*
Integration of an East
African Commercial
Empire into the
World Economy
ABDUL SHERIFF

Zanzibar Under Colonial Rule
Edited by ABDUL SHERIFF
& ED FERGUSON

*The History and Conservation of
Zanzibar Stone Town*
Edited by ABDUL SHERIFF

*East African Expressions
of Christianity*
Edited by THOMAS SPEAR
& ISARIA N. KIMAMBO

*The Poor Are Not Us**
Edited by DAVID M.
ANDERSON
& VIGDIS BROCH-DUE

* forthcoming

Contents

Contents

Maps, Photographs & Tables

Contributors

Christopher Comoro is Senior Lecturer and Chair of the Department of Sociology and Anthropology at the University of Dar es Salaam. Dr Comoro received his PhD from Carleton University in Ottawa, Canada. He is principal researcher in the Kagera Aids Research Project of the Swedish Agency for Research Cooperation (SAREC) and has written extensively on topics related to medical anthropology. He also acts as consultant to the Open University of Tanzania for religious studies.

James Giblin is Associate Professor of History and African-American Studies at the University of Iowa. He received his PhD in History from the University of Wisconsin. Dr Giblin has written extensively on environmental history and epidemiology (most notably, *The Politics of Environmental Control in Northeastern Tanzania*) and edited *Custodians of the Land* with Gregory Maddox and Isaria N. Kimambo. He is currently working on a history of Njombe District in southern Tanzania since the 1940s.

Francis Kimani Githieya teaches religious studies at St Leo's College, Atlanta, Georgia. A Presbyterian pastor, he received his PhD in religion from Emory University and is the author of *The Freedom of the Spirit: African Indigenous Churches in Kenya*.

Ronald Kassimir is the Programme Director for Africa at the Social Science Research Council. Before joining the SSRC, Kassimir was the Assistant Director of the Institute of African Studies at Columbia University, where he also taught African politics. He holds a PhD in Political Science from the University of Chicago, and conducted field research in Uganda from 1989–91.

Isaria N. Kimambo is Professor of History at the University of Dar es Salaam, having served previously as Chief Academic Officer. He received his PhD in history from Northwestern University and is the author of *A Political History of the Pare of Tanzania, Mbiru: Popular Protest in Colonial Tanzania,* and *Penetration and Protest in Tanzania* as well as the editor of *A History of Tanzania* (with A. J. Temu), *The Historical Study of African Religion* (with T. O. Ranger), and *Custodians of the Land* (with Gregory Maddox and James Giblin).

Anza A. Lema received a PhD in history at the University of Dar es Salaam in 1973 and a DSc in Educational Theories and Practices from the University of Geneva in 1979. He has served as Director of the Institute of Education at the University of Dar es Salaam; Associate General Secretary of the Lutheran World Federation in Geneva, Switzerland; Director of the Christian Social Services Commission, Dar es Salaam; and Coordinating Secretary of the Tumaini University Planning Office of the Evangelical Lutheran Church in Tanzania.

Gregory H. Maddox received his PhD in history from Northwestern University. He is the author of several articles on the history of central Tanzania and the editor of *The Gogo: History, Customs, and Traditions* by Mathais E. Mnyampala and *Custodians of the Land* (with James Giblin and Isaria N. Kimambo). He has taught at the University of Dar es Salaam and is currently Associate Professor of History at Texas Southern University.

Josiah R. Mlahagwa is Associate Professor in history at the University of Dar es Salaam. A southern Africanist who received his PhD from the University of Dar es Salaam, he has written on southern African history and colonial economy. He is also a leading member of the fellowship movement in Dar es Salaam.

C. K. Omari is a Lutheran pastor and Professor of Sociology at the University of Dar es Salaam. He received his theological training at Makumira, the Lutheran School of Theology, and Union Seminary, and his academic training at the University of East Africa. His numerous books and articles on theology, African religion, church and society, development, and the family include *Strategy for Rural Development, Essays on Church and Society in Tanzania* (ed.), *Youth and Development* (ed.), *Social Problems in East Africa* (ed.), *God and Worship among the Pare,* and *The Church in Africa.*

David Sandgren is Professor of History at Concordia College in Minnesota. He received his PhD in history from the University of Wisconsin; has conducted extensive field work in Kenya on local religious and social history; and is the author of *Christianity and the Kikuyu.* He is currently working on a collective biography of Kenyan high school students from the 1960s.

Contributors

John Sivalon is a sociologist and Maryknoll priest educated at the Maryknoll School of Theology, the University of Dar es Salaam, and the University of St Michael's College, Toronto. A lecturer in sociology at the University of Dar es Salaam, he has conducted research and written on the church and education, *Ujamaa*, economic crisis, social services, and political change.

Kathleen R. Smythe is Assistant Professor of History at Xavier University in Ohio. She has done research on women and church membership in western Kenya and most recently on childhood in southwestern Tanzania. Her dissertation, 'Fipa Childhood: White Fathers' Missionaries and Social Change in Nkansi District, 1910–1980', was completed at the University of Wisconsin in 1997.

Thomas Spear is Professor of History at the University of Wisconsin, where he received his PhD and directs the African Studies Program. The author of histories on *Zwangendaba's Ngoni*, the Mijikenda (*The Kaya Complex*), eastern Kenya (*Kenya's Past*), *The Swahili* (with Derek Nurse), and most recently, Arusha and Meru (*Mountain Farmers*), he is also the editor (with Richard Waller) of *Being Maasai* and of the *Journal of African History*.

Richard Waller is Associate Professor of History and International Relations at Bucknell University in Pennsylvania. He received his PhD from Cambridge University and has taught at Chancellor College, Malawi, the University of North Carolina-Chapel Hill, and the University of Virginia. He has published extensively on Maasai history, ecology, and socio-economic relations in the nineteenth and twentieth centuries, and is the editor (with Thomas Spear) of *Being Maasai*.

Ernest Wamba-dia-Wamba is Associate Professor of History at the University of Dar es Salaam. He studied philosophy, economics and the history of ideas at Brandeis University. A member of the Executive Committee of the Council for the Development of Social Sciences in Africa (CODESRIA), he formerly served as CODESRIA's president and coordinated its research on social movements and democracy in Africa. He has conducted research and published numerous articles on African philosophy, historiography, the history of capitalism, and the history of Central Africa and the Great Lakes as well as editing (with Mahmood Mamdani) *African Social Movements and Democracy*.

Acknowledgements

The articles published here are the results of a collaborative research project conducted by the University of Wisconsin-Madison and the University of Dar es Salaam. Bringing together academic and church scholars, Africans and Americans, our discussions ranged widely as we struggled to understand African expressions of Christianity during a century in which a host of individuals interpreted the faith and appropriated it for themselves. Our discussions were exciting, and we trust some of that excitement is conveyed in the articles published here.

Our research, the workshops in Dar es Salaam and Madison, and publication in Tanzania were made possible by a generous grant from the Ford Foundation for strengthening African studies through promoting collaborative research projects between American and African scholars. Administrative support at Wisconsin was provided by James Delehanty and Robert Houle of the African Studies Program, while Kathleen Smythe contributed valuable editorial assistance.

In addition to the authors published here, others who contributed to the workshops and to the ideas developed here included the following:

Dorothy Hodgson, 'Engendered encounters: men of the Church and the "Church of Women" in Maasailand, Tanzania, 1950–93';

Sharon Hutchinson, 'The Nuer "Crocodile Man": resisting the state through prophecy in the Southern Sudan';

Paul Landau, 'Other worlds: the spirit in Southern Africa';

Anne Lewinson, 'Translating models of Christian marriage and commitment in Dar es Salaam';

Timothy Longman, 'Christian churches and the organization of political life in Rwanda';

Bishop Zakayo Majige, 'Understanding Sukuma society in relation to Christianity';

Michael Schatzberg, 'Seeking the political kingdom in Kenya';

Jan Vansina, 'Notes on Catholicism in Kongo and Angola, 1484–c. 1867'.

Our special thanks to all the participants, who made this such an exciting and rewarding endeavour, and to Kevin Ward for his perceptive and productive comments on the manuscript.

Thomas Spear
Isaria N. Kimambo

I am a free man and own no master; but I have made myself every man's servant, to win over as many as possible. To Jews I became like a Jew, to win Jews; as they are subject to the Law of Moses. I put myself under that law to win them although I am not myself subject to it. To win Gentiles, who are outside the Law, I made myself like one of them, although I am not in truth outside God's law, being under the law of Christ. To the weak I became weak, to win the weak. Indeed, I have become everything in turn to men of every sort, so that in one way or another I may save some.

I Corinthians 9:19–22

For God has no favourites: those who have sinned outside the pale of the law of Moses will perish outside its pale, and all who have sinned under that law will be judged by the law. It is not by hearing the law, but by doing it, that men will be justified before God. When Gentiles who do not possess the law carry out its precepts by the light of nature, then, although they have no law, they are their own law, for they display the effect of the law inscribed on their hearts. Their conscience is called as witness, and their own thoughts argue the case on either side, against them or even for them, on the day when God judges the secrets of human hearts through Christ Jesus.

Romans 2:11–15

Circumcision has value, provided you keep the law; but if you break the law, then your circumcision is as if it had never been. Equally, if an uncircumcised man keeps the precepts of the law, will he not count as circumcised? He may be uncircumcised in his natural state, but by fulfilling the law he will pass judgement on you who break it, for all your written code and your circumcision. The true Jew is not he who is such in externals, neither is the true circumcision the external mark in the flesh. The true Jew is he who is such inwardly, and the true circumcision is of the heart, directed not by written precepts but by the Spirit; such a man receives his commendation not from men but from God.

Romans 2:25–29

I

Introduction

The topic of African Christianity is a complex one, and the literature on it is enormous. The two opening chapters provide an introduction to the topic, focusing on the ways in which Africans have interpreted Christianity for themselves and appropriated it within the context of their own experiences and beliefs. Spear's essay first discusses the development of African Christianity as a series of linked processes, from those involving the mission enterprise itself through those relating to Africans' conversion to Christianity and the critical role played by African catechists, evangelists and translators in interpreting the new faith and conveying it to others. He then considers the struggles between missionaries and their converts that resulted from these interpretations and the missionaries' continued control over the Church; the emergence of African prophetic and healing movements drawing on both African and Christian traditions; and the widespread phenomenon of revival as Africans seized control of their own spiritual destiny. Each of these processes is exceedingly complex, and many of his suggested approaches are discussed at greater length in the case studies that follow.

Spear then surveys the historiography of Christianity in East Africa, focusing on several case studies to illustrate the processes identified previously. In the well-known case of Buganda, early Christian 'readers' effected a wide-ranging 'Christian Revolution' that not only transformed Ganda politics but also resulted in the development of a vibrant 'indigenous missionary movement', ongoing struggles between missionaries and converts, the rise of local prophetic and healing movements, and a wide-ranging series of revivals that spread throughout eastern Africa. Similarly, Haya men and women in western Tanzania initially evangelized by Ganda creatively reinterpreted Christian beliefs and mission institutions to reflect their own religious concerns and social needs.

A different history developed in central Kenya, where initially the first

1

generation of Kikuyu converts were alienated from their own societies, but then gradually reintegrated themselves to become leaders in the drives for cultural, religious, and political autonomy from oppressive white control, creating in the process their own schools, a diverse array of churches, and new political parties. Among the new Kikuyu churches were the charismatic Arathi, or Spirit Churches, similar to the Holy Spirit movement that emerged in western Kenya among Christians influenced by the earlier indigenous spread of Christianity from Buganda. Under the guidance of charismatic prophets, the movement simultaneously fused and transformed Luo, Luyia and Christian beliefs in a culmination of almost a century of Christian history in the area.

Most of the movements detailed by Spear were popular movements, initiated by individual Christians and communities as they struggled to incorporate Christian teachings in their own lives. Such struggles, and the movements they gave rise to, did not escape the attention of mission and African priests and pastors, however, as they also sought to disentangle Christianity from its Western trappings and reinterpret Christian theology in the context of African cultures, beliefs and historical experiences.

This 'search for the universal' is the subject of Maddox's chapter on the development of African theology, as African theologians simultaneously criticized the Western cultural particulars incorporated in mission Christianity while calling for 'adaptation' to or 'inculturation' with African cultures and conditions. Those advocating inculturation, then, call for the radical restructuring of the message to address local contexts. An alternative view, however, argues that Christianity, as universal, is already 'incarnate' in African societies, and thus has little need for further adaptation. While the debate continues within both the Protestant and Catholic churches, however, Maddox notes an unanticipated side effect of the African critique of Christianity in the marked ecumenism within African Christianity, as African theologians pay less regard to the European denominationalism and more to the search for the universal within African Christianity as a whole.

One

Toward the History of
African Christianity

THOMAS SPEAR

It has become commonplace to think of the Christian churches in Africa as alien institutions, the cultural agents of colonial and capitalist powers who helped subdue Africans to European domination. Christian missionaries brought, and enforced, specifically European cultural norms of religious, social, moral and economic behaviour and sought to mould African individuals and societies to them. Similarly, African conversion to Christianity has been seen largely in materialistic and instrumental terms as individuals sought to gain political allies, land, education, medicine and jobs in the new colonial order through the missions.

Such views neglect the manifold ways Africans interpreted and appropriated Christian scriptures, practices and institutions for their own purposes within the contexts of their own values and needs. Confronted with new epidemic diseases, natural disasters and widespread political and economic destruction in the wake of colonial conquest, Africans sought new religious concepts to regain moral control over their lives. Later, they would employ Christian ideas of equality to assert their rights to religious and political independence. And today Christian church leaders are among the leading critics of political corruption, while writers like Ngugi wa Thiong'o infuse their radical political critiques with Christian imagery and values.

The abundant literature on the dramatic spread of Christianity in Africa in the late nineteenth and twentieth centuries thus suffers from several critical absences concerning the religious experiences of African Christians, especially those within the historical churches.[1] While the literature is comparatively rich on the growth of missions and the subsequent development of independent African Christian churches, we have little information regarding the practices and beliefs of Africans generally. Social histories of mission and national churches are rare, ethnographies of African Christian religious practice virtually non-existent, biographies of early Christian converts and catechists exceptional, and analyses of African Christian beliefs

3

scarce. Yet Christianity may well be the most important single legacy of colonialism and, far from dying with it, has gone on to become one of the most dynamic social movements in Africa today.[2]

It is thus critical that we probe deeply into the experiences of African Christians themselves as they explored the new faith in all its complexity, interpreted it in their own cultural and historical contexts, and appropriated it as their own, forging in the process African churches distinctive from the European Christianity of the missionaries. This process has been explored most fully in the case of the independent Christian churches established by African church people and prophets as they sought to reinterpret Christianity within their own contexts. Yet, as Barrett notes perceptively, the independent churches represented only the tip of the iceberg of the development of African Christianity, leaving parallel developments within the historical churches and the emergence of African churches obscured below the waterline of schism and independence.[3] Our concern in the studies presented here is thus to explore more fully the experiences of African Christians and the emergence of African churches throughout East Africa from the earliest days of mission enterprise.

Perspectives

Such a task is a daunting one for wide-scale social and religious phenomena that transform people's lives and are themselves transformed in the process. We start with a descriptive model, a schematic map of the territory, intended to identify critical features in the development of African Christianity in order to provide a context for the individual studies that follow as well as to provoke further research and analysis.

The historical development of Christianity in Africa might be seen as involving six interrelated historical processes – mission, conversion, popular evangelism, struggles for control, charismatic prophecy and healing, and revival – each of which comprised a complex set of interrelated factors of its own.

Mission

The first general process was that of mission, in which European missionaries sought to convey the Christian message as they interpreted it to Africans they viewed as 'heathen'. The historical context was that of triumphant European power married to evangelical revival, and the overall goals were Livingstone's famous trio – Christianity, commerce and civilization – in which Africans were to be saved so as to become developed and civilized. Fuelled by nineteenth-century evangelical fervour and pietistic Christ-centred concerns, Protestant missionaries focused on gathering small flocks into Christian villages and preaching individual salvation, the confession of sin, the constant struggle between God's word and Satan's, and the coming end of the world. At the same time, Catholic missionaries

4

from predominantly rural and working-class backgrounds emphasized neo-scholastic theology, liturgical conformity, and Ultramontanist beliefs heavily influenced by such folk practices as the veneration of saints, Marian devotion and worship at healing shrines. Early Protestant concerns were thus largely individualistic and eschatological in their religious orientation, while Catholics were corporate and focused on developing their own institutionalized ritual community. While a few struggled to understand African beliefs and concerns, most paid them little heed except in so far as they were deemed antithetical to Christian ones as they interpreted them.[4]

The process of mission, however, was a complex phenomenon, involving a number of interrelated factors. The mission movement itself was not a monolithic one, containing within it a bewildering array of different denominations, sects and orders, each possessing its own theology, ritual practices and strategies for conversion. Each was also composed of different nationalities and ethnicities with their own attendant languages and cultural values. Thus British Anglicans vied with Scottish Presbyterians, American Baptists, and German, American and Scandinavian Lutherans, while French White Fathers competed with German Benedictines, French and American Holy Ghost Fathers, British Mill Hill Fathers, American Maryknolls and Irish Pallottines.[5] It was not purely in jest that many Africans viewed the missions as European 'tribalism', a view that bears reiterating in the light of a frequent tendency to essentialize Christianity, mission and the Church in the literature.

The roles of individual missions and missionaries also varied enormously depending on the colonial context and their relations with colonial authorities. The intensity of conquest and rule, together with Africans' calculations of their own self-interest and comparative strength, were important factors behind their receptivity to missionaries and the Christian message.[6] Similarly, missionaries' roles varied according to their relations with local people as influenced by their willingness to learn the local language, their degree of social and cultural tolerance, and their personal relations with individual Africans.[7]

The study of mission must thus take careful account of the historical specificity of each mission, including the beliefs, practices and strategies of the missionaries; their individual backgrounds and personalities; the colonial context in which they found themselves; their relations with the colonial authorities on one hand and local people on the other; their cultural and linguistic proficiency; and the length of time they spent in the field.[8]

Conversion

If Christianity was selectively transmitted by missionaries, it was also selectively received by Africans as they listened to the Christian message, interpreted it, and imbued it with meaning within the context of their own values and experience. Conversion was a classic dialectical process, involving the dynamic interaction between potential converts and missionaries, with their differing beliefs and practices. Whatever European missionaries intended, they could not dictate the terms of African acceptance, especially as African converts gained increasing access to vernacular Bibles and could make their own scriptural interpretations independent of those of the missionaries.[9]

Vernacular translations of the scriptures also inculturated the faith in indigenous cultural meanings, while problems of translation sometimes obscured the distinctiveness of the Christian message as missionaries sought to convey such unique Christian concepts as God, the Holy Spirit or the Virgin Mary through vernacular words for Creator, ancestral spirits or a circumcised woman, thus causing potential confusion and conflict.[10]

Translation was the operative concept, as missionaries sought to convey their own cultural values and religious beliefs in terms of the words, values and beliefs of others. Meanings shifted in unpredictable ways as different Christian theological concepts flowed across cultural and linguistic divides to acquire new meanings in the minds of African converts. Missionaries themselves often spoke local languages poorly or not at all, and thus were subject to translations made by local intermediaries or the audience themselves, while African catechists were usually fluent in the local language, but their understanding of Christian doctrine was filtered through their own interpretative processes.[11]

Nevertheless, conversion to Christianity also involved a fundamental reorientation of African religious beliefs and practices. While African religions tended to be this-worldly, unitary and instrumental, Christian beliefs were other-worldly, dualistic and expressive. If African worlds were 'enchanted', European ones were radically secular.[12] Each met different needs, leading many Africans to balance Christian concerns for individual salvation with African ones for health and moral regeneration in an attempt to close the epistemological gap between the two faiths, while others radically reinterpreted mission Christianity to focus more on Christ's healing ministry than on his ultimate sacrifice.

Potential converts differed widely in their status, gender and social identity, leading individuals to be drawn to a Christian faith by very different religious, social and political needs. For many the initial attractions were more socio-political and materialistic. Missions provided potential political alliances for ambitious young men, land for former slaves or those dispossessed by white settlers, education and jobs for young people seeking to take advantage of new economic opportunities, or places of refuge for women fleeing unwanted marriages. But for others the appeal was more spiritual, as missions also provided new religious powers to help people cope with disastrous new diseases, rising infertility rates or increasing social conflict.[13]

Conversion was thus a complex and protracted process of individual social *and* religious change involving a wide range of possible shifts in religious affiliation and conviction as 'converts' changed from 'traditional' to mixed beliefs, from nominal to fervent Christianity, from one denomination to another, from Christianity to Islam, or from a mission church to various forms of independency.[14]

Popular evangelism

The initial African Christians converted by European missionaries were few, often limited to those drawn to the mission stations, but they soon became an expanding corps of catechists, teachers and evangelists themselves, settling in villages, teaching school and forcefully preaching the Gospel in the vernacular to increasing numbers of their fellows.[15] Local evangelists travelled so widely, in fact, that in many areas of Uganda and western Kenya missionaries found local catechists and Christian homesteads already in place before they arrived.[16] In the course of this indigenous missionary movement, the Christian message shifted subtly from that of a profoundly nineteenth-century European Christianity to a twentieth-century African one, rooted in vernacular Bibles and the catechists' own cultural interpretations, thus sowing the seeds for the development of African churches to come.

The critical role of African catechists and evangelists has rarely been fully appreciated, but they were instrumental in translating the scriptures, interpreting the Christian message and conveying it to others. They were the first African interpreters of the Gospel and, without them, Christianity would not have spread as it did. From a small beleaguered band of poorly educated 'readers', they grew to a legion of teachers and preachers culling the countryside for converts, while European missionaries increasingly withdrew into specialized administration.[17] Far more successfully than their European colleagues, African evangelists understood the relevance of the Christian message to their own lives, and they could preach it forcefully to their friends as few Europeans could.

Struggles for control

As the number of catechists, outstations and converts proliferated, European missionaries feared the worst and sought to reassert their control through imposing new institutional rules of behaviour, belief, baptism, ordination and the direction of the church. Not surprisingly, those Africans actually responsible for building the local church (many of whom were excluded from baptism, communion or ordination by the new rules) chafed at this reassertion of European authority, giving rise in some areas to independent 'Ethiopian' churches under African leadership and in most to the development of semi-autonomous local churches increasingly distant from mission control, while adherence to mission churches fell precipitously.[18]

African churches emerged early in Tanzania following the deportation of German missionaries during the First World War. Placed under the nominal control of other missions, the 'orphaned' missions thrived so well under the de facto leadership of their own teachers and evangelists that, when the Germans returned after 1926, they found their followers less amenable to European direction than before. And, when the Germans were again deported during the Second World War, Africans reestablished their leadership and successfully maintained it until they were freed from formal mission control in the 1950s and 1960s.[19]

While other East African missions were more successful in maintaining overall control through the colonial period, missions everywhere were dependent on local catechists and teachers to run their local churches and schools, and the struggle for power – and its daily exercise by Africans within local churches – began everywhere long before Europeans relinquished final authority. We must thus pay close attention to the activities of local congregations if we are to understand the slow emergence of African churches from their European forebears decades before any formal declarations of religious independence.[20]

Charismatic prophecy and healing

African struggles for control extended to matters of doctrine as well, as African prophets, seized by the Holy Spirit, acquired charismatic gifts and established their own prayer groups and spirit movements. Such prophets built on the traditions of the Old Testament and Christ's ministry as much as on African prophetic traditions and quests for spiritual power to contest the European monopoly on God's word. While such prophets were frequently derided by missionaries as unorthodox and ultimately driven out of the mission churches, the compatibility of African and Christian prophetic traditions enabled African prophets to reclaim the prophetic essence of Christianity from the missionaries, indicating the degree to which Africans were successful in separating Christian messages from those of their European messengers and making them their own.[21]

African prophecy was nothing new.[22] But the messages of the Christian prophets were, and they require close study to establish the provenance, theology and practices of the African churches. The problem of evil had long concerned Africans. Evil was seen to reside in immoral witches and spirits that destroyed life. By attacking 'traditional' religion as the work of the Devil, however, missionaries inadvertently incorporated African doctrines of evil within Christianity, leading African Christians to adopt prayer and baptism by the Holy Spirit as means of combating witchcraft in general.[23]

Nor were the religious communities that the prophets established new, but they provided 'a place to feel at home' for people whose lives had suffered from the disruptions of colonialism.[24] As Hastings has noted: 'The quest for the Independent Church was the quest for a ritual, a belief, a realized community in and through which immediate human needs, social, psychological and physical could be appropriately met.'[25]

Revival and popular Catholicism

At the same time, spiritual movements such as the East African Revival (or Balokole) flourished within mission churches and transformed them from within. While such lay movements often accorded with the other-worldly pietism and evangelicalism of the missionaries themselves, they were initially opposed by European missionaries and African clergy alike as potentially divisive and as challenges to their own ecclesiastical and spiritual authority.[26] Subsequent history has proved differently, however, and today many Protestant church leaders are themselves members of the Revival or fellowship movement, while popular Catholic movements flourish within and outside the bounds of the Catholic Church. Little, however, has been written about such movements within the historical churches, and they are now expanding dramatically, together with evangelical crusades and Pentecostal movements, forcefully reminding us of the diversity and vibrancy of theology and practice within African Christianity.[27]

Historiography

The historiography of Christianity in East Africa has long focused on the initial spread of Christian missions in the late nineteenth and early twentieth centuries, on the role of the missions in 'cultural imperialism', and especially on the sociological and material factors – education, employment, land and cash crops – behind the dramatic expansion of Christianity during the colonial period.[28] By the 1960s, however, nationalism and increasing interest in African agency caused historical attention to shift to independent churches. No longer seen as unorthodox apostates, independent churches came to be seen as part of a dynamic and creative movement drawing on African religious concerns and practices to root Christianity firmly in African cultural soil.[29]

Most studies have thus focused on the processes of mission and charismatic prophecy and healing identified above. What has been missing, however, is careful study of the religious dynamism and agency involved in the intermediate processes of conversion, popular evangelism and the struggle for control, especially the critical roles played by African teachers, catechists and translators in the process of interpreting Christianity and appropriating it to African religious and social concerns. Earlier studies focused on instrumental reasons for conversion thus need to be expanded to explore the multiple social *and* religious meanings Christianity had for African converts in responding to the socio-political and moral crises of colonialism.[30] Focusing on processes of conversion, evangelism and the struggle for control raises crucial issues relating to the translation of religious meanings across cultural boundaries; the historical values, beliefs and practices in terms of which Africans interpreted and appropriated Christianity; the religious as well as social appeals of the new faith; and the vital roles of African catechists, evangelists, pastors and priests in the spread of Christianity and development of an African church.[31]

Recent studies of African Christianity have begun to focus on just these issues. In a sweeping reassessment of the development of Christianity historically, Lamin Sanneh argues that translatability and radical cultural pluralism – the ability of Christianity to transcend cultural boundaries – constitutes the essence of historical Christianity from the very beginning of the church, thus placing the development of African Christianity firmly within the history of Christianity as a whole.[32] Sanneh's focus on Paul's concept of radical cultural pluralism has also been at the centre of Catholic thinking since Vatican II stressed the principle of God's 'incarnation' in all cultures and the need for the church to become 'inculturated' in African culture.[33] Similarly, Richard Gray and Adrian Hastings stress the vital roles played by Africans and African culture in the transformation of mission Christianity to portray the development of African churches as indigenous movements of Christian renewal.[34]

A crucial shift in focus is thus occurring in the study of Christianity in Africa. Few, however, have taken up the critical sociological and theological issues involved if we are to define precisely how Africans interpreted the Christian message and appropriated it in terms of their own historical and cultural experiences. Studies of independent churches have come closest, perhaps because many were largely made by religious historians, but academic studies of the historical or mainstream churches have tended to assume rather mechanical models of conversion that focus on socio-political and economic factors rather than on religious belief and practice.

Toward a History of African Christianity in East Africa

Several provocative case studies point the way to the future. Processes of mission, conversion, popular evangelism, struggles for control, and revival have been explored in notable depth in the cases of Buganda, Kikuyu and Buhaya, while the process of charismatic prophecy and healing is notably developed in new studies of the Holy Spirit movement in western Kenya.[35] Few have begun to look at the situation today, however, but some indicators emerge from the increasing role of Christianity in politics and contemporary African thought.

The 'Christian Revolution' in Buganda

The rapid acceptance of Christianity in Buganda and its subsequent spread to neighbouring areas of Uganda and western Kenya provide a particularly well-known example of the wide range of socio-political, economic and religious factors accompanying the expansion of Christianity in East Africa. Early studies by Low, Wrigley and Rowe focused on the socio-political and economic issues as Kabaka Mutesa invited Muslim traders and later British Protestant and French Catholic missionaries to the court to bolster his waning power in the region. Pages in the highly competitive Ganda court were drawn by the secular benefits offered by the carriers of the new religions to become 'readers' with the Muslims, Protestants and Catholics

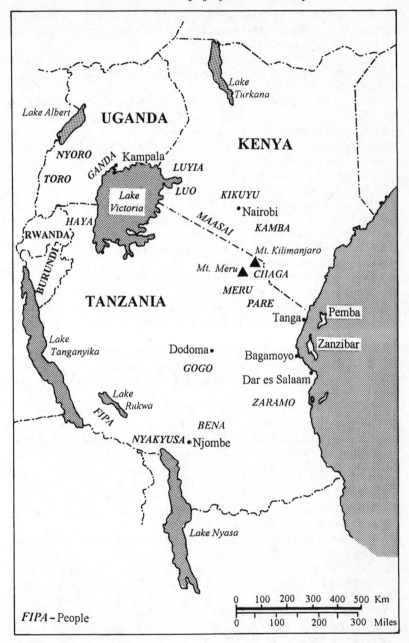

1.1 Eastern Africa

in turn, who were often identified in national, as opposed to religious, terms. As rising chiefs converted, so did their followers, and eventually the religious leaders and their chiefly allies constituted powerful political factions in the court, overthrowing Mutesa's successor, Mwanga, and entrenching themselves in power as a landed Christian aristocracy allied with the British colonial regime.[36]

In the view of these writers, the 'Christian Revolution' was a classical political revolution in a thoroughly secularized society led by a temporal monarch. As Brierley points out, however, such views neglected critical religious dimensions of the revolution, from the attempts by Mutesa to enlist the spiritual aid of the foreign religious to help stem a disastrous series of diseases and military defeats afflicting the kingdom (and his increasingly desperate appeals for spiritual help in combating his slow and painful death from gonorrhoea) to the moral collapse of the kingdom on his death and the successive martyrdoms of both Muslim and Christian converts.[37]

In the aftermath of the 'Christian Revolution', the African Anglican church, under the leadership of the Mengo Church Council, effectively became the established state church in all but the few districts set aside for Catholics and Muslims. That Ganda Protestants took their new faith seriously was attested by their enthusiastic evangelization of the surrounding areas as an 'indigenous missionary movement'. Energized by a local revival in 1893–4, Ganda catechists eagerly volunteered to proselytize as far afield as Nkore, Koki, Toro, Bunyoro, Busoga, Acholi, Teso and Sukuma. Ganda Catholics soon followed suit, while Luo converts residing in Buganda carried their new faith home with them to western Kenya, where they established local prayer houses prior to missionaries advancing into the area.[38]

Rising anti-Ganda sentiments fuelled by Ganda sub-imperialism and the continued use of Luganda and the Luganda Bible by the evangelists slowly led to Baganda being displaced by local Christians and the establishment of local churches throughout southern and western Uganda. The infusion of large numbers of new European missionaries in the early 1900s displaced more Baganda, and the paternalistic 'policy of leading strings' of the new missionaries, their lack of support for village catechists and their reluctance to ordain African clergy stunted the growth of the Ganda church to the point where some 75 per cent of Ganda Anglicans were denied communion, largely because they had married according to local instead of church law.[39]

The ongoing struggle for control soon led to the development of autonomous movements both in and outside the church, including the East African Revival (or Balokole), the Society of the One Almighty God (Bamalaki), and the African Greek Orthodox Church. The first revival was conducted in 1893–4 as a deliberate attempt by the missionaries to revive the flagging fortunes of the church, and it was repeated periodically thereafter. But it was the East African Revival, arriving from Rwanda in the 1930s, that took hold within the Ganda church. Stressing mutual confession of sins, the acceptance of Christ as one's personal saviour, the importance of dreams, speaking in tongues, and community prayers and hymn singing, the Revival signalled a return to the homestead churches of the 1880s, as small groups of lay brethren established their own fellowships autonomous from European or clerical control. Originally opposed by the mission hierarchy for its exclusivist piety and potential for dividing congregations, the Revival has since become an increasingly central part of the church, with many of the Ganda clergy and leadership active members, and parallel charismatic movements have spread to the Catholic Church in Uganda as well.[40]

While mission and church were ultimately largely successful in containing the Revival within their precincts, other movements burst the boundaries of European control and doctrine to establish themselves as independent African churches. Some, such as the African Greek Orthodox Church, remained within the historic churches. Founded by Reuben Spartas as a biblically based church free of European control in 1929, it immediately established institutional links with the Garveyite African Orthodox Church in the United States and ultimately with the Greek Orthodox Church. Others, such as the Bamalaki, founded in 1914, developed their own interpretations of Christian doctrine based on careful study of the Luganda Bible. Founded in opposition to the post-Agreement Christian aristocracy and politico-ecclesiastical order by an early Christian convert and senior chief, Yoswa Kate, the church was based on injunctions against the use of medicine found in the Luganda Bible, immediate baptism, a ban on eating pork, recognition of Passover, a Saturday Sabbath, and acceptance of polygamy, and some adherents even went so far as to embrace Mosaic laws fully by identifying themselves as Jews (Bayudaya).[41]

As illuminating as this material is for exploring a range of different perspectives on Christianity in Buganda, it would be hard to argue that anything like definitive histories exist for the early Anglican and Catholic missions; the subsequent development of African churches; the production, translation and impact of the early Luganda Bible used throughout the region; the struggles within the Anglican and Catholic churches that lay behind Taylor's grim portrayal of a moribund church or the experiment in Africanization in the Catholic diocese of Masaka under Bishop Kiwanuka; or the dramatic rise of Pentecostalism from the early 1960s. Aside from John Taylor's classic study of the Anglican church at the parish level, twentieth-century history continues the earlier emphasis on religion and politics, and little analysis has been done on independency since Welbourn's narrative account.[42] And, as in studies of other parts of Africa, the history of Catholicism is barely touched upon in spite of important Catholic roles in the 'Christian Revolution' and subsequent politics, the fact that Catholics actually form a majority in the area, the Masaka experiment in establishing an African church, the impact of Vatican II's call for greater cultural pluralism, and the critical role played by the *African*

Ecclesiastical Review in the development of African Catholic theology and practice.[43] In short, the full history of Christianity in Buganda remains to be written, and, if that is true for Buganda, what can we possibly say for the rest of East Africa?

Religious conflict in Kikuyu

A particularly illuminating case study of mission, conversion, popular evangelism and the struggle for control is provided by Sandgren's study of the Africa Inland Mission and independency in Kikuyu.[44] Established in 1895, the non-denominational AIM was, perhaps, one of the most extreme examples of individualistic Protestant pietism. Individual missionaries funded themselves, were chosen on the basis of their personal conversion experience, and tended to be strong-willed men and women with a passion for evangelism, answerable only to God. With their almost exclusive stress on personal conversion, the AIM showed little interest in education or medicine, and they viewed the persistence of African customs as the work of Satan that had to be overcome at all costs.

While many of the first Kikuyu 'readers' (or Athomi) were drawn to the mission by material desires to acquire land, avoid colonial taxes and labour, gain an education or get a job, they soon found themselves alienated from their kin, who saw them as responsible for bringing disease, drought and famine to the land by breaking social conventions, burning sacred trees, destroying divination tools and disinterring their ancestors. Challenged from without, the Athomi developed into a tight-knit community, dependent on the missionaries and smugly superior to their fellow Kikuyu.

By 1920, however, Athomi began to leave the confines of the mission community to establish outstations in the wider community. Colonial policies had taken their toll of Kikuyu society, and people were now more interested in education and Christianity. At the same time, Athomi in the outstations themselves became subject to increasing colonial demands for land, labour and taxes, and slowly rejoined the wider social and ritual community. As a result, they began to criticize the missions for their insensitivity to local needs, their lack of support for education and their attacks on sacrifice and polygamy. As catechists began to make common cause with Kikuyu politicians, the missionaries imposed strict new rules and discipline requiring all converts to obey the missionaries, abstain from politics and devote themselves exclusively to preparing themselves for the life to come. While older Athomi remained loyal to the mission, many of the younger catechists in the outstations identified more with their parishioners and defended their schools.

Tensions between the missionaries and local Christians continued to increase over the years, exacerbated by the mission's continuing attacks on polygamy and circumcision. They were countered by Kikuyu appeals to the Kikuyu Bible in which the patriarchs were polygamous, Mary was identified as a circumcised woman (*muiritu*), and, it could be argued, circumcision of both men and women (*irua*) was prescribed. The AIM responded by seeking to impose a mandatory Loyalty Oath in 1928, but this time all but a few of the older Athomi left the mission. Calling themselves Aregi ('those who refused'), in contrast to Kirore ('thumbprint', signifying those who had sworn allegiance), over 95 per cent of Christians left the mission, allied with non-Christians in defence of Kikuyu customs and outstation autonomy, and ultimately established their own churches and schools. Nineteen years later the remaining Athomi left as well, in opposition to the AIM's continuing paternalistic control, lack of support for education and resistance to ordaining African pastors.

While the independent churches remained largely conventional in their doctrines, one group of Aregi joining the African Orthodox Church and another loosely associating with Anglicanism, a third group struck decisively out on its own. Known as Arathi ('those filled with the Spirit') or Aroti ('Dreamers'), they fiercely opposed both European and Kikuyu culture, putting their faith in dreams and revelation, baptism by the Holy Spirit and strict adherence to Hebraic dietary laws.[45]

In the end, then, while most Kikuyu became Christians, Christianity sharply split the Kikuyu community over issues of education, cultural tolerance, church governance, ordination and doctrine. Such splits were later manifested within the Mau Mau movement and the struggle for independence, with Aregi largely siding with the Kikuyu Central Association (KCA), Kirore allied with the government, and Arathi militantly opposed to both. Christianity had become more deeply embedded in Kikuyu society, politics, and belief than anyone suspected as the struggle for the Kikuyu soul became a struggle for the people and ultimately the nation. Christianity lay at the very core of those struggles throughout, a fact that is inexplicably neglected in the extensive literature on Mau Mau and nationalism in Kenya.[46]

The Holy Spirit movement in western Kenya

The case of the Arathi, or Spirit churches, raises a host of other issues, theological as well as sociological, that are developed in fascinating studies of charismatic prophecy and healing among the Holy Spirit (Roho) movement in western Kenya by Hoehler-Fatton and Rasmussen. According to Hoehler-Fatton, Christianity first entered western Kenya from Buganda, conveyed by Luo migrants who had studied in Buganda and subsequently returned home to establish their own prayer houses, gathering their Christian followers around them in new homesteads (*dala*) in the Luo fashion.[47] Thus, an indigenous Christianity was already established in Luo before the first pioneers of the Church Missionary Society (CMS) settled in Maseno in 1906, and the missionaries continued to rely heavily on Luo catechists to spread the faith. With only the Luganda Bible to guide them, the catechists drew on their own religious experience to establish their own autonomous communities, and after the Holy Spirit struck Ibrahim Osodo in 1912, many communities became increasingly charismatic in spite of opposition from the mission.[48]

Alfayo Odongo Mango was first possessed by the Holy Spirit shortly thereafter, following a long illness and his conversion to Christianity in a local prayer group. He established his own prayer house, became an active preacher, and soon attracted the attention of the mission. He was appointed a deacon, sent to Freretown to study for ordination, and subsequently returned to become a local pastor and establish his own following on his ancestral lands at Musanda. It was not long, however, before Mango, a Luo, came into conflict with local Luyia authorities, who claimed his land, together with local Anglicans, who did not share his intense beliefs in prophecy, healing and the Holy Spirit. Physically attacked by their neighbours, members of his beleaguered community withdrew into prolonged fasts and prayer meetings, during which they experienced repeated visitations by the Holy Spirit, received millenarian prophecies predicting Mango's death and the end of European rule, and appointed Mango's successors. Thus, when Luyia attacked the compound again in early 1934, immolating Mango as he stood with his Bible raised to the heavens and his house collapsed around him, the community instantly believed their prophecies had been confirmed. Taking Mango as their prophet, Musanda as their shrine, and his sacrifice as their origin myth, members of the Roho movement split with the CMS and subsequently formed a number of independent Holy Spirit churches throughout Luo areas in Western Kenya.

Stressing the primacy of religious belief and practice, Hoehler-Fatton's conclusions are as interesting as they are arresting. She sees Mango's sacrifice as the pivotal event in Roho history and belief, fusing Luo and Christian beliefs while simultaneously transforming them. Sacrificing his life for Africans, Mango created the African church and bequeathed it the Holy Spirit to mediate between the living community and the divine. As such, it represented the culmination of the development of an 'indigenous charismatic Christian' movement among Luo from early in the century, a movement that had drawn as heavily on Luo religious experience as on the plethora of new Christian beliefs and movements that permeated the countryside. Far from being a schismatic split from the European mission movement, as commonly thought, the Roho movement represented the slow emergence of indigenous Luo Christianity under the charismatic leadership of local Luo.

Further, its emergence was deeply influenced by the experience of women. Prominent in the early movement as evangelists, healers and warriors, women actively defended the Musanda community. Charismatic fervour provided a unique opening for women's empowerment, but its subsequent routinization has allowed the restoration of patriarchal authority. Nevertheless, women continue to be active in the movement today, finding peace and self-fulfilment in its woman-centred theology. Finally, contrary to contemporary accounts that the movement was essentially the product of a land dispute between Luo and Luyia, Mango's politics are viewed as specifically religious in origin, stemming from the political implications of the founding of a new (religious) community, or *dala*.

The Holy Spirit movement was not confined to Luo, however. It also developed among Luyia to the north, where similar religious communities emerged within the Friends African Industrial Mission. In a detailed account of the movement's religious beliefs and ritual practices there, Rasmussen shows how these flowed out of Luyia religious experience as members interpreted new ideas brought by Christianity for themselves.[49]

The Friends missionaries were evangelical American Quakers, not unlike their pietistic Protestant counterparts elsewhere. They enjoyed only moderate success initially, but, after the pioneer missionary Arthur Chilson first preached the message of Pentecost in 1927, the Annual Meeting was seized by the Spirit. Students responded enthusiastically and carried the doctrine of baptism of the Holy Spirit and confession of sins home with them, founding a number of semi-autonomous spiritual fellowships. Ostracized and expelled from the mission two years later, they slowly transformed their informal communities into a series of independent Holy Spirit churches in the years that followed.

Relying solely on faith and prayer, members of the Holy Spirit churches rejected education and medicine. Their services were loosely structured and combined enthusiastic hymn singing, rituals to purify the church and public confession to purify themselves, prayers for personal healing and well-being, intermittent preaching, and possession by the Holy Spirit. In the endless battle between good and evil, confession purified the body, drove out evil demons, and made way for the Holy Spirit. Similarly, charismatic gifts of speaking in tongues, dreams and visions, and prophecy were all valued as means of personally receiving and being baptized by the Holy Spirit. The role of Christ's sacrifice in bringing redemption was minimized; instead, his death was seen as paving the way for the Holy Spirit and the attainment of final salvation. Christ's death did not end evil, but provided a means of combating it. Combining Luyia and Christian beliefs and practices, the Holy Spirit churches reinterpreted Christianity and reintegrated sacred and secular beliefs in ways that were meaningful to their members.

The interpretation of Christianity in Buhaya

The personal account of the Lutheran church in Buhaya by its ex-Bishop, Bengt Sundkler, vividly captures many of the religious dimensions of Christianity in East Africa.[50] Based on extensive oral interviews and his own personal experience, Sundkler's study of the development of the Haya Lutheran Church paints a dramatic picture of the church at the personal and parish level.

Exiled Ganda evangelists established the first Christian communities some twenty years before the arrival of German Lutheran missionaries in Buhaya in 1912. The Germans were deported soon thereafter, however, and Haya Christians saw the mission through successive trusteeships by Baganda and South Africans, the return of the Germans, and the final takeover by Swedes following the Second World War.

Conversions proceeded slowly at first, but, after the Haya kings finally converted in the early 1920s, the churches became symbols of adaptation and modernization, and the people followed *en masse*. Conversion remained a long and complex process, nevertheless, according to early Christians. 'When the foreign missionaries came, they did not preach to people with heads like empty boxes. No, these people had their religion, their way of life, their social philosophy, their medicine, their traditions and their history', noted Bishop Kibira later. First-generation Christians could only experience Christianity through Haya eyes in the form of visions and dreams, rituals and prayers. Similarly, Pastor Tinkaligaile stressed the appeal of the Old Testament 'faith of men' where ritual, rhythm and movement dominated, not ideas, thought and vision.

Since the only Bibles before 1930 were in Luganda and Swahili, early Haya Christianity remained an oral religion, dominated by proverbs and 'a spirit-filled and animated world', as the Haya language shifted unfamiliar Christian meanings to familiar Haya ones. In time, however, Haya meanings too began to shift, as dreams made the new faith personal. The Revival introduced the cleansing power of the Holy Spirit, the intense fellowship of the brethren and the personal acceptance of Christ as saviour at a time when venereal disease, prostitution and the breakdown of the family threatened to destroy the moral community. Local churches became rooted in their local communities, led by lay teachers and farmers and ministered to by pastor-farmers.

Larsson's study of Haya women in the Catholic church adds a further dimension to our understanding of Haya Christianity by detailing the intensely spiritual roles of women in the church.[51] French White Fathers first entered Buhaya in 1892 and were followed by White Sisters a decade later. Women were attracted to the mission from an early stage as it provided protection (*busirika*) to royal 'slaves', girls escaping unwanted or unhappy marriages, and women fleeing widowhood. Many subsequently entered an unofficial sisterhood (Bashomesa) whose members took annual vows and served as teachers, nurses and evangelists in the community. Others joined the Revival-like Catholic Action, the locally established lay Association of Charles Lwanga (Banyakaroli), or the official Order of St Teresa. Sisterhood became more popular than priesthood, as women sought to join a universal motherhood and spiritual family. Similarly, Protestant women joining the Revival frequently did so in response to female life crises or in order to establish new spiritual partnerships with their husbands and families.

Church, state and society in East Africa today

We have focused thus far on the genesis and early development of African Christianity in East Africa, but what of Christianity in Africa today? Unfortunately, this is largely a neglected subject, and what there is tends to return us to the theme of the role of religion in politics.[52]

The prominent role assumed by church leaders in recent Kenya politics is an example. Schooled in the conservative evangelical tradition of the Protestant missions, Kenya's church leaders tended to side with the colonial and national state until they became alarmed by the threats posed to the churches and their members by the increasingly 'paranoid style' of politics of President Moi. Drawing on both African and Christian religious experiences, they then began to develop their own 'theologies of power'. Rev. Timothy Njoya stressed human dignity as understood in African cultures; Bishop Henry Okullu focused on Christian justice; Bishop David Gitari emphasized 'a prophetic ministry of judgement'; and the Catholic Justice and Peace Commission cited justice and human rights in developing pragmatic theological principles for judging state policies and actions.[53]

Christianity has also influenced contemporary political thought, from nationalist justifications of independence to Nyerere's political philosophy and Ngugi wa Thiong'o's radical critiques of nationalist politics. Led by educated Christians, the nationalist movement drew on Western liberal as well as Christian principles of justice, equality and freedom to advocate independence from colonial rule, but the Christian role is rarely acknowledged in the extensive literature. Similarly, little has been written on the influence of Catholic and liberation theology on Julius Nyerere's thought,[54] and Ngugi's critics have tended to focus on his radical politics while ignoring the Christian metaphors deeply embedded in his novels.[55]

Afterthoughts

My conclusions regarding the vital need to probe the ways in which Africans have interpreted Christianity and appropriated it for themselves if we are to understand their historical experiences have been developed throughout this chapter; so I will close simply with some afterthoughts about the nature of the task.

Questions of religious belief pose problems for academic social scientists, many of whom are made uncomfortable, for example, by Sanneh's conclusion that, while the missionaries themselves may have failed, God's mission (*missio Dei*) in Africa succeeded.[56] We need to cross the boundaries between academic and religious scholarly discourses if we are to understand those converts who say that, while they were initially attracted by the schools and jobs, they were captured by 'the poetry of the religion'. How else, after all, can we understand the sacrifice of the Buganda martyrs, the motivations of catechists who laboured for the church with scant material rewards, the philosophic basis of Nyerere's concept of *ujamaa*, the abundant religious symbolism contained in Ngugi wa Thiong'o's *Matigari*, the principled political opposition of Kenya's churches, or the resurgent dynamism of the faith today?

The study of African Christianity in eastern Africa has drawn variously on church history as well as on academic history, anthropology and religious studies, but the differences between them have not been as dramatic as might be imagined. Nor have there necessarily been great differences between scholars writing from within and from outside the churches.[57] Thus, while it was largely academic historians (such as Oliver, Temu, Strayer and Hansen) together with some church historians (Taylor, Pirouet, Kieran and Lema) who pioneered revisionist studies of missions, it was primarily church historians (Sundkler, Welbourn, Barrett and Murray) who rejected mission condemnations of the independent churches to stress their fundamental Christianity. Conversely, academic scholars (Kimambo, Ranger, Sandgren, Robins, Larsson, Rasmussen and Hoehler-Fatton) have been forthright in developing African religious history, but church historians (Sundkler, Hastings, Waliggo, Githieya, Ward and Benson) have probed African religious ideas in great depth. Thus the most significant fault lines in the literature have been not religious but political, functions of the changing political climate over the past century as concerns have shifted from metropolitan and ecclesiastical to nationalist and African religious history.[58]

There are, however, fundamental differences between church and academic history in the ways in which each views time and history. Christianity is a profoundly historical religion, and Christians see history as the unfolding of God's plan for the world to the end of Time. Academic historians, by contrast, see history as simply the unfolding of human events through time, with no teleological implications. Thus, Sanneh employs both these notions when he contrasts the very human faults that caused Christian missions in Africa to fail in historical times with the success of God's Mission in universal Time. Similarly, while church historians are prone to talk of the Church as universal, academic historians focus on different churches and denominations as Christian doctrines and institutions have developed through real time and feel that focus on the Church universal obscures the real, everyday experiences of Christians that they seek to understand.

As plain as these differences are, however, they are ultimately differences of faith and do not intrude on our common concerns for understanding the historical development of Christianity in Africa. In real life, church historians writing on Christianity in Africa have paid just as close attention as academic historians to the experiences of real people and the ways in which Christian beliefs and institutions have slowly become rooted in their lives and thought. And academic historians have struggled to make sense of people's faith as it influences their actions. But the world of religious faith and practice is a very difficult and mysterious world to explore; we can only do so with empathy for the beliefs of those whose experiences we seek to understand.

Notes

* My thanks to the participants in the workshops on 'African Expressions of Christianity' (Madison, 1996) and 'Africans Meeting Missionaries' (Minneapolis, 1997), particularly Jan Vansina and Richard Waller, for their perceptive comments and suggestions.

1 My focus here on the immediate precolonial and colonial periods neglects, of course, the earlier spread of Christianity to Ethiopia, North Africa, the Kingdom of the Kongo and elsewhere, but much of the analysis is applicable to those cases as well. See, for example, for the early Kongo, Richard Gray, *Black Christians and White Missionaries* (New Haven, 1990); Wyatt MacGaffey, *Religion and Society in Central Africa* (Chicago, 1986); and Jan Vansina, 'Notes on Catholicism in Kongo and Angola, 1484–c.1867', unpublished paper, workshop on African Expressions of Christianity, Madison, 1996.

2 The dramatic expansion of Islam in Africa represents a similar phenomenon and is even less well understood than that of Christianity. See, for example, N. Levtzion (ed.), *Conversion to Islam* (New York, 1979); Robert Launay, *Beyond the Stream* (Berkeley, 1992); Louis Brenner (ed.), *Muslim Identity and Social Change in Sub-Saharan Africa* (Bloomington, 1993).

3 David B. Barrett, *Schism and Renewal in Africa* (Nairobi, 1968), 4–7, 179–86.

4 Adrian Hastings, *The Church in Africa, 1450–1950* (Oxford, 1994), 242–72; Robert W. Strayer, *The Making of Mission Communities in East Africa* (London, 1978), 5–9.

5 Sometimes significant differences even occurred within a single denomination or mission. Thus various Anglican missions competed with one another within Tanzania. The Anglican Church Missionary Society was split between Low Church Australian missionaries in central Tanzania and High Church British elsewhere. Adrian Hastings, *A History of African Christianity, 1950-1975* (Cambridge, 1979), 167. German Lutheran missions within Tanzania varied widely as well. Marcia Wright, *German Missions in Tanganyika* (Oxford, 1971), 3–14, 86–130.

6 As shown, for example, by the relative lack of conversion among Mijikenda along the Kenya coast both before and after colonial conquest, compared with that among Kikuyu in the Central Highlands following a brutal conquest, widespread land alienation and harsh labour policies.

7 Compare, for example, the roles of the White Fathers in Fipa with those of the Lutherans in Zaramo and Chaga or the AIM in Kamba detailed in the studies by Smythe, Kimambo, Lema and Sandgren in this volume.

8 T. O. Beidelman, *Colonial Evangelism* (Bloomington, 1982), 8–30; John and Jean Comaroff, *Of Revelation and Revolution*, Vol. I (Chicago, 1991).

9 Vernacular translations of the Bible thus became critical factors in the subsequent establishment of independent churches, according to Barrett, *Schism and Renewal*. Cf. Christopher Hill, *The English Bible and the Seventeenth Century Revolution* (London, 1994).

10 Lamin Sanneh, *Translating the Message* (Maryknoll, 1989); David Sandgren, *Christianity and the Kikuyu* (New York, 1989), 73–74; F. B. Welbourn, *East African Rebels* (London, 1961), 34.

11 Wendy James, *The Listening Ebony* (Oxford, 1988), 221–41; Wendy James, 'Uduk faith in a five-tone scale: mission music and the spread of the Gospel', in D. Johnson and W. James (eds), *Vernacular Christianity* (Oxford, 1988), 131–45.

12 Karen Fields, *Revival and Rebellion in Colonial Central Africa* (Princeton, 1985).

13 See, for example, Paul Landau, *The Realm of the Word* (Portsmouth, 1995) and Dorothy Hodgson, 'Engendered encounters: men of the Church and the "church of women" in Maasailand, Tanzania, 1950–1993', unpublished paper, workshop on African Expressions of Christianity, Madison, 1996.

14 Emefie Ikenga-Metuh, 'The shattered microcosm: a critical survey of explanations of conversion in Africa', in Kirsten Holst Petersen (ed.), *Religion, Development, and African Identity* (Uppsala, 1987), 11–27. See also, Robert Hefner, 'Introduction', in R. Hefner (ed.), *Conversion to Christianity* (Berkeley, 1993), 3–44; Steven Kaplan, 'The Africanization of missionary Christianity', *Journal of Religion in Africa*, 16 (1986), 166–86; Gray, *Black Christians and White Missionaries*, 70–8.

15 Roland Oliver, *The Missionary Factor in East Africa* (London, 1952), 182–202; John V.

Taylor, *The Growth of the Church in Buganda* (London, 1958), 63–80; Strayer, *Mission Communities*, 52–68; Louise Pirouet, *Black Evangelists* (London, 1978); Sandgren, *Christianity and the Kikuyu*, 37–61; Hastings, *Church in Africa*, 438–56; T. O. Ranger, 'Protestant missions in Africa: the dialectic of conversion in the American Methodist Episcopal Church in Eastern Zimbabwe, 1900–1950', in T. D. Blakely *et al.* (eds), *Religion in Africa* (London, 1994), 275–313.

16 Pirouet, *Black Evangelists*, 11–22, 41–64; Cynthia Hoehler-Fatton, *Women of Fire and Spirit* (New York, 1996), 14–16.

17 As noted by Sandgren regarding AIM missionaries in Kamba, Chapter 8 below.

18 Sandgren, *Christianity and the Kikuyu*, 61–87; Oliver, *Missionary Factor*, 207–22; Taylor, *Growth of the Church in Buganda*, 125–41, 177–87; Welbourn, *East African Rebels*; F. B. Welbourn and B. A. Ogot, *A Place to Feel at Home* (London, 1966); Barrett, *Schism and Renewal*; Sandgren, Chapter 8 below

19 Thomas Spear, *Mountain Farmers* (London, 1997), 158–72; Wright, *German Missions*, 137–214; Kimambo, Chapter 4 below.

20 Strayer, *Mission Communities*, 68–95. See also the studies in this volume by Kimambo, Lema, Maddox and Waller.

21 While generally the Christian elements of African prophetic and healing movements have been neglected in the literature, they are stressed in the studies here by Comoro and Sivalon, Kassimir, Mlahagwa and Githieya.

22 See, for example, Douglas Johnson, *Nuer Prophets* (Oxford, 1994); David M. Anderson and Douglas H. Johnson (eds), *Revealing Prophets* (London, 1995).

23 Gray, *Black Christians and White Missionaries*, 99–113; Birgit Meyer, '"If you are a devil, you are a witch, and if you are a witch, you are a devil": the integration of "pagan" ideas into the conceptual universe of Ewe Christians in south-eastern Ghana', *Journal of Religion in Africa*, 22 (1992), 98–132; Ane Marie Bak Rasmussen, *Modern African Spirituality* (London, 1996), 129–35, 148–51; Kassimir, Chapter 12 below.

24 Welbourn, *East African Rebels*; Welbourn and Ogot, *A Place to Feel at Home* ; Barrett, *Schism and Renewal*; Fields, *Revival and Rebellion*.

25 Hastings, *History of African Christianity*, 72.

26 Max Warren, *Revival* (London, 1954); Catherine Robins, '*Tukutendereza*: a study of social change and withdrawal in the Balokole revival of Uganda' (PhD, Columbia, 1975); Kevin Ward, '*Tukutendereza Yesu*: the Balokole revival movement in Uganda', in Z. Nthamburi (ed.), *From Mission to Church* (Nairobi, 1991), 113–44; George K. Mambo, 'The Revival Fellowship (Brethren) in Kenya', in D. B. Barrett *et al.* (eds), *Kenya Churches Handbook* (Kisumu, 1973), 110–17; Kevin Ward, 'The Church of Uganda amidst conflict', in H.B. Hansen and M. Twaddle (eds), *Religion and Politics in East Africa* (London, 1995), 74–7; Hastings, *History of African Christianity*, 127–8; Mlahagwa, Kassimir, and Comoro and Sivalon, this volume.

27 The links between evangelical/Pentecostal movements and developments within African Christianity go back at least to the 1920s. T. O. Ranger, 'Religion, development, and African identity', in Petersen, *Religion, Development, and African Identity*, 29–57.

28 See, for example, Oliver, *Missionary Factor*; Taylor, *Growth of the Church in Buganda*; Wright, *German Missions*; Robert MacPherson, *The Presbyterian Church in Kenya* (Nairobi, 1970); A. J. Temu, *British Protestant Missions* (London, 1972); Holger Bernt Hansen, *Mission, Church and State in a Colonial Setting* (London, 1984); John Kieran, 'The Holy Ghost Fathers in East Africa, 1863–1911' (PhD, London, 1966); B. G. McIntosh, 'The Scottish mission in Kenya, 1891–1923' (PhD, Edinburgh, 1969); A. A. Lema, 'The impact of the Leipzig Lutheran Mission on the peoples of Kilimanjaro, 1893–1920' (PhD, Dar es Salaam, 1975); F. Nolan, 'Christianity in Unyamwezi, 1878–1928' (PhD, Cambridge, 1976).

29 See, for example, Welbourn, *East African Rebels*; Welbourn and Ogot, *A Place to Feel at Home*; and Barrett, *Schism and Renewal*. There was also new interest in African religious movements generally: for example, T. O. Ranger and I. N. Kimambo (eds), *The Historical Study of African Religion* (London, 1972).

30 See, for example, Jean Brierley and Thomas Spear, 'Mutesa, the missionaries, and Christian conversion in Buganda', *International Journal of African Historical Studies*, 21 (1988), 601–18; Spear, *Mountain Farmers*, 61–74, 158–72.

31 See, for example, Strayer, *Mission Communities*; Bengt Sundkler, *Bara Bukoba* (London, 1980).

32 Sanneh, *Translating the Message*. Cf. comments on *Translating the Message* by Marilyn Waldman, Olabiyi Babalola Yai, and Lamin Sanneh in *Journal of Religion in Africa*, 22 (1992), 159–72.

33 See special issue of *African Ecclesiastical Review* on 'Inculturation', 22 (1980), 321–400, especially Eugene Hillman, 'Missionary approaches to African cultures today', 342–56. Cf. Kassimir, Chapter 12 below.

34 Gray, *Black Christians and White Missionaries*; Hastings, *The Church in Africa*.

35 T. O. Ranger's forthcoming book on Masasi promises to add to these cases.

36 D. A. Low, *Religion and Society in Buganda, 1875–1900* (Kampala, 1955); C. C. Wrigley, 'The Christian Revolution in Buganda', *Comparative Studies in Society and History*, 2 (1959), 33–48; John A. Rowe, 'Revolution in Buganda, 1856–1900: Part One: The Reign of Kabaka Mukabya Mutesa, 1856–1884' (PhD, Wisconsin, 1966); J. A. Rowe, 'The purge of Christians at Mwanga's court', *Journal of African History*, 5 (1964), 55–72; Hansen, *Mission, Church and State*.

37 Brierley and Spear, 'Mutesa, the missionaries, and Christian conversion'. See also Benjamin Ray, *Myth, Ritual and Kingship in Buganda* (New York, 1991).

38 Taylor, *Growth of the Church*, 63–8; Pirouet, *Black Evangelists*; Hoehler-Fatton, *Women of Fire and Spirit*, 14–16.

39 Taylor, *Growth of the Church*, 71–97, 177–87.

40 Taylor, *Growth of the Church*, 96–103; Robins, '*Tukutendereza*'; Ward, '*Tukutendereza Yesu*'; Ronald Kassimir, 'Catholics and political identity in Toro', in Hansen and Twaddle, *Religion and Politics*, 120–40.

41 Welbourn, *East African Rebels*.

42 Taylor, *Growth of the Church*; Welbourn, *East African Rebels*.

43 Hastings, *History of African Christianity*, 61, 234–7. I have not seen, however, the important theses by John M. Waliggo, 'The Catholic Church in the Buddu Province of Buganda, 1848–1975' (DPhil, Cambridge, 1976) and Ron Kassimir, 'The social power of religious organization: the Catholic Church in Uganda 1955–1991', (PhD, Chicago, 1996).

44 Sandgren, *Christianity and the Kikuyu*. On the Kikuyu churches generally, see also, Welbourn, *East African Rebels*; Strayer, *Mission Communities*; Valeer Neckebrouck, *Le Onzième Commandement* (Immensee, 1978); *idem*, *Le Peuple affligé* (Immensee, 1983); John Gratton, 'The relationship of the Africa Inland Mission and its national church in Kenya between 1895 and 1971' (PhD, New York University, 1974); Jocelyn Murray, 'The Kikuyu circumcision controversy' (PhD, University of California at Los Angeles, 1974).

45 For an insightful account of Arathi thought, see Francis Githieya, *The Freedom of the Spirit: African Indigenous Churches in Kenya* (Atlanta, 1997) and Chapter 11 below.

46 While the extensive literature on Mau Mau acknowledges the roles played by the independent churches in 'cultural nationalism', it generally neglects their spiritual roles or the degree to which divisions within the struggle stemmed from earlier conflicts within the missions. Lonsdale comes closest to considering the religious component of Mau Mau in his penetrating studies of Kikuyu thought and Kenyatta's theology: John Lonsdale, 'The moral economy of Mau Mau', in B. Berman and J. Lonsdale, *Unhappy Valley* (London, 1992), 315–504 and 'Jomo, God, and the modern world', African Studies Association, 1977. Interestingly, Ngugi wa Thiong'o employs extensive Christian imagery in his radical reassessment of the aftermath of Mau Mau, *Matigari* (Portsmouth, 1987).

47 Hoehler-Fatton, *Women of Fire and Spirit*. For other Luo religious movements, see also Welbourn and Ogot, *A Place to Feel at Home*; Peter Dirven, 'The Legio Maria: The dynamics of a breakaway church among the Luo of East Africa' (Miss. D., Pontificia Universitas Gregoriana, 1970); Marie-France Perrin Jassy, *Basic Community in the African Church* (Maryknoll, 1973); Nancy Schwartz, 'World without end' (PhD, Princeton, 1989).

48 Interestingly, the Anglican missionaries resisted translating the Bible into Luo until the late 1930s for fear that the Old Testament would provide Luo with justification for polygamy. Hoehler-Fatton, *Women of Fire and Spirit*, 25.

49 Rasmussen, *Modern African Spirituality*; *idem*, *A History of the Quaker Movement in Africa* (London, 1995). For other movements among Luyia, see Audrey Wipper, *Rural Rebels* (Nairobi, 1977); Gideon Were, 'Politics, religion and nationalism in Western Kenya, 1942–1962: Dini ya Msambwa Revisited', in B. A. Ogot (ed.), *Politics and Nationalism in Kenya* (Nairobi, 1972), 85–104; Walter Sangree, *Age, Prayer and Politics in Tiriki, Kenya* (London, 1966).

Parallels might also be drawn with the militant Holy Spirit Movement in Uganda today. See Heike Behrend, 'Is Alice Lakwena a witch? The Holy Spirit movement and its fight against evil in the north', in H. B. Hansen and M. Twaddle (eds), *Changing Uganda* (London, 1991), 162–77; *idem*, 'The Holy Spirit movement and the forces of nature in the north of Uganda', in Hansen and Twaddle, *Religion and Politics*, 59–71; Tim Allen, 'Understanding Alice: Uganda's Holy Spirit movement in context', *Africa*, 61 (1991), 370–99.

50 Sundkler, *Bara Bukoba*. See also Lesley Stevens, 'Religious change in a Haya village, Tanzania', *Journal of Religion in Africa*, 21 (1991), 2–25; Wilson Niwagila, 'From the catacomb to a self-governing church' (thesis, Hamburg, 1988).
51 Brigitta Larsson, *Conversion to Greater Freedom?* (Uppsala, 1991).
52 But see Barrett, *Kenya Churches Handbook*, for an exception. Several studies in this volume address different aspects of contemporary Christianity, including those by Mlahagwa, Comoro and Sivalon, Giblin, and Wamba-dia-Wamba.
53 G. P. Benson, 'Ideological politics versus biblical hermeneutics: Kenya's Protestant churches and the *Nyayo* state', in Hansen and Twaddle, *Religion and Politics*, 177–99; David Throup, 'Render unto Caesar the things that are Caesar's: the politics of church–state conflict in Kenya, 1978–1990', in *ibid.*, 143–76; Louise Pirouet, 'The churches and human rights in Kenya', in *ibid.*, 247–59. For another study of the impact of Christianity on current politics, see Timothy Longman, 'Christianity and crisis in Rwanda' (PhD, Wisconsin, 1995).
54 See Per Frostin's unpublished paper cited in Hansen and Twaddle, *Religion and Politics*, 10 and C. Legum and G. Mmari (eds), *Mwalimu* (London, 1995).
55 Such as *Devil on the Cross* (Portsmouth, 1982) and *Matigari*.
56 Lamin Sanneh, *West African Christianity* (Maryknoll, 1983). See also Barrett, *Schism and Renewal*, 154–58, 264–78, where he notes a critical failure of love (*philadelphia*) by European missionaries.
57 For a comparison of church history and academic approaches, see T. O. Ranger and J. Weller (eds), *Themes in the Christian History of Central Africa* (London, 1975).
58 Strayer, *Mission Communities*, 1–6.

Two

African Theology &
the Search for the Universal

GREGORY H. MADDOX

Although Christianity has been present in Africa since its origins as a formal religion, the forms of Christianity explored here grow out of the missionary enterprise that originated in Europe in the nineteenth century. While Christianity since St Paul has been a universal and universalizing religion, in eastern Africa it came as a faith and as a specific set of institutions, part of the dominance of European states over African peoples. From the start, new adherents as well as missionaries have asked how much Africans have had to change to become Christian and how much Christianity has had to change to become African.

A fundamental problematic emerges in the chapters of this book. Most of the chapters, especially those by secular academics, situate religious practice and faith within broader fields of social practice and change, often linked to particular communities. The chapters by church people, however, usually concentrate on relating the extent to which a definable body of belief and practice, Christianity, has embedded itself in and hence transformed communities. For the former, Christianity remains an expression of power, fundamentally alien.[1] But, for the latter, Christianity operates as a source of liberation – one, however, that has to be stripped of much of its cultural and institutional baggage in the form of its mission origins. Both tendencies often result in a dualistic presentation contrasting the Christian with the local or African.

These tendencies reflect the broader scholarship about Christianity in Africa. Much of the secular scholarship has concentrated on independent or prophetic movements that are influenced by specific versions of Christianity. Christianity is often treated as if it is nothing beyond its locally specific manifestation. Conversely, religiously oriented historical writing has often assumed the existence of a Christianity and concentrated on the building of an institution – the Church in some form – that transcends the local. Both approaches are profoundly unsatisfying. The secular approach ignores the extent to which the process of becoming Christian involves an ongoing dialogue with both institutions and a body of writing that emphasizes the universality of the faith. Much religiously oriented writing, however, falls back on essentializing constructions of African identities and traditions that become the opposite of Christian practice. In short, Christianity exists as a faith, and can be analysed as such, to the extent that Christians in Africa engage in this dialogue. At the same time, Christian belief and practice, and churches as institutions, have to be analysed in specific contexts, not just in reference to generalized assertions about African traditions.

The spread of Christianity has to be placed within the context of colonial domination of Africa and the racial justification that explained colonialism. Colonialism in practice mandated that most Africans could never become citizens but would always remain subjects in the colonial order. They were permanently marginalized as different from the civilized order, of which Christianity remained one of the implicit supports. Hence, to be Christian, even for some missionaries, was in a sense a contradiction of being African.[2] Yet Christianity in practice subverted this very difference.

As a result, as Africans confronted the fundamental contradiction between the Word and the vessels in which it came, they developed particular intellectual responses to these practices. These responses were revealed in a variety of contexts. Many gave rise to various forms of independency movements, but, as churches became more institutionalized within African communities, African church men and women also developed their own discourse about Christianity within the language of the churches. African theology draws on these discourses in response to the contradictions of universalizing faith and local contingency.

The attraction of the universal embodied in Christianity for some Africans lies in both the general need in humans to create continuity in the face of almost random contingency and the failure of previous or competing systems of thought to explain the new contingencies.[3] Benedict Anderson has noted:

If the manner of a man's dying usually seems arbitrary, his mortality is inescapable. Human lives are full of such combinations of necessity and chance.... The great merit of traditional religious world-views (which naturally must be distinguished from their role in the legitimation of specific systems of domination and exploitation) has been their concern with man-in-the-cosmos, man as species being, and the contingency of life. The extraordinary survival over thousands of years of Buddhism, Christianity or Islam in dozens of different social formations attests to their imaginative response to the overwhelming burden of human suffering – disease, mutilation, grief, age, and death.[4]

During the nineteenth and twentieth centuries, Christianity did not provide the only answer in Africa. Islam increased its number of adherents, and

Africans adapted existing religious traditions. African theology, though, self-consciously attempts to integrate African contingencies with one strand of universalism.

The central theme of theology from and about Africa is the search for the universal transcending both a created division between African and Western and the different African contexts. Theology from and about Africa has sought to distinguish the message of Christianity from the cultural trappings of the West. Likewise, much of the formal, academic theology has tried to identify an essentially African religion.[5] Both of these projects begin, perhaps, as a matter of faith, but in the historical arena both projects represented the intellectualization around which a very important institution and linkages were built.

This brief essay is an exploration of the tension between the universal and the particular in Christianity in eastern Africa. It arises out of the conjuncture of two recent syntheses on Christianity in Africa with the dense empirical studies presented at the 'African Expressions of Christianity' workshops and the literature they referenced. The first section examines Lamin Sanneh's discussion of the transcendence of the Christian message in the context of Africa.[6] The second examines John Parratt's review of theologizing about Africa in which he examines the possibility of a distinctive African theology.[7] The conclusion then comes back to the central question of this piece, the search for a universal narrative in Christianity in Africa.

Finding the Universal in African Christianity

Although missionary efforts accompanied the earliest Portuguese contacts with sub-Saharan Africa, the effort died out with the rise of the Atlantic slave trade.[8] The renewal of missionary efforts coincided with the anti-slavery drive of the early nineteenth century. Mission expanded dramatically in the late nineteenth century, and many missionaries were influenced by the Social Darwinism and scientific racism of the time. Most saw a clear distinction between civilized and uncivilized, and condemned a wide variety of African practices as unchristian. While churches preached doctrines of spiritual equality and allowed Africans to advance into positions of responsibility in larger numbers and usually more rapidly than in colonial political hierarchies, a real cultural colour bar remained throughout much of the twentieth century. Indeed, churches practised their own form of indirect rule. In the hands of missionaries, support for adaptations of the faith to African cultures often became another means of denying Africans power both institutionally and intellectually.[9]

The attitudes and practices of most nineteenth-century missionaries and mission organizations seem at odds with the message of Christianity as a universal religion in which all people are God's children. Mission churches generally locked African adherents in subordinate positions both institutionally and spiritually. In eastern Africa, the debate over circumcision reveals this complexity. Many missions condemned the practice outright, while others sought to transform various initiation rituals into Christian rituals, sometimes under the control of a missionary.[10] The debate in mission churches themselves over the degree of adaptation resulted in a message that Africans must renounce much of their cultural past to become Christian, but could never become the masters of their own faith. This duality has continued to shape African responses to mission in Africa. It is the one constant that runs through almost all theologizing about and from Africa.[11]

Between the 1930s and 1950s, at least, much church practice shifted formally to 'adaptationism', adapting the faith to local cultural conditions. This shift in nomenclature, although the practice goes back to the origins of most missions, came in part because Africans had begun to move into positions of responsibility within churches. Mission theology also began to reflect this shift. African church leaders, as well as an increasing number of expatriate church workers, sought ways to make the Christian message relevant to larger numbers of people. Yet one of the appeals of mission Christianity remained its universalizing narrative, and much writing from within churches remains more or less locked in a mode that celebrates mission.[12]

As will be discussed below, though, both secular and theological writing on the issue of the adaptation of Christianity to African cultures has continued to postulate a duality between African cultures and Christianity. As the terminology has shifted from adaptationism to inculturation to incarnation, theologians have continued to argue about the means of Africanizing Christianity.[13] Secular scholars have focused relatively more attention on various forms of independent churches than on the development and institutionalization of churches of mission origin.[14] Both of these views ignore the reality of the faith of millions of Africans.

Lamin Sanneh has offered an intellectual way out of the trap of either denying the legitimacy of Christian faith in practice or seeing the diversity of practices labelled commonly as Christianity as so dissimilar as to make the term meaningless. In *Translating the Message* he goes further than theologians concerned with Christianity in Africa who isolate the message from the changing context of the messengers: he also identifies methods through which the message transcended the messengers.[15]

Sanneh argues, first, that the nature of the message drove missionaries from the beginning to make it relevant for new converts. He argues that the Pauline dispensation itself makes the Christian message one that can insinuate itself into any cultural and historical situation. He then goes on to argue that the history of Christianity has always seen this drive to the transcendental at work.[16]

Sanneh finds in translation the medium of this cultural transcendentalism. He notes:

Societies that have been less broken up by technological change have a more integrated, holistic view of life, and language as complete cultural experience fits naturally into this world view. Missionary adoption of the vernacular, therefore, was tantamount to adopting indigenous cultural criteria for the message, a piece of radical indigenization far greater than the standard portrayal of mission as Western cultural imperialism.[17]

Translation gave adherents the tools to create their own faith. That Catholic and Protestant churches differed in their attitudes towards the actual scriptures mattered little. The Catholic emphasis on translating catechisms produced the same result as the Protestant emphasis on the Bible, especially as Bible translation usually occurred anyway.

As noted above, missionaries often ignored the way in which the message subverted the very institution of mission. Not only did the emphasis on translation provide Africans with direct access to the teachings of the church and the Bible, but translation required local mediators. These mediators became more than consultants; they often became the real evangelists from the earliest days of the missions. Sanneh puts the matter in a rather lyrical form:

> Faced with this bewildering situation, Africans began earnestly to inquire into the Christian Scriptures, which missionaries had placed in their hands, to see where they had misunderstood the gospel. What they learned convinced them that mission as European cultural hegemony was a catastrophic departure from the Bible. They met the original irony with one of their own: they went on to claim the gospel, as the missionaries wished them to, but in turn insisted that missionary attitudes should continue to be scrutinized in its revealing light.[18]

Two examples, one very localized and one that eventually has influenced all of eastern Africa, will have to suffice of the ways in which early converts took control of the message themselves. Key intermediaries, more than missionaries, often determined the process of the implantation of Christianity both as faith and as institution. Yohana Malecela converted at the Church Missionary Society station at Mpwapwa at some point before 1902. Noted as a rainmaker before his conversion, he helped establish the Mvumi station of the mission that became its largest in central Tanganyika. He served as a senior teacher before the First World War, even using part of his salary to pay an extra junior teacher. He was scheduled to be ordained before war broke out, but a work stoppage by teachers in the Ukaguru branch of the mission over pay and then the commencement of hostilities disrupted his plans. The Germans imprisoned him during the war. After it, he continued to teach and was finally ordained in the 1920s. A later generation regard him as the founder of the Anglican tradition in the region, and his family has continued to play a prominent role in the church as well as in politics.[19]

In the second example, from the 1890s, a movement known generally as Revival has spread across eastern Africa. The term covers a variety of movements, often not institutionally connected with one another, that operated as a fellowship outside but not in opposition to established churches. Beidelman has provided a description of its operation in Ukaguru, describing it as a movement that called believers to public confession in meetings, often led by teachers or African clergy but outside the confines of the mission church. The mission churches often sought to use and control the movement, but in many cases they recognized the drive for autonomy it expressed.[20] Today the movement has become broad, as Josiah Mlahagwa reveals in Chapter 14 below. Its conferences bring together bishops and clergy from many denominations as well as lay people.[21]

These two examples show the way that Christians in Africa controlled the actual process of translation, despite the attempts by missionaries to remain the final arbiters. In almost all missions, in theory from the beginning, Africans could become clergy. Although the numbers ordained in the mission churches remained small throughout Africa until at least the Second World War, in practice the greater part of pastoral care in most missions actually was carried out by Africans very early. Typically, missionaries first established stations, which also housed medical and educational facilities, which then became centres of Christian communities under the direct control of the missionaries, but the number of converts in these communities often remained small. By the beginning of the twentieth century, however, missionaries began to send African teachers, catechists and preachers out to establish outposts that then became the centres of popular conversion, with the missionaries increasingly concentrating on administration, overseeing translation and maintaining church discipline.

The treatment of African church workers, and especially of African clergy, reveals the dual nature of mission Christianity. As well as receiving salvation Africans could also accept a calling to bring the message of salvation to others. The encouragement to do so and the independence with which most African church workers operated gave great latitude to Africans to begin to domesticate the new faith. Yet the declaration of theoretical equality for those called came with many restrictions. For Catholics, Africans ordained as priests received the same education and were held to the same rules as other priests. Yet not only were very few ordained before the Second World War, but most who were could not become brothers of the missionary orders that controlled the mission churches. They either became diocesan clergy or joined separate African orders. Women likewise usually had to became members of separate orders.[22] Although ordination eventually became more widespread in many Protestant missions, missionary societies often maintained a sharp division between local and mission clergy as well.[23]

The role of African clergy and other church workers points to another result of the spread of Christianity. In a rather ironic way, the spread of Christianity often accompanied a secularization of life in many African societies. One must tread carefully here because the process was never complete and was always contested. Often those most secularized became members of the new power structures established by colonial administrations, while popular resistance often included an appeal to elements of traditional religion. Examples abound, from the Xhosa cattle killing to the Maji Maji rebellion, from Mau Mau to the Zimbabwe liberation struggle.[24] Yet the spread of Christianity did disrupt the holistic view of life often promoted in African communities.[25] The breaking of the links between the spiritual world and everyday life was the religious aspect of the disruption of social organization that occurred throughout Africa during the colonial era – as much in Muslim or other communities in which Christianity made little headway as in colonies where Christian influence was strong.

The great debate for almost all missions was not whether to adapt to local cultures, but how to do so. Very few missionaries before the last half of the twentieth century would go so far as translating African religions beliefs into a pre-Christian form of religion. Many shared belief in the spirits Africans saw, but claimed they emanated from evil.[26] Most regarded African practices as merely superstition. Even today, African Christians and theologians remain divided on these issues.

From the beginning, missionaries and Africans debated the requirements of Christianity. To a degree unknown in contemporary Western Christianity, missionaries and African Christians sought to define the external signs of the faith. Although some mission leaders saw the goal of mission as the creation of indigenous churches under indigenous control, missionaries disagreed strongly over the degree to which community rituals could be integrated into Christian life and practice. The initiative, though, in this discourse remained with the missionaries – or perhaps more accurately, as the colonial era wore on, with the church – as interpreters of the acceptable and unacceptable. Such attitudes towards adaptation come through as late as the 1970s.[27]

Only in the 1950s did official churches begin to take African religious thought seriously. In particular, the works of Bengt Sundkler and Placide Temples began the serious analysis of African religious thought in theological terms. By that time, however, the intellectual initiative had passed from the missionaries, and African intellectuals within and outside church circles were challenging the domination of the highest realms of the church by persons of European descent.

The first wave of African theologians often asserted their right to approach the universal on the same terms as the missionaries. They often sought to and succeeded in becoming more Christian than their erstwhile guides. Both missionaries and critics of mission Christianity have often derided such attempts, but in them lies the beginning of the strongest theological critique of mission Christianity.

Finding the African in African Christianity

Since the late nineteenth century, African Christians have called for a Christianity stripped of its Western cultural baggage and Africanized. This call has continued to be made in matters of ritual, dogma, practice and theology. The call to Africanize Christianity is perhaps the only thing that unites African theology. As Parratt notes, the earliest African proponents of Christianity – Samuel Ajayi Crowther, Edward Blyden and James Johnson – all wrote of the need for the church to become African.[28] As African theologians have emerged, especially since the Second World War, such calls have appeared regularly and, indeed, in almost every published source on African theology. Ironically, during the heyday of mission Christianity, missionaries also often made such calls, and usually saw themselves as engaged in 'adapting' Christianity.[29]

That almost all sides of this debate have called for a greater penetration of faith into society would seem to indicate that Christianity has remained external to African consciousness. Yet Christianity has been Africanized in that it has become the faith of millions of Africans. Different churches and communities in Africa have achieved this in very different ways. The discourse of Africanization is part of a power struggle within institutions more than a reflection of reality. It speaks less to the practice of Christians than to the perceived division between Christian and African. The central question then is perhaps less what is Christian than what is 'African'.

The response to the tension between the African and the Christian takes two general forms. One form redirects the message. In theological terms it posits a new revelation directed specifically at Africans or a people in Africa. The other form retains the message. Relying primarily on scripture, it challenges both power and dogma in mission churches. Sundkler first described this distinction as between 'Ethiopian' and 'Zionist' type movements.[30] African theologians within churches of mission origin (and, until very recently, this meant all formally trained African theologians) have themselves struggled with the same contradictions that have driven these movements. For theologians, these have become the debates over adaptation or inculturation, and incarnation.

The first response is one of radical restructuring of the message to fit local conditions. This restructuring often takes the form of a prophetic movement that brings a message directly to a particular people. As Wamba-dia-Wamba's article here demonstrates again, these movements usually emerge where Christianity has become an important element in local discourse but is unable to answer the felt need for community or individual healing. Such situations became common during the colonial era and have continued in many parts of Africa. Some of these movements remain very close to the scriptures, with particular calls for Africans or an ethnic group as a new chosen people. Examples include the Kimbanguist church, John Chilimbwe's Watchtower movement, and the Zionist movements in South

Africa.[31] Others add a great deal new in their revelation that contradicts or supersedes the scriptures, for example the Church of the Bakongo and the Holy Quaternity movements discussed in this volume.

Independency movements are often reactions to structural domination and put into practice an Africanization formal theologians still only debate.[32] Elizabeth Isichei, noting that Kenya alone has 300 independent churches, says:

> They enriched not only African Christianity, but Christendom as a whole by the richness and creativity of their liturgies, and by their exploration of an insight that the West has often lost sight of but is now rediscovering: the unity of health of mind and body.[33]

Yet, even if the base of the message is entirely scriptural, these movements often come under attack from theologians as heretical. At the deepest level, the reason for this contradiction lies in theologians' purpose in transforming institutions, not just finding theological truth.[34]

These movements all link a particular experience to at least part of the universal embodied in Christianity. For Christians in the mission churches a more subtle problem arises: the necessity of relating the universal to the particular. Because the churches both make claims to the universal and are institutionally larger than the local, these claims are important. In particular, despite the missionary attitude towards African beliefs in general, the discontinuity with some element of the universal presented by churches and elements of almost every African culture leads to a persistent trope of duality in writing about Christianity.

The source of this duality is partly external and institutional. The structures of racial and colonial domination coincided with the spread of various churches. In southern Africa, particularly, theologians have confronted this domination openly; varieties of black and liberation theology have gained a degree of currency there not found as strongly elsewhere in the continent. Such theologies addressed the very real political struggles in that region; the duality lay between the oppressor and the oppressed, and the central theological problem was how to manifest God's justice as well as God's grace.[35]

In Africa north of the Zambezi, though, the central problem after the 1960s became not political liberation but a sense that spiritual and cultural independence had not followed political independence. As a result, African theologians began to call for more than adaptationism or inculturation, asserting incarnation as a basis of Christianity in Africa. Incarnation could mean very different things, though. In a statement issued at the Roman Synod of 1974, the Bishops of Africa and Madagascar rejected adaptation and stated that, 'Theology must be open to the aspiration of the people of Africa, if it is to help Christianity to become incarnate in the life of the people of the African Continent.'[36]

For others, such as F. Eboussi Boulaga, incarnation means not just finding the Gospel incarnate in pre-Christian people and societies, but also finding an African salvation beyond Christianity. His charge is that the Catholic Church remains so locked in dogma and alien to Africa that an African Christian cannot but have a sense of alienation. The way out (or through) is the relation of a Christic model of rebellion and rebirth in community to Africans' lived experiences. For Boulaga, this new faith will have to recognize the 'complex pluralistic' modern world of Africa, while the Church will have to recognize that the Bible is 'only ... a local historical manifestation, not an absolute'.[37]

Although few African theologians follow Boulaga in rejecting the organized church, many phrase their critiques in similar terms. Most accept the historicity of Christianity as revealed in the Bible and the history of the church. In general, most concern themselves with the institutional position of African churches. They seek to empower African communities within churches. The drive for empowerment comes out most clearly in the application of elements of liberation theology in South Africa.[38]

Part of the problem with theologies that seek to define an autonomous African Christianity is the difficulty in defining 'African'. Boulaga takes the view that there must be many forms of African Christianity reflecting the many African communities. Others – such as Benézét Bujo, Harry Sawyerr and John Mbiti – seek to define an African essence drawing on concepts such as Negritude and the thought of Placide Temples. Such approaches can easily be attacked on empiricist grounds, yet they respond to the totalizing reality of the modern world.[39] Churches, perhaps more even than the political institutions of colonialism, defined adherents as African first. As a result theologians have tended to search for the universal in Africa as well as in the Bible.

Finally, African Christians have tended to emphasize ecumenism. Churches cooperate with each other both practically and theologically. As the essay by Mlahagwa in this collection shows, a variety of fellowship movements operate across arbitrary denominational lines. Even the Catholic–Protestant division receives less emphasis in Africa. Cooperation has become an emphasis because churches of mission origin, especially in East Africa, operate in truly pluralistic societies. The most important religious division is not between denominations but between Christianity, Islam and more traditional faiths. Missions themselves encouraged this feature in practice by dividing mission fields and, in the Protestant case, operating schools and seminaries cooperatively.

Conclusion

Where does this leave Christianity in Africa and the study of Christianity in Africa? First, as much as theology is a search for the universal, religious practice and theorizing about that practice operate within specific historical conditions. African Christianity and theology reflect the struggles and divisions within African societies. Yet Christianity and its theology represent one field drawing Africans together. Theological discourse keeps alive a sense of African identity. Christian practice acts as one factor that encourages a sense of community beyond the immediate setting. This element is what gives Christianity its power in Africa.

Given that power, a sense of irony emerges from comparing theology for and about Africa with the practice of Christianity. Churches and faith have become embedded in many African contexts. African Christians have defined their own faith and developed their own practices. The difference seems much more institutional than a matter of faith. Yet theology still seems caught in debates first aired at the turn of the century.

So that leaves the central question – is there a universal in African Christianity? The first answer is that millions of Christians in Africa believe they are members of, in the words of the Nicene Creed, the 'holy catholic church, apostolic and universal'. More to the point, Sanneh's work reminds us of the critical role of the Word itself in creating that unity. Yet, as the debates about African theology show, a tension remains. A senior Catholic priest from Tanzania once told me that missionaries made people feel dirty. Such tensions reflect the power, both political and cultural, that accompanied the spread of mission Christianity. And that structure is still with us.

Notes

* I would like to thank the participants in the workshops on 'African Expressions of Christianity in Eastern Africa', held in Madison, those in the conference on 'Africans Meeting Missionaries: Rethinking Colonial Encounters' at Minnesota, and Tamara Giles-Vernick for their comments on the paper.

1 T. O. Beidelman has written: 'Christian missions represent the most naive and ethno-centric, and therefore the most thorough-going, facet of colonial life. Administrators and planters aimed at limited ends such as order, taxation, profits, cheap labor, and advantages against competing Europeans; and in that quest they sometimes attempted psychic domination as well. Missionaries invariably aimed at overall changes in the beliefs and actions of native peoples, at colonization of heart and mind as well as body.' *Colonial Evangelism* (Bloomington, 1982), 5–6.

2 See Mahmood Mamdani, *Citizen and Subject* (Princeton, 1996) for a discussion of this concept. Mamdani totally ignores the role of Christianity in the continuing transformation of Africa, however.

3 In the penultimate chapter of *Paths in the Rainforests* (Madison, 1990), entitled 'Death of a tradition', Jan Vansina discusses this conflict in terms that cast doubt on the possibility of developing a compelling synthesis. He writes: 'The peoples of the rainforests began first to doubt their own legacies and then to adopt portions of the foreign heritage. But they clung to their own languages and to much of the older cognitive content carried by them. Thus they turned into cultural schizophrenics, striving for a new synthesis which could not be achieved as long as freedom of action was denied them.... The transition to independence occurred, however, without the guidance of a basic new common tradition. Today that is still the situation, and the people of equatorial Africa are still bereft of a common mind and purpose.' 247–8.

4 Benedict R. O'G. Anderson, *Imagined Communities*, 2nd edition (New York, 1991), 10.

5 John S. Mbiti, *Introduction to African Religion*, 2nd edition (Portsmouth, 1991); Aylward

Introduction

Shorter, *African Christian Theology – Adaptation or Incarnation?* (Maryknoll, 1977).

6 Lamin Sanneh, *Translating the Message* (Maryknoll, 1989).
7 John Parratt, *Reinventing Christianity* (Grand Rapids, 1995).
8 Richard Gray, *Black Christians and White Missionaries* (New Haven, 1990).
9 Elizabeth Isichei, *A History of Christianity in Africa* (Grand Rapids, 1995), 84–8.
10 Marcia Wright, *German Missions in Tanganyika 1891–1941* (Oxford, 1971).
11 Parratt, *Reinventing Christianity*, 6–8.
12 See, for example, Carl-Erik Sahlberg, *From Krapf to Rugambwa* (Nairobi, 1986) and Elisabeth Knox, *Signal on the Mountain* (Canberra, 1991). These works are not hagiographies, but they do celebrate the role of missions in the expansion of the church.
13 See Parratt's discussion, *Reinventing Christianity*, 8–9.
14 See, for example, Benjamin C. Ray, *African Religions* (Englewood Cliffs, 1976), 193–215.
15 Sanneh, *Translating*, 31–32.
16 Sanneh does not go into great detail on one case that seems to contradict his thesis, the spread of Catholicism in Latin America. See Robert H. Jackson and Edward Castillo, *Indians, Franciscans, and Spanish Colonization* (Albuquerque, 1995).
17 Sanneh, *Translating*, 3.
18 Sanneh, *Translating*, 163.
19 See Knox, *Signal*, 102, 165; Ernest Kongola, *Historia mfupi ya Mbeya ya 'Wevunjiliza' toka 1688 mpaka 1986: 'Mbukwa Muhindi wa Cimambi'* (Dodoma, 1986), 18; *idem, Ybile ya almasi ya Dayosisi ya Central Tanganyika* (Dodoma, 1987), 6–7; Church Missionary Society Archives, G3 A8/01 1903, Bishop Peel, 'Notes on a Visit to Usagara and Ugogo', Oct. 6, 1903; and Gregory H. Maddox, '"Leave, Wagogo! There is no food!": famine and survival in Ugogo, Central Tanzania, 1916–1961' (PhD, Northwestern, 1988), Appendix; interviews with Job Lusinde and Nafali Lusinde.
20 Beidelman, *Colonial Evangelism*, 108.
21 See also Brigitta Larsson, *Conversion to Greater Freedom?* (Uppsala, 1991), 144–67.
22 Elizabeth Isichei, *History of Christianity in Africa* (Grand Rapids, 1995), 87; Larsson, *Conversion to Greater Freedom?*, 69–81.
23 See Beidelman, *Colonial Evangelism*, for example.
24 John Iliffe, *A Modern History of Tanganyika* (Cambridge, 1979); Terence Ranger, 'The death of Chaminuka: spirit mediums, nationalism, and the guerilla war in Zimbabwe', *African Affairs*, 81 (1982), 349–69; John Lonsdale, 'Mau Maus of the mind: making Mau Mau and remaking Kenya', *Journal of African History*, 31 (1990), 393–422; J. B. Peires, 'The central beliefs of the Xhosa cattle–killing', *Journal of African History*, 28 (1987), 43.
25 See John Comaroff and Jean Comaroff, *Of Revelation and Revolution* (Chicago, 1991); Paul S. Landau, *The Realm of the Word* (Portsmouth, 1995).
26 Wright, *German Missions*; Roland Oliver, *The Missionary Factor in East Africa* (London, 1952).
27 See Shorter, *African Christian Theology*, 149–53 for a discussion of the Roman Synod 1974 on evangelization. Shorter's own view, although phrased in terms of dialogue, comes through as one still of Catholic dogma as the standard around which African practice fluctuates, 1–19.
28 Parratt, *Reinventing Christianity*, 5–7.
29 Sanneh, *Translating*, 25.
30 Bengt Sundkler, *Zulu Zion and Some Swazi Zionists* (Oxford, 1976).
31 Ray, *African Religions*, 193–4; Ian Linden and Jane Linden, 'John Chilembwe and the New Jerusalem', *Journal of African History*, 12 (1971), 629–51.
32 Sundkler, *Zulu Zion*.
33 Isichei, *History of Christianity*, 253.
34 Parratt, *Reinventing Christianity*, 6.
35 Parratt, *Reinventing Christianity*, 163–91.
36 Quoted in Shorter, *African Christian Theology*, 150.
37 Quoted in Parratt, *Reinventing Christianity*, 120.
38 Parratt, *Reinventing Christianity*, 169–91.
39 Parratt, *Reinventing Christianity*, 28–49, 122–36.

II

Mission

Our case studies start with the evangelization of East Africa from the nineteenth century by European and American mission societies. Focused on the early years of mission activity in Zaramo, Kilimanjaro and Maasai, these studies run contrary to the triumphalism of many mission studies to highlight the initial difficulties and failures of mission in Africa. In spite of the traumatic moral crises provoked by disease, famine and political violence in the later nineteenth century, which fundamentally challenged Africans' beliefs, Africans were repelled by the cultural arrogance and intolerance of missionaries, their linguistic *faux pas*, and the seeming irrelevance of their message. The first Christian converts thus tended to be few and drawn largely from the ranks of ex-slaves, refugees, alienated youth or women fleeing unhappy marriages.

This is a remarkable set of conclusions, especially for the Kilimanjaro area where Chaga subsequently converted to Christianity in large numbers, but as Lema, himself a prominent Chaga Lutheran, shows in his detailed study of Chaga religion and the early Leipzig missionaries, the initial stages were fraught with peril. The lack of congruence between late nineteenth-century German Lutheran Christianity and Chaga religion and the cultural chauvinism of the missionaries limited their appeal to a few opportunistic outcasts, who were then shunned by wider Chaga society. Only later, as the missionaries broadened their appeal and the advantages of Christianity in the expanding colonial order became more obvious, did Chaga convert in any numbers.

Kimambo's study is even more critical, as the Berlin missions collaborated with colonial officials and employed non-local Swahili-speaking agents to proselytize unsuccessfully among Zaramo. Faced with meagre results from the very beginning, the mission struggled in the face of adversity brought by the Maji-Maji rising, the First World War and the peripatetic presence

37

of missionaries thereafter, and it never did achieve much success when compared with the spread of Islam throughout the area.

Waller's analysis of the Africa Inland Mission among Kenya Maasai is similarly critical of the approaches of the missionaries, but in placing their activities within the broader context of contemporary Maasai politics and the experiences of the first Maasai Christians, he moves beyond essentialist views of mission and Maasai 'conservatism' to show how Christianity failed to meet the needs and aspirations of Maasai themselves, Christian and non-Christian alike. His detailed account of the approaches and experiences of the early AIM missionaries, conveyed through their theology, policies, practices and personalities; of the lived experiences of the first Maasai Christians; and of the conflicts between the missionaries, Maasai and the colonial administration all show the critical need to understand African Christianity in the very specific historical contexts in which it developed, contexts in which African Christians themselves played a dominant role in its potential success or failure.

Given these studies, one might interpret the early history of missions in East Africa in fairly dire terms, but later studies in this volume point to a broader range of possible interpretations. In contrast to the cultural arrogance and intolerance noted above, Smythe's study of the White Fathers in Fipa points to a greater degree of congruence between Fipa and Catholic beliefs and practices, as well as to greater cultural tolerance shown by the priests as they adopted familiar roles within Fipa society as fathers and patrons. This left Fipa freer to interpret the faith for themselves, and they were remarkably quick to allow their children to be baptized, even as adults continued to resist the Christian message.

Sandgren's study of the AIM in Kamba further emphasizes the significant differences between individual missionaries and mission strategies, with the linguistically fluent and sympathetic Rhoad much more successful than his culturally arrogant AIM colleagues, whose lack of sympathy for Kamba social practices and educational aspirations contributed to massive defections from the AIM to the independent African Brotherhood Church. He also notes a broad range of Kamba responses; while many were drawn to the church for the educational and other secular opportunities it provided, others responded on spiritual grounds to the Christian message.

The overall process of mission in Africa thus incorporated an array of very specific historical processes that varied enormously in the individual contexts in which they actually took place. If we are to understand the process broadly, then, we must first appreciate it narrowly, paying careful attention to the attitudes, beliefs, practices and strategies of the individual missions and missionaries; the historical context in which they encountered their potential converts; and their relations with both colonial authorities and local peoples as well as the beliefs, practices, experiences, needs and aspirations of their potential followers.

Three

Chaga Religion &
Missionary Christianity
on Kilimanjaro

The Initial Phase, 1893–1916

ANZA A. LEMA

In order to appreciate the culture of another society, one should be able to study and understand the basic principles of its cultural life, including its religion. It follows, then, that the analysis of creeds and dogma, of sacred writings, and of theological treatises are of great importance in explaining the social, economic, moral and political life of a people.

Equally valid is the more circuitous, but often more fundamental approach that begins at the opposite end, where the basic structures and patterns of community life are analysed in detail. The fundamental beliefs and assumptions that undergird the life of that society emerge by implication. For what the people believe about the nature and existence of God, about themselves as men and women, about their individual and community destiny, about their world and the significance of its inanimate objects and its manifold life forms determines the basic patterns of community life.

This second approach has proved particularly interesting and useful for studying religion in traditional African societies. The very nature of religion in communities like that of the Chaga precluded the possibility of studying it as a separate entity. Traditional Chaga religion was informal, natural and all-pervasive. It did not originate in the mind or from the experience of any particular individual at a given point in history, as was the case with many other religions. Rather, it represented the communal wisdom and experience of the Chaga people accumulated over time.

It was passed on from generation to generation, partly through specific oral teaching and partly through the example given by adults. There were no written records of any kind, no sacred scriptures embodying the story and teachings of a great religious leader or a holy man or woman, no dogma or creeds laid down, and no historical documents or theological writings to help trace the growth of religious beliefs and ceremonies. As a

39

result, no formal literary study of Chaga religion has been possible. Instead, the social historian has to rely on oral traditions: the still-remembered songs, prayers, proverbs and religious lessons. Older people's memories of dances, of traditional rites and ceremonies, and of the day-to-day life of the community as it was lived are also invaluable. Indeed, a study of everyday life has proved essential for a proper understanding of religion in Chaga society. The creed of the Kilimanjaro people was engraved, so to speak, not on paper leaves nor on tablets of stone, but in the life of the community.

Chaga Religion – An Overview

Chaga religious concepts

Life, as viewed by Chaga, was to be lived and experienced as a whole entity. It was never compartmentalized into artificially isolated spheres, each demanding a separate function from the individual. The arbitrary division of community life into political, economic, social and religious compartments, each operating more or less independently of the others, was unknown. The Western dichotomy between the sacred and the secular was also an inconceivable idea to Chaga. Religion was embedded in all. The spiritual and the physical were inseparably interwoven aspects of the same whole.[1] This conception of religion as the essence of all life proved to be a powerful unifying force.

As a distinctive community group, Chaga had their own religion. Though it had much in common with the religious experiences of other communities throughout East Africa, Chaga religion was nevertheless a unique expression of the common life of the various communities living on the slopes of Kilimanjaro. The body of religious beliefs and practices was passed on from generation to generation of the community. New ideas and rites were sometimes absorbed from other communities; at other times modifications were introduced in response to changing circumstances. But one community never attempted to force its religion on another. Chaga religion had no proselytizing objective: there were no missionaries or messengers and there were no converts, in the formal sense of the word, from other faiths.

Each mature Chaga, through informal childhood learning and specific instruction in initiation school, knew and understood the religion of his or her people. Religion was never a matter for argument in the community. There were no discussions or debates about the existence of God. On the whole, there were no people who thought of themselves as sceptics, agnostics or atheists. Rather, each person accepted his or her role as a religious being in a religious community almost as naturally as becoming a husband or wife, or a father or mother. Indeed, the roles could not be separated. The individual's existence as a man or woman and his or her status as an adult depended on acceptance of the community's beliefs and participation in its ceremonies, rituals and festivals. To reject the common belief or to disregard the community's practices was an act of voluntary excommunication that cut the individual adrift from every part of the community's life, a fate almost as bad as death.[2]

The explanation – God (Ruwa)

Chaga songs and stories, praise names and proverbs, prayers and religious ceremonies all attest to the community's belief in a God who was worthy, above all life forms, to be worshipped. He was regarded as the Supreme Being, the source of all life. Yet the names people used to address God imply that his essential nature and character eluded them. He remained a mystery to them, a Being beyond the reach of their minds to imagine or describe. Dr Bruno Gutmann, one of the early Leipzig missionaries in Kilimanjaro, recorded that God was addressed in the prayers uttered by a Chaga man as the sun rose each morning to begin a new day as 'the man of heaven or chief whose name we do not know'.[3] For Gutmann, 'this address expresses the awe of the one who is incomprehensible because that which one can name one can master'.[4] The expression 'man of heaven' or 'man of the sky' also occurred several times in Chaga initiation lessons recorded by Gutmann. Such names provide a clue to the basic Chaga ideas about God. Although they recognized that God was involved in various ways in the affairs of men and women on earth, Chaga thought of God as dwelling permanently in the sky, alone and beyond the reach of human beings.

The most common Chaga name for God implied not only that he was an inhabitant of the heavens but also that he was the source of all light and power. In East and Central Kilimanjaro, God was referred to as 'Ruwa', while, in West Kilimanjaro and especially in Machame and Masama, he was known as 'Iruva'. But *ruwa* or *iruva* was also the Chaga name for the sun. In western Kilimanjaro the name commonly used for the sun was *kyendesa* (giver of light), though sometimes the sun was referred to as *iruva lyivaa* (God that shines).[5]

Some of the early Christian missionaries insisted that Chaga considered that God was the sun, and vice versa. The question of whether Chaga actually regarded God and the sun as one and the same being can be as complicated as the Christian theology of the triune God. Most recent commentators, however, would be inclined to accept Professor Mbiti's view that *ruwa* was used as the name for the sun chiefly because it symbolized so vividly the source of life and light, everlasting power, omniscience and endurance, all qualities that Chaga attributed to the being of God.[6]

In traditional thinking Ruwa was an invisible and spiritual being, rather than a physical being. There is no evidence in oral traditions that Chaga thought of God as possessing a human body. Nor were there any attempts to portray him visually in a picture or a carving. The characteristics attributed to God were never deduced by a process of theoretical or logical reasoning, but they became apparent in people's experience of God at work in their own lives. Down through the generations his character remained steadfast and unchanging.

The Chaga concept of the omniscience of God was stressed in a concrete human metaphor; God was the eternal watcher or 'silent observer'.[7] Nothing human beings did in the secret places of the forest, within the walls of their own huts, in the darkness of the night, or in the innermost recesses of their hearts escaped the scrutiny of God. From his home in heaven, he saw, heard and knew all that happened on earth.

To Chaga, God was everlasting and omnipotent. His presence filled and overflowed all the experiences of an individual. Traditional proverbs in almost all parts of Kilimanjaro suggest that Chaga regarded Ruwa as possessing boundless capabilities, strength and power. He was supreme over all. In his early account of Chaga, Charles Dundas, a former British district officer in Moshi, stressed that the Chaga God was all-knowing, all-powerful and eternal:

> Ruwa has power to do all things. Ruwa does not change, as Ruwa was of old so he is now. Nor does he lie, as he says so he will do. If a man does evil, though it be at night, Ruwa sees him. If the chief and his warriors surround a man, they cannot kill him if Ruwa does not permit it. When a man sickens and goes to the diviners and slaughters many goats and oxen (for sacrifice), he will not be cured if Ruwa does not wish it.[8]

This description by Dundas illustrates the way Chaga deduced the nature of God from his activity in the world. His infinite greatness was revealed in his work as Creator, Sustainer and Judge of all. Everything in the universe that had come into being was governed and sustained by God's hands. His power and wisdom had formed the heavens; brought into creation mountains, lakes and plains; carved and fashioned each plant and animal; and created man and woman. To Chaga, Ruwa's work involved not only the physical creation of the human being, but also the shaping and moulding of each individual's character and destiny. The ultimate power of life and death was his; no man, woman or child died unless Ruwa willed it. Each new child was a blessing, for which God was thanked.

The way Chaga identified Ruwa with the sun, the source of light and warmth so necessary for life and growth, illustrated one aspect of this. Ruwa was also regarded as the giver of the other vital ingredient for plant and animal growth, rain. Chaga delighted in the sound and the feel of the rain, sensing its promise for a good season in which they harvested plenty and prospered. The beginning of the rainy season was always greeted with great joy. In some oral traditions, rain was called God's spittle or saliva, the sign of his special favour and blessing. For in many African societies spittle was a symbol of health, happiness, prosperity and well-being.[9]

Ruwa's providence not only ensured proper growth of pastures and crops, but it also bestowed health and fertility on livestock and human beings. An individual whose herds increased rapidly and who was the father or mother of many children was blessed by God. Thus Ruwa's continuing work in the world was to provide for the well-being of people. His gifts were enjoyed in a concrete way in the lives of his people. For the most part, they believed that God's providence did not entirely depend on a person's good behaviour or propitiatory sacrifices. Rather, Ruwa bestowed life and the means of life impartially, according to his own unchanging will and purpose.

What happened when famine, disease or other disasters threatened a community's prosperity and health? When sudden calamity struck? In such times, people turned to God for explanation and guidance. Special sacrifices and prayers were offered imploring God's help in their distress. In cases of sickness and barrenness, especially, people turned to God, hoping that he would grant healing and fertility. And, if a sick child recovered, a barren woman conceived, or drought-breaking rain fell, people gave thanks to Ruwa for his deliverance or healing, even when other agents had also been involved. When, however, disease or calamity proved fatal, Chaga were left to try and explain how far Ruwa was to blame. They regarded Ruwa as fundamentally the originator of all the good in the world. Could he also send suffering and misfortune to people? Yet, ultimately, they believed life could end only if Ruwa decreed it.[10]

In some instances the dilemma of Ruwa's involvement in calamity or death could be explained in terms of his work as the judge of people. His ultimate justice, they believed, was fair and impartial. In situations where community leaders were called upon to pronounce or execute judgement, Ruwa's justice was often invoked. Chaga also had a strong sense of the immediacy of Ruwa's judgement in daily life. Thus, when sickness or misfortune befell a family, people declared that it was punishment for misdeeds committed by a member of the family. Parents warned their children that Ruwa would surely punish anyone who disobeyed or showed disrespect to the elders or who broke the laws of the community. Conversely, the person whose field, cattle and family prospered was being rewarded by Ruwa for his or her upright life. In this way, the concept of Ruwa as a moral judge was used to uphold social sanctions, strengthen accepted patterns of behaviour and reinforce the solidarity of communal life.[11] Dundas explained this aspect of Chaga belief in detail:

> If a child is sent by its parents, and that child refuses to obey or if a child quarrels with parents and people seize the property of the parents, such a child is rejected by Ruwa and will die before he marries. And a robber who steals and kills people, such a man cannot hide himself, there will come a day when Ruwa will place him in the hands of the judge and [he] will die with all his clan.[12]

The Chaga concept of Ruwa's relationship with humankind cannot be fully appreciated apart from the paradox of his simultaneous transcendence and immanence. Many Chaga proverbs and oral traditions implied that God was beyond human reach, having no direct communication with people. Many early missionaries maintained that Chaga ignored Ruwa in their everyday lives when things were going well. They seemed to acknowledge him mainly in times of dire necessity when all other appeals had failed, directing frequent sacrifices and prayers to the spirits instead. When

Dundas questioned people about this assertion their reply indicated clearly that they regarded the spirits as Ruwa's emissaries in the world. They felt that the spirits who had power to influence their lives needed to be appeased with frequent sacrifices.[13]

Chaga clearly felt that Ruwa was an abiding presence in the world. True, Ruwa did not speak or manifest himself directly to them, but this was not proof of his non-existence or impotence, nor even of his permanent separation from his creation. Rather, it was an indication that his divine activity was understood most fully in the unseen, unheralded life force that filled the whole cosmos. They never formulated any theological doctrine about the life of God as such. Yet they acknowledged Ruwa's help and providence in their everyday affairs. Their very lives were an ongoing response to his continuing presence and power in the world. They felt that they could come to him in prayer and worship in any place at any time.[14] Professor Mbiti has suggested that this paradox of God's immanence and transcendence in black Africa could best be understood as an attempt to acknowledge two different aspects of African experience of God.[15] When they reasoned about Ruwa, they appeared to be awed by his transcendence, his existence above and beyond human beings. In terms of concrete reality of everyday living, however, they knew him to be close. He was omnipresent in the world he had created and still sustained.

Chaga legends of creation, of humankind's origin, and of their relationship with Ruwa highlighted this paradoxical experience. Perhaps, indeed, these stories handed down from generation to generation were intended to explain it. Though there were conflicting accounts of just how human beings were created, all the legends stressed that human beings, both male and female, were the climax of God's creation. Indeed, one of the Chaga terms for addressing God was 'God who allowed human beings to burst forth' (*Iruva mwitaswa vandu*). The title stemmed from an old myth that maintained that humankind had originally been sealed within a vessel that God opened. Humankind was thus enabled to burst forth and live. Another legend declared that originally God had created the first people in his heavenly home. They then descended to earth by means of a thread spun by a spider.[16] This latter story stressed the divine origin of humankind, giving them a place of pre-eminence above the rest of creation. It also explained the beginning of God's separation from humankind. Humankind came down to dwell on earth while Ruwa remained in the heavens.

Humankind was the focal point around which the rest of the universe revolved. In contrast to European attitudes, however, Chaga never viewed a person as an individual, but only as an integral part of a whole community. A person was never considered as a separate entity, apart from his or her family and society. His or her safe birth was seen as the culmination of the efforts and activities of many people among his or her immediate family and kin. Chaga survival depended on the physical, emotional and spiritual support of other people in the community, both forebears and contemporaries. The joys of one person at his or her marriage or at the birth of an offspring were the joys of the whole community. The sorrows and sufferings on occasions of sickness, disaster and death were equally shared by kin and neighbours. A person could become aware of his or her existence and significance as·an individual being only if he or she were meaningfully related to others. The traditional developmental rites of ear piercing, tooth extraction, circumcision and initiation were highly dramatic and effective means of incorporating individuals more deeply into society. In Professor Mbiti's words, an African could explain his or her existence only by saying 'I am because we are; and since we are, therefore I am.'[17] In Chaga society, the family constituted the central component. For family was the space in which life was lived, in which rights were claimed and exercised. The dimensions of family vary from place to place, often extending beyond the basic nucleus of father, mother and children. It was the place, more than any other, in which solidarity, communion and interdependence were experienced.

'Warumu' or the living dead

Belief in the departed, *warumu*, as integral and influential members of the living community was a vital aspect of traditional religion. Many Christian missionaries used the term 'ancestors' when speaking of the dead of earlier generations, and they described the religious rites associated with the departed members of the community as ancestor worship. Otto Raum of the Leipzig society recognized the extension of the family and community beyond death and made constant reference to the ancestors. He stressed their educative role and described how parents and the community appealed to them as disciplinary agents in helping to mould the young into socially acceptable patterns of behaviour. Again, Professor Mbiti has argued that the term ancestor in this regard was a misnomer. The dead who continued to be accepted as part of the living community were not, strictly speaking, a person's forefathers in direct genealogical line, but they included brothers, sisters, uncles, aunts and even children – any member of the family who had been taken by death. The recently deceased were thus best described as the 'living dead'.[18]

Chaga believed that when a person died he or she did not pass immediately into total oblivion or non-existence. The dead remained alive in several ways. They continued to be regarded as people who had lived in some form and were supposed to be important members of the living community, perpetuated in the persons of their children and grand-children. In the memory of the family, kin and contemporaries, the person remained alive: hence the significance of the term 'living dead', for though physically dead and buried they remained present in the hearts and minds of the living. Initially, the name of a recently dead person would be frequently mentioned, as members of the family and friends remembered his or her character and personality. With the passing of years, the name became mentioned less and less as fewer and fewer people were left alive who could refer to him or her by name. And the person who had no family or relations, no living offspring, could not hope to prolong his or her existence in this way.

The 'living dead' were associated with a great number of communal rites and ceremonies that revolved around birth, initiation, marriage and death. Many were designed to strengthen the ties that bound the 'living dead' and their surviving relatives together into the community. Libations of beer and milk and the offering of choice cuts of sacrificed animals should not, however, be interpreted as ancestor worship. Rather, they should be regarded as a dramatic act of remembrance, communion and fellowship. They symbolized a common meal that living members of the family shared with their 'living dead'. It was believed that the 'living dead' remained closely interested in the affairs of the family and the community. In some places, oral traditions said that the 'living dead' could be heard performing dances at the time of the finger millet harvest when local beer was plentiful.

The 'living dead' could have a profound effect on the family in the present life. Thus, if an individual wanted to live a long and happy life, he or she had to be careful to keep in harmony with the 'living dead'. They were the guardians of family life, upholding traditional customs and morality within the family circle. Tremendous pressure was put on an individual to remain loyal to traditional beliefs and practices of the community and not to turn to new beliefs and ceremonies that would eventually disrupt both the individual's and the community's union with the 'living dead'.[19]

The role of the 'living dead' in community life stemmed from a dual level of existence. Because they had a spiritual rather than a bodily form, they belonged to the world of spirits. Thus, they were closer than living persons were to Ruwa. Yet they still continued to inhabit the physical world in the bodily form of their heirs in succeeding generations and in the memory of their family and friends. Thus they were regarded as living links between Ruwa and humankind. Chaga were conscious that the 'living dead' had until recently been involved in the business of living. Yet now their spirit forms gave them direct communication with God. Consequently, people felt it was easier and more effective to direct their everyday prayers and requests to the 'living dead' rather than to the remote, detached figure of Ruwa.

Spirits — the divinities

In the ontological hierarchy of life, Ruwa represented the pinnacle of the pyramid, the highest form of spiritual being, while at its base were natural phenomena and objects not endowed with biological life. In between were all forms of animal and plant life, above which were the 'living dead', a transitional level between humankind and spirits or those closest to God in terms of communication, but no longer recognized as human beings. This last form of survival beyond death represented not the fulfilment and maturation of individual life, but the shrivelling of the pride of humankind into a shadowy depersonalized collective existence.

Not all spirits, however, had once been human beings. Some, it was believed, had been spirits from the beginning. Indeed, in Chaga thinking, the whole of the universe they knew – the world of trees, animals, mountains, lakes, rocks and streams that surrounded them – was filled with spirits. Such spirits were regarded as powerful and significant forces in their particular environments. A spirit had power to punish people with whom he had had close relations. Some spirits revealed themselves in dreams to diviners (*mmasya*), medicine men and magicians, whose work required that they be perceptive to spiritual forces at work in the world.[20]

These spirits were regarded as neither intrinsically good nor evil. Rather, they were agents of God who punished or rewarded human beings according to their merits. As Dundas wrote:

> The spirit is the deputy of Ruwa who sends it to do his work. To cast sickness on people, to give them children, to bring famine, to mock bad men, to demand cattle, goats, and sheep and to take them to Ruwa and to bring smallpox and war into the country, to kill such and such a one by sickness and to kill all those who Ruwa wants.[21]

Their close links with Ruwa gave the spirits more than human influence on the world. People feared the spirits' capacity to bring misfortune into their lives. Many went to great lengths to propitiate the spirits to their own benefit. Since Chaga felt that they had little direct communication with Ruwa, they regarded the spirits as an invaluable group of intermediaries between themselves and God. When Dundas asked Chaga why they appeared 'to fear and obey the spirits more than they did Ruwa', he was told:

> When the chief sends to demand something that is his due, and on that day you have naught to give, who will you try to appease, the chief or his messenger that he may speak well of you to the chief and the chief may have mercy on you? And if you give bad words to the spirit who is sent to you, or refuse him that which the diviner had counselled you to give (i.e. sacrifices), that spirit will go to Ruwa and accuse you and Ruwa will be angered and will send another spirit, a foreign spirit, who is not of your ancestry, to afflict you greatly and to kill you. For this reason we honor and fear the spirits more.[22]

The importance of the physical world

In contrast to the view of some Asiatic religions, which deny and reject the physical world in order to gain the spiritual one, Chaga made no attempt to distinguish between the physical and spiritual worlds. They saw both worlds as integral aspects of the unity of the universe, and so their sensitivity to the spirit world did not prevent them from taking special delight in the physical realm. In all that they did they affirmed the value and validity of the physical experiences of living. According to many oral traditions, they prayed daily to Ruwa for the blessing of a long life. After death they sought to prolong their contact with the light, vigour and warmth of life on earth.[23] God, they believed, had created the physical world for humankind's benefit and enjoyment. Thus they regarded the world around them, the heavens above and the earth beneath, as living proof of God's power to create and sustain life. He alone had shaped the myriad forms of animals and plants and put his life into them.[24]

Although the earth was regarded as humankind's domain, certain natural phenomena were closely associated with religious rites and practices. Mountain peaks reaching towards heaven were regarded as especially sacred, the dwelling places of God when he came down to earth. Thus, many Chaga faced the great dome of Kibo whenever they addressed Ruwa in their morning prayers. In some communities, people always slept facing the mountain. Streams and running water were often associated with a natural symbol of cleansing, purity and growth. Certain plants and animals also gained religious significance. Goats, sheep and cattle were used for sacrifices. In some areas, the great fig tree, *mfumu*, was regarded as sacrosanct.[25] Any person who dared to cut off even one of its branches had to sacrifice a black ram to appease the anger of the disturbed divinities. Otherwise he or she could expect to be punished in many ways for the rest of his life.

Personal causation for events in life, family, and community

For Chaga, there was one grave and inexplicable flaw in the world Ruwa had created for them. The problem of evil, in the form of misfortune, sickness and ultimate death, was puzzling and deeply disturbing. The matter became more acute because of the Chaga view that nothing happened by chance. They held no scientific explanations for events in terms of physical, chemical and biological reactions. Instead, they believed that every event or phenomenon, from an earthquake to the death of a cow, or from a sick child to the failure of crops, had a personal cause. Even a nightmare or sleeplessness must, they believed, have been caused by someone.

To say that crops were ruined because of a locust plague caused by favourable weather conditions in breeding grounds a hundred or more miles away only led to more questions. Why did the favourable weather conditions occur? And why at this particular time? Why were their fields, and not their neighbours', affected? There could be only one convincing answer. Someone, somewhere, must have caused it. Perhaps it was done because of an inadvertent misdeed or neglect of duty. Or perhaps it was done deliberately through witchcraft or the defiance of community customs.

Similarly, parents could never be content with the idea that their child had contacted tetanus through a cut he or she received after tripping on a stone. To them the most pertinent questions would still remain unanswered. Why did the child trip? Why did the disease affect the cut and not similar cuts of other children? Somebody must have caused it by evil charms or witchcraft. Hence, whenever people were confronted by misfortune or sickness, they were desperately anxious to know what being, whether living, 'living dead' or spirit, was responsible.[26] Only then could palliative measures be taken to try to root out the evil that afflicted them.

Some evil could be explained as the natural and inevitable consequences of breaking laws that were the very foundation of community life. Many proverbs and stories, for instance, warned children that, if they showed disrespect toward their grandparents or disobeyed their parents, they could expect to be overtaken by misfortune in adult life. Barrenness and miscarriage, sickness and madness were often explained in this way. A young person who fathered an illegitimate child could fail to produce a legitimate heir.

Logically, such a consequence would have to be attributed to Ruwa, the ultimate upholder of moral law. Yet, on the whole, Chaga rejected the idea that Ruwa had created evil, for they believed he was all good and beyond the scope and knowledge of evil.[27] Yet they felt compelled to explain some of their personal and community experiences in terms of God's punishment.

Breaches of communal law, such as rape, murder and theft that seriously undermined the community's safety and well-being, came to be regarded as offences against Ruwa. But he did not execute punishment. Instead, he sent spirits as his agents to bring evil and misfortune upon those who deserved it. Ruwa's justice was always worked out in the span of a person's lifetime. There was no suggestion that punishment was suspended to take effect in a life beyond death.

In all the critical events of life – childbirth, circumcision, initiation and marriage – healing rites included propitiatory sacrifices and appeals to the spirits for their active aid and support. When misfortune or trouble did strike, people often employed a diviner to discover what spirit had been offended. They then decided what propitiatory rites and sacrifices of explanation needed to be performed in order to restore peace and harmony.[28]

The need to find a convincing personal causation for every evil act led to fear of witchcraft and magic. Most of the evil experienced in everyday life was ascribed to the general malevolence and deliberate malefaction of one human being against another. Many traditional customs were designed to safeguard an individual and his or her family from witchcraft and the evil eye.

The family priest

In Chaga society there were no priests ordained or specially set aside for religious duties. Every mature Chaga man was a priest for himself and his family. His obligations as head of the household and defender of his wife and children were linked with his responsibilities as the religious leader of the family. Whenever it was necessary to offer sacrifices, prayers or libations, the father presided at the rites. He was responsible for perpetuating the memory and authority of the 'living dead', offering sacrifices and libations to ensure that their benign influence would bring uninterrupted blessings and happiness to the family. In times of sickness and disaster, he made sacrifices to propitiate the offended spirits. Thus he was the acknowledged mediator between his family on earth and the realm of the 'living dead', the spirits and even the supreme being.[29] The health and prosperity of the family depended on his effective mediation.

Traditional worship

Just what did these traditional religious rites and ceremonies involve? When did they take place? What was their nature and function? Usually they were not bound to a particular time and place, as the Christian pattern of Sunday worship in church tends to be. True, some Chaga ceremonies were performed with unfailing regularity, according to long accepted and inherited traditions, or at places of special religious significance, and some were celebrated according to the cyclic patterns of nature and community life.

Traditional worship was not so much a meditation through words and thoughts as a drama of deeds and acts. Body and spirit together expressed faith and commitment in a concrete way through songs and dances, symbolic meals, sacrifices and offerings.[30] When words were used they usually consisted of brief invocations, songs and proverbs, and curses or blessings. Preaching, exhortations and exposition were unknown. Goats, cattle and sheep were the usual Chaga animals of sacrifice. Often they had to be of a special type to suit the occasion – all black, for example, or pure white and unspotted. After the animal had been slaughtered at the burial place of the 'living dead' (*kifu*), part was set aside as the sacrificial meat. Libations of milk and banana beer were also prepared. In some instances, offerings of plants, fruits and vegetables were made.

Most sacrifices, libations and offerings were made to the spirits and the 'living dead' to ensure their continuing good will and cooperation.[31] The shared food was a symbol that the 'living dead' remained in fellowship with surviving members of the family.[32] The first act performed by every mature Chaga man when he arose in the morning was to go outside the hut, face the snow-covered summit of Kibo, spit twice into the sky, and invoke Ruwa in a simple brief prayer: '*Iruva Nndumi, ringa mmba yakwa*' (God Almighty, protect my family). Many children became aware of the abiding presence of Ruwa when, grasping their father's right hand, they first heard the words of his morning prayer. Gutmann explained that when Chaga prayed in this way 'at sunrise and were touched by the cool breeze which comes up in the morning they felt themselves invigorated by the heavenly blessing'.[33] Thus, in fulfilment of his role as family priest, the first person a Chaga man spoke with each day was God.

Religious rites

The religious rites recurring each year in connection with agriculture involved the whole community. When the time for planting came, every family prepared its field but no one planted until the traditional ceremonies had taken place. On the appointed day, the ritual leader of the community took some grains and mingled them with various symbols of fertility as he intoned adjurations to the soil to promote the seeds' growth. Then a magic liquid was sprayed over the fields to prevent insect pests from ruining the crop. About a month before harvest, other rites were performed to ensure a final spurt of growth and successful ripening of the crops. People joined in dances enacting the various activities involved in farming.

At the end of harvest came the rite known as 'separating the year'. All the uncircumcised teenage children of the community were led to the spot where the canals that watered their families' fields began. Wading into the canal, ritual leaders sprinkled the assembled children with water from the canal. The next day the houses of the participating children were adorned with dracaenas.

Circumcision and initiation rites were always preceded by prayers and sacrifices. When arrangements had been finalized for a girl's circumcision, for example, an unblemished goat was sacrificed to the 'living dead' at the place where her father's parents were buried. The father recited prayers, praying that the girl should not disgrace the family but pass the test of womanhood with honour and be granted a safe recovery. Similarly, just before a boy was circumcised his mother's brother poured out a pot of banana beer as a libation to the 'living dead', praying that the boy be protected from infection. As the boy left the river after bathing in its cold water in the early morning, his father offered a libation to all the male 'living dead' for a safe, speedy recovery.[34] Traditional prayers were also recited before the initiation lessons. At the beginning of the initiation, the teacher, after climbing up a tree above his pupils, called upon God in a praise name such as 'God of the permanent seat, who infest the firmament'.[35] Similarly, before an old woman began the day's initiation instruction on a tally stick, her assistant spat four times at the stick and four times up into the sky as the woman uttered prayers for Ruwa's blessings.[36]

Chaga rites for the dead had a two-fold, paradoxical purpose. On one hand, they were a lament for a human being who had passed from the full experience of living and a ritual preparation for the dead person's entrance into the spiritual realm. On the other hand, they stressed the dead person's continuing existence with the corporate life of the family. A person's spiritual immortality depended first on his or her continuing existence as a 'living dead', and, second, on the bodily form of children and grand-children he or she had. In the death rites, as in the ceremonies described earlier, the religious significance lay in the symbolic acts performed rather than in the spoken words or prayers.

Many Western observers have commented on the apparent functional nature of Chaga religious rites. The term 'worship' is not used here because in many ways it is an anachronism – a Christian term retrospectively imposed, in the belief that Chaga prayers and sacrifices were comparable in purpose and significance to Christian worship. Chaga showed no special preoccupation with the person of Ruwa; there was none of the old Hebrew thirsting after Yaweh and no seeking after God as the perfection and fulfilment of being. As long as the seasons were good, harvests plentiful, children healthy and their numbers increasing, and the community peaceful, it seemed that God, too, was happy. When sickness or death desolated a family, however, or when war, famine or disaster shattered community life, people were quick to make their appeal to Ruwa. Perhaps this existence of God as a functionary of their own need could be best understood in terms of the Chaga concept of Ruwa as dwelling beyond them in the sky, remote from their experience here and now. Yet such an interpretation overlooks the complementary Chaga awareness of the immanence of Ruwa as Creator and Sustainer of all life on which, in a dramatic and concrete way, so many of the religious rites of Chaga life were centred.

The Coming of Christianity and its Impact

Into this tightly knit community life with its own distinctive, rather highly developed and all pervasive religion came Christian missionaries representing the Leipzig Missionary Society, preaching a new faith. Though there were a number of vital points of contact, the basic differences between the two religions need to be understood in order to appreciate fully the impact of Christianity on Chaga beliefs.

In determining the initial impact Christianity had on the people of Kilimanjaro, the missionaries' cultural bias was probably even more important than their distinctively Lutheran doctrines. Many revealed a total inability to separate the essence of the Christian gospel from the European cultural mores that had penetrated it for over a thousand years. The missionaries sought to eradicate what they regarded as 'primitive', 'pagan', 'heathen' or 'savage' from religious life and to wipe out a superstitious reliance on witchcraft as the means of restoring harmony and health to life, replacing the latter with the supposedly more advanced, rational and objective explanations of European technology and science. They strove to develop a European mental outlook that divided life into separate compartments of secular and sacred. Many of them never paused to appreciate the awareness of the universalism of all life that arose out of the way Chaga lived in their environment.

In this, the attitude of nineteenth-century Lutheran missionaries in Africa contrasted sharply with the attitude of the missionaries of the first century. The early apostles faced the same problem of cultural bias in presenting the Gospel to the people of Rome, Greece and Asia Minor. How far should converts from non-Jewish backgrounds be expected to accept the cultural concomitants of Judaism that had nurtured the faith of Jesus and his disciples? The issue came to a head over circumcision, the distinguishing mark of all Jewish males and symbolizing their covenant with Yaweh. Should gentile Christians be forced to undergo this Jewish rite before they could be accepted as Christians? Saints Peter and Paul, the leaders of the early church, did not think so. The living truth of Christianity was to be free to express itself in different ways in different cultures. The power of the Holy Spirit and the love of God could not, they believed, be chained to the cultural traditions of one people. Thus St Paul could say:

> For though I am free with respect to all, I have made myself a slave to
> all, so that I might win more of them. To the Jews I became as a Jew,
> in order to win Jews. To those under the law I became as one under
> the law, so that I might win those under the law.... To the weak I became
> weak, so that I might win the weak. I have become all things to all people
> that I might by all means save some.[37]

When preaching to Jews, St Paul had thought, felt and spoken as a Jew.
When in the cities of Asia Minor and Greece, he strove to adopt the
language and philosophical outlook of ordinary Greek.

Unfortunately, nineteenth-century Lutheran missionaries showed none
of the vital faith and flexibility of their predecessors. They revealed little or
no capacity to preach the critical essence of their Christian faith and allow
their students to express it most meaningfully for themselves in their own
cultural terms. No wonder many African academics still consider the
Christian Church as a powerful outpost of Western imperialism, functioning at the expense of African cultures.[38]

The political dominance of Europeans throughout the world had led
European missionaries to the largely unconscious and quite unjustified
assumption that their culture was superior. In their own minds their
supremacy in art, commerce, technology, science and other aspects of
culture was attributed to the fact that theirs was a Christian society. Such
arrogance is not hard to find in the European literature:

> Only a Christian civilisation ... can benefit the people of that continent
> [Africa]. And if among the religions of the world we are to choose a
> power fit, able, strong enough for the work of the moral and spiritual
> regeneration of a whole continent, we shall find that power in the
> religion of Jesus Christ, *and find it only there*. Practically the fact remains
> that we can find nothing better.[39]

Elsewhere the same writer says:

> I have twenty-one years' experience among natives. I have lived with
> the Christian native, and I have lived and dined and slept with
> cannibals. But I have never yet met with a single people that civilisation
> without Christianity has civilised.[40]

Few Leipzig missionaries took the trouble to observe Chaga life in depth
or detail. Most of them failed to realize that, for Chaga, religion was not
a limited set of personal beliefs about worship of a Supreme Being that
could easily be isolated from a person's general way of life. Life, which is
the ultimate goal of the gospel, was also the major concern of Chaga
religion, but missionaries did not recognize the way traditional beliefs and
practices pervaded every aspect of the community, deepening and en-
riching it. Instead, they saw only the most dramatic or sensational religious
rites, some of which repulsed and horrified their refined European

sensibilities. Their feelings were well described by Charles Dundas, when he noted that missionaries refused to discuss the rites of the initiation camp because the 'practices are indecent and repulsive'.[41]

The missionaries began their work on assumptions drawn from superficial contacts, assumptions that eventually proved to be dangerously inadequate for effective missionary work. Without taking the trouble to acquaint themselves with the Chaga way of life, missionaries assumed that the people were hungering for the Christian gospel of salvation. In the words of James Stewart: 'Yet repulsive and unpromising as African paganism looks, it is an excellent field for missionary work. Its very misery makes it welcome relief. Its utter darkness makes it glad of light.'[42] They preached about the new faith with the expectation of having eager listeners who were dissatisfied with their own religion. When they were ignored or rebuffed, they lost no time in condemning 'natives' as godless heathens.[43]

Perhaps because it was so different from their own experience, they never understood the distinction in Chaga thought between Ruwa, the spirits and the 'living dead'. Chaga sacrifices and libations that were offered to the 'living dead' or were left on family graves were wrongly interpreted as animism and ancestor worship. The Leipzig missionary historian, Paul Fleisch, writing as late as 1936, dismissed Chaga religion, in a word, as 'animism'. He did concede, however, that 'belief in a Creator was still effective, even though apparently declining'.[44]

Thus, out of ignorance or cultural prejudice, missionaries belittled traditional religion by dismissing it as savage, barbaric and beneath their standards. The most conservative of them felt that traditional religion was the work of the devil, which they were called to root out of the society. Only then could the fallow soil be replanted with the seeds of Christianity germinated in European culture. As mission historian Donald Fraser noted in 1911:

> A full understanding of the significance of the Cross of Christ cannot be expected among a people who have little or no sense of sin. Before the power of Christ to redeem a man from sin can be realized in the mind of the pagan, many steps have to be climbed. Some sense of sin has to be created.[45]

The Lutheran missionaries in Kilimanjaro were not much different from the majority of other Europeans who worked in non-European cultures. They were not prepared to engage in a genuine encounter with existing religion and philosophy.[46] This fact, more than any other perhaps, explains why, in the early years, Christianity proved to be a destructive and not a creative force in the Chaga community.

In all fairness, it should be said that not all the Leipzig missionaries had such extreme views about Chaga religion. A tiny minority were willing to listen and try to understand. Two or three early missionaries laboured tirelessly to preserve local culture by committing ancient stories to writing, translating them, and making them known to the world. One of these was the missionary scholar Dr Bruno Gutmann, who came to Kilimanjaro in 1910. His prolific writings on Chaga traditional life included a wealth of useful information on Chaga customs. He came closer than most of the Leipzig missionaries in the area to appreciating the value and validity of Chaga community life and to understanding the function and significance of its religion. After analysing the differences between historical and natural religions in *Christusleib und Nachstenschaft*, he went on to declare:

> natural religion must not be considered as contrary to spiritual religion. Exactly that which lives in a natural religion and builds it up is spirit, people's spirit which, in the last analysis, originates from God. At least it should be mentioned that natural religion and historical religion are not exclusive contrasts.[47]

Gutmann seemed to be suggesting that Christian missionaries, instead of destroying traditional religion, could use it as a meaningful and effective basis for preaching Christianity. Had such an approach been adopted, Christianity might have quickly become a more meaningful and creative force in Chaga society. The message of the Christian gospel would not then have been presented to Chaga in a completely foreign idiom. Had it been possible for missionaries to see that at the heart of every culture there was a religious or world view that presented a general understanding of the nature of the universe and the place of human beings in it, the task of relating to non-Christians might have been more rewarding.

Chaga responses to mission

To suggest that there was a single pattern in which Chaga as a whole responded to the Christianity introduced by the Leipzigers would be a gross oversimplification. Reactions varied from place to place and among different communities, each of whom had their own particular reasons for gratefully accepting, disdainfully ignoring or vehemently opposing missionary teachings.

Initially, suspicions and misapprehensions about the white missionaries were rife. They were seen as prophets of doom, who either failed to appreciate Chaga dynamism or shrank back in fear of it. The people most vocal in their opposition to the missionaries were often the elders of the community. They, perhaps, were the ones who stood to lose most from any breakdown of community life, and this new teaching, they instinctively felt, threatened the whole structure of Chaga society. They feared that if the younger generation accepted it, their authority would be greatly undermined and the ties of family and community would be severed. Thus many elders felt it was their duty to speak sternly to those few individuals who presented themselves to the missionaries for instruction in the new faith and to warn them of the consequences that would follow their continued association with the missionaries. Where the warnings were ignored, intimidation was used. The renegades were accused of being responsible for evil afflicting the community. Ruwa and the spirits, it was said, did not approve of people who collaborated with foreign gods. The spirits were sure to punish severely all those who disobeyed their elders. Anything that an individual did that could be construed as placing the community in danger of being afflicted by the anger of the spirits was severely condemned by the elders.

Given Chaga ideas about personal causation, it was hardly surprising that strangers who condemned the old beliefs and practices in order to replace them with their own were themselves regarded as a source of evil. The community's medicine men and diviners could, with impunity, place the blame for all sickness, disaster and misfortune that befell people on the white man's malevolent influence. Partly because of these unfounded suspicions, and partly because Christianity in many ways represented a totally different approach to life, very few people initially were interested enough to listen to what the missionaries had to say. Few parents were prepared to send their children to the schools established by the missionaries. And when they did, it was to learn how to read and write, not to be taught the new religion. Thus during the first few years of work among Chaga, the missionaries were unable to convince many to accept the new faith.

Even more effective a deterrent was the attitude adopted by the community toward the few who dared to defy the elders and associate with the missionaries openly. Many of the older people interviewed stressed how much the first adherents and converts were hated for deserting the religion and tradition of their people. At worst, the rest of the community rejected them as despised outcasts who could no longer take part in community life. They dared not speak in public for no one would listen to them. They were rejected by their families and sometimes driven from their land, which meant they had nowhere to call home and no source of food. The first Chaga to take religious instruction at the mission stations were regarded as lazy and deceitful liars. This idea arose out of the missionary practice of preaching and teaching in the daytime. Chaga considered preaching to be story-telling, which, according to their customs, always took place in the evening. People who told stories in the daytime were ridiculed as lazy and sluggish. As a disciplinary measure to teach them better habits, they were refused food.

To some, however, especially the poor, the mission station provided a refuge and a home. At first, it was not so much the theological doctrines of Christianity that proved to be particularly attractive to the common people, but what the missionaries did in practical ways to help improve the living conditions of ordinary Chaga. The gifts of food and clothes that missionaries offered to those who came empty-handed to settle around the mission station convinced them that they would be better off in the benevolent care of the missionaries. The poor found consolation, too, in the Christian hope of finding a better life beyond death in God's Heavenly Kingdom.

Stories like those of Adam being driven out of Eden for eating a forbidden fruit, or Lot turning into a pillar of salt for looking back, or Jonah being cast into a storm and swept to sea while trying to escape the call of

God appealed to Chaga. This was the way people expected God to act, imposing immediate punishment upon those who dared to disobey his instructions. The technique of telling stories in order to teach an important truth about life was also an accepted educational practice among Chaga. Thus potential converts were keenly appreciative of stories like the Sower and the Seed and the Lost Sheep.

The accounts of Jesus healing diseased bodies by the power of his touch were also accepted without question, as were the incidents in which Jesus restored the tortured minds of men by driving out the unclean or evil spirits that inhabited them, for was not God meant to heal? But Jesus also embodied new and foreign concepts, which at first Chaga found hard to grasp. They had little difficulty in accepting him as a son of man, a charismatic leader and a teacher of his people. But the events of his crucifixion, and even more so of his resurrection, remained an enigma to them. The interpretation of his death as a sacrifice that reconciled humankind to God or the possibility of a man conquering death to return from the grave in a new body went beyond the traditional wisdom of the community.

Missionaries did their best to try to eradicate the supposedly pagan rites of Chaga. Distinctively African forms of worship were replaced with Christian patterns, fundamentally German in outlook and expression. A regular Sunday service replaced the simple daily prayer of recognition, the spontaneous cry for help in time of need, and the recurring community celebrations of songs, dances and feasts. This ceremony demanded that people sit and be passive for most of the time (one to two hours) as they listened to the reading of the Bible, the preaching and the recital of the liturgy. In most cases these were a straight translation of German prayers of adoration, confession, petition and intercession. Such long, formal and verbose ceremonials were typical of European word-dominated culture. But they were quite alien to Chaga, who expressed their deepest feelings, thoughts and beliefs in actions more often than in words.

The only ways in which a congregation could participate in Christian worship were by repeating the creeds and brief liturgical responses, by singing the hymns and by receiving the sacraments. Almost without exception, the hymns introduced by the missionaries consisted of German verses translated awkwardly into Chaga speech rhythms and intonations. They sounded discordant and unfamiliar to ears attuned to the rhythms and harmonies of African drum music. But the missionaries refused to use traditional music for fear its association with pagan beliefs and practices would encourage backsliding and apostasy. Moreover, the ears of many of the missionaries were so attuned to European forms of music that they could not recognize Chaga songs and their accompanying noises as genuine music.

Probably the sacraments of Christian worship came closest to the Chaga spirit of expressing beliefs in ritual action. The sacrament of baptism with its use of water as a symbol for cleansing and new life was a meaningful ceremony for Chaga. Water was used with similar significance in some of their own rites. But the celebration of the Lord's supper as a symbolic meal, held two to three times a year in Lutheran tradition, must have seemed rather strange and meaningless after the abundance of traditional feast days.

Thus the missionaries did little either in the organization of the congregation or in the forms of worship to make Chaga feel that the Christian church was, in the now famous phrase of Ogot and Welbourn, 'a place to feel at home'.[48] The European forms and idioms made the service dull and irrelevant to Chaga in the early days. African responses to this Christian worship clothed in European dress is perhaps only now becoming apparent in the African Independent churches. Freed from the foreign service, Africans are now finding their own ways to express the truths of the Christian faith. For worship in the Independent churches involves body, soul and spirit as well as mind; its demand is not for passive listeners but for active participants. The whole congregation joins in music and songs of Christian faith, which are truly African in presentation, phrasing, rhythm and music. Clapping, dancing, laughing and shouting for joy, they offer their worship to the glory of God in ways most meaningful and significant to them.

Thus in the early years the missionaries found themselves unable to make significant headway with Chaga. Their work was limited to people who were outcasts and despised by society, some of whom had lost contact with the communities into which they had been born. Others, through poverty or misfortune, had little or no standing in society. It was easier for such people to cut their ties with Chaga religion and embrace a new one because they had little to give up materially or socially.

The response by chiefs and their advisers to Christianity was more subtle and sophisticated. Many chiefs were shrewd enough to realize that it was politic to accept and even appear to welcome missionaries to work among their people. As Germans, the Leipzig missionaries were clearly linked in Chaga minds with the power of German colonial authorities. As a result, many chiefs both feared and respected them, anxious to avoid an open clash with German officials that could end in their own deposition or execution. The missionaries had appeared among them with a far more friendly, generous and helpful attitude than the government officials. The chiefs, therefore, felt that the missionaries might be useful allies in getting the best possible deal from the colonial authorities. When, however, they came to realize that Christianity itself was not a magical source of political power, but rather opposed many fundamental traditions of the community, their initial enthusiasm waned. While they often continued to support the educational work of the mission, they steadfastly refused to commit themselves to the new religion.

Christianity and Chaga religion

For the chiefs and other important personalities in Chaga society, the great stumbling block to their acceptance of Christianity was not just the faith itself; rather it was the criteria that the missionaries insisted upon as a pre-condition for baptism. Many things that were at the very centre of community life were forbidden to would-be converts. They were not, for instance, permitted to attend local ceremonies, even when intimate family matters were concerned. Converts were forbidden to eat meat of an animal that had been slaughtered in the traditional way for fear that the meat had been consecrated to pagan gods or the 'living dead'. Converts were forbidden to take part in traditional ceremonies and feasts linked with elemental events in a human being's birth, circumcision, marriage and death. Nor were they allowed to join in the songs and dances, *ngoma* and *iringi*, some of the most pleasant experiences of community life.

Perhaps the most adamantine obstacle of all was the regulation against polygamy. This was one that caused the most heartache, especially among older people. Few of those who already had many wives were prepared to disown all but one wife, leaving the others to destitution and ignominy. Most of those with only one wife continued to regard the taking of other wives as both the right and the duty of a man, as well as the primary means of amassing prestige, wealth and power.

A number of fundamental Christian doctrines presented considerable difficulty for they held no parallel in Chaga thought. When missionaries spoke of the Holy Spirit, for instance, it conjured up Chaga beliefs in the spirits and the 'living dead'. Casting aside these old associations while trying to grasp the new idea of the Spirit coming to dwell in the hearts of all who accepted God as the guide and protector of their lives was difficult for Chaga. And the concept of Iruva, as God, the Father, Son and Holy Spirit, 'one in three and three in one', was even more unsettling.

Furthermore, Chaga religion and Christian doctrine had fundamentally different understandings of morality and evil. For Chaga, righteousness involved not so much a human being's direct relationship with God, but rather the individual's relationship with others. It was not qualities of the character that mattered so much as the way a person actually behaved in the life of the community. A person's action was morally good if it strengthened the community and conformed to traditional patterns of life, if it built up healthy relationships between individuals and families within the community. A person's action was morally evil if it violated community customs and regulations or shattered relationships between parents and children, between a husband and a wife, or between their families. A deed was condemned if its consequences shattered traditional relationships or destroyed the possibility of life for succeeding generations.[49]

In Chaga society a person never transgressed alone. The guilt of one individual involved the guilt of his or her entire household as well as his or her animals and property. Moreover, any act of immorality was considered an offence against the whole community, both the living and the dead. Both the offender and the immediate family had to accept legal and ritual punishment from the elders of the community and expected fearful retributions, such as poverty, sickness, madness and barrenness, from the spirits. For, although Ruwa was regarded as the ultimate upholder of moral law, he was not believed to be directly involved in enforcing it.[50]

To some Lutheran missionaries the Christian gospel and Chaga religion appeared to be so diametrically opposed to each other that for them there was no room for the gospel to be inculturated or indigenized. Chaga responses, however, were different. Slowly and imperceptibly, they responded by accepting some Christian aspects, rejecting others, and modifying or adapting others to their environment and way of life. Chaga were able to find meaningful relationships between their own and Old Testament attitudes to life, although these were in no way highlighted by the missionaries.[51] Yet there were numerous other aspects of Chaga religion that local Christians clung to as providing vital and valuable insights, particularly in the expression of religious beliefs and their application to everyday life.

Over the years, Chaga have come to distinguish between the basic truths of Christianity and its European dress. Hence, Chaga Christians began to adapt the Christian faith they received from the Leipzig missionaries to their own cultural values and practices. Drum music and African tunes can now be heard in many churches on Sunday morning. The order of service has changed, and body language is more visible in Sunday worship services.[52]

Christianity and culture

While Christian missionaries often pointed to the dangers of syncretism, with its blending and fusing of diverse or opposing religious activities, Chaga did not view syncretism as a serious threat since they see all religions as admixtures of concepts and elements with diverse origins. Religious tolerance is one of the values that Chaga bring to the unity of faith.[53] Missionary accusations of syncretism and compromise must thus be challenged in order to defend the right of people to explicate the meaning and message of the gospel in terms that make sense to them. There is a real need for a new discussion to take place on the issue of gospel and culture. While it is a fact that missionary work among Chaga was accompanied by colonization and Westernization, the confidence that the colonizers had in the superiority of their own culture and religion led them to reject the culture of the people to whom they had brought the gospel.[54]

The Leipzig missionaries must have known that the gospel was being taken to people who had different cultural traditions, and they must have been aware that those who took the gospel to other lands carried their own cultures with and in themselves. Why then was there no exploration of the meaning and significance of the cultures they encountered? Why was an understanding of gospel and culture not at least a part of missionary strategy? Part of the answer lay in their fear of syncretism and compromise with other religious belief systems. This made a positive approach to other religious traditions impossible. It reduced all traditional religions, beliefs and practices to a single level of activity that stemmed from and participated in human sinfulness. Therefore, there was no room for the gospel to be inculturated or indigenized.[55] Persons of other faiths had to be called to leave both their religion and culture in order to belong to an alternative community that came out of the self-revelation of God in Jesus Christ.[56]

This understanding leads one to ask the question: is there a specific Christian culture? It would be impossible to come up with a convincing argument that a particular culture is a Christian culture. Christian experience all over the world affirms that no culture is closer to Jesus Christ than any other. According to David M. Paton, 'Jesus Christ restores what is truly human in any culture and frees us to be open to other cultures.... He offers us liberation from attitudes of cultural superiority and from self-sufficiency. He unites us in a community which transcends any particular culture.'[57]

A few Leipzig missionaries, such as Bruno Gutmann, Yohanes Raum and Paul Rother, pointed to high spiritual attainments within Chaga culture. They spoke of points of contact between Christianity and Chaga religion. They went even further and talked about the enrichment to Christian faith that could result from a positive relationship with Chaga religion. Yet most of the missionaries could not bring themselves to the level of identifying with the people they were evangelizing as Christ identified himself with the human community. They did not see any good in coming to an informed understanding of the beliefs of others, not only to see the points of contact, but also to know what others actually believed.[58]

The universal truths of the Christian faith need to find natural and spontaneous expression in the language, the art, the music and the dance forms that each group has developed as its own. People need to be able to hear and speak the truths of the Christian faith in their own native language and culture. Every church has to find its own unique place in a concrete cultural situation. Only in that way can it be the transforming salt of the earth.[59]

Notes

1 John S. Mbiti, *African Religions and Philosophy* (London, 1969), 2–3.
2 Yusto Manai, Interview, January 1972.
3 Bruno D. Gutmann, *Christusleib und Nachstenschaft* (Feuchtwangen, 1931), 208.
4 Bruno D. Gutmann, *Die Stammeslehren der Dschagga*, Vol. II (Munich, 1935).
5 Mikael G. Mushi, 'The life of Mangi Gedion Mushi of Siha', unpublished manuscript (Arusha, 1971).
6 Mbiti, *African Religions and Philosophy*, 52.
7 Gutmann, *Die Stammeslehren der Dschagga*, Vol. II, 12.
8 Charles Dundas, *Kilimanjaro and Its People* (London, 1968), 122.
9 Mbiti, *African Religions and Philosophy*, 41.
10 John Warneck, 'Studies of African religions', *The International Review of Missions*, 2 (1913), 591.
11 *Ibid.*, 123.
12 Dundas, *Kilimanjaro and Its People*, 122.

13 *Ibid.*, 123.
14 Yusto Manai, Interview, January 1972.
15 Mbiti, *African Religions and Philosophy*, 108.
16 Yese Maeda, Interview, April 1971.
17 Mbiti, *African Religions and Philosophy*, 108.
18 *Ibid.*, 9, 25–7, 83–5.
19 Yese Maeda, Interview, April 1971.
20 Yona A. Nsami, Interview, April 1971.
21 Dundas, *Kilimanjaro and Its People*, 122.
22 *Ibid.*, 123.
23 Sebastian S. Moshi, Interview, July 1971.
24 Yese Maeda, Interview, April 1971.
25 Manai Yusto, Interview, January 1972.
26 Mushi, 'Life of Mangi Gedion Mushi', 5.
27 Yusto Manai, Interview, January 1972.
28 Rev. Kaleb Mangesho, Interview, April 1972.
29 Otto F. Raum, *Chaga Childhood* (Oxford, 1940), 111.
30 Mbiti, *African Religion and Philosophy*, 197–203.
31 Raum, *Chaga Childhood*, 119–26.
32 Yona A. Yona, Interview, September 1971.
33 Gutmann, *Christusleib und Nachstenschaft*, 208.
34 Raum, *Chaga Childhood*, 209.
35 Mushi, 'Life of Mangi Gedion Mushi'.
36 Raum, *Chaga Childhood*, 356.
37 *The New Revised Standard Version*, I Cor. 9:19–22.
38 Andre Karamaga, 'Problems and Promises of Africa', in Margaret S. Larom (ed.), *Claiming the Promise* (New York, 1994), 24.
39 James Stewart, *Dawn in the Dark Continent* (Edinburgh, 1903), 28, italics in original.
40 *Ibid.*, 26.
41 Dundas, *Kilimanjaro and Its People*, 270.
42 Stewart, *Dawn in the Dark Continent*, 45.
43 Donald Fraser, *The Future of Africa* (London, 1911), 173.
44 Paul Fleisch, *Hundert Jahre Lutherischer Mission* (Leipzig, 1936), 268.
45 Fraser, *Future of Africa*, 174.
46 Mbiti, *African Religions and Philosophy*, 232.
47 Gutmann, *Christusleib und Nachtenschaft*, 205.
48 F. B. Welbourn and B. A. Ogot, *A Place to Feel at Home* (London, 1966).
49 Bruno Gutmann, *Das Seelenleben der Dschagga-Negger* (Leipzig, 1909), 46–8.
50 Emil Muller, *Madschame, die altest Leipzinger Station am Kilimanjaro* (Leipzig, 1936), 4.
51 Yusto Manai, Interview, January 1972.
52 Karamaga, 'Problems and promises of Africa', 29.
53 Jane Mutambirwa, 'African religious traditions', in Larom (ed.), *Claiming the Promise*, 91.
54 Karamaga, 'Problems and promises of Africa', 29.
55 Mutambirwa, 'African religious traditions', 92.
56 Wesley Ariarajah, *Gospel and Culture* (Geneva, 1994), 34.
57 David Paton (ed.), *Breaking Barriers, Nairobi 1975* (Geneva, London, and Grand Rapids, 1976), 79.
58 *The New Delhi Report: The Third Assembly of the WCC* (London, 1962), 98.
59 Ariarajah, *Gospel and Culture*, 9.

Four

***

The Impact of Christianity among the Zaramo

A Case Study of Maneromango Lutheran Parish

ISARIA N. KIMAMBO

A number of Lutheran churches in Tanzania have recently celebrated a hundred years since the arrival of the first missionaries in their areas. The Maneromango parish celebrated its centenary in 1995 in a ceremony attended by church leaders and Christians from many parts of the Eastern and Coastal Diocese; yet, unlike the parishes whose celebrations this writer has witnessed in the Northern Diocese, the Maneromango congregation remains quite small. The story told here is thus that of a relatively less successful mission story than some of the other examples in this volume.

Four factors explain the slow development of the Maneromango mission. First, the earliest missionaries arrived at the same time as the colonialists, and their work accompanied and facilitated that of the colonizers. Second, whereas in many areas missionary education eased the transition to Western culture and Christianity, this did not happen quickly in Zaramo. As a result, there remained protracted resistance to Christianity within local culture. Nor were local Africans able to appropriate the message and become active agents in spreading it to their own people.[1] A third factor was the mission's reliance on Swahili as a means of communicating and translating the Christian message. By not using Zaramo, the missionaries lost the opportunity of translating the message into the vernacular, while at the same time reinforcing the local dominance of Swahili Muslim culture.[2] The final factor was that the missionaries depended almost entirely on non-Zaramo African agents, often freed slaves, in their early evangelistic work among the Zaramo.

Missionary work in Zaramo thus remained largely dependent on the missionaries themselves, and when they left there was a noticeable decline. Only in recent years have Zaramo pastors and evangelists come to the fore, thus creating the possibility that their presence, together with that of the Revival, might help to overcome prior Zaramo resistance to Christianity.

The Missionary Background

The Evangelical Mission Society for German East Africa (EMS), was founded on 4 May 1886. Its name and founding suggest a close connection with the German imperialist organization of Carl Peters, the German Colonization Society. The suggestion for its founding had come from Peter's relative, Countess Martha Pfeil, who suggested in 1884 'it was the duty of the German Evangelical Motherland, as soon as possible, to begin with the building up of an evangelical church in the newly acquired colony'.[3] And it was strongly influenced in its early years by the emphasis of the colonization society on education for work on German plantations and on medical work for company personnel, both of which were strongly criticized by other missionary societies and contributed to its lack of success on the coast in the early years.[4]

The original constitution of the EMS was based on the Lutheran Augsburg Confession, although the constitution was changed to be confessionally non-committal in January 1887 in accord with its imperial mission. The first inspector, C. Buttner, was a nationalist whose views predominated in the mission, but F. V. Bodelschwingh, a more pietistic and humanistic person, was appointed inspector in the 1890s and was able to improve external relations with other mission societies, but the confessional position of the EMS remained unchanged until it handed over Dar es Salaam and its hinterland to the Berlin Mission Society in 1903.[5] After that the positions of the two societies in terms of their emphasis on evangelism were probably indistinguishable.

The EMS came to be known as Berlin III because there were already two other missionary societies based in Berlin: the Berlin Mission Society (Berlin I) and the Gossner Mission (Berlin II). Its first missionary, Rev. Johann Jakob Greiner, arrived in Dar es Salaam in July 1887 at the time Carl Peters was trying to extend the occupation of the coastal area by the German East Africa Company. Greiner's work establishing a missionary centre in Dar es Salaam was interrupted by the Abushiri Uprising, but his work progressed more smoothly after the German government took over the administration of the colony in 1890. The connections between the colonial administration and the mission continued for some years.

Establishment of Maneromango Mission Station

Greiner first visited Maneromango in 1892 in the company of the colonial governor, von Soden. He had already bought land for a mission station in Kisarawe, and, while Kisarawe was being developed as a settlement for freed slaves, the mission inspector, Rev. Winkelmann, recommended the establishment of an additional centre at Maneromango away from the coast in the heart of Zaramo country. Zaramo is a vast territory that stretches from the Swahili settlements on the Indian Ocean in the east to Bagamoyo and the Kwere and Khutu country in the north, the Luguru mountains in the west, and the Ndengereko territory in the south towards the Rufiji valley.

The site of the parish headquarters in southwestern Zaramo was chosen by Greiner for its fertile land, nearby wells and available building materials, especially timber and stones. The following year, Inspector Winkelmann confirmed Greiner's judgement. Rev. W. Göttmann was designated to open a station, but he died early in 1894 before he was able to move from Kisarawe to Maneromango. The arrival of a missionary was then further delayed by a famine in the region in 1894–5, and Rev. Bernhard Maass did not arrive in Maneromango until 15 June 1895.

Maass's arrival created a new situation for the people around Maneromango. While local leaders had requested a missionary previously, in anticipation of the benefits one might bring, missionaries had only visited Maneromango for short periods before.[6] The Kisarawe mission station 45 km away was already well established by this time, and a town or a mission station would provide a market place for exchanging surplus agricultural produce for cash to buy other requirements.

Having arrived alone, Maass lived in a tent while seeking the assistance of the local population to clear the land and build a house, thus providing some local employment. Deacon Bokermann from Kisarawe also spent some months with him in this early period, and soon Maass had a temporary hut to live in. It appears that Maass was well received by the local people: 'There was definite response from the people, for when he fell sick they crowded to his hut and Chief Mwinyimkuu Ulembo even brought some local medicine which took away his fever.'[7] Maass was ready to move into a permanent house within three months of his arrival, and he inaugurated construction of a church the following month. By the time he was joined by a second missionary, Rev. August Peters, in March 1896, six students were residing at the station, and the building programme included a stone residence and a shelter for animals.

Peters was impressed by the behaviour of the Maneromango people:

> They exhibited a very correct and democratic behavior at meetings, even when these were held in, what for them must have been strange surroundings, the church. The women were not relegated to an inferior position as women were at the coast, but took part in the discussions and exhibited no shyness.[8]

The main problems noticed by the missionaries among the Maneromango people were a fear of evil spirits and drunkenness, especially after the harvest, 'when [the] new harvest was used to brew beer and one party followed another'.[9]

Zaramo Society

The mention of 'Chief Mwinyimkuu Ulembo', 'fear of evil spirits' and 'drunkenness' reveals how little the missionaries understood Zaramo culture in the early years of their work.[10] Zaramo had settled a vast territory over an extended period of time, establishing dispersed villages located near sources of water. Each village consisted of people, often related by clan or lineage, and each had its own leader, known as *mndewa*. While slave raiding in the second half of the nineteenth century resulted in villages being stockaded, there was no centralized authority.

Following conquest, the Germans centralized a number of villages under *akida*s, usually literate coastal Swahili Muslims from outside the Zaramo area, and local *jumbe*s. Maneromango mission was placed under *jumbe* Ulembo. From the beginning, the missionaries maintained good relations with Ulembo's family, and Ulembo also recognized the benefits of maintaining good relations with the foreigners. Many local Zaramo leaders had established stopping points along the caravan routes from the middle of the nineteenth century. Kibasila, south of Ulembo, had done this, but Ulembo was off the established caravan routes. The coming of German missionaries to his area thus gave him an opportunity to benefit from their influence with the German rulers.

The alleged 'fear of evil spirits' indicates also how little missionaries understood Zaramo religion. Zaramo believed in a creator, whom they called Kyumbe or Mulungu.[11] This creator had authority over human beings, though he was far removed and it was his various agents who were more closely involved with the living members of society. Perhaps the closest agents were the spirits of the ancestors who were respected by the living members of their lineages. Once a person died, his spirit (*kungu*) continued to be near the living members and was appeased for a few generations. Unless he subsequently appeared as a particular named spirit (*mzimu*), thus becoming a taboo (*mwiko*), however, the ancestral spirit would soon be forgotten and would go on to join the general group of ancestral spirits who populated the world in great numbers. These were categorized according to the ways they interacted with the living and the ways they had to be propitiated so that they would not bring harm. Thus the *mizezeta*, *mwenembago*, *kinyamkera* and *majini* represented different kinds of spirits that interacted with living members. Some of the religious rituals conducted by Zaramo *waganga* (medicine men or ritual specialists) were intended to protect living members of society from harm that could be caused by lack of attention to these spirits.

From the beginning of contact, missionaries regarded Zaramo traditional rituals as pagan worship and prohibited their catechumens and converts from participating in them. Rituals intended for general spirit propitiation might be forgotten, especially since missionaries introduced Western medicine to treat some of the diseases treated through ritual, but those involving rites of passage, such as circumcision for men (*jando*) and seclusion for women (*mwali*), were harder to ignore. For a while it seemed as if the relationship between missionaries and their Zaramo converts was good, but there was an underlying tension between them that would come to the surface when the missionaries left after the First World War, as we shall see.

Finally, missionaries criticized Zaramo 'drunkenness'. Zaramo commonly prepared two types of alcoholic drinks (*pombe* and *tembo*), the former fermented from cereals and the latter juice collected from coconut palms. Almost all rituals involved drinking *pombe*.[12] One of the first African teachers and later a pastor, Martin Nganisya, argued that it was impossible to prohibit drinking of alcohol among Zaramo because celebrations of rites of passage could not be done without *pombe*.[13] And the initiation rites of men and women were considered so important that it would have been impossible for the society to exist without performing them. Some Christians were excommunicated for drinking, and later Nganisya himself got into trouble with the missionaries over this issue.[14]

Beginnings of Maneromango Congregation

Maass and Peters surrounded themselves with a number of boys at the mission, and the first baptism took place in 1897. This involved Abdallah, a young man who had accompanied Peters from Dar es Salaam when he first took up his assignment at Maneromango. Abdallah came from the Great Lakes area, probably Uganda.[15] He had been employed in Dar es Salaam by a German military officer who returned to Germany in 1895. Abdallah then obtained a job as a cook at the Dar es Salaam mission station hospital, and, after meeting Peters there, he agreed to accompany him to Maneromango as his cook. On settling in Maneromango, Abdallah became a member of Zaramo society, probably by being absorbed in an existing clan. Abdallah subsequently decided in 1896 that he wanted to become a Christian and, after a period of instruction, he was baptized at Pentecost before a huge crowd that included the German district commissioner, von Strantz, and took the baptismal name Barnaba Duakikaa.[16]

The congregation had begun. A second baptism of a young man, Salehe Mkubwa, was celebrated on Christmas Day that same year, and the two converts became a great help to the missionaries in teaching and translation. The missionaries also noted that the people needed to be taught improved nutrition and clothing; based on their recommendations, the Mission Board agreed to establish a technical training centre at Maneromango where women would be instructed in weaving and spinning and men would learn carpentry and woodwork.[17]

Rev. Worms and his wife then moved to Maneromango to oversee these new activities. Worms's thorough knowledge of the Zaramo language and the ability of his wife to teach women stimulated interest in the mission, and the number of pupils soon increased from 30 to 60. Among the new pupils were two sons of Mndewa Ulembo, and two of his daughters attended Mrs Worms's school. Mama Anna, a liberated Yao girl who had been entrusted to Greiner in 1888, was then sent from Dar es Salaam to help Mrs Worms. Worms is remembered as a person who translated hymns into Zaramo, and Nganisya notes that he had also wanted to conduct worship in Zaramo.[18] But, unfortunately, the work started by the Wormses ended abruptly with his sudden death in 1899. Mrs Worms left soon thereafter, and Mama Anna returned to Dar es Salaam, thus ending the girls' training project for the next 30 years. 'This neglect in women's work may seem to be one of the reasons for the weakness of the Church in Uzaramo.'[19] The technical training of young men for employment also ended. The departure of Rev. and Mrs Worms thus brought an end to the hopes of a congregation which had seemed to be progressing so well up to that point.

The period between 1899 and 1903 was a difficult one for the Maneromango congregation. There were frequent changes of missionary personnel, and at times there was no missionary at the station at all. Some of the young converts, without guidance from missionaries in their new faith, found themselves participating in traditional religious activities and losing their Christian faith. Von Sicard reports that the period would have been a bleak one for Maneromango 'were it not for the amazing dedication and zest of one man, Daniel Kassuku, the caretaker and teacher in charge at Maneromango'.[20] Kassuku was one of the liberated slaves at Kisarawe, freed by district police while his caravan was camping near the mission. Originally a Dengereko by the name of Saidi, he decided to stay with Rev. Greiner at Kisarawe after his liberation for fear that he would not be able to trace his mother's house. Saidi was quick in learning; he was baptized in 1896 and sent to Maneromango as a teacher by 1900 during the difficult years. He quickly became responsible for conducting Sunday services and visiting Christians in their homes. There was an increase in the number of school children as well as in those who wanted to be baptized. When Rev. and Mrs Dupre arrived in September 1900, 19 adults and some children had been baptized, and by 1902 the number of school children had reached 90. Another African teacher, Mika, was subsequently moved from Kisarawe to assist Kassuku.[21]

By 1902 the EMS was facing a crisis in its work on the coast. Sixty-five missionaries had been employed in the coastal stations of Tanga, Dar es Salaam, Kisarawe and Maneromango, but the results of 15 years of work amounted to only 270 Christians and 74 catechumens, meagre results indeed when compared with the high cost and the growing influence of Islam.[22] The Mission Board eventually decided to withdraw from Dar es Salaam and its hinterland (Kisarawe and Maneromango), concentrating on Tanga and the Usambara Mountains instead. The Dar es Salaam and hinterland stations were then handed over to the Berlin Mission Society (Berlin I), which had been working in the Southern Highlands since 1891.

In withdrawing from Maneromango, the EMS acknowledged the failure of its work in Uzaramo. Their collaboration with the colonial administration tended to make conversion to Christianity less spiritual. The use of Swahili as a means of communicating the Christian message removed the power of translation and associated the mission with Islam and the Swahili towns of the coast. While Muslim influence was not yet great at

Maneromango, translation of the Christian message into Swahili in such a situation tended to favour Islam, the dominant culture on the coast, because Muslims 'could claim that translation conceded the inferior status of the message whose original is to be encountered in the pristine, untranslatable Arabic of the Quran'.[23]

Maneromango was still a rural environment in 1899–1903. Even though Swahili was spoken locally, the use of African catechists like Daniel Kassuku helped to spread the message faster because of their ability to communicate in Zaramo. Yet, as Rev. Yohana Marko recalls, the opportunity to employ the vernacular fully was lost at a time when it was still the main means of popular communication. More recently, the vernacular has lost currency, and attempts to translate some books of the Bible produced negative results because people saw this as a step backward and were not willing to read them.[24] Misunderstanding of the role of Zaramo rituals also made conversion superficial because people had to keep their rituals underground while still attending church.

Maneromango under the Berlin Mission Society

The Berlin Mission Society was an older society, having been founded in 1824. It had longer experience in mission work and was better financed with its 'well established support in the Prussian Church of the Union'.[25] It had also been involved in the formation of EMS, but, because of the latter's abandonment of the Augsburg Confession, its nationalism, and its involvement in medical work instead of evangelism, the two had subsequently severed connections. But the BMS was willing to take over the work of the EMS in Dar es Salaam and its hinterland because it represented a natural expansion of its work in the Uluguru mountains and Southern Highlands.

The first BMS missionary on the coast, Rev. Martin Klamroth, recommended that Maneromango should become the centre for mission work at the coast. Noting after his first tour that 'Dar es Salaam had no traditional claim on Zaramo loyalty, but was an artificial center planted in Zaramo territory and its ministry should not be confused with the evangelization of Uzaramo', he felt that work at Maneromango was more hopeful.[26] It was there that he sensed a 'congregational and evangelistic spirit' not noticeable at Kisarawe. This spirit was shown in the way Christians cared for one another and in the way they witnessed to those outside the mission in order to bring them to church. He thought the difference came from the way the Gospel had been presented to the people, referring specifically to the work of Daniel Kassuku and Martin Nganisya, who had succeeded him.

Rev. Siegfried Wentzel arrived at Maneromango early in 1904 as the first resident missionary under the BMS. He is remembered at Maneromango for having introduced the keeping of cattle, sheep, pigs and ducks at the mission station.[27] He is also remembered for giving jobs to the surrounding people so that they could get relief during famine periods. This also was an incentive for people to come to church and, when no jobs were available, some of them also ceased to attend church services. Rev. J. Kupfernagel joined Wentzel for a short time towards the end of 1904, but he was transferred to Dar es Salaam in February 1905 after Rev. Hermann Krelle arrived at Maneromango as the second missionary. After a period during which there had been no resident pastors, sixteen persons were baptized during Easter in a spirit of new life.

This hopeful picture was abruptly interrupted again in 1905–6 during the Maji Maji rising. People in southern Uzaramo had been involved in the communal cotton cultivation project introduced by the German government, and Zaramo in that area had been required to spend two days per week on the communal plots. When the number of days was extended, von Sicard notes, 'the people refused to obey'.[28] Consequently, all the headmen (*wandewa*), including Chief Kibasila of Kisangire, were punished with a month's imprisonment in Dar es Salaam, and, after they were released, the tension between the people and the colonial government increased.

Only Krelle was at the Maneromango mission station at this time, Wentzel having gone on leave. On 12 August 1905, Krelle noticed that something unusual was happening when a number of Zaramo came to him wanting to sell their hens, ducks, sheep and goats. 'The Christians told Krelle that the God of the Zaramo, Kolelo, had told them to get rid of them for they were *mwiko* – taboo.'[29] Kolelo was a widely venerated spirit, not only among Zaramo but also among Luguru and Kutu, and Krelle learned that people were selling and killing livestock in preparation for a ritual in honour of Kolelo. By the next day, people were flocking to Kibasila to pay tribute to Kolelo instead of paying taxes to the Germans, and Kisangire had become a centre for the distribution of powerful 'water' that would protect people against German bullets. Kisangire was within the Maneromango *akida*'s area, so Krelle conferred with Akida Minimbegu on how best to protect the Christians. It was rumoured that war would begin with an attack on the mission station, and the *akida* became even more frightened when some Zaramo, who had not paid their taxes, were arrested while taking their money to Kolelo. Their supporters 'turned up in force at the Akida's house and freed their leaders as well as retrieved Kolelo's money'.[30]

Intense consultation between Krelle, the *akida* and the district officer ensued. After German agents discovered that the people from southern Uzaramo had left their houses and gone into the bush, and Interpreter Osman returned wounded and died a few hours later, Krelle called the Christians together in the stone mission house. When the information reached Kisarawe on 16 August, Rev. Kniess collected 25 men to help the Maneromango Christians defend themselves. Eventually, German troops arrived, and the punitive expedition moved south from Maneromango, burning a number of villages to the ground. Kibasila was said to have assembled a force armed with some 1,500 guns.[31] He put up a strong resistance, but, in confronting the better-armed German troops, the German bullets did not turn into water, many Zaramo lost their lives and Kibasila fled. He was subsequently apprehended by Akida Minimbegu in March 1906 and sent to Dar es Salaam, where he was executed.

The Maji Maji crisis demonstrates three important points about the nature of European penetration in rural Zaramo. First, the Maneromango station was closely associated with the colonial government. At the same time the mission station was also near the *akida*'s residence, and Mndewa Ulembo, the local *jumbe*, enjoyed a good relationship with the missionaries. Southern Uzaramo was therefore already influenced to some extent by Christianity.

Second, local Christians already felt they were a community that needed to care for one another and looked upon the mission station as their place of protection. They reported moves by non-Christians and thus weakened the resistance movement. It is interesting to note that Christians from Kisarawe, though not as strong at this point as those in Maneromango because many had gone into railway construction, helped defend their fellow Christians at Maneromango.

Third, Kibasila's forces appeared to be opposed to Christianity. Von Sicard reports that Wentzel had asked Kibasila 'if he would want a school at Kisangire' in early 1905.[32] Kibasila turned him down, noting that he already had a Quran school. Kibasila's area had been a stopping point on one of the minor caravan routes and subsequently had been influenced by Islam. But even this influence was superficial, as shown by the continuing importance of the Kolelo ritual, one of the main Zaramo religious rituals, which was used to unite people against oppressive German rule.[33] It was not accidental that the rebels identified Maneromango mission station as their first target because it would have been difficult to distinguish government agents from missionary agents.[34]

After Maji Maji, new evangelistic vigour was required to restore things to normal in the Maneromango area. Thus, Klamroth, who earlier had been impressed by the congregation, moved to Maneromango in November 1905. Klamroth felt that adult converts who resulted from Christians witnessing to one another were more spiritually mature than children who came through school programmes. The first method had been used in the Southern Highlands, where Klamroth had served previously, and it had seemed to help congregations withstand times of difficulty, such as Maji Maji. He thus suggested that some Christians move to non-Christian villages and witness there, not by preaching but by example. Four families agreed to settle at Mhalaka by July 1906, and soon the headman, Kombe, and two other persons asked for Christian instruction.[35]

Work was also started at Mengwa, where Mika, a Christian from Maneromango, had settled with his family. This area had been influenced by Islam during the caravan period, but Klamroth was pleased when two persons from Mengwa joined the catechumens at Maneromango. It is significant that the Maneromango congregation celebrated the first anniversary of 'delivery from Kibasila' by thanksgiving 'not only for the strength they had received to stand firm in the storm, but also for the strength to witness to those around them in a purposeful way'.[36]

The mission continued to expand. Permanent schools and preaching stations were established not only at Mhalaka and Mengwa but also at Kitonga and Msegamo. It is not clear, however, whether witnessing among non-Christians continued to be employed. One of Klamroth's most valued assistants, Martin Nganisya, was critical of the idea of 'witnessing by residence': 'Zaramo Christianity is still young. Thus, among non-Christians, instead of being light, they are more likely to be absorbed back to traditional religion.'[37] In addition to bringing superficial conversions, Nganisya also claimed that the residential system did not work in the long run because most of the 'Christian ambassadors' felt they were wasting their time and soon returned to their homes in Maneromango, in contrast with full-time teacher/evangelists who remained, fully occupied, in the rural areas.

The mission also built a permanent church. The stones used for the building had been collected during the famine of 1898–9, when people had been asked to bring them to the mission station in exchange for food. Christians had previously met for worship in a small church built in traditional style, but, after the large residential house was finished in 1903, they moved into the old missionary residence, which was also used for a school. Building the church required use of German technicians, but this also provided an opportunity to train local masons and carpenters, who then easily obtained jobs in Dar es Salaam after the church was completed three years later. One of the happiest memories among Maneromango Christians was the colourful ceremony dedicating the new church on 6 February 1910, during which 18 persons were baptized, among whom was Mwinyimkuu Ulembo, the Mndewa of Maneromango, who took the name of Abraham.[38]

Mndewa Ulembo's conversion must have encouraged Christians throughout the region. Before the outbreak of the First World War, there were further calls for stations at Kidunda, near the Ruvu river, and at Kisangire. Significantly, the call from Kidunda had come from Kambangwa, Kolelo's agent in the area, and Kisangire was Kibasila's centre, but neither call could be implemented before the war because of an urgent need to open a teachers' training centre in Morogoro.[39]

The Period of Stress: 1917–26

Thus, just as evangelical work in Maneromango was expanding, the First World War broke out in Europe and then in German East Africa. The German mission stations were affected from the early period of the war as some of the missionaries were required to join the war effort. There were four missionaries at Maneromango and Kisarawe according to Nganisya, and two had to join the war, while Krelle remained at Kisarawe and Heil stayed at Maneromango.[40] Later, when the British took over from the

Germans, all the German missionaries were sent home. Before leaving, however, they ordained Martin Nganisya to take care of pastoral work in Dar es Salaam, Kisarawe and Maneromango. His work required touring all three mission centres, but the main work at each was conducted by local teachers who served without pay. Three teachers handled the work of teaching and preaching at Maneromango: Yosia Mkumbalu, Anton Misokia (a freed slave from Kisarawe) and Daniel Mwenesano.[41]

Together with Pastor Nganisya, the teachers had to overcome a number of problems brought on by the war. The most serious was the occupation of the mission by British troops, during which the British did not allow worship services to be conducted. Later, when the British colonial administration was established, it sought to have the Anglican Bishop from Zanzibar take over the mission, but Nganisya and his teachers stood firm in opposition. Eventually it was agreed that American Lutheran missionaries would take over the 'orphan missions', but they could not field enough missionaries to replace the Germans. Nganisya recalled the tour of 'Missionary Hult' in 1924, but no permanent missionary came until Krelle was finally able to return in 1926.[42]

When Krelle returned, he noticed a number of positive results from the African leadership of the mission. Over one hundred persons were enrolled as catechumens.[43] Many people, including non-Christians, were attending services, and there were twenty youths in the confirmation classes. Yet all those who have written on this period agree that the period between 1917 and 1926 saw strains in the development of Christianity in Zaramo resulting from weak leadership, the expansion of Islam and cultural conflict between Christian and non-Christian Zaramo.[44]

Nganisya had been given a heavy burden without adequate training. Even though he toured the congregations regularly, he often created more conflicts than he could handle. Some of the local church leaders also failed to remain faithful to their faith and gave up their work. Chuma reports that a number of Christians took second wives, following the examples of some of their leaders.[45] When Krelle returned, some of the Christians also accused Nganisya of moral misbehaviour and drunkenness, although Nganisya himself denied the accusations.

These moral problems, as seen by the returning German missionaries, were complicated by the expansion of Islam in the area. Islamic influence in the southern part of Zaramo had been limited before the war, but German colonialism had seemed to favour Islam in the use of Muslim *akidas*, Nubian soldiers, most of whom were Muslims, and even Muslim names for those who were not Muslims. When British soldiers occupied the mission stations during the war, they reinforced the impression that most Africans in the army were Muslims. Rumours even circulated that the British themselves were Muslims or preferred Muslims. All these factors favoured Islamization immediately following the First World War. The spread of Islam may have started earlier elsewhere.[46] Kisarawe, being nearer the coast, had faced these problems earlier than Maneromango,

73

where the stronger influence of the German missionaries and Muslim involvement in Maji Maji delayed Islamic expansion until the period when the congregation was left without strong leadership.

The Islamic factor interacted with the third factor causing strain in the mission: cultural conflict between Christianity, as presented by missionaries, and Zaramo culture. We have seen how the missionaries earlier tried to suppress Zaramo rituals as pagan worship. There is evidence that the Mission Board had decided as early as 1896 to establish monogamy as the norm and to prohibit circumcision. Von Sicard notes that 'the Lutherans came to differ from the Anglicans who allowed circumcision under Christian supervision'.[47] The missionaries also tried to prohibit the seclusion of girls at puberty on the basis that the rituals involved, including drinking alcohol, were not compatible with the Christian faith. There are reports of Christians excommunicated for preparing alcoholic drinks and of other Christians emptying their pots when they learned of the approaching visit of a missionary.[48]

Even though things had seemed to be going well before the missionaries had left, these conflicts came out into the open while they were away. The spread of Islam increased the trend of backsliding. In Maneromango there were reports that Mndewa Abraham Ulembo, who had been taken a prisoner of war and interned in Nairobi until the end of the war, became Muslim after he returned home, encouraging other Christians to follow suit.[49] Even some church leaders are said to have adopted polygamy. Perhaps the most serious of these conflicts involved the African agents themselves. Nganisya, having been given responsibility for pastoral care, felt that it was his responsibility to warn Zaramo Christians about the consequences of violating the norms established by the German missionaries. He criticized those who openly organized circumcision ceremonies for their sons, and he complained about teachers in Kisarawe who allowed these ceremonies to take place on the mission ground.[50] In response, the teachers accused him of immoral behaviour and drunkenness. Nganisya denied the accusation of immorality, but he defended his drinking, claiming that many Zaramo Christians had not given it up and no African could survive socially without drinking.

It is tempting to see this conflict in terms of Zaramo versus non-Zaramo, since Nganisya was a freed slave from Nyasaland. One writer has claimed, in fact: 'Because of strong tribal feelings Africans from other ethnic groups were not received well by the Zaramo.'[51] Yet Nganisya was not the only non-Zaramo teacher; Anton had also been a non-Zaramo freed slave.[52] It may also be true that drinking became a problem for Maneromango Christians during this period, but, taking into account the vigour with which Nganisya tried to enforce the ban on circumcision, one suspects that the crux of the problem lay elsewhere. *Jando* and *mwali* were important rites of passage in Zaramo society. Their prohibition by missionaries had not been accepted by Zaramo, and there are reports that they continued surreptitiously among Christians. Thus the conflict has to be understood as one of broader cultural conflict between Zaramo and the missionaries. Even Nganisya, an African, was unable to enforce unacceptable European norms at a time when Zaramo felt free to make their own adjustments.

Restoration and Further Development

When the German missionaries returned in 1926, the first task was to restore Christian discipline in the church. After arriving in Dar es Salaam, Krelle travelled to Maneromango without taking Nganisya with him. Apparently Nganisya's colleagues in Maneromango had already made accusations against him to Germany, and he was instructed to stay in Dar es Salaam before proceeding to Nyasaland on leave. Thus Krelle had a good opportunity to investigate the accusations without the presence of the African leader. Krelle then organized a meeting of representatives of Christians in Maneromango and Kisarawe for 18–21 March 1927.[53]

The outcome of the meeting was far-reaching. Although Nganisya continued as pastor after receiving further practical training with the Moravians in the Southern Highlands, his work was restricted to Dar es Salaam (especially the Kigamboni area) because it was clear that he was not acceptable in Kisarawe and Maneromango.

Secondly, following the recommendations of Zaramo Christians, the missionaries accepted both *jando* for boys and *mwali* for girls, provided they were conducted under Christian supervision. For *jando*, this meant that the extended period of seclusion of boys in the bush had to be given up; it had to be an open affair, supervised by church leaders, and instruction had to be given without its attendant rituals. A similar recommendation was made regarding *mwali* for girls. It was to be supervised by Christian women and its period, which had tended to be months and even years, shortened. In cases of schoolgirls, it was to be limited to 'a nominal period of a few days'.[54] The position taken on drinking is not as clear. According to some informants, the missionaries were still opposed to drinking and participation in what they considered 'pagan celebrations', but perhaps they were not as strict in enforcing their opposition as before.[55]

After restoring harmony in the Maneromango congregation, Christian activities became vigorous again. Outposts that had been abandoned before the war were resumed, and more teachers were trained to expand teaching programmes in the outlying areas. By the time Krelle was joined by Walter Reckling early in the 1930s, there were eight outposts and eight teachers.[56] Krelle then moved to Morogoro to continue his efforts there.

Two things stand out in the development of the Maneromango congregation in the 1930s. The first was the rapid growth of membership. Unfortunately no statistics for the 1920s have been seen by this writer, but, if one takes into account the acknowledged backsliding during the period of stress, the few statistics available create a memorable impression. The membership for the years 1933, 1934 and 1935 were 604, 641 and 682 respectively, indicating a congregation growing to a good size.

Part of the success in the 1930s stemmed from renewed emphasis on education. The lower schools run by catechists increased in number, while a proper primary school was started with trained teachers from Marangu Teachers' College. The Maneromango Primary School became the only school in the area catering for Christians and non-Christians alike. A Technical Training Centre was also established at Maneromango early in 1930, and it continued to function until the German missionaries were again removed during the Second World War.

The technical school was an expansion of the earlier carpentry and craft school that had operated in Dar es Salaam and Kisarawe before the First World War. It was reopened in Maneromango in 1926, and subsequently became an important technical training programme under Reckling's leadership. Students made chairs, doors and windows and later 'set up home workshops' and trained others.[57] Reckling is also remembered as having encouraged 'special training in ebony wood carving'. Starting from traditional carving skills 'the missionaries encouraged the Zaramo to carve as their imagination led them'.[58] Reckling also brought in a few Makonde carvers, while trying not to influence Zaramo style. Human figures and birds were the first attractions, then animals, especially elephants and giraffes. There was a special fascination with the chameleon 'because they thought it was from him that all animals obtained their poison'.[59]

The technical school for boys had a number of advantages for Christian youth. It kept them occupied so that they would not be involved in non-Christian activities. It also prepared them for employment. Those who did not want to work in the rural area could easily obtain employment in urban centres. So, even though the training centre collapsed when the Second World War broke out, many of the technical and carving skills survived. Outside dealers, such as Indians from Nairobi and Dar es Salaam, employing Kamba promoters, enabled this activity to become economically worthwhile in the 1960s, and Zaramo carvers even formed a cooperative society in 1965.[60]

The missionaries also tried to adapt the *mwali* (seclusion) tradition to train Christian girls for adult life. An industrious female missionary, Anna von Waldow, established the Mwali Centre, a residential programme intended to keep Christian girls confined as they would have been traditionally, but introducing them to Western education, domestic science, child care, home craft, reading, writing and Bible knowledge. From the missionaries' point of view, they hoped this Christian programme would replace the traditional *mwali* programme, and Christian women were invited to give the girls lessons in good motherhood. While all informants praised the *mwali* programme and many young Christian men preferred to get their wives from the Mwali Centre, no Christian parents were willing to give up the traditional rite altogether.[61] In most cases the *mwali* rite started in the family before the girl was released to the mission boarding school.

Western medical services manned by European medical practitioners were also introduced at Maneromango from 1930. The establishment of hospital (or dispensary) services was greatly appreciated by the Zaramo. It was the only hospital available in the area, and people travelled long distances to be treated there. By 1934 the hospital was treating over 800 patients a month, and patients included both Christians and non-Christians.[62] Wide use of missionary hospital services by Zaramo Christians did not mean, however, that they abandoned the services of traditional practitioners. While missionaries condemned Zaramo medical practitioners as 'pagan' rituals, Zaramo continued to use both, even though they had to conceal this from the missionaries.

The Second World War and the Evolution of Local Leadership

The outbreak of the Second World War again threatened the mission's progress, but the local situation had improved greatly since the First World War. A teachers' training centre had been established at Schlesien in the Uluguru mountains before the First World War.[63] It received its first students just before the war broke out, after which teacher training shifted to Marangu Teachers' College and later to Kinampanda Teachers' College established by the American Augustana Mission. Schlesien then became an important place for training pastors, and it was there that the first Zaramo pastors were trained, including Yosia Mkumbalu at Maneromango, Andrea Kirumbi at Kisarawe and Andrea Ndekeja (a non-Zaramo) at Kigamboni.[64]

Thus, when the German missionaries were again deported at the start of the Second World War, the Maneromango congregation was bigger, it had more mature Christians, and above all it had an industrious local leader in Yosia Mkumbalu. Mkumbalu worked for a long time without any salary, and he encouraged the teachers and evangelists to do likewise. The American Augustana mission sent missionaries to tour and assist, and by 1942 they were contributing funds to pay for some of the Zaramo workers. There were also short visits by missionaries from Sweden. Thus work continued until a permanent missionary from Finland, the Rev. Martin Peltola with his wife Ingeli, finally arrived in 1948.

By the early 1950s, a number of the services that had been suspended during the war had been revived. The first were medical services. With the closure of the Lutheran Dispensary during the war, many people had been denied treatment, but the colonial government subsequently established a small replacement dispensary in the Maneromango area. In 1950, Sister Maria Telitu, a missionary from Finland, arrived, mission medical services resumed, and Christians cooperated in carrying stones and building materials to establish the hospital facilities still in use today.[65]

In the meantime, Peltola built a primary school, staffed by qualified teachers trained at Marangu (such as Yohana Andrea Sagamba and Samuel Yesaya Lukela) and Kinampanda (including Nathaniel Yosia Povi, Aron Tuheri Abraham and Namsifu Nahori Chuma), catering for non-Christian children as well as Christian ones. The Finnish missionaries also revived the homecraft school for girls in 1956. Even though the intention was to revive the *mwali* programme of the 1930s, it adopted a broader educational programme. It still taught home economics, but it added academic subjects to prepare younger girls to continue to middle schools after passing the required Standard IV examinations.[66] For older girls, it still prepared them in the same way as the *mwali* programme, and some girls left the school to get married.

The Maneromango congregation of the 1950s was thus still heavily influenced by the missionaries. Yet these were years of rising political awareness as the Tanganyika Africa National Union (TANU) proclaimed that Tanganyikans were ready to rule themselves. The Lutheran missionaries throughout Tanganyika had already seen a need to involve African leadership. As early as 1952, they brought the various missionary fields – Northern, Tanga, Usambara, and Uzaramo – together and formed the Mission Coordination Committee, composed mainly of missionaries. By 1956, they acceded to African demands for the formulation of a new constitution of the MCC incorporating African leaders. By this time, the Lutheran Theological Seminary had started at Luandai and then moved to Makumira; more African pastors were being trained; and the Lutheran Bible School had also been established at Mwika to train evangelists. African church leadership grew apace. In the Northern Synod it was possible to have an African leader by 1960, but in the Zaramo Uluguru Synod, a missionary was appointed until a qualified African pastor could be found, while Yosia Mkumbalu was chosen as the Vice-President.

When one compares the church politics of the 1950s with those of the 1920s, one finds in the later era no tensions comparable to those of the earlier. Yosia Mkumbalu, the first Zaramo pastor, was now a mature

Table 4.1 *Membership Figures for the Maneromango Church*

Year	Membership
1969	600
1970	600
1973	600
1974	800
1993	462
1994	468
1995	328

Source: Reports to Synod meetings and the last three from Parish Register. Commenting on the figures, Rev. Yohana Marko, a retired Assistant Bishop of the Eastern and Coastal Diocese of the Lutheran Church, said that the 1969–74 figures are mere estimates, which can be inaccurate. The last three thus indicate the true trend.

person, and his leadership was appreciated by both missionaries and Zaramo Christians, but Maneromango was still very much a mission centre with the hospital and Homecraft Centre both manned by missionaries. Things were soon to change. The Maneromango congregation said fare-well to their last missionaries, E. E. Carlson and Margret Gramzow, in 1964. This was the end of the Homecraft Centre as well, and Rev. Mkumbalu retired the following year and was replaced by Rev. Daudi Bundi (a non-Zaramo).

Available statistics suggest that membership figures started to decline soon after the departure of missionaries (Table 4.1). While it has been difficult to assess the reasons for the decline, Rev. Bundi suggests that some tension was still felt among the members of the congregation after the long missionary presence; other informants note that older problems still plagued the church.[67] Economically, the Maneromango mission had been a market for locally produced commodities, such as vegetables, eggs and chickens, but the departure of missionaries led to the demise of the market because the African pastor lacked the financial resources to maintain it.

Political calls for a national culture also exacerbated earlier cultural tensions. There was a general trend for revival of traditional *ngoma* (dances), but Maneromango Christians had already adjusted their traditional rites to Christian requirements. And as long as Christians continued to live in communities with Muslims and followers of *kipazi*, or traditional religion, the presence of different world views presented an ongoing problem.

Drinking also remained a problem. We have seen that Nganisya claimed in the 1920s that no African could avoid social activities that involved drinking. While many older Zaramo in Maneromango testify that they had already overcome this problem, drinking is again becoming a problem among youth, though some hope the Revival movement, which seems to touch youth more than older people, will help to alleviate this.

A final problem is what people call *woga wa chuuchawi* (fear of witchcraft), or, as the missionaries noted earlier, 'fear of evil spirits'. The image of a world full of spirits that can cause harm has not disappeared among Christians, but continues as a struggle in strengthening the Christian faith through better understanding of the Bible. Sometimes embarrassing scenes appear when a pastor has to remove amulets from a child who is being baptized and burn them in front of other members of the congregation.

Conclusion

The history of the Maneromango Parish is an interesting case study of acculturation, the meeting of Western and Zaramo cultures in circum-stances quite different from normal exchange. Prior to German coloniza-tion, Zaramo incorporated people from many directions. That was the way the numerous Zaramo clans were formed. Even following the introduction of Christianity, a number of freed slaves came to be absorbed among

Zaramo communities. But Zaramo strongly resisted colonial and mission influences. The circumstance under which these cultures met were new. A few European missionaries, backed by European imperial power, sought to convey the Christian message to Zaramo. It took some time before the Europeans understood Zaramo culture, however, and because of this there was a long period of resistance to, and only a slow acceptance of Christianity.

African agents – teachers, evangelists and pastors – emerged much more slowly in Zaramo than in other areas such as Kilimanjaro. Even when they did, Christianity lacked the local character created by the translation of the message into the vernacular.[68] Underground resistance to the missionaries persisted in the early period and came into the open in the 1920s, when the missionaries were absent, but later acculturation was made easier when the European missionaries became better informed about Zaramo culture. Yet the picture of a declining congregation reveals a relative failure of mission. Perhaps the successes under the missionaries were not realistic, for, even when they were present, people responded according to the benefits offered. If there were jobs they attended church, but, once opportunities ceased, they no longer went. Yohana Marko likened this superficial conversion to employment in urban firms. Young Zaramo would go to Dar es Salaam to work, but once the job was done they returned home.

The situation was complicated by the predominance of Islamic culture. Many Zaramo Christians were also given a Muslim name when they were born. It was easy (and sometimes considered respectable) to revert to the dominant culture whenever occasion demanded. That was why it became so difficult to have stable Zaramo agents for Christianity. According to Yohana Marko, not until the arrival of von Sicard in 1956 to head the Eastern and Coastal Synod was an effort made to train a second generation of pastors to succeed Reverends Mkumbalu and Kirumbi. And, even then, it required strong revival efforts to counter local resistance. Now a number of young Zaramo pastors and evangelists have entered the ministry.[69]

The Christians of Maneromango, however, appreciate the role of the missionaries in bringing the message to them. They point to the related services of medicine and education which have been enjoyed by all residents of the region regardless of their religious beliefs. They realize that, without the Berlin Mission, it probably would have taken a long time for government services to reach them.

Notes

* The first draft of this chapter was presented at the Workshop on African Expressions of Christianity in Eastern Africa at the University of Wisconsin-Madison, 23–27 August 1996. I would like to thank the organizers for inviting me and giving me funds to finance the research for this chapter. I would also like to thank Dr S. von Sicard for reading a draft of this chapter and making useful suggestions.

1 Richard Gray, *Black Christians and White Missionaries* (New Haven, 1990).
2 See Lamin Sanneh, *West African Christianity* (Maryknoll, 1983); J. F. A. Ajayi, *Christian Missions in Nigeria 1841–1891* (London, 1965).
3 S. von Sicard, *The Lutheran Church on the Coast of Tanzania, 1887–1914* (Uppsala, 1970), 53.
4 *Ibid.* See also Roland Oliver, *The Missionary Factor in East Africa* (London, 1952), 96.
5 Von Sicard, *Lutheran Church on the Coast*, 56.
6 *Ibid.*, 134.
7 *Ibid.*
8 *Ibid.*, 135.
9 *Ibid.*, 136.
10 See Marja-Liisa Swantz, *Ritual and Symbol in Transitional Zaramo Society* (Uppsala, 1970); Lloyd W. Swantz, 'The role of medicine man among the Zaramo of Dar es Salaam' (PhD, Dar es Salaam, 1974); Lloyd W. Swantz, 'The Zaramo of Tanzania: an ethnographic study' (MA Thesis, Syracuse, 1965).
11 L. Swantz, 'The Zaramo of Tanzania', 59; L. Swantz, 'The role of medicine man among the Zaramo', 48.
12 Rev. Yohana Marko claims that only cereal *pombe* was used for rituals. Interview, 27 January 1997.
13 Martin Nganisya, 'Habari ya Mission katika Uzaramo', MS written in 1931, available in Lutheran Archives, Luther House, Dar es Salaam.
14 Interview with Rev. Ajuaye A. King'homella in his Kariakoo Office, 1 August 1996. Rev. Yohana Marko thinks excommunication referred to drinking related to ritual only.
15 Von Sicard, *Lutheran Church on the Coast*, 136.
16 The Maneromango Centenary report identifies him with the retired Assistant Bishop, Rev. Yohana Marko: E. Mpelemba and Z. Harani, 'Historia ya Ushirka wa Maneromango' (Maneromango Centenary Report, 1995), 4. Yohana Marko, whose grandfather was also called Barnaba, belongs to the Chuma clan related to Ulembo's group. He thinks the report is wrong (interview 27 January 1997), but it has not been possible to identify Barnaba Duakikaa's clan.
17 Von Sicard, *Lutheran Church on the Coast*, 138.
18 Nganisya, 'Habari ya Mission katika Uzaramo', 4, 5.
19 Von Sicard, *Lutheran Church on the Coast*, 140.
20 *Ibid.*, 142.
21 *Ibid.*, 143.
22 *Ibid.*, 163.
23 Lamin Sanneh, *Translating the Message* (Maryknoll, 1989), 187.
24 Yohana Marko, Interview, 27 January 1997.
25 Von Sicard, *Lutheran Church on the Coast*, 53.
26 *Ibid.*, 171.
27 Mpelemba and Harani, 'Historia ya Ushirka wa Maneromango', 6.
28 Von Sicard, *Lutheran Church on the Coast*, 186.
29 *Ibid.*
30 *Ibid.*, 187.
31 *Ibid.*, 188.
32 *Ibid.*
33 L. Swantz, 'The role of medicine man among the Zaramo', 75.
34 Conversely, von Sicard reports that Muslim participation in Maji Maji set back the spread of Islam in the Maneromango area for some time. *Lutheran Church on the Coast*, 188.
35 *Ibid.*, 189.
36 *Ibid.*, 190.
37 Nganisya, 'Habari ya Mission katika Uzaramo', 7.
38 *Ibid.*, 191. See also Mpelemba and Harani, 'Historia ya Ushirka wa Maneromango', 7. Rev. P. Duge, in his 'Ulutheri Katika Wilaya ya Kisarawe' (Maneromango, final paper for his theological training, 1993), quotes a different figure, presumably from oral sources: 50 persons baptized, among whom were Ulembo, his wife, and Rev. Krelle's child. He also says that Ulembo's marriage received Christian blessing on the same day. All these need checking from surviving records.
39 Von Sicard, *Lutheran Church on the Coast*, 192–3; Mpelemba and Harani, 'Historia ya

Ushirka wa Maneromango', 7–8.
40 Nganisya, 'Habari ya Mission katika Uzaramo', 15.
41 *Ibid.*, 21; Rev. Charles Chuma, 'Maneromango Berlin Mission', notes taken from Maneromango files while on visit in Berlin, 1978 (Dar es Salaam, in Rev. Chuma's possession).
42 Nganisya, 'Habari ya Mission katika Uzaramo', 23–4; Chuma, 'Maneromango Berlin Mission', 1.
43 Chuma, 'Maneromango Berlin Mission', 2.
44 Nganisya, 'Habari ya Mission katika Uzaramo'; Chuma,'Maneromango Berlin Mission'; and L. Swantz, 'The Zaramo of Tanzania'.
45 Chuma, 'Maneromango Berlin Mission', 2.
46 J. S. Trimingham, *Islam in East Africa* (London, 1964), 53, 59. See also Swantz, 'The Zaramo of Tanzania', 43–7.
47 Von Sicard, *Lutheran Church on the Coast*, 157.
48 Interviews with Rev. C. A. Chuma at Kariakoo Lutheran Parish, 30 July 1996 and Rev. A. King'homella, Kariakoo Lutheran Regional Office, 1 August 1996.
49 Chuma, 'Maneromango Berlin Mission'; L. Swantz, 'The Zaramo of Tanzania', 77; S. von Sicard, 'The Lutheran Church on the coast of Tanzania: the war years, 1914–1920', *The African Theological Journal* 15/2 (1986), 97.
50 Nganisya, 'Habari ya Mission katika Uzaramo', 25.
51 L. Swantz, 'The Zaramo of Tanzania'.
52 Von Sicard, *Lutheran Church on the Coast*, 127.
53 Chuma, 'Maneromango Berlin Mission', 4.
54 L. Swantz, 'The Zaramo of Tanzania', 42.
55 Chuma, interview. The question of cultural conflict should not be taken as an unusual phenomenon among the Zaramo. In Kilimanjaro there were problems of a similar kind, though, because of more frequent visits by American missionaries , they never reached the same level of seriousness. In Gutmann's own congregation of Old Moshi, for example, a number of young men were placed under suspension for being circumcised, one of them being the writer's own father. And, when Gutmann returned at the same time as Krelle, he abolished the regulation. Among the Kikuyu in Kenya, an even more agonizing controversy involving female circumcision in 1929 caused serious divisions within a number of Protestant churches in the area. See John Middleton, 'Kenya: administration and changes in African life', in *History of East Africa* (Oxford, 1965), V. Harlow and E. M. Chilver (eds), II:362–73; David Sandgren, *Christianity and the Kikuyu* (New York, 1989).
56 1933 Maneromango Annual Report, ELCT. Eastern and Coast Diocese Archives, Luther House, Dar es Salaam.
57 L. Swantz, 'The Zaramo of Tanzania', 82.
58 *Ibid.*
59 *Ibid.*
60 *Ibid.*, 83.
61 Interviews with Chuma and King'homella; Rev. D. Bundi interviewed at his Mkuza residence, 20 January 1996; Nikodemo Mindu interviewed at his house in Maneromango, 10 February 1996.
62 Hospital Report, 1934, Diocese Archives, Luther House, Dar es Salaam.
63 Von Sicard, *Lutheran Church on the Coast*, 220.
64 Mpelemba and Harani, 'Historia ya Usharika wa Maneromango', 8. After the war, Schlesien was not revived as mission centre. It came to be known as Morning Site and was given to the University of Dar es Salaam, Faculty of Agriculture, and later Sokoine University of Agriculture as a suitable place for coffee experiments.
65 *Ibid.*, 10.
66 At that time a majority of pupils ended their education at Standard IV. Only a few were chosen to go to middle school.
67 Rev. D. Bundi, Interview; Aron Tuheri and Daniel Chuma, both interviewed at Maneromango, 10–11 February 1996.
68 See Sanneh, *Translating the Message*, 51–4.
69 Yohana Marko, Interview.

Five

They Do the Dictating &
We Must Submit

The Africa Inland Mission in Maasailand

RICHARD WALLER

In 1938, Meshak Naitore, part-time Christian evangelist and headmaster of the small school at Kerarapon near Ngong, placed his views on progress before the elders of the Kajiado Local Native Council. Amongst other things, he thought that employment should be found for school leavers: 'They should not be left doing nothing only wasting their time in the Reserve.' Under-age drinking should be banned as 'this is the chief hindrance of civilization'. And he wanted more mission schools because being taught about God was 'the only way which will bring good manner, politeness, honesty, faithfulness, obedience, sincerity among our people'. He received an acknowledgement from the district commissioner, but his letter was not placed on the agenda.[1]

At this time, Maasai who became Christians were marginal figures, often accused of being 'aliens', not Maasai, poor and unconfident, divided amongst themselves and lacking the 'respect' that was the mark of Maasai social order. Much of their energy was spent in trying to make a place for themselves in Maasailand. While they shared many of the concerns of the wider community with the maintenance of proper behaviour and Maasai identity, and with the defence of Maasailand itself, they had little voice in the debate.

One obvious reason for the insignificance of Maasai Christians was that there were simply too few of them. Church membership in Maasailand barely reached treble figures during the period.[2] Most Maasai Christians were living either outside Maasailand altogether or concentrated in small semi-agricultural settlements on its fringes. The autonomous expansion of congregations and out-schools found elsewhere as an expression of local identities and rivalries had no counterpart in Maasailand at this time; and no 'critical mass' of converts existed.[3]

Why did missions have such a slight impact on Maasailand over a period of nearly 40 years of effort? In so far as the question has been addressed at all, it has often been assumed that Maasai were simply inaccessible, either because of the practical difficulties involved in their evangelization or because the social and belief systems of pastoralists were in some way incompatible with Christianity.[4] This chapter suggests that an approach which also considers why *some* Maasai *did* convert is likely to be more fruitful than one that focuses only on why *most* Maasai did not. It makes three general points: first, that the particular character of the AIM enterprise in Maasailand did have an important bearing on its failure to gain adherents; second, that a study of the Maasai Christian community which none the less emerged shows that converting Maasai was not impossible, although it also suggests its difficulties; and, third, that there were indeed incompatibilities, but they lay not so much between 'Christianity' and 'pastoralism' as such, as in the more complex discrepancies and contradictions between the social and economic aspirations of the converts and the position they actually occupied, and between these aspirations and the values and concerns of the mission, of the larger Maasai community and of the colonial administration.[5]

The Africa Inland Mission

We must begin with the Africa Inland Mission (AIM), in whose sphere Maasailand lay, for it was not Christianity in the abstract but its particular cultural embodiment in the AIM that the Maasai generally encountered before the 1940s.[6] The distinction is an important one: the separated and self-sufficient community of faith envisioned by the AIM was not the only model of a Christian community, and it was not ultimately the one that most of the converts sought.

The Africa Inland Mission was founded by Peter Cameron Scott in 1895, and its first station was established at Nzawi in Ukambani at the beginning of the following year. By the middle of 1899, however, only one of the original party of seven was still in the field. Several, including Scott, had died and the rest had left the mission. It was essentially re-founded when the overseeing body, the Philadelphia Missionary Council, appointed C. F. Hurlburt as Director. Hurlburt went out to Kenya with a new party of missionaries in October 1901 and laid the foundation for a more systematic and organized effort.[7]

The AIM was a non-denominational Protestant evangelical mission. It differed from other Protestant missions in Kenya, notably the Church Missionary Society (CMS) and the Church of Scotland Mission (CSM), not only in its governance, structure and theology but also because it was directed and largely staffed from America. Several features of the mission, its personnel and its message are relevant here. Born out of the evangelical fervour of middle-class urban revivalism in late nineteenth-century America, the mission had as its central tenets of belief a conviction of the sole efficacy of salvation through a personal experience of Christ and an acceptance of Divine Revelation in matters great and small, the inerrancy and primacy of Scripture, and an absolute abhorrence of 'modernism' (which included almost any kind of scriptural reinterpretation, the 'social Gospel' and a wide range of personal habits). Like Moody himself, the commanding figure of American revivalism in the 1870s, and the Student Christian Volunteer Movement that he founded and from which it recruited, the AIM eschewed political and social activism. Its vision was inward-looking and narrowly focused on 'soul winning'. As one of its later members put it bluntly: 'The church does not engage in social reform....'[8]

Its central beliefs were endorsed by the missionaries the AIM chose, though as individuals they interpreted these beliefs as variously as did any other body of missionaries. All of them were required to give evidence of personal conviction, and for many this seems to have emerged out of dramatic or disorienting incidents. They expected salvation to be an equally traumatic and socially alienating experience for their converts.[9] Many of the missionaries came from small-town backgrounds in rural America, though their first experiences of evangelism were often among white industrial and commercial workers in big cities. This confirmed their sense of being both elected and embattled, set apart from the evils and pervasive unbelief of modern life, but it hardly helped them to embrace the realities of rural and colonial Kenya. While they were neither would-be squires in search of a deferential peasantry nor offshoots of a discontented petty-bourgeoisie, alienated from industrial capitalism and in search of a lost social hierarchy, they did bring to Africa a particular nostalgic and defensive vision of a close-knit Biblical community, ordered by faith and shaped as a peculiarly American pastoral.[10]

This nostalgia did not extend, however, to the African past, which they interpreted as a nightmare of backwardness and ignorant superstition.[11] Nor did it foster an appreciation of the culture of others. Many of the missionaries held narrow and somewhat Manichean views of the world. Few evinced much interest in learning about or understanding the African cultures and traditions that they encountered, since these were unworthy, if not actively evil, and destined to wither in the light of the Gospel.[12] AIM missionaries thus arrived in Kenya with little or no preparation for work in Africa and with equally little idea of what the reality of working in a colonial state and with Africans might be like. They made up for this with the firm belief that they were individually and exclusively mandated by God to bring light to 'savage heathendom' and to 'win lost souls for Christ'.

This was uncomfortable baggage, for missionaries and their future converts alike. It meant that the inevitable disappointments, disputes and crises of the mission field would be attributed to failures of personal faith – or to the wiles of Satan, who was everywhere in evidence, working through Africans, administrators and, sometimes, fellow missionaries. It meant that missionary attitudes towards their converts would be rigid and authoritarian, rather than simply paternalistic, and their interactions simultaneously highly charged and personalized and yet curiously detached and insensitive. It meant that the mission itself would be poised institutionally between an extreme individualism, almost an evangelical anarchy, characterized by bitter personal disputes, and an anxious social conformity, reinforced by 'testimony' and public confessions of sin. It also meant that official and social relations between the AIM, other missions and the colonial administration would often be tense and suspicious.

Early Encounters and Assumptions

The AIM had not, in fact, been the first mission to make contact with the Maasai, and not all Maasai Christians were AIM adherents. Early missionaries had kept away from the troubled interior, believing Maasai too dangerous to work with, but the situation had been changed by the devastating rinderpest and smallpox epidemics of the early 1890s and the consequent dislocation of Maasai society. Indigent Maasai had taken refuge with mission settlements on Kilimanjaro, at Taveta and at Kibwezi, and some became Christians. Orphans or runaways had been adopted by the missions and sent to school.[13] This seemed to offer an opening. Bishop Tucker was not alone in thinking that the crises through which the Maasai were passing would make them more amenable to 'civilization'. Once bereft of their immense herds and forbidden to raid for more, they would have to 'turn their spears into spades and their swords into reaping hooks – or starve', as Johnston had foretold in 1885.[14] Under such circumstances, missions and their native evangelists might reach them. They were a prize worth striving for. Maasai were still a significant presence in Central Kenya and were thought to be especially fitted for evangelization by reason of their character and intelligence: 'a chosen people for a chosen purpose', as one missionary put it.[15]

The CMS had had plans for a Maasai mission of its own. By 1900, McGregor, who had been transferred from Taveta to Kikuyu partly because of his prior experience with Maasai, was claiming 'oversight' of Maasai in the vicinity. He was learning Maa and hoped to begin work in the area near the camp of the *laibon* and 'Paramount Chief', Olonana, with the help of Josiah, a Maasai convert from CMS Taveta.[16] The work continued until at least 1903, and by then one member of Olonana's entourage was at school at Kabete.[17] In the event, the CMS never established a permanent presence among the Maasai, but they, and more particularly the CSM, continued to show a cautious interest in the areas closest to their own spheres, the latter overseeing a school at Kerarapon (the first in the Masai Reserve), which catered for the children of the Ngong community.[18]

Thus, in somewhat fortuitous ways, a number of Maasai had gained an early experience of Christianity and education. Few of them, however, stayed long with the missions. Some put their skills and knowledge to work as 'converts for hire' – much as others became *askaris* – moving from mission to mission and into government or private employment depending on where the best opportunities lay; others simply disappeared, at least from the record.[19] Some of them, like Enoch,[20] Josiah Shanga[21] and Justin Lemenye,[22] passed through the AIM at various times as teachers and evangelists. Lemenye's autobiography, the only one from this period that we have, captures the sense of transience, eclecticism, movement and opportunity that infused the lives of the earliest converts, but it is significant that Justin structured it as a narrative of return (to Parakuyu), not as a journey outwards to a new life, despite its editor's intention that it should stand as a model of progress.[23]

This Maasai 'diaspora', as King terms it,[24] hardly represents a community 'response' to Christianity, but the circumstances of the early converts do suggest two characteristics that would inhibit mission growth in the future. The first was marginality. Those Maasai with whom missions first came into contact were people whose circumstances had already taken them beyond their community. In the 1890s, they were ex-slaves, orphans and famine refugees. Later on, they would often be immigrants in search of an identity and a place to live. The AIM offered both, but only within a closely bounded and tightly controlled world of its own that alienated its adherents from their surroundings. The second characteristic was expediency. Missions offered survival and protection in a very uncertain world, but once conditions improved or other opportunities arose, settlements melted away. Converts expected to better their fortunes by joining a mission, and some, like Justin Lemenye, did so, but the AIM discouraged such aspirations. It expected its adherents to live simply and self-sufficiently, and not to concern themselves with material things, which the mission neither could nor would provide. Thus, demands for more pay and status were often interpreted as merely being greedy and 'unspiritual'. Poverty and marginality could be found in any new mission area in East Africa at the turn of the century, but the AIM in Maasailand never advanced beyond that. In an important sense, it remained an enclave community of the sort that had always attracted temporary refugees from pastoral economy and society.

Beginnings: the Mission at Rumuruti

AIM evangelism among the Maasai began brightly enough, however, late in 1903, when John Stauffacher first arrived from Illinois to join the newly established mission headquarters at Kijabe.[25] By the end of the year, he had made his first contacts among Keekonyukie Maasai around Naivasha and the Kedong Valley and had acquired two Maasai to help him learn the language. One of them was Molonket ole Sempele ('Mulungit'), with whom Stauffacher developed a close, if often fraught relationship that lasted until Stauffacher left Maasailand for good nearly 40 years later. The

5.1 *Molonket ole Sempele, c. 1912*

young missionary's first reaction to the Maasai was ecstatic, an unstable combination of intense romanticism and a sense of urgent mission, which quickly became focused on and through Molonket himself. This led Stauffacher at one point to suppose that Heaven itself would be a disappointment if Molonket were not there to share it with him and at another to declare that the boy would share his house and home.[26] By the end of 1904, Stauffacher had met and gained the approval of Olonana, who invited him to locate near his camp and promised to send him boys to teach. 'About 25' Maasai had attached themselves to the Kijabe mission and there were plans for education and for a permanent settlement. It was a promising beginning, again not unlike the early days of missions elsewhere.[27]

After some hesitations caused by the uncertainties of the first Maasai Move (splitting the Maasai between two reserves), the mission established itself near Rumuruti, in the Northern Masai Reserve (Laikipia), and began work in the immediate vicinity.[28] Although no pupils had materialized from the meetings with Olonana and his elders, Florence Stauffacher opened a school with ten boys. They were paid Rs1.50 with food and were expected to cultivate and work on the mission property as well as to learn. Later, the

5.2 *The Stauffachers*

mission was invited to provide literacy classes and church services for the *askaris* at Rumuruti *boma*, and it was through this connection that the AIM acquired its second major Maasai convert, Taki Oloposioki ole Kindi, a Keekonyukie like Molonket.[29]

Preaching and teaching remained the mission's focus throughout its short existence in the Reserve. It was closed at the end of 1911, ostensibly because the second Maasai Move (re-consolidating all Maasai in a single reserve south of Nairobi and west of the railway) threatened to remove its flock, but also perhaps because the AIM wished to shift its resources into more rewarding areas. Some evangelism continued intermittently, largely through the efforts of Taki, but until 1918 missionary work in Maasailand was largely allowed to lapse.[30] The Stauffachers, however, were long gone. They had left at the end of 1908, for home leave and then for the Congo.[31] The mission at its first attempt had lasted eight years – slightly less than the earlier Maasai mission settlement at Taveta in the 1890s. It had made three permanent Maasai converts – Molonket, Taki and Suapei ole Meitame, another Keekonyukie from the same boys' group as Molonket – and had perhaps influenced a dozen more, among them chief Masikonte, his two sons who were sent to school but did not subsequently join the mission, and Mariani ole Kirtela, who became a strong supporter of the church at Nairage Ngare, where he became headman in the 1930s.[32] This was hardly impressive, since the mission staff at Rumuruti had included up to six missionaries and several Maasai teacher/evangelists.

It will be useful to take advantage of the hiatus to examine the broad implications of mission policy and practice as they developed on Laikipia and continued in the Masai Reserve. One pressing and practical problem was how to reach Maasai. Earlier experience was no guide here, for no Kenya mission had yet worked amongst a sparse and mobile population. The standard local model of evangelism – that of establishing a mission station in a selected area and working outwards from it – was unhelpful since it presupposed a settled and fairly dense population from which converts might be drawn. In Laikipia, there was no obvious strategic location, and no centre of population. The site near Rumuruti was chosen partly at the convenience of the administration and partly because the Pesi Swamp offered the possibility of irrigation agriculture, which the mission hoped would provide an incentive for Maasai to settle. Maasai camps soon moved beyond the reach of the mission station, however, as they dispersed throughout the Reserve to find grazing and water.[33]

Earlier experience had also been misleading. Assessments of the prospects of mission work in Maasailand were based partly on generalizations from what missionaries and others had observed of Maasai responses to very specific conditions. Once conditions changed, these assessments lost their validity. McGregor had already warned that it seemed almost impossible for the 'present [Maasai] generation to settle down ... and cultivate like other tribes...'. If they could not, he thought, again echoing Johnston, they would either be 'greatly reduced by chastisement from the government' or, if their herds were again struck by disease, they would starve.[34] In the event, neither quite happened, but the warning that disaster might not have chastened or transformed the Maasai went largely unheeded. In part, this was because these assessments were rooted in much deeper assumptions – strange in proponents of a religion that drew many of its images of redemption from journeyings in the wilderness and the rejection of Ur and Egypt – about the necessary relationship between civilization, sedentarization and the humbling or even extinction of once proud nomadic peoples. Stauffacher's own writings echoed these assumptions. Like others at the time, he believed that the 'traditional' Maasai way of life was doomed and that 'It is only as the Masai begin cultivation and industry, that they can hope to exist as a tribe.' By implication, they would have to lose their wealth to gain salvation. And so the unfortunate link between conversion, cultivation, sedentarization and impoverishment, which was to be characteristic of mission in Maasailand, was forged.[35]

At the outset, the AIM wavered between two alternative approaches: to recruit and train native evangelists to cover Maasailand, using Kijabe as a base, or to establish a mission settlement inside the Masai Reserve and attract Maasai to it.[36] Once Stauffacher moved to Laikipia, the decision in favour of the second option had in effect been taken. Instead of travelling widely in the Reserve, the missionaries concentrated their attention on Maasai living in and around Rumuruti itself. A pattern established itself of Maasai coming to the mission rather than the mission going to the Maasai. This restricted its scope and, as Stauffacher admitted, made the mission dependent on Maasai – not merely on their passive willingness to listen to itinerant preachers, but on their active wish to receive education and to work.[37] Itineration diaries do show the development of a programme of regular visits to selected camps, together with more or less random encounters with, for example, wandering *murran*, but they also indicate the limitations of this strategy.[38] At the beginning of 1908, for example, four camps were visited regularly, but by June most of the camps had moved because of drought, and visiting seems to have ceased after July. Most of the audience were women – not surprisingly, since most men were out herding. Attempts to reach *murran* and elders were not very successful, and, with the exception of Masikonte – and on one occasion ole Galishu – none of the leading elders or spokesmen were contacted. Work centred on the mission itself and here too rewards were meagre. The mission did not become a way-station and focal point, as Stauffacher had intended, the hoped-for agricultural colony never materialized, and only about four pupils remained regular attenders at school. The AIM could hardly be said to have developed a presence on Laikipia and, given the narrow radius of its itinerations, it is likely that the majority of Maasai had no clear idea of its existence.

A fixed mission station had failed to reach the Maasai, yet it was not clear what practical alternatives there were. Before the advent of motor transport, the Word of God, like that of government, moved at the speed of a walking man; both were easily avoidable in Maasailand, and the AIM did not have the resources to invest in a more extensive and intrusive enterprise. Although Stauffacher initially intended to use Siyabei as a centre for outreach, a combination of financial limitations, Maasai indifference and suspicion, government discouragement, and his own increasing ill-health and disillusion led him to concentrate on the one settlement. He had also come to believe that Maasai would only be drawn to the church through innate and individual conviction, and that this might take a very long time.[39] The Stauffachers soon more or less ceased itineration, and they put little effort into the establishment of out-schools and churches, even in areas such as Ngong where there was both a settled community and a demand for mission education. At Siyabei, as at Rumuruti, the mission relinquished much of its field almost before it began.[40]

In 1923, another AIM couple, the Shaffers, arrived in the field. They were younger, better-funded, more energetic – and possibly more plausible.[41] They disliked what they saw of the introverted life of Siyabei and proposed an active programme of itineration and outstations – 'Cowpen Crusades', as Ruth Shaffer put it. In their view, the community at Siyabei was already over-evangelized; the future lay with 'Gospel Centres', staffed by Native Evangelists and supervised by travelling missionaries. The mission would go to the Maasai and not the Maasai to the mission.[42] It was through their initiative that a Maasai evangelist was placed at Lassit in Loitokitok to create a nucleus around which they would build a second mission station. Yet the establishment of Lassit was still predicated on the old assumption that settled cultivation was almost a pre-requisite for conversion – though in Loitokitok, unlike Narok, sedentariza-tion long pre-dated the mission.[43]

Another major issue was the social standing of converts. Again, a pattern was established early and persisted throughout the mission's career. With the possible exception of Chiefs Masikonte at Rotian and Kulale at Loitokitok (neither of whom converted), the mission gained no supporters among leading Maasai elders of the pre-1940s generations. Stauffacher came to recognize and regret this, but his determination to create a Christian cultivating community, together with the difficulties of itineration among the cattle camps, largely determined who would fall under mission influence and who would not. Yet it was not merely that the mission could not attract Maasai of 'good standing'; it quickly gained the opposite reputation. Children were forbidden to approach, girls who visited the school were ridiculed, and men saw preaching as something only for women.[44] Moreover, the mission's insistence that its enquirers should do 'station work' for their education established a link between conversion and dependence, which was reinforced by the fact that only 'the poorer class of Masai' remained settled in the Rumuruti area or later attached themselves to the mission at Siyabei.[45] In Maasai terms, converts were not only *il ashumpa* ([like] whites) but also *isingan* (menials). When the mission moved, this pattern of recruitment continued, and, as it became identified as an enclave of poverty and deviance, its social isolation was reinforced.

Two other issues affected the standing of converts and their influence in the community. One was the nature and consequences of conversion itself. Given the missionaries' central belief in personal salvation, it was logical that they should insist on a convert's complete separation from his or her past. This was symbolized by the adoption of Western clothes instead of 'skins', residence or regular attendance at the mission and a confession of sin.[46] The conversion of Molonket in 1906 was the ideal model.[47] After a period of intense and wrenching internal struggle, he renounced his leadership of the Keekonyukie *murran* on Laikipia and attached himself permanently to the mission, despite attempts by his family, his age-mates, elders and the administration to dissuade him. In a series of distancing and even transgressive acts, he began to grow potatoes, sought a Kikuyu mission wife, and sold cattle to finance a trip to America. It was a heroic effort, but also a disaster, not only for Molonket personally but also for the mission, for Molonket's wider influence was largely destroyed.[48] More than that, it demonstrated very clearly that the mission was setting itself up as a rival authority to family and elders.

Understandably, the mission was seen as an opposed world, a place from which Maasai did not return unscathed. Indeed, ostracism at home ensured that those who actually joined the mission could not return.[49] In the long run, the mission's insistence that converts renounce their former identities in order to assume new ones would be a source of great tension within the mission community. Converts did not always share the missionaries' conviction that the new identity was both essential and superior to the old, and those who were attracted to the mission were often those whose present identity as Maasai was most uncertain. Stauffacher described them, presciently, as 'that class who wander about not knowing whether they will be able to hold to their own customs'. Having joined the mission as a way of settling in Maasailand, they were faced with the demand that they cease to be Maasai, a paradoxical choice that few were willing to make absolutely.[50]

Apart from raising the larger issue of the apparent impossibility of being 'saved' and being 'Maasai' simultaneously, the conversion of Molonket and the attempt to create a separated community had political implications. The first years of the mission coincided with a period of internal crisis in Maasailand over the Moves. The AIM leadership took a firm line in refusing to allow its members to intervene on behalf of the Maasai. An attempt to involve Molonket was firmly squashed by the Field Director, who made it clear that 'our policy is to work in harmony with the Administration'. When the Maasai took the government to court, the plaintiffs and their lawyers did have the help of some educated Maasai – but they were not AIM adherents.[51] Stauffacher had left Rumuruti before the Second Move took place, but his own views are not in doubt. He was well aware that the Moves were intensely unpopular and he sympathized with Maasai attempts to resist.[52] He seems to have been much less aware, however, that Maasai might have had their own reasons for encouraging and befriending him and of how his attempt to attract converts might then come to be perceived as part of a general assault by whites on Maasai. Before the first Move, camps began to move onto mission land at Kijabe, probably in search of a place to shelter from eviction rather than out of a desire for enlightenment, but after Molonket and Taki joined the mission, the *murran* became very hostile; Taki's wife later recalled how her husband and other evangelists had been called 'deceivers and crazy ones.... Men of propaganda and followers of the *Lashumpa*'.[53]

Its narrow angle of vision made it difficult for the mission to understand the motives and actions of its supporters and opponents within their wider, secular context and to respond to their concerns. But, while missionaries operated in a political and social vacuum, their converts did not. Protection and patronage were important, and the AIM was perceived as failing to honour its obligations. Stauffacher failed to defend Kikuyu converts from eviction from Maasailand, and he refused to act the part of patron, a role in which he was inevitably cast as head of his own community at Siyabei.[54] The daily record shows the missionaries unpredictably denying reciprocity and rebuffing attempts to engage them in networks of obligation, not because they were especially ungenerous but because they did not recognize these approaches for what they were. Misunderstanding increased when they in turn reacted angrily to refusal, which they saw as 'betrayals' by their converts. Confused, and denied support by the mission, erstwhile clients looked for alternative patrons in other missions, in the administration and in outside associations.[55]

The main problems affecting the prospects of evangelism among Maasai were thus largely internal, but government too played a part in the blunting of mission outreach. Its delay over both Moves had made it difficult for the mission to begin work, and when the Maasai were finally settled, official support for mission activity was lukewarm. The administration realized quickly that the AIM would not be an effective tool for the expansion of elementary education and development in the Reserve and was perhaps content to see the mission sealed in an enclave of its own.[56]

The administration was also wary of a church which threatened to disrupt familiar patterns of social control, by campaigning 'in a crude militant spirit' against female circumcision, for example.[57] Something deeper was at issue than an official distaste for religious enthusiasm. Administrators and missionaries were competing for authority, albeit of different kinds, over the Maasai. One view of Maasai development held by administrators called for a gradualist approach to modernization and for the exclusion of undesirable outside influences until Maasai were strong enough to resist them. Under this policy of 'managed Maasainess', the community would slowly transform itself under the protective guidance of enlightened administrators. It was a vision of progress, perhaps, but one entirely antithetical to mission plans for a new Christian society, wrenched away from its Maasai pagan past, which demonized rather than acknowledged 'tradition' and which placed pastors rather than paternalists in control.[58] In its dealings with the mission, the administration preached patience and toleration, but patience was the prerogative of power since it implied both authority and understanding. As a 'discourse', 'managed Maasainess' was both convenient and effective in defining, controlling and separating pastors and pastoralists.[59] The mission could hardly look for official support for its attempts to propagate an opposed, and equally totalizing, ideology. At Loitokitok, especially, where the Headmaster of the Masai School, Whitehouse, was the de facto administrator and an enthusiastic 'Maasai-izer', there were bitter personal clashes over the demarcation of spheres of influence as the mission made converts at the school and interfered in domestic affairs, and as Whitehouse moved from being 'royal and kind and frank' to 'a dictator' (who wanted the Shaffers removed from his bailiwick).[60]

Missionaries claimed to be speaking for Maasai and in their interests, but what did Maasai themselves think? Their general attitude is hard to estimate, given the low level of mission activity and penetration and the nature of the sources.[61] Their public actions generally suggest indifference and disdain rather than active hostility. Chief Masikonte was reportedly 'wholly disgusted' with affairs at Siyabei in the mid-1920s, but he took no action.[62] Missionaries were not attacked in Maasailand, and, although church adherents sometimes were, they were being disciplined for individual acts of disobedience rather than being punished for simply wishing to convert to Christianity.[63]

Just before Christmas 1936, *murran* dragged off a girl from the Lassit mission. She had defied paternal authority by refusing to be led to the *manyatta*, as she should be, and the *murran* were acting as a posse (*empikas*) to enforce their elders' commands, as they were expected to do. Although the girl's (somewhat hesitant) defiance was perhaps a consequence of her involvement with the mission, the elders dealt with the affair as a domestic dispute. Public hostility was not directed explicitly against the mission itself until, after a series of similar incidents, local elders lost patience, confronted the Native Evangelist in charge in the missionaries' absence, told him and the mission to get out and, in a gesture of contempt and rejection, turned their cattle into the mission garden. Yet, within a short time, the mission returned without further incident.[64] In general, Maasai elders probably did not perceive the mission as a threat. It was too powerless and isolated to warrant much attention. Its adherents seemed more pathetic than polluting and, however subversive its doctrines might have been, they were not advocated by persons with standing or authority and could therefore be ignored.

Two concerns do surface, however, which tend to confirm the view that the mission attracted attention only when its actions impinged directly and specifically on sensitive areas. One was with land ownership. Local elders were unwilling to allow plots to be acquired by outsiders. Their experiences during 1904–13 had convinced them that requests for land led to dispossession, and the administration was bound by treaty to support their refusals – indeed, it faced similar difficulties in getting elders to release land.[65] But, even when local elders agreed to school or church plots, they sometimes made it clear that the mission itself would not be welcome.[66] The other concern was the impact of mission teaching on women. Interest in church was thought by elders to be a female fancy, but as it also distracted and 'spoiled' women it was potentially disruptive of proper domestic relations.[67] At Lassit, some women were forbidden to visit the mission from the start, and missionary attempts to shelter girls from the demands of men confirmed elders' suspicions that their domestic authority was being questioned, and they caused the withdrawal or removal of more, bringing 'girls' work' temporarily to an end.[68]

Where the mission attempted to establish itself in an existing population centre, its reception may have been determined by local rivalries. In Loitokitok, Shaffer's first request for a mission site had been turned down by the elders in 1929, but a second approach two years later was welcomed by headman Kulale, a leading but unpopular 'progressive' in the Rombo-Lassit area, whose support came from poorer Maasai but whom Shaffer mistakenly assumed was the senior chief. Kulale may have seen the mission as an ally against his opponents among the Loitokitok elders, as a possible material resource, and perhaps as a useful counterweight to Whitehouse and the government Maasai school. Work began, despite local opposition that forced the Shaffers to withdraw for a few months. But Kulale's enemies struck back in 1934, accusing him and another 'progressive' of procuring the deaths by sorcery of ex-Chief ole Nkoju and his successor Mako, both mission opponents and members of a different clan faction in Loitokitok. The administration supported Kulale and the matter blew over.

Kulale continued his support and publicly associated himself with the mission by the gift of an ox for its chapel dedication ceremony in 1935, but he was again challenged and forced to resign in 1937. An influential spokes-man, acceptable to all factions, but with no record of mission involvement, was elected chief. Here what mattered was not the mission itself, though the 'Sofi affair' and other disputes cannot have helped, but local perceptions of who was associated with it and why.[69] Loitokitok, however, had a mixed population and unusually volatile politics. Kilgoris, in Trans-Mara, where the AIM began work in the late 1930s, was similar, but the mission made no headway in more homogeneous areas where the authority of ruling elders remained unbroken.

Returns: the Mission at Siyabei and Lassit

The Stauffachers returned to the Masai Reserve in the middle of 1918 and established a new mission settlement on the Siyabei river, a few miles from Narok, the district headquarters. Taki and Molonket were waiting for them. A fresh start seemed possible.[70]

In the next few years, most of the families that would comprise the core of the community arrived. Their motives were as diverse as their points of departure. Some had prior knowledge of or contact with the mission; for others it was an unknown destination. Some were heads of households who came with herds and possessions; others came alone or with very little.[71] Some had been forced out of Kikuyuland by the same pressures, hopes and fears that were taking others into the Rift Valley, their putative Maasai connections suggesting an alternative to squatting on a white farm. Others had been looking for a place since leaving Laikipia or even since the 1890s, when they had been washed up as orphans by the tidal wave of disasters.[72] For a few, living with other Maasai Christians may have been the major attraction, but for many the mission primarily offered security and a chance to build an identity, for, various though they were, the settlers brought with them common experiences of upheaval, fragmentation and insecurity. Their claims to a Maasai identity were often tenuous – some perhaps had never been Maasai at all – and they fitted awkwardly into reserves where rights of residence were determined by proven kinship or ethnicity. Settle-ment at Siyabei and membership of the mission seemed a convenient way of obtaining Maasai registration and of establishing their claims.[73]

Their destination was as peripheral as they were. Unlike Lassit/ Loitokitok, Siyabei was empty land, probably depopulated during the early 1890s and subsequently passed over by Maasai coming down from Laikipia. Although maize and vegetables could be grown on land irrigated by the river, it was poor cattle pasture, vulnerable to drought and off the main track of transhumance.[74] It was a poor base for those who wished or needed to move out of pastoralism – precisely the shift advocated by the mission. Produce could be sold in Narok, but the town was small, unlike the burgeoning urban market open to Ngong farmers. Richer or more enterprising residents left for places like Ngong or Nairage Ngare, where agricultural and trading prospects were better, or took up part-time cattle dealing and shopkeeping, enterprises which were disapproved of by both missionaries and officials.[75] In 1928, the administration estimated that about a hundred 'half-bred [i.e., half-Kikuyu] Masai' cultivated 50 acres and herded 250 head of cattle. This was not impressive in Maasai eyes; well-to-do elders in Narok District had larger family herds of their own.[76]

Those who joined the mission also hoped for access to education, often the greatest resource that mission Christianity had to offer. However, the provision of African education was one of the AIM's weakest spots, as some of its missionaries came to recognize. The AIM was not hostile to education, but it did regard it as of decidedly secondary importance. Literacy enabled Africans to read the Bible and to communicate it to others; it was not provided for private gain or idle speculation – 'polished paganism', as the Home Secretary put it. Mission education in Maasailand conformed to this mould and thus failed to meet the expectations of its would-be supporters.[77] Moreover, in contrast to Kikuyuland, where missions had a virtual monopoly of lower education, more Maasai boys were learning the rudiments of literacy in government schools than through the mission, whose contribution seemed so 'negligible' in comparison that a 1939/40 out-school scheme completely ignored it.[78] This increased the distance between government and mission and further isolated its adherents.

Limited opportunities and the contrast between aspiration and reality bred discontent, and were probably reflected in the low level of financial support for the church.[79] Slender finances contributed to conflicts with teachers and evangelists over pay and support, which, in turn, made the latter aware of their poverty and subordination and less enthusiastic proselytizers. In 1934, Stephen Sitoiya, a young Siyabei teacher, lost his small cattle herd to drought and, facing starvation, decided to go to Rumuruti to find work (presumably as a herder on a Laikipia ranch). The mission offered him Shs8 a month to stay, half what his education might have brought him elsewhere, and he accepted, but a few years later he refused to open up an outpost at Kilgoris without a firm salary agreement. For this he was called a 'hireling' by the Field Director.[80]

Siyabei's isolation was reinforced by its physical distance from the nodes of interaction in a dispersed and mobile society. While this may have provided an unusually closed and controllable space for the imposition of mission discipline, it also cut the community off from 'news' and the wider currents of affairs.[81] Moreover, in a small enclosed community, resentments festered and were pursued.[82] In the Maasai world outside, disputes could be solved by formal discussion, which enabled aggrieved parties to appeal for support within the wider community, or by moving away. At Siyabei, these options were largely ruled out: the first required the structured and responsible opinion that could be found in a Maasai locality but not among the families in the settlement, the second was often impractical. Confession, the mandated substitute in missionary eyes, was unpredictable in its operation, tainted by its association with church discipline and rarely seems to have led to closure.[83]

But, if Siyabei was alienated from its surroundings, it was still part of a wider colonial world over which it had no control. Within months of their arrival, the Stauffachers were reminded of this when the Purko Rising broke out. Troops hunting *murran* camped on their doorstep and the missionaries, with other non-officials, left the Reserve for a short period.[84] The Masai Reserve was a closed district, entry to and deportation from which was at the discretion of the administration, acting as trustee for the Maasai. Government controlled and ultimately policed the field in which the mission operated. Elsewhere, in areas where missions were more numerous, well-entrenched and better connected, missionary opinion could be brought to bear on government, but in Maasailand the mission had few supporters and no security of tenure.

Missionaries and their flock all lived within a hierarchy of vulnerability shaped by race, influence, ethnicity and gender. The missionaries themselves, being white, had to be treated with some consideration but, being powerless, they could get none for their flock. Nor could they influence policy, and their work depended on the continued acquiescence of Maasai themselves. On at least three occasions between 1930 and 1932, at the height of the tensions over female circumcision, the mission elders threatened to have the missionaries removed.[85] For the converts, vulnerability was symbolized by the *kipande*, their registration paper which certified that they were officially 'Maasai'. Those who did not have this were liable to deportation without notice, and even those immigrants who did might have their credentials challenged and overturned. During the 1920s and 1930s, the administration put increasing pressure on 'aliens' (here Kikuyu) and regarded Siyabei, not without cause, as a major point of Kikuyu infiltration.[86]

Beyond ethnicity was sectional identity. Siyabei was in a Purko-dominated area, under the jurisdiction of a Purko chief, but many of the residents were Keekonyukie. At times of tension, this too could be used as a threat.[87] Then came the vulnerabilities of gender. While missions might be perceived as welcoming to women, they were themselves patriarchal institutions. At Siyabei, there was no escape from male authority. When Odupoi repeatedly beat his daughter for refusing his choice of husband and running away to her lover, a mission teacher who had already been fined for abduction, both the church elders and the administration refused to intervene. The Stauffachers were reduced to threatening to close the school 'until they decide to stay by Masai customs and not be Kikuyu'. Odupoi continued to beat his daughter and to veto her choice. Maasai elders may have worried that missions encouraged female insubordination; Christian wives and daughters might not have agreed.[88]

All these graduated insecurities were reflected in community and mission politics. They made it certain that the ban on female circumcision would provoke a crisis, but equally certain that it would not lead to a separatist church, as there was nowhere to go. They were also at the heart of the central dilemma: how to be both Maasai and Christian in a world divided between two classificatory and value systems – 'cabbages vs cattle' as one administrator put it.[89] As Christian converts they were 'Kikuyu camouflaged as Masai ... an undesirable type of native' in administrative eyes, liable to deportation, but, if they attempted to follow Maasai custom in defiance of mission rules, they might be expelled from the mission, which was their only place in Maasailand.[90] Isolated from the Maasai mainstream and often at odds with the mission, neither the local politics of ethnic patronage nor the paternalism of missionaries could protect them; only a secure community of their own could perhaps do that.

Making such a community, however, was not easy. Unusually for Kenya, the Siyabei community was not formed by attracting families from surrounding areas of settlement. It had to be created from scratch, and there were few available models of organization beyond those already framed by the structures of mission discipline.[91] Maasai Christians faced two tasks: they had to build a community structure, and they had to ensure that it was under their own control – and not that of the mission. One possibility was to adopt the structures of Maasai society, to which they claimed to belong and which would give them 'ethnic credibility'; another was to work within the model of Christian life, which was required by the missionaries, but which was seen as fundamentally opposed to Maasai culture. Neither alternative was presented as a coherent whole. Few of the Siyabei household heads had personal experience of the entire cycle of Maasai organization. They had not been publicly circumcised, lived in a *manyatta*, or been formally graduated to elderhood. Maasai culture thus came to them partly as memory and partly as a timeless ideal. This made them outcasts in the eyes of other Maasai, and it also raised difficult questions of leadership within the community itself. Mission teaching, on the other hand, was a present reality, but it came piecemeal in the form of Biblical texts, hymns, rules, admonishments and, presumably, sermons, which the converts had to configure for themselves in contexts that are now difficult to recover.[92]

The first issue was leadership. The mission established a Council of

Elders to deal with the daily affairs of the community; outside, the community was represented by a paid headman, recognized by the administration within the system of Maasai local government. Two questions arose: who were elders and who should lead? While Taki was alive, his overall authority was recognized by converts and missionaries alike. For the former, he occupied the 'correct' position within Maasai organization. He had been properly initiated into an age-set, probably Il Dwati from which the current ruling generation was then drawn, had served as a *murran* and exhibited the qualities and behaviour that marked him as an elder with 'respect'. For the latter, he had always been a model native Christian. His accidental death in July 1923 robbed the community of the only leader who could transcend the factions into which Siyabei was dividing and bridge the widening gap between mission and community.[93] Molonket then became headman, but his position was challenged by other elders with claims to lead, including Suapei, Enoch and Mpaayei.[94] None of the leading elders was, in fact, properly an elder, since they had neither been initiated nor graduated publicly: nor, of course, had any of their juniors.

But, if legitimate authority could not, or did not, come with age in a community effectively excluded from the ceremonies and practices that gave such authority meaning, from where was it to be derived?[95] Spiritual qualifications, though important to missionaries, were both too contentious and too abstract and intangible to form a basis for leadership by themselves – and even the missionaries had difficulty in determining who was and who was not a good Christian at Siyabei. Both Molonket and Suapei had longevity in the mission, but their worthiness was open to question, as they lacked the twin Maasai virtues of wealth and wisdom. Mpaayei was more prosperous and more centrally placed in public opinion. He perhaps better exemplified the kind of success, as a Maasai Christian, to which others in the community aspired. The question of leadership within the community was never fully resolved, and, while it remained disputed, Siyabei could neither conform to Maasai notions of proper behaviour nor fully control its own fate.

Conflicts over leadership reflected factionalism inside the community and the difficulties of establishing legitimate secular authority in the absence of an overarching age organization. Arguments over church membership involved the mission as well, raising questions about the limits of religious authority and who might wield it. The AIM recognized three levels of mission involvement, from 'church attender' through 'enquirer' or catechumen, which implied a wish to join the church, to full church membership, initiated by baptism and continued by participation in Communion. The importance of church membership and the need for disciplinary procedures to maintain its integrity was shared ground at Siyabei. It was, after all, the church that framed the community and was its official *raison d'être*. But who would act as the gatekeepers, admitting members and, when necessary, imposing sanctions on them? In so far as church and community membership was the same – and the core families seem to have accepted that this was so – control over church rites of initiation, promotion and affirmation thus implied a wider authority in the community and provided the main areas of argument between the mission and its elders. On occasion, baptisms were contested on points of 'fitness'.[96] It was not always the missionary denying and the elders insisting, since the latter could use challenges to individual baptisms as a form of elders' sanction. At the beginning of 1929, Stauffacher agreed to hold baptismal meetings for all who 'know their hearts are right'. The elders complained that they had not been consulted and 'knew something [detrimental] about all the candidates'.[97] Here, as with confession/testimony, they were reshaping mission practice to create resources of power, which they otherwise lacked.

It was admission to Communion that caused the greatest difficulties. Communion was seen by both mission and community as the central act of membership and worship. Its centrality, as a communal practice and as an arena of conflict, is especially clear in the years of crisis in the early 1930s. Although the crisis centred on the practice of female circumcision, it was expressed partly in terms of attendance at Communion. When the 'rebels' held their first independent church service in February 1930, with the Stauffachers present, Molonket read Paul's condemnation of those who caused confusion in the community by perverting the Gospel, a general reference to the missionary ban on female circumcision, but Christopher Tameno, who had previously sided with the mission, chose as his text Mark's account of the Last Supper and declared that 'they here [at Siyabei] have the seal of Christ on them and can take the supper just as well as the apostles of old', a very specific comment on practice at Siyabei.[98]

Communion both as a practice in itself and as an expression of underlying beliefs is particularly rich in levels of meaning and interpretation. At one level, monthly Communion was a community ritual that united and reconciled church members, including missionaries. In February 1930, at the height of the schism, the elders demanded that the Stauffachers take Communion with them. It was probably intended as an attempt at reconciliation – which was refused because the missionaries did not accept the elders' authority to hold Communion.

Communion required inward preparation and examination, and here interpretations differed. For the missionaries, only those members 'in good standing', that is, those not guilty of breaking mission rules, could partake. Early in 1929, only two or three elders were eligible, the rest being 'on probation' – a matter of church discipline. But some at least of their flock developed an alternative view: that Communion 'wipe[d] out sins' and was therefore also a cleansing ceremony. It was precisely those who had sinned who stood in most need of Communion; those at least who had been brought up in Kikuyu would have been aware of pollution and the need to cleanse it, usually through a sacrifice.[99] Mission teaching emphasized Christ's sacrifice of himself as atonement and also used the tag 'Washed in the Blood of Jesus' in its evangelizing. At the same time, Communion, as a reenactment of the Last Supper, drew attention to the use of 'blood' as a central part of the commemorative ritual.[100] The two streams of thought may have fused to produce first the belief that Communion cleansed sin and second that the deliberate withholding of Communion condemned individuals to a state of dangerous pollution, a frightening prospect. This was especially contentious in cases where the mission had imposed the sanction of exclusion for acts that were perfectly acceptable, or even prescribed, in Maasai belief.[101] Thus struggle and attempted negotiation over Communion involved different levels of belief and understanding, some shared, others not. Communion was simultaneously a rite of reconciliation and of cleansing. Individuals could abstain, but they should not be excluded. Church elders were willing to forbid baptisms, but not to expel members from Communion, the very act that the missionaries regarded as an important and essential sanction within the church.

The Circumcision Crisis at Siyabei

Many of these issues and conflicts at Siyabei were folded into the circumcision crisis of the early 1930s – the community's bid to join the mainstream of mission history. The crisis in the AIM was precipitated by the decision of its Annual Conference early in 1930 to follow the lead of the CSM in declaring a formal ban on the practice of female circumcision amongst its members and then in requiring that church members must sign a public declaration of support for the mission's 'stand' in order to remain 'in good standing'.[102] In fact, female circumcision had already been forbidden at some mission stations, including Kijabe; what was new was the determination to enforce a universal ban and to insist that Christians make a public choice.

Despite the agreement to ban, however, neither converts nor missionaries nor missions themselves were unequivocally in support of making the rejection of female circumcision a prerequisite for church membership. Nor was it always missionaries who took the lead; in some places, church elders struck first, for or against, and missionaries followed. Moreover, although there were connections between Siyabei and Kikuyuland, the local crisis was not simply imported from outside.[103] Events at Siyabei must be seen against a background of division and ambivalence in the church in which the course the crisis took in any community was largely determined by local personalities and circumstances. While Siyabei Christians shared concerns with communities elsewhere, they also had their own problems and perceptions.[104]

At Siyabei, no confrontation occurred before 1930. There had been earlier discussions, and Florence Stauffacher had been preparing her women's meeting and girls' class to resist circumcision and 'leave the things of the Masai', but the circumcision of Ruth Oloisenke passed off without incident in July 1928. Three out of four eligible girls were circumcised the following year, again with 'nothing definite' being done by the mission.[105] After the conference resolution, positions hardened. When Stauffacher approached the elders to discuss the matter in February 1930, he was met with a complete rebuff: '… ALL said they were going to circumcise their girls and they'll have their own church in this building!!!' (emphasis in original).

The mission then temporarily suspended school and catechism classes. An intermittent and selective boycott of school and church meetings followed, as the elders attempted to take control and to organize their own church, while still leaving the door open for reconciliation. Under great tension, five girls were circumcised later that year.[106] Stauffacher did not, however, ask people to sign the public declaration against circumcision until September 1931.[107] In Kikuyuland, the AIM had lost 95 per cent of its members by the end of 1930, most of whom never rejoined. At Siyabei, few actually left the mission permanently. Uncertainty prolonged the crisis long after it was effectively resolved elsewhere, but negotiation ultimately produced a tacit compromise.[108] In a sense, the 'rebels' won, since they returned to church membership without having to renounce female circumcision.[109]

Stauffacher had returned from the Kijabe Conference 'more or less with fear and trembling'. He was aware that applying the rules at Siyabei would probably 'drive native Christians wholly away from us'. While personally opposed to female circumcision, he believed that the ban was premature, unwise and even unfair. In his view, it was wrong to punish people for defending a custom which the mission had hitherto accepted, however reluctantly, and which they did not see as 'un-Christian'. For him, the '*kidole*', not circumcision itself, was the main issue.[110] It strained loyalties too far, and it forced missionaries to expel church members whom they believed were otherwise faithful adherents and to withdraw patronage and guidance from communities 'recently come out of the rankest heathenism'. Thus, he confessed, 'My heart goes out strongly sometimes to the natives.'

He was also aware that he would get no support from the local administration; that, if the mission school closed, government might take it over; and that, should the 'rebels' succeed in organizing their own church, the mission itself might be shut out of Maasailand. As events unfolded in 1930, Stauffacher expressed his despair at the destruction of his life's work and his criticisms of the AIM policy in letters to the Home Secretary: 'I am afraid you don't see much loyalty on my part to the stand taken by the missionaries.…'[111]

Florence Stauffacher was markedly less sympathetic. Entries in her diary suggest that husband and wife differed significantly, but probably silently, in their attitudes to female circumcision and in their perceptions of what was at stake. This raises the issue of gendered perception, both specifically in the 'circumcision crisis' (where it seems oddly absent) and more generally in the mission field. The evidence from the AIM suggests, broadly, that, while male missionaries focused on the issue of church discipline, female missionaries empathized with the plight of the girls concerned and saw the ban on female circumcision as crucial to their conception of marriage and 'Christian Womanhood'. Both Ruth Shaffer and Florence Stauffacher were prepared to intervene directly to save 'their girls' from being circumcised and 'sold'. Yet, however sympathetic they might be, female missionaries themselves had little authority of their own. Their response should thus be placed within the context of mission patriarchy, and may indicate that, to some degree, within a colonial hierarchy of race which divided more deeply than gender united, they perceived similarities between their own position and that of their female 'charges'.[112]

Despite their united front at the beginning of 1930, the church elders were equally concerned about the rupture of social relations and just as apprehensive about the wider implications of the crisis. Their position was also insecure, one cause of which revealed itself immediately. Once the elders announced that they would hold their own services in the church, Stauffacher appealed to the DC. The official response satisfied neither side and indicated that, while the administration had no intention of getting involved in the mission dispute, it did have an agenda of its own. The DC refused the elders permission to use the church or school, but raised no objections to their conducting services or forming their own church. He appointed two elders to keep order, but he also posted *askaris* to protect mission property. More ominously, he announced that all Kikuyu would be deported, and his *askaris* began to hunt for illegal immigrants.[113]

The elders held their ground, partly because they believed that Stauffacher himself would capitulate, as his willingness to negotiate and listen seemed to indicate, and partly because they were aware that the mission depended on them, but also because they did not, in fact, want a schism.[114] What they envisaged was not a radically new 'Maasai' church – their religious thinking seems to have remained almost entirely orthodox[115] – but one in which the respective roles of missionary and elders were reformulated, with themselves in control, advised but not commanded by the missionary. They were willing to return to church membership provided that their authority over both the church and the community was confirmed. In this way, they might demonstrate good citizenship, escape deportation and acquire a voice in Maasailand.[116]

Here, however, a second difficulty emerged. At the end of 1929, Stauffacher had ascertained that a group of younger men would support the ban on circumcision. In the event, only three did so consistently after 1930: Steven Sitoiya, Peter Kuyioni and Milaon Sairogua. All three were unmarried teacher/evangelists, closer to the mission and less immediately susceptible to community pressures.[117] Generational difference was a feature of the circumcision crisis generally, but, whereas elsewhere it tended to be the first generation of converts who supported the mission and younger men who opposed, here the position seems reversed. Younger men may have had less to lose from abandoning circumcision, since they had no families of their own, and they may also have understood their separation from Maasai society in different terms. What seems clear in retrospect is that the elders intended to maintain their authority over their juniors as well as to impose it on the mission, and that this generational tension at Siyabei reflected the world outside, where Maasai *murran* were resisting attempts by the ruling elders to further circumscribe their activities.[118]

The circumcision crisis was thus a crisis of authority at several different levels, and it was played out in those areas where authority could be challenged or asserted – in the policing of ethnicity, over church membership and ritual, within the household and even in the school.[119] The challenge to the ban was grounded in an appeal to Biblical authority, just as admission to Communion had been. Recognition of the authority of the Bible provided common, if contested, ground between those who boycotted mission services at Siyabei and those who attended them. There is no need to assume, as missionaries did, that KCA men could not be believers.[120] The question was not the authority of the Bible itself, but who would determine what that authority said. Elders told the Stauffachers that they were false teachers and that it was they, the elders, who now alone held to the truth; the missionaries thought that their interlocutors were perverting the Bible for their own ends.[121] Just before the crisis, Stauffacher had told the readers of *Inland Africa* that African Christians studied their Bibles assiduously and argued well and carefully: 'Mr Native is not as stupid as some of us took him to be.'[122]

The observation pointed to a serious difficulty. Missions were on weak ground in attempting to argue that female circumcision transgressed God's Word: the texts were, at best, contradictory.[123] The AIM, with its basis in Biblical literalism, its belief that God's Word was open to all believers, and its insistence on the necessity of Bible Study, found it especially hard to adopt the position of final arbiter of the Word. When Siyabei Christians '[took] the 10 Commandments for their rule and only them and [said] they do not say *Do not circumcise*' it was difficult to fault them.[124] They were also supported by the vagaries of Bible translation. In the Maa translation of the Nativity, the Virgin Mary appears as a circumcised woman. This was not so much an error in translation, as Sandgren suggests in a similar argument about the Kikuyu Bible, as a translation of culture. In St Matthew's Gospel (1:20–3), the angel appears to Joseph and tells him: 'fear not to take unto thee Mary, thy wife'. In Maa, the phrase '*miureyu irik esiangiki ino Maria*' indicates the proper 'leading' of a bride in marriage and the word for 'wife' used here (*esiangiki*) implies that she has been circumcised. However, in the quotation from Isaiah, 'Behold, a virgin shall conceive...', which immediately follows, the word used for 'virgin' (*entito*) implies an as yet uncircumcised and unmarried girl. While Maasai were aware that girls sometimes got pregnant, it would take more than an angel to convince them that a man might then marry such a girl without circumcision. However miraculous the conception, Mary could not be married and a mother and still be uncircumcised without implying a far greater social solecism than the Gospels intended.[125]

Arguments over Biblical circumcision bring us back to the centre of the crisis. Why was *female* circumcision such an issue at Siyabei? It was partly a matter of domestic authority, as we have seen in relation to events in Lassit. More specifically, it related to marriage, for female circumcision was the preparation a father made before handing his daughter over to the authority of a husband. The operation made a girl marriageable, but its proper performance also demonstrated the 'marriage-worthiness' of her family. To give an uncircumcised girl in marriage would not only be a sinister perversion in itself, it would also destroy the social credit of her family.[126] That marriage itself was a sensitive issue is perhaps indicated by the fact that church marriage was the last major Christian ceremonial to be instituted at Siyabei, the first marriage being Peter Kuyioni's in 1933 after his return from Bible School.[127]

The linkage between circumcision, marriage, domestic authority and social credit was a powerful and evocative one, especially since the story of Mary and Joseph seemed to indicate that the Holy Family had trodden the same path of propriety. Evidence again is slender, but it may help to explain why it was fathers especially, rather than husbands, who resisted and did 'nasty things especially about the sale of their girls', and why the intimidation of younger mission supporters like Sitoiya and Kuyioni took the form of blocking their marriages, thus signally demonstrating the continued power of elders over the young – an idea and a practice that would have been strongly endorsed by non-Christian Maasai elders as well.[128] Control over marriage, and maintaining circumcision, was made easier because the 'marriage pool' at Siyabei was so small. As one informant put it bluntly, those who had Maasai wives had either married before they converted or had found one among the families at Siyabei, for they had no chance of finding one outside. Inevitably, too, younger men had to accept circumcised brides if they wished to marry at all – even Sitoiya married Noolmisheni *after* her circumcision.[129]

By the mid-1930s, the crisis was over, though Siyabei remained a troubled station. Despite its small scale, the crisis had an important effect on the development of Christianity in Maasailand. By forcing division and putting both 'Maasai' and 'Christian' as concepts to the test, it had begun to clarify the question of who Maasai Christians were and what they stood for. The successful assertion of authority in church, community and house-hold gave Christians the confidence that they too might find a way to responsible elderhood, while internal conflicts had perhaps helped to draw a line between an older identity as 'Maasai *manqué*', the familiar refuge of failed pastoralists, and an emerging, if as yet incompletely formulated, positive identity as 'new (or modern) Maasai'.

The Predicament of the Maasai Christians

After the Stauffachers had retired, the AIM summed up a quarter-century of continuous presence in Maasailand: 'It has been possible to gather only small groups of adherents from among the Masai, and often the work has been very discouraging.'[130] Was this simply because missions were unreceptive to Maasai, not Maasai to Christianity, as Hodgson has perceptively suggested?[131] Certainly, the strategies and attitudes of the AIM and its missionaries, combined with those of the local administration, left much of Maasailand effectively un-evangelized. Whether a different mission would have been more successful is impossible to say. Early Catholic attempts in Tanzania fared no better, but a comparison between Siyabei and Ngong suggests that the separation and isolation of the former were an important factor. Arguably, Ngong was the most successful Maasai Christian community. Its members were mostly CMS and CSM adherents. It was richer, more cosmopolitan and more self-confident. Many educated Maasai gravitated there, attracted by the proximity of Nairobi, better economic opportunities (including individual land title) and, very possibly, the absence of resident missionaries. It was, however, on the fringes of Maasailand.[132]

Yet the AIM did attract some Maasai; so why did the few not become the many, as they often did elsewhere? In an attempt to address the question without becoming mired in circular arguments about 'Maasai conservatism', innate or induced, Neckebrouck has argued that missions had nothing to offer that Maasai thought valuable. If anything, they were perceived as being part of a world that Maasai consciously and with reason rejected. However problematic this approach may be, it does at least place Christians in context and suggest ways of exploring their relation to the wider society.[133]

Missions themselves did not spread Christianity; African Christians did. Why was the picture of Christianity presented by Maasai Christians so unattractive? The crux of the problem, as the Christians themselves were acutely aware, was their lack of success and legitimacy as Maasai. If Christians were not good Maasai, why should good Maasai become Christians? Their failings lay in three areas: their ethnic identity was ambiguous; they were 'outside time';[134] and they were poor and not fully 'people of cattle'.[135] To Maasai observers it might seem that the three were but different aspects of the same defect: that Maasai Christians lacked 'respect'.[136] Without this, they could have no voice, and without a voice they had no chance of shifting Maasai opinion in their favour, of establishing Christianity as an option rather than a deviation and of creating a 'critical mass' of local Christians.

Maasai Christians could not help their origins, nor could they entirely follow 'Maasai custom' – which, indeed, they hoped to change – but they could attempt to find a voice and a constituency. Maasai society and opinion were far less monolithic than outsiders have assumed, and being 'Maasai' was no longer what it had been or what officials still insisted that it was. During the inter-war years, the dominant, and exclusionary, definition of 'Maasai' was set by ruling elders, in somewhat uneasy alliance with the local administration. But elders themselves were divided over the future, aware of change and the need to control it. They understood what Meshak Naitore was saying, even if they did not agree with his remedies.[137]

There were other audiences, created by the main fault lines of age and gender running through Maasai society. One was women, as Hodgson has shown. Ruth Shaffer was aware of women's religious devotion, especially with regard to fertility, but an appeal to women was problematic within a patriarchal context. Maasai Christians themselves did not support a 'Church of Women', and missionary intervention placed women whom they attracted in an impossible position as pawns in a struggle between rival male authorities.[138] Another was the *athomi* (Sw: 'readers'), younger men who had acquired some education. They began to coalesce as a group in the Masai Association of the early 1930s and then in the significantly named *Ol Turrur l'ol Maasai Oisomate* (OLO: 'Educated Maasai Group') a decade later.[139] Many became Christians, though not necessarily of the AIM. Indeed, the mission's isolation again worked against it, for it lay at the very end of a chain of transmission which stretched out through Ngong or over the Mau from the central foci of 'progressive' discussion in Nairobi and the Rift Valley towns. Except perhaps between 1930 and 1932, Siyabei was not at the centre of Maasai political activism.[140]

In order to make space for themselves, educated Maasai, like their counterparts elsewhere, were engaged in an imaginative project in which Christianity could play a key role. In some societies, men were using Christianity as a glass through which to envision their own ethnic destinies. Kikuyu *athomi* were coming to assert that Christianity marked the completion, not the negation, of Kikuyu civilization, and they saw 'Kikuyu' as something more than the sum of its customary parts. Ancient Kikuyu had created a world out of wilderness. In the new colonial wilderness of towns, wayward women and undisciplined youth, Christian virtues supported the older civic virtues of responsible wealth and productive labour.[141]

Maasai Christians, less well-situated and less confident, were none the less moving, albeit with great difficulty, in similar directions. Because they were isolated from Maasai discourse, they had to develop an idea of 'Maasai' that was not defined entirely in terms of a social experience they did not share. Their room for conceptual manoeuvre was limited by existing social and ethnic boundaries and assumptions, and these had gradually to be redrawn and rethought. There were immediate drawbacks to political association, since this laid *athomi* open to accusations of being Kikuyu and lost them supporters among the Maasai establishment.[142] A differently focused politics might become acceptable if it spoke to specifically Maasai concerns.[143] AIM fundamentalism threatened to alienate Christians entirely from their surroundings. Yet church membership might support Maasai ethnicity if it could be shorn of the old connotations of marginality and expedience.[144] The persuasiveness of the advocates of modernity depended crucially, however, on their being able to demonstrate its benefits to themselves first.

In a sparsely populated, minimally administered and closed reserve, peripheral to the main centres of the colonial economy and in which there were virtually no non-governmental institutions other than the AIM itself, it was difficult to advance or even to earn a living outside pastoralism.[145] Moreover, education, which elsewhere opened up horizons and, indeed, made *athomi* what they were, here closed them down. If mission education for Maasai was barely at the level of the 'dame school', government education, at least in its first decade, was not much better.[146]

The problem was not the provision of schools but the type of education that was offered and the uses to which it could be put. Both mission and government had a sense of how education shaped the community, and a determination to direct the skills of the educated in ways they thought fit, but they were different communities, and the contrasting peaks of the two educational systems reflected this. For the mission, it was Kijabe Bible School, which created the native evangelists and teachers who were the backbone of evangelism. For government, it was the Ngong Veterinary Training School, which taught its pupils how to be 'better pastoralists'.[147] The view from neither peak was especially entrancing to those Maasai who scaled it. Both the divergences and the similarities between government and mission were significant: the first because the AIM did not offer the kind of education that would strengthen the appeal of conversion; the second because *no* education on offer in Maasailand provided a firm material basis for the community of 'new Maasai'.

Thus the issue was not ultimately one of 'conversion and conservatism', but of finding a voice, an audience and an identity. We cannot know how Maasai in general might have responded to Christianity – too few of them had the opportunity to judge for themselves – but we can see how a variety of factors combined against the success of its advocates. Christians in Maasailand were squeezed between three authorities: that of the mission, which attempted to enforce their separation from Maasai; that of the ruling elders, who despised them for their poverty and deviance; and that of the colonial administration, which disapproved of or ignored them. In the longer term, however, their efforts were not without significance. They suggest some of the complexities, conflicts and discontinuities which existed in even such an apparently unified field as Maasailand; and they illustrate a side of Maasai history that has been obscured, and yet is important to our understanding of the present.

Maasai, Missions and Historiography

Stauffacher and his church saw themselves as 'pilgrims in a barren land'. Narratives of evangelism and Christian conversion, like those of national-ism, have often been shaped as journeys towards salvation. But what of those left for dead along the way? The case of Maasai Christianity is a difficult one to frame because it is excluded from two dominant historical narratives: of Maasai 'conservatism' and Christian 'progress'.

Previous studies of Maasailand have stressed its failure to develop economically and politically under colonial rule. This emphasis fits into the conventional frame of colonial history, with its somewhat Whiggish emphasis on class, progress and politics. It presents Maasailand as a negative case that serves to throw developments elsewhere into greater relief. Ironically, historians have accepted the fact of Maasai conservatism, but have turned it on its head, making it the result rather than the cause of colonial neglect and leaving Maasai as victims rather than opponents of modernization. Maasai indifference to missions and education appears as part of a package of characteristics associated with marginalization, whether enforced or actively embraced, which requires no further investigation.[148]

Obviously, the narrative of marginalization is not entirely misconceived. One of the major themes in the colonial history of Kenya is the reordering of the economy around the poles of African capitalism and commercial agriculture, and the consequent displacement of pastoralism from the centre of regional networks of exchange and accumulation. This placed new constraints on Maasai economy and society, and left Christians and 'new Maasai' with little ground on which to build their community.

Another theme is the struggle for primacy between the written and the spoken word. By 1930, the written word and its proponents, the *athomi*, had won in Central Province and perhaps in Nyanza, but in Maasailand they had not. The latter's failure marked a significant point of divergence in what had hitherto been a very close-knit regional history, and left Christians without a voice.[149]

Most *athomi* were or became Christian and had learned to 'read' in mission schools. Christianity became almost inseparable from the written word in Kenya, and was deeply embedded in the imagination of new communities and, later, new nations. The narrative of Christianity is thus woven into that of the nation, and both, understandably, emphasize 'progress'. Mission historiography, especially, has tended to take the high road, if not always to Government House then at least to the council chamber, partly no doubt to appear on the winning side, but also because it has been influenced by the teleological concerns of mission narratives themselves.[150] While some missions did play an important role in stimulating African mobilization by providing encouragement and the tools of literacy, however, others had different priorities. Because they did not fit the frame of 'religion and politics', or contribute significantly to the making of an African middle class, their concerns have previously been overlooked within the dominant paradigms of mission historiography. The AIM is an example. Maasai Christians, already defined out of the main current of Maasai history, have found no place in the history of mission Christianity either.[151]

With the merging of foreign missions and local African churches, and with the marriage of church and state gone sour, other perspectives have emerged. Recent studies present African Christians, not as mission 'converts' – a significantly loaded term – navigating between two worlds, but as active intellectual and social innovators consciously creating a new culture, not so much by assimilating and adapting what was already there as by formulating new ideas and practices to meet needs, which they themselves identified and which did not necessarily conform to a 'modernizing' agenda. This reconceptualization and the empowerment of African Christianity, focusing on individual experience, have begun to separate the history of Christianity from that of missions and to decouple both from the grand narratives of colonialism.[152]

This approach still proposes a narrative of Christian progress, however, albeit one in which the journey is directed towards different goals and in which the pilgrims do their own dictating. It addresses the present state of Maasai Christianity rather better than its past. The field of evangelism has been transformed as Maasailand has been incorporated into the modern state and as church denominations have proliferated. By 1970, 'new Maasai' were finally coming into their own, and their civilizing project was finally being realized. Churches now have much larger Maasai member-ships, and the two worlds are no longer so obviously opposed. Yet there is still a conceptual as well as a chronological gap between the isolated world of pre-war Siyabei and the expanding and confident churches of modern Narok and Kajiado that will remain unless the narratives of Maasai and mission can be made to meet and interrogate each other.[153]

Why Christians failed to become an effective presence in Maasailand is less clear than might at first appear. Rethinking their history outside the frames of 'progress' vs. 'conservatism' and 'empowerment' will give them a place, and perhaps suggest different narratives of Christianity and colonialism in Maasailand, narratives that challenge assumptions about their mutual opposition and essential seamlessness.

Notes

* I am grateful to the participants at the Madison seminar in August 1996, where a preliminary version of this chapter was presented, for their helpful comments, and especially to Tom Spear and Dorothy Hodgson.
Note on the papers of the AIM: The Billy Graham Center, Wheaton holds only the papers from the American office of the mission, as Collection 81. They are cited here as AIMBGW with file reference. Additionally, the Center now holds the Stauffacher papers [SP] including Florence Stauffacher's Diaries [FSD], as Collection 281. Much material remains in the Nairobi headquarters, but is not fully accessible to researchers. For the local papers, I am indebted to the AIM staff in Nairobi (papers cited as AIMN with file reference), to the History Department, University of Nairobi, which holds copies of notes taken by Kenneth King (cited as AIMK), and to Kevin Ward who allowed me to see his

own notes of papers shown to him by the mission (cited as AIMW).

1 Naitore to President, Kajiado LNC, 14 Dec. 1938, Kenya National Archives [KNA]: DC/KAJ 2/6/1.

2 In 1934, there were 30 church members at Siyabei and the same number at Lassit, though the latter also had 90 'enquirers' and a Sunday service attendance of 70. AIM, *Annual Report* (1934), AIMBGW: 20/12. By contrast, the Anglican community in Kabete alone was over seven thousand strong in the mid-1930s. H. R. A. Philp, *A New Day in Kenya* (London, 1936), appendix IV.

3 Arguably, church influence was beginning to grow and spread by the late 1930s. Missionaries claimed a 'decided awakening', and there is evidence of community church-building, informal evangelizing and church baptisms. Shaffer to Nixon, 24 June 1938, Report of Field Director: Kenya Field, Dec. 1938, 'Echoes from Masailand' [Shaffers' Prayer Letters], Sept. 1939–April 1940, all in AIMBGW: 24/9, 13/14, 24/10. However, these remained highly localized phenomena, and it was not until the 1970s that anything like 'mass conversion' occurred in Kenya Maasailand.

4 In 1966, Fr Donovan told his bishop that 'the relationship with the Masai ... is dismal, time-consuming, wearying, expensive and materialistic'. After seven years of effort, there were no adult Maasai Catholics in Loliondo, parochial school-leavers had simply lapsed, and it seemed impossible to preach directly to the people. Fifty years before, a fellow-Catholic had assessed mission prospects among the Maasai in similar terms. V. J. Donovan, *Christianity Rediscovered* (Notre Dame, 1978) 14–5, 55; Fr Wall letter, Feb. 1913, *St Joseph's Foreign Missionary Advocate*, Summer, 1913. For a Marxist analysis which reaches the same general conclusion, see P. Rigby, *Persistent Pastoralists* (London, 1985), Chapter 5.

5 Some of these points are addressed in V. Neckebrouck, *Le Onzième Commandement* (*Nouvelle Review de Science Missionaire*, Supplementa, Vol. 27) (Immensee, 1978), Chapter 20. I am grateful to Tom Spear for bringing this to my attention.

6 Studies of the AIM have been few and often critical, partly perhaps because their particular religious perspectives have not been shared by their critics and partly because the antipathy shown by some members of the mission to scholarly enquiry has been reciprocated. For assessments, see K. Ward, 'The development of Protestant Christianity in Kenya' (PhD, Cambridge, 1976) (which I have been unable to consult); D. P. Sandgren, *Christianity and the Kikuyu* (New York, 1989).

7 K. Richardson, *Garden of Miracles* (London, 1968) 21–49.

8 Quoted in Sandgren, *Christianity and the Kikuyu*, 23. See generally, W. G. McLoughlin, *Revivals, Awakenings and Reform* (Chicago, 1978), Chapter 5; M. L. Bell, *Crusade in the City* (Lewisburg, PA, 1977), 19–20 and Chapters 11–12; R. L. Tignor, *The Colonial Transformation of Kenya* (Princeton, 1976), 116–24.

9 Sandgren, *Christianity and the Kikuyu*, 18, 22; Richardson, *Garden of Miracles*, 23–7, 43–4. For vignettes of traumatic conversion, see the mission magazines *Hearing and Doing* [HD] and *Inland Africa* [IA].

10 See T. O. Beidelman, *Colonial Evangelism* (Bloomington, 1982), especially Chapters 1 and 8. Mission biographies echo the themes of family and faith, e.g. J.H. Westervelt, *On Safari for God* (Kijobe, nd); G. Stauffacher, *Faster Beats the Drum* (Kijobe, 1977).

11 The introduction to *Garden of Miracles*, the official AIM history, republished in 1976, gives a dystopic view of un-evangelized Africa which would not have been out of place in mission publications of a century earlier.

12 Sandgren, *Christianity and the Kikuyu*, 23–4; Tignor, *Colonial Transformation*, 119–20; R. W. Strayer, *The Making of Mission Communities in East Africa* (London, 1978), Chapter 5. An early AIM missionary had written: 'The more we know of the Wakamba, the more vile, naturally, do they appear to us.' Allen to Home Council, 14 Aug. 1897, *HD*, 2:10 (1897). There are few positive references in missionary writings to any aspect of Maasai life. One described the *murran* system as 'hellish': '[It] has secured a death grip upon the people, dragging them further and further down into the quagmire of sin and hopelessness.' 'Echoes from Masailand', March 1936, AIMBGW: 24/9. However, Ruth Shaffer's recollections, written much later in retirement, are both better informed and more sympathetic to Maasai, with whom she worked for 35 years. R. T. Shaffer, *Road to Kilimanjaro* (Grand Rapids, 1985). See also D. T. Priest, *Doing Theology with the Maasai* (Pasadena, 1990).

13 R. Waller, '*Emutai*: crisis and response in Maasailand, 1883–1902', in D. Johnson and D. Anderson (eds), *The Ecology of Survival* (London, 1988), 94–101. Francis Hall, administrator at Kikuyu, sent a group of 23 Maasai orphans to Kibwezi mission, of whom four were accepted by Freretown CMS school at the Coast. Hall to Father, 5 July 1894, Hall Papers, Rhodes House, Oxford; B. G. McIntosh, 'The Scottish mission in Kenya, 1891–1923 (PhD, Edinburgh, 1969), 108–10; Minutes of Finance Committee, Freretown, 12 March 1895, CMS [Archives, Birmingham] G3 A5/O 1895. The list of pupils at Mahoo school (Taveta) for 1895 shows 11 Maasai, who had been there for up to three years and of whom at least five were subsequently baptized. CMS: *Taveta Chronicle*, 1 (Easter, 1895).

14 A. R. Tucker, *Eighteen Years in Uganda and East Africa* (London, 1908), 212, 356; Tucker to Stock, 26 Oct.1892, CMS: G3 A5/0 1892; Steggall to Baylis, 4 Jan.1895, CMS: G3 A5/0 1895; H. H. Johnston, *The Kilima-Njaro Expedition* (London, 1886), 406–7, 426.

15 Stauffacher to Culley, 31 March 1905, *HD*, 10:4 (1905). He could not 'help but believe that our greatest hope for native evangelists is in the Masai'. *Idem*, nd, *HD*, 9(1904).

16 Tucker to Baylis, 4 Dec. 1897, CMS: G3 A5/0 1897; McGregor to Baylis and to Peel, both 24 Nov. 1900, CMS: G3 A5/0 1901. Josiah Aramato was either a debt pawn or a famine refugee separated from his family who had been brought to McGregor at Taveta by his 'owner' in 1893. He was baptized and subsequently sent to Freretown, Mombasa 'with a view to future work in Masailand'. McGregor to CMS, 1 Oct. 1899, CMS: *Annual Letters*; *Taveta Chronicle*, 5 (July 1896); Hamshere to Baylis, 18 May 1899 and McGregor to Baylis, 27 March 1899, both CMS: G3 A5/0 1899.

17 McGregor to CMS, 27 Nov. 1901 and 12 Dec. 1902, *Annual Letters*; memo by Canon Leakey, in Kenya Land Commission, *Evidence and Memoranda*, Vol. I (HMSO, London, 1934), 851.

18 Arthur to Hurlburt, 13 Jan.1912, Arthur to Downing, 16 Jan. 1929, AIMK; G. R. Sandford, *An Administrative and Political History of the Masai Reserve* (London, 1919), 67. The Catholic Mill Hill fathers also announced a mission to the Maasai, based on Naivasha, but nothing came of this either. Plunkett letter, 15 Dec. 1906, *St. Joseph's Foreign Missionary Advocate*, Spring 1907.

19 All the Maasai boys at Kibwezi eventually absconded, as did several of the first AIM pupils. McIntosh, 'The Scottish mission', 110; Stauffacher to Minch, 13 March 1904, SP; entries for 27 Dec. 1906, 1–3 and 9 Aug. 1908, FSD.

20 Enoch ('Boy') Kahare was a runaway slave released to the CMS in 1890 and baptized in December 1891, the first Maasai to be so. After working on the Coast, he was sent to Kikuyu as a 'non graded agent' early in 1902. Stauffacher met him a few years later, and in 1907 he turned up at the Rumuruti mission looking for work. Stauffacher took him in, and he worked intermittently as a teacher and translator until 1924, when he was dismissed by the Field Council for polygamy. Hooper to CMS, 25 Oct. 1892, *Annual Letters*; Burt to Baylis, 21 Feb. 1902, and Resolution 48, Mombasa Executive Committee Minutes, 21–22 Jan. 1902, both in CMS: G3 A5/0 1902; Leakey to CMS, 7 Jan. 1903, *Annual Letters*; J. Stauffacher, 'The prodigal son', *HD*, 12/4(1907); Stauffacher to Hurlburt, 16 Jan. 1908, AIMN: FC/90; Shaffer, *Road to Kilimanjaro*, 43, 45–6.

21 Stauffacher engaged Shanga as a teacher early in 1905. Within months, however, he had disappeared, only to reappear a year later. He remained unhappily at the mission until a final break occurred in April 1908. Stauffacher to Minch, 1 March and 16 May 1905, SP; Stauffacher to Cully, 11 July 1905, *HD*, 10:5 (1905); entries for 17–18 Sept.1906 and 16, 18 April 1908, FSD. He may be the same as Josiah Aramato (see fn. 16 above) but, if so, he gave Stauffacher a different account of his life, including a Somali mother, a visit to England, baptism in Uganda, and a death scene with the Rev. Pilkington in Busoga in 1897.

22 Justin Lemenye was born a Parakuyu near Mazinde, but had been sent to live with the Maasai. When rinderpest struck in 1891, he fled to Chaga and was eventually handed over by *mangi* Rindi of Moshi to the CMS with other refugee children. When the CMS left Moshi, Justin went with them to Taveta, probably at the end of 1892. He was baptized in the following year and worked as a pupil–teacher until he was sent to Freretown for training. On his return, he was put in charge of the work at Kikoro. At the end of 1902, he met Hollis who employed him to help with the Maasai grammar he was then compiling. In 1904, he was appointed Maasai interpreter at the newly opened government station at

Rumuruti and remained there until he resigned and returned to Taveta in 1907. He was invited to work for the AIM and did so from 1908 to 1911. He then returned home to Parakuyu, eventually being appointed headman for the Parakuyu in Same District in 1923. *Maisha ya Sameni ole Kwasis yaani Justin Lemenye* (Dar-es-Salaam, 1953), translated as H. Fosbrooke (ed.), 'The life of Justin', *Tanganyika Notes and Records*, 41 (1955), 31–57 and 42 (1956), 19–30. See also, biography in *Taveta Chronicle*, 16 (June 1899); Hurlburt to Lemenye, 16 July 1907 and 28 Jan. 1908, AIMN: FC/90; and Hurlburt letter, 29 April 1908, printed in *HD*, 14:1 (1909).

23 See R. Waller, '"Whose life is it anyway?" Biography and autobiography reconsidered', paper presented to Biography in East African Historical Writing Workshop, Oxford, June 1995.

24 K. King, 'The Maasai and the protest phenomenon, 1900–1960', *Journal of African History*, 12 (1971), 119.

25 Biographical details in Stauffacher to Culley, 14 June 1903, *HD*, 7:3 (1903). He married Florence Minch in 1906 and, except for leaves and six years in the Congo, the couple remained in Kenya until their retirement in 1940.

26 Stauffacher to Minch, 30 March, 29 April, 9 June 1904, SP. Such youthful sentiments could not survive elderhood and domesticity. By 1914, proper racial practice prevailed, at least on Earth; Molonket was sleeping in the storehouse and eating in the kitchen. Entry for 2 July 1914, FSD.

27 Stauffacher to Cully, nd., *HD*, 9 (1904); Stauffacher to Minch, 8 Dec. 1904, 13 June 1905, SP. There were at least two meetings with Olonana, the first in mid-1904; the second, a year later, was a formal conference in Nairobi with leading elders, Sub-Commissioner Ainsworth, and a representative from the CMS also present. At the second meeting, Stauffacher was promised a ten-acre mission site near Olonana's land at Ngong and up to 40 pupils, to be selected by the *laibon* with the backing of government and to remain under his control. These meetings have to be read against the background of the politics of the Maasai Moves, and are an indication that, in 1904–5 at least, but probably not much later, the mission was being taken seriously as a potential political resource by both government and Maasai.

28 Stauffacher to Cully, 28 Sept. 1905, *HD*, 10:7 (1905). The original plan had been to remain near Kijabe, but this seems to have been ruled out by difficulties over land and then by the government's refusal to allow Maasai to remain in the area. The Ngong offer was never implemented. Stauffacher to Minch, 8 Dec. 1904, 12 Jan. and 22 March 1905, SP; Stauffacher to Cully, 11 July 1905, *HD*, 10:5 (1905). For the Maasai Moves of 1904 and 1912, see M. P. K. Sorrenson, *The Origins of European Settlement in Kenya* (Nairobi, 1968), Chapter 12.

29 Stauffacher letter, 21 July 1906, *HD*, 11:3 (1906); entries for 24 April and 1 May 1908, FSD. Taki was a slightly older man, already a circumcised *murran*, who had been a government *askari* at Rumuruti since its establishment. He joined the mission permanently in 1909 and remained with it until his death in 1923. See O. L. Burbridge, *Taki: Soldier, Evangelist, Translator* (London, nd) and obituaries by Simpson and Stauffacher in *IA*, 7:9, 12 (1923).

30 AIM, *Annual Reports* (1912, 1914, 1916), *HD*, 18:1 (1913) and 20:2 (1915) and *IA*, 1:11 (1917); Westervelt, *On Safari*, 148–51. Molonket had left Kenya for school in the USA in 1909 and did not return until 1912. Westervelt, *On Safari*, 95; Downing letter, nd, *HD*, 18:9 (1913). The AIM seems to have taken a justifiably more pessimistic view of the prospects of winning the Maasai to Christ. After Stauffacher's departure, magazine coverage of the Laikipia mission becomes more circumspect, and, although the *Annual Report* for 1912 promised that the mission would be reopened when the 'state of unrest' in Maasailand was resolved and Hurlburt applied for a mission plot at Narok when the Reserve was established, nothing was done until the Stauffachers returned. Narok District, *Annual Report* (1914/15), KNA: DC/NRK 1/1/1.

31 The Stauffachers returned briefly to Rumuruti in 1910/11 and departed for the Congo in April 1912. They did not return to Kenya until 1918. J. Stauffacher, 'History of the Africa Inland Mission' (MS, nd), 36, 39–43, AIMBGW: 12/45; entry for 29 March 1918, FSD. Stauffacher's decision to leave Maasailand for the Congo is difficult to explain. Tignor implies that he simply abandoned the Maasai work, an accusation made by some

of his fellow missionaries. Yet Stauffacher shared Scott's founding vision of a chain of mission stations advancing into the interior of Africa, and it is evident from the record that the Stauffachers had determined to move on, perhaps even before they left Rumuruti in 1908. Opposition from Hurlburt and the Field Council, which led to their threatening to resign from the AIM, delayed their departure. His later letters from Rumuruti, however, suggest that Stauffacher had lost his initial enthusiasm for work among the Maasai – he quotes the image of the Suffering Christ apparently in relation to himself – and this may have had an influence on his decision to push for the Congo and, later, on his attitude to mission work at Siyabei. Tignor, *Colonial Transformation*, 141–2; Riebe to Hurlburt, 30 March and 10 Aug. 1911, AIMN: FC/90; memo for 1908, entries 11 and 31 Dec. 1910, 13 Feb. and 10 Aug. 1911, 9 Feb. 1912, FSD; Stauffacher to Downing, 2 Aug. 1911, AIMN: FC/88; Stauffacher to Hurlburt, 22 Jan. 1911, and *Minutes of General Council*, Kijabe, 6 Sept. 1911, AIMW; extract from Stauffacher letter, nd (mid-1908?), *HD*, 14:2 (1909); J. Stauffacher, 'Side tracked for 2,000 years', paper to Kijabe Conference, *HD*, 17:4 (1912); Stauffacher letter, 7 Jan. 1907, *ibid.*, 12:1 (1907).

32   Entry for 4 June 1908, FSD; Laikipia District, *Survey of Events*, KNA: DC/LKA 1/1; Narok District, *Annual Report, op.cit.*

33   Stauffacher to Cully, 28 Sept. 1905, *HD*, 10:7 (1905). Stauffacher was correct in thinking that the Reserve would prove insufficient for the Maasai. Stauffacher to Minch, 12 Jan. and 22 March 1905, SP; Sandford, *History of the Masai Reserve*, 26–7.

34   McGregor to Baylis, 24 Nov. 1900, CMS: G3 A5/0 1901. See also, *Taveta Chronicle*, 13 (Sept. 1898).

35   Stauffacher to Minch, 30 March and 9 June 1904, SP; Stauffacher to Cully, 31 March and 11 July 1905, *HD*, 10:4, 5 (1905). Stauffacher was aware that cultivation would attract only poorer Maasai, but this seemed to be 'God's Plan' for the regeneration of the people. Stauffacher to Culley, 28 Sept. 1905, *HD*, 10:7 (1905). Significantly, the Mill Hill Fathers' later negative assessment was based partly on the observation that the Maasai were conservative and '*very rich*' [emphasis in original]. Fr Wall letter, Feb. 1913, *op. cit.* Officials saw a similar connection between stock wealth and conservatism. See R. Waller, 'Pastoral poverty in historical perspective', in D. Anderson and V. Broche-Due (eds), *The Poor are Not Us: Poverty and Pastoralism in East Africa*, forthcoming.

36   See fn. 28 above and Stauffacher to Minch, 10 July, 22 Oct. 1904, and 16 May 1905, SP. For the important role to be played by native evangelists in the general mission strategy, see Hurlburt's remarks in AIM, *Annual Report* (1923), *IA*, 8:7 (1924).

37   '[T]hey do the dictating and we must submit' – but what could one expect from people 'steeped in sin and vice for centuries' [note the change in tone from 1904]. Stauffacher letter, 7 Jan. 1907, *HD*, 12:1 (1907).

38   Itineration diaries for Jan.–July 1908 are in FSD. Parts for 1910–13 (Taki) can be found in SP, and others are printed in *HD*, 16:3 (1911) and 17:1 (1912).

39   Stauffacher letter, 6 July 1918, *IA*, 2:10 (1918); *ibid.* to Johnston, 2 Nov. 1920 and 22 Feb., 18 March 1921, AIMW; Stauffacher to Campbell, 19 Nov. 1929, AIMBGW: 13/10.

40   Between 1919 and 1939, only three safaris are noted in FSD. In 1919 and again in 1932, the CSM asked the Stauffachers to take over at Ngong, but beyond visits nothing transpired, and the school continued independently, even though there were some AIM adherents in the area and close contacts between the two communities. Unlike the community at Siyabei, the Ngong area residents were willing to raise money for buildings and a teacher's wages. Entries for 17 July 1919 and 27 Sept.1923, FSD; Davis to Campbell, 11 June 1932, AIMBGW: 10/5; Masai Province, *Annual Report* (1931), KNA: PC/SP 1/2/1.

41   Roy and Ruth Shaffer also came from mid-West farming communities, but Roy had served as an army medical orderly in France in 1917–18, and Ruth's family had moved to Chicago. Shaffer, *Road to Kilimanjaro*, especially Chapter 5. Their relations with the Stauffachers were often strained, for they belonged to another mission generation with different experiences and expectations, and had different visions of the Maasai Christian community they wished to build, as well as different ideas of how to realize it. A full discussion of their differences, which affected converts as well as missionaries, is beyond the scope of this chapter, but see correspondence in AIMBGW: 24/9, 24/16, and entries for Sept. and Oct. 1939 especially in FSD.

42 R. Shaffer, *Report to Field Council* (1928), AIMW; Shaffer, *Road to Kilimanjaro*, Chapter 11; Stauffacher to Campbell, 7 Feb. 1928, Mrs Shaffer to Campbell, 27 Feb. 1931, AIMBGW: 13/10, 24/9; 'Echoes from Masailand', Feb. 1940, SP. In 1925, the DC Narok noted that Shaffer, then missionary in charge, had recommended its closure 'being now of the reluctant opinion that most of the grapes in this "vineyard of the Lord" are sour ones'. The somewhat stagnant atmosphere at Siyabei was evident to others. A decade later, the Kikuyu evangelist then in charge preached on the need for a revival at Siyabei. His chosen text was the story of Jonah and the whale: the Christians were like Jonah, and Siyabei was the sinking ship. Narok District, *Annual Report* (1925) KNA: DC/NRK 1/1/2; Downing letter, nd (1937), *IA*, 22:1–3 (1938).

43 Kajiado District, *Annual Reports* (1931, 1932) KNA: DC/KAJ 2/1/1; Shaffer to Davis, 12 Feb. 1932, AIMK; Shaffers to Campbell, 8 July 1932, AIMBGW: 24/9. For Loitokitok settlement, see Waller, '*Emutai*', 94, 100.

44 Florence Stauffacher to Mrs Minch, 20 April 1908, SP; Slater letter, 5 Feb. 1908, *HD*, 8:1 (1908); entries for 14 and 16 April 1912, Taki Itineration Diary, SP. Men would not sit with women to listen to preaching and were surprised when Taki 'talked to God', something that women did. Extract from Barnett letter, 28 Sept. 1909, *HD*, 15:1 (1910). See further in D. Hodgson, 'Engendered encounters: men of the church and the "church of women" in Maasailand, Tanzania, 1950–1993', Workshop on African Expressions of Christianity. Madison, 1994. I am grateful to Dorothy Hodgson for access to this paper, which was originally presented at the Madison workshop.

45 Stauffacher letter, 7 Jan. 1907, *IA*, 12:1 (1907); entries for 1, 3, 9 Aug. 1908, FSD; Staffacher to Campbell, 19 Nov. 1929, AIMBGW: 13/10. Maasai initially refused to work for wages for fear of losing status, yet they demanded to be paid to attend school or to listen to preaching. Stauffacher letter, 21 July 1906, *HD*, 11:3 (1906); Florence Stauffacher letter, 1 Sept. 1919, *IA*, 4:2 (1920). Demands for gifts were a normal part of the currency of reciprocity, as the Stauffachers understood, but, by categorizing learning and (listening to) preaching as something imposed that required direct payment in return, Maasai may also have intended pointedly to exclude evangelism from the realm of '*enkiguana*' (debate/discussion), where juniors properly listened while seniors spoke, and to deny the inequality between preacher/teacher and 'listener' which the missionaries saw as implicit in their message of salvation. Working for another clearly implied dependence; listening to another was more ambiguous.

46 Clothes seem to have been a shared means of symbolic communication between missionaries and Maasai. Soon after Stauffacher met Molonket, he gave him and his companion a set of Western clothes, 'and now they look quite like men'. Later, Molonket switched from shirt to *shuka* and back as he wrestled with the decision to convert, and he signalled 'that he's no Masai anymore' by washing and putting on clothes again. In reverse, a girl who left the mission sent back her dress. Stauffacher to Minch, 13 March 1904, SP; entries for 1 and 14 Sept. 1906 and list of pupils in diary for 1908, FSD. For 'testimony' and confession as a method of disciplining converts, see, for example, Hurlburt letter, nd, *HD*, 11:2 (1906); Downing, 'Discipline in the Native Church', *ibid.*, 18:1 (1913).

47 The official AIM version of Molonket's conversion is in J. Riebe, 'The story of Mulungit', *HD*, 12:1 (1907) and Westervelt, *On Safari*, 36–48, 78–83, but there is also a later, more reflective, journal account by Stauffacher himself among his papers, which does not seem to have been intended for circulation. There are daily references in FSD, Aug.–Sept. 1906. Molonket himself left no record. See also, K. King, 'A biography of Molonket Olokorinya Ole Sempele', in K. King and A. Salim (eds), *Kenya Historical Biographies* (Nairobi, 1971), 7–11. The various texts would repay closer comparison and analysis as conversion narratives.

48 Molonket was the exception to the usual pattern of converts. He was apparently from a wealthy family, and had been picked out early as spokesman for the Keekonyukie *murran*. In time, he would probably have become senior spokesman for the age-set as a whole, as well as Keekonyukie government chief. As it was, Molonket was circumcised privately in hospital and never graduated to senior *murran*hood. It was a heavy price to pay for a position of minor responsibility in the mission, and he came to resent it. Apart from the loss of status, absconding from his responsibilities, as his age-mates saw it, and then selling stock made for difficulties in recovering cattle from his father's herd and may have

contributed to his poverty in later life. King, 'Molonket', 2, 11–12, 22; Stauffacher letter, nd, *HD* 12:2 (1907); Stauffacher to Hurlburt, 16 Jan. 1908, AIMN: FC/90; Florence Stauffacher to 'Dear Ones", 1 May 1930, SP; interview with Johanna Nyenjeri s/o Njeroge, St Paul's Limuru Research Papers [LRP], file KIK (2), seen by kind permission of K. Ward; entries for Sept.1918; Siyabei interviews, esp. M(aasai)T(ext)/M/KE9.

49 Stauffacher letter, 7 Jan. 1907, *HD*, 12:1 (1907); Farnsworth letter, nd, *IA*, 13:12 (1929); replies to Evangelism Questionnaire, 1944/45?, AIMBGW: 13/13. Similar feelings of loss and separation were evoked by government education.

50 *Ibid.* Stauffacher identified 'affinity for their own tribe' as the greatest difficulty in attracting Maasai to the mission. Only those already detached 'dared' to come to the mission.

51 Downing to Hamilton, and Downing to Home, both 13 Sept. 1912, and papers enclosed in Downing to Hollis, 1 Oct. 1912, all enclosed in Belfield to Harcourt, 12 Oct.1912, Public Record Office: CO 533/107; Sorrenson, *European Settlement*, 261, 266–7. Their stance may have been prompted partly by a desire as foreigners to appear 'responsible' in the eyes of the British administration. For the Masai Case, see T. H. R. Cashmore, 'Studies in district administration in the East Africa Protectorate, 1895–1918' (PhD, Cambridge, 1965), 303–8.

52 Stauffacher to Minch, 9 June, 15 July 1904, 12 Jan., 22 March 1905, SP. The Maasai response to the Moves has not yet been fully studied, but see Cashmore, 'Studies in district administration', 261ff.

53 Hurlburt letter, 30 Oct. 1903, *HD*, 8:1 (1904); Stauffacher to Minch, 22 Oct., 10 Nov., 8 Dec. 1904, SP; Slater letter, March 1910, *HD*, 15:3 (1910); interview with Hannah w/o Taki ole Kindi, LRP: file MAASAI.

54 Informants unfavourably contrasted the AIM with other missions in this respect. See, e.g., MT/M/KE9.

55 The search for patrons explains in part why, in 1929, the Siyabei elders approached the CSM and then government to provide a teacher, claiming that the mission 'has done nothing', and why a year later they invited (Maasai) members of the Kikuyu Central Association (KCA) to act as mediators in the dispute over female circumcision. The Stauffachers were outraged by this 'sneaky business', and the level of mutual misunderstanding is evident. Entries for 11, 22 Jan., 2–3, 13 Feb., 27 April 1929; Florence Stauffacher to Aunt Ann, 16 March 1929, SP; King, 'Maasai and protest', 127–8, 131.

56 Comments in district annual reports are uniformly negative. While admitting the unreceptive attitude of the Maasai and the practical difficulties of work in Maasailand, the Officer-in-Charge in 1930 called for a mission with 'a high standard of discipline in connection with religious teaching' to take up the educational work which was being neglected by the AIM. A later comment was more direct: 'As in every other form of work amongst the Masai, the qualities of enthusiasm, personal influence, gaining confidence and making a lengthy stay are absolutely essential in a missionary, and these qualities the present missionaries of the AIM have not got...' Masai Province, *Annual Reports* (1930, 1936). The administration initially refused to allow evangelizing in the government school, and Shaffer, at least, was convinced that the administration covertly put pressure on Maasai to refuse mission extensions. Entries for 5, 9 April 1922 and April memo, FSD; Shaffer to Davis, 28 Nov. 1931, AIMK.

57 Masai Province, *Annual Report* (1937). Official policy towards female circumcision in Maasai was, in effect, to avoid the issue. See DC Kajiado to Officer-in-Charge, Masai Reserve [OiC], 12 May 1931 and OiC to Chief Native Commissioner, 18 May 1937, KNA: DC/KAJ 2/1/12.

58 R. Waller, 'Acceptees and aliens: Kikuyu settlement in Maasailand', in *Being Maasai* (London, 1993), T. Spear and R. Waller (eds), 239–41. Missionary views could be uncompromising: 'The objection we are up against is due to the fact that we object to native Christians singing objectionable heathen songs, piercing ears, circumcising, and a long list of definitely sinful things.... The policy of the [government] school ... is in direct opposition to the policy of the mission with respect to several moral issues....' Shaffer to Davis and Downing, 4 Jan. 1938, AIMK.

59 E.g. OiC to Stauffacher, 4 Jan. 1937, KNA: DC/KAJ 2/1/12; entries for 18, 31 Dec. 1936, FSD. Missionaries were aware of the disingenuousness of these claims, but could

Mission

not challenge them directly: 'If nothing may be done without the father's consent, how does [Whitehouse] get 100 boys in his school?' Entry for 10 Feb. 1937, FSD.

60 Shaffer to Davis, nd (1932?), Shaffer to Nixon, 10 July 1939, AIMK; AIM, *Annual Report* (1934). Disputes centred on attempts by the mission to control the marriages of their converts and, possibly, to foment opposition to Whitehouse among his own teachers and pupils. Shaffer to Nixon, 12 June, 10 July 1939, AIMK; MT/M/KA19-20. See also below, pp. 95-6.

61 Virtually no contemporary non-Christian perspective survives. Even as late as 1945, missionaries had no clear idea why Maasai were so unreceptive, beyond their inherent sinfulness. The only theological objection mentioned was horror at the idea of the Resurrection of the Dead. Replies to Evangelism Questionnaire, AIMBGW: 13/13.

62 Stauffacher to Campbell, 7 Feb. 1928, AIMBGW: 13/10. His objection was to incessant feuding between the residents, not to their evangelism.

63 One father, a local seer, first moved camp when his sons showed an interest in the mission rather than in herding, and then disinherited them as a last resort. Shaffer, *Road to Kilimanjaro*, 2-3. But, with the debatable exception of the public cursing of Molonket in 1906, nothing resembling the killing of the first Lutheran missionaries by Arusha *murran* or the 'war against converts' in Meru occurred in Maasailand, despite Maasai willingness to attack other agents of colonialism. In both these cases, and others, however, public violence was being used to cleanse the land of pollution, restore moral order, or to destroy a potent source of evil in the community. See T. Spear, *Mountain Farmers* (Oxford, 1997), 65-74; J. A. Fadiman, *When We Began, There Were Witchmen* (Berkeley, 1993), Chapter 9.

64 Entries for Nov.-Dec. 1936 and 7 Nov. 1937, FSD. The *murran* took the opportunity to make a public demonstration of their own sphere of influence, as much to the elders as the missionaries. Entry for 16 Dec. 1936, FSD.

65 DC Kajiado to OiC, 15 April 1931, DC/KAJ 2/3/13. Stauffacher complained that his attempts to build outside Siyabei were prevented by the elders. On one occasion, the elders peremptorily ordered him to leave the area, and, when appealed to, the DC informed him that the Maasai were in the right. Stauffacher to Campbell, 19 Nov. 1929, AIMBGW: 13/10.

66 In 1939, for example, a meeting of leading Nairage Ngare residents, some of whom were church members, including headman Muneria and Mpaayei ole Kinaiya, an ex-member of the Siyabei Council of Elders, agreed to set aside a plot for church use, but they stipulated that granting the plot in the name of the AIM should not imply permission for the establishment of a mission station. 'Meeting of Local Natives, Nairage Ngare', note 28 Oct. 1939, KNA: DC/KAJ 2/1/11.

67 Shaffer to OiC, 12 March 1932, AIMK. This perception took hold even before the mission began to campaign against female circumcision and for Christian marriage, and was, perhaps, sparked by small but symbolic acts. At Lassit, for example, the Shaffers attempted to persuade women who visited the mission to remove *sekengei*, their wire coil ornaments. This may have been interpreted as an attempt to single out women and as a public challenge to male authority. Mrs Shaffer to Davis, nd, AIMK.

68 Steiner to Campbell and Lanning, 2 April 1935, AIMBGW: 24/18; Nixon to Campbell, 18 May 1938, Shaffer to Nixon, 5 June 1939, AIMK. The bizarre 'Sofi affair' was one example, in which the Shaffers attempted to prevent the daughter of a Christian from being circumcised and sent off to the *manyatta* prior to marriage by (allegedly) spiriting her away to Kijabe. That Sofi was also the headman's niece complicated matters. The 'plot' was 'betrayed' to Whitehouse by the Stauffachers, who disapproved of their colleagues' actions, but Sofi remained under mission protection for some time despite attempts to have her returned to her father's custody. Entries for Sept. 1936 to Feb. 1937, FSD; Stauffacher to Field Council, 30 Sept. 1936; Shaffer to Downing, 30 Dec. 1936; Shaffer to Campbell, 2 April 1937; AIMBGW: 24/9.

69 Kajiado District, *Annual Reports* (1929-30, 1934); *idem* (1935), KNA: PC/SP 1/5/1; Masai Province, *Intelligence Reports*, Nov. 1934, Feb., June 1935, Aug., Sept., Nov. 1937, KNA: PC/SP 3/1/1; Shaffer to Davis, 10, 17 Oct. 1931, 12 Feb. 1932, Shaffer to OiC, 12 March 1932, AIMK; Steiner to Campbell, 21 Oct. 1934 and 2 April 1935, AIMBGW: 24/18; 'Echoes from Masailand', Jan.-March 1932, Shaffer to Campbell, 4 Dec. 1934 and Shaffer to Field Council, 24 Jan. 1938, AIMBGW: 24/9; Loitokitok interviews.

70 Stauffacher, *Faster Beats the Drum*, 118.
71 In July 1918, there were seven hundred cattle at Siyabei, though this number soon dwindled. Taki had cattle, an ox wagon, and household goods worth Rs50 or more. When Kashisha Wapary arrived with his father, mother, grandmother and two children, he was able to pay Rs60 for a field of maize. Entries for 15 June, 9 July 1918, 5, 8 Aug. 1919, FSD; Simpson letter, 23 Oct. 1918, *IA*, 3:5 (1919).
72 See T. Kanogo, *Squatters and the Roots of Mau Mau* (London, 1987), 11–29; Waller, 'Emutai', 96–101.
73 Paragraph based on references in FSD and on field interviews. The stories of Mpaayei ole Kinaiya, 'Kamuni' Kinana and Isiah Oloisenke will serve for many. The three men were friends who came to Siyabei from the Kijabe area in the early 1920s. They had been brought up in Kikuyu households after being left as small children in the 1890s. Kinaiya and Oloisenke were Keekonyukie and members of the same circumcision group. Kinana was slightly older and had originally come from Loitokitok. All belonged to the same clan, however. Isiah had heard about Siyabei through attending Kijabe mission. He told the others, and went ahead to investigate. All were attracted by the idea of being Maasai again while remaining 'a bit civilized'. Kinana had been working as a tribal policeman and forest guard – not popular jobs locally – and Mpaayei was having problems with his father-in-law on whose land he was living. They gathered families and possessions and made their way across the plains and over the Mau, arranging with the border post to let them all through even though they only had one pass. Once in Maasailand, they had to prove their identity to register as 'Maasai'. The mission could not help, but Molonket knew what to do, and Christopher Tameno, who was working as a government clerk and who knew of them as part of the Maasai refugee community in Kikuyuland, vouched for them. MT/M/KE5, /KL3, /P29.
74 See R. Lamprey and R. Waller, 'The Loita-Mara region in historical times: patterns of subsistence, settlement and ecological change', in P. Robertshaw (ed.), *Early Pastoralists of South-western Kenya* (Nairobi, 1990), 20–5. Despite the river, herd owners at Siyabei still had to move their stock. Shaffer letter, nd, *IA*, 9:9 (1925); Stauffacher letter, nd, *ibid.*, 13:6 (1929); entry for 5 March 1939, FSD.
75 Entry for 22 April and 17 Aug. 1928, FSD; Narok District, *Annual Report* (1925). See also, R. D. Waller, 'Uneconomic growth: the Maasai stock economy 1914–1929', unpublished paper, Cambridge, 1975, 18–19. Mpaayei, one of Siyabei's most prosperous residents, eventually moved permanently to Nairagie Ngare, where there was already a Kikuyu squatter settlement and where he and others organized a church of their own. Several other people, including Tameno and Molonket, had acquired land at Ngong.
76 Masai Province, *Annual Report* (1928).
77 Johnston to Fletcher, 30 Nov. 1921, AIMK; AIM, *Annual Report* (1923), *IA*, 8:7 (1924); D. M. Miller, 'The strategic value of the rural school', *ibid.*, 11:12 (1927); Campbell to Maynard, 4 Aug. 1926, AIMBGW: 10/5. The official (but never unanimously agreed) policy of the AIM was to provide education geared to the needs of evangelism only, and to refuse government education grants-in-aid, since 'entering into contracts' compromised the faith basis of the mission. See Field Council to Home Council, 27 Aug. 1936 and reply 21 Oct. 1936, Downing to Campbell, 5 Nov. 1936, Campbell to Nixon, 11 Aug. 1939, AIMK; Tignor, *Colonial Transformation*, 122–4. Stauffacher supported this policy. Stauffacher to Campbell, 23 Feb. 1927, AIMBGW: 13/10.
78 Masai Province, *Annual Report* (1923); Headmaster, Loitokitok School to Director of Education, 10 April 1938, KNA: PC/Ngong 1/17/1. The school at Siyabei opened in 1918 with six pupils (only one of whom was a Maasai). When the Narok Government School opened in 1921 with 96 pupils, Siyabei enrolments had reached 33. Within ten years, the numbers in government education had doubled, with the opening of another school at Kajiado in 1926 (transferred to Loitokitok in 1929). Out-schools followed in the late 1930s. This achievement was not matched by the AIM, however, whose education did not significantly expand in either scope or quality. Tignor, *Colonial Transformation*, 279–87; entries for 12 Aug. 1918 and 31 Oct. 1921, FSD; Report of Chief Inspector of Schools, April 1940, AIMW.
79 Shaffer to Nixon, 5 July 1938, AIMK; Masai Province, *Annual Report* (1931). Annual contributions from the 18 members, 15 'inquirers', and 65 (average) Sunday church

attenders at Siyabei totalled Shs33, less than Shs2 per church member. By contrast, the 113 members at Eldama Ravine (some of them Uas Nkishu Maasai) contributed Shs700, over Shs6 each. *Statistical Report: Kenya, IA*, 11:8 (1927).

80 Entries for 2–3 April 1934, FSD; Shaffer to Nixon, *op. cit.* and reply, AIMK. See also, Stauffacher to Woodley, 14 March 1921, AIMK. The AIM generally paid its African staff less than other missions – and less than they might have got in secular employment. Stauffacher to Johnston, 22 Feb. 1921, AIMW; unsigned (Kijabe) to Johnston, 13 July 1920, AIMK; AIM, *Annual Report* (1923).

81 The word for 'news', *ilomon*, is the word for 'visitors', the channels of communication throughout Maasailand. At Siyabei, few 'visitors' are recorded, although out-patient figures, where they are provided, give an indication. In 1934, only 376 patients appeared for medical treatment at Siyabei, compared with almost ten times that number at Lassit, where there was a trained nurse at the time. AIM, *Annual Report* (1934), AIMBGW: 20/12.

82 Florence Stauffacher's daily record is full of references to half-revealed feuds over dowries unpaid, adulteries and trespasses committed or denied, and bad words spoken. Since much of daily experience consisted of simply living and working together, these quotidian and apparently trivial concerns constitute the very texture of life at the mission within which religious concerns and conflicts were shaped and embedded.

83 Downing to Campbell, 26 Sept. 1928, AIMW. Mission rules made public confession ('testimony') a prerequisite for taking Communion (q.v. below). Some, like Bridget, accused of sleeping with a teacher in 1928, tried unsuccessfully to avoid this by claiming that private confession to God was sufficient. On other occasions, confession was used by the young to cut a dash in public – 'swank' – and to assert themselves against their elders, or by individuals to air private grievances: '[one evening] a strange thing happened.... We went to praying and ended in a wrangle [over cattle trespass]'. Entries for 5 June 1939, 30 Sept.–7 Oct. 1928, 16–17 Sept. 1928, 13–18 Aug. 1920, FSD. There may be an interesting parallel between the spoken 'confessions' of young Christian men and the dramatizing of thinly disguised exploits and affronts to elders in songs sung by *murran* and girls during dancing.

84 Florence Stauffacher letter, 13 Nov. 1918, newspaper cutting in SP; AIM, *Annual Report* (1918–19), *IA*, 3:10 (1919). They were temporarily ordered out again during the 1922 disturbances.

85 E.g. entry for 21 Aug. 1932, FSD: 'They threaten they'll get us out of here if we protect any girls.' See also entries for 20, 27 May 1930, 7, 12–14 April 1931, FSD and Stauffacher to Campbell, 11 Feb. 1930, AIMBGW: 13/10.

86 Entries for 4 Oct., 10–19 Nov. 1923; Florence Stauffacher to Aunts Lora and Ann, 16 Nov. 1923, newspaper cutting in SP; Masai Province, *Annual Reports* (1925, 1935). Kikuyu were again being cleared out during the circumcision crisis in 1930 (q.v. below). For background, see Waller, 'Acceptees and aliens', 234–7.

87 See entries for May 1930, FSD.

88 Entries for 6–8 April 1931, FSD. The ethos of the AIM was highly patriarchal, as its own publications make clear, and its interventions to 'protect' women can be seen as an attempt to place them under a different but still male authority. An article on 'The heathen women of Africa' [*IA*, 2:2 (1918)], while explaining that the mission school was a place of refuge for girls when home was 'undesirable or unsafe', went on to regret, using a commonly assumed (but wrongly drawn) parallel with freed slaves during the Reconstruction era, that such girls often felt 'under no restraint'. However, freedom from a father's or husband's authority did not mean 'idleness nor disobedience...[to "those in authority"]'. After a particularly trying time with the mission girls at Lassit, even Florence Stauffacher confided that she wished that Sofi would be circumcised – so that she could be married and out of the mission. Entry for 8 Aug. 1937, FSD. I am grateful to Leslie Patrick for discussing the American parallel with me. See also, T. F. Gossett, *Race: The History of an Idea in America* (Dallas, 1963).

89 DC Narok's [hostile] comments on the Land Commission Report, encl. in OiC to Colonial Secretary, 29 Aug. 1934, KNA: DC/Ngong 1/7/7; Narok District, *Annual Report* (1939), KNA: DC/NRK 1/1/3.

90 Narok District, *Annual Report* (1925). Expulsion was the final sanction within the community for 'trouble-makers' and 'backsliders'. Entries for 21–22 March and 27 April

1921, FSD.

91 See Strayer, *Making of Mission Communities*. One exception was the community of freed slaves established on the Coast at Freretown in the 1870s. *Ibid.*, Chapter 2.

92 For configuring, see, for example, J. and J. Comaroff, *Of Revelation and Revolution* (Chicago, 1991); P. S. Landau, *The Realm of the Word* (Portsmouth, 1995). We need to be aware of the dangers of post-modern glosses and solipsistic interpretation here. Although we can inspect the texts that they used, we often cannot know how and what missionaries actually preached or what their listeners really understood them to be saying.

93 '...Tagi was the one around whom our hopes for the evangelization of the Masai centered'. Field Director to Green, 24 Sept. 1923, AIMBGW: 22/8. *Inland Africa* [1:3 (1917)] had earlier told its readers that Taki's Christian life was 'characterized by obedience'. Official and oral accounts confirm his authority and 'respect'. See Westervelt, *On Safari*, 151–2; Stauffacher, *Faster Beats the Drum*, 125; interview with Johanna Nyenjeri, *op. cit.* and MT/M/P27.

94 Stauffacher to Campbell, 7 Feb. 1928, AIMBGW: 13/10; Florence Stauffacher to Aunts Lora and Ann, 16 Nov. 1923, *op. cit.* In 1928, Masikonte settled the disputed headmanship in Molonket's favour, but the elders refused to pay his salary and he was replaced by Mpaayei a year later. Entries for 7–9 Feb., 3–4 March 1928 and 7 March 1929, FSD.

95 It seems likely that some practices continued, secretly, at Siyabei, but the references are rendered so opaque by the mission perspective that it is impossible to determine what they were. See, for example, 'wickedness' in the 'kraal', which may have been a pre-circumcision boys' gathering or merely dancing. Entries for 26 April and 21 Sept. 1920, FSD.

96 This is to use an analytical terminology more applicable to the society beyond the mission boundaries, but, just as becoming a Maasai is a continuous process, monitored by patrons and marked by ritual stages, so was becoming a Christian in the AIM.

97 Entry for 13 Jan. 1929, FSD. A similar conflict occurred in 1935. This time the elders rejected some but insisted on others who, in Florence Stauffacher's eyes at least, were unfit. Entries for 27 Nov., 4 and 8 Dec. 1935, FSD.

98 Entry for 16 Feb. 1930, FSD and Florence Stauffacher to 'Dear Ones', 18 Sept. 1930, SP. The texts were Galatians 1:6–9 and Mark 18:17–25. In fact, the passage which establishes Communion specifically as a commemoration comes in Luke's account (Luke 22:19–20), but is omitted in some modern translations.

99 Entries for 23 Feb. and 18 June 1930, FSD; Florence Stauffacher to Aunt Ann, 16 March 1929, SP; Stauffacher letter, nd, *IA*, 13:6 (1929). David Sabean has explored conflicts between village pastors and their flocks over the meaning and significance of Communion in post-Reformation Germany in similar ways. He argues that a reason for non-attendance at Communion was the peasants' belief that to take Communion in a state of anger was ritually dangerous. D.W. Sabean, *Power in the Blood* (Cambridge, 1984), Chapter 1. I am grateful to Jay Goodale for discussing this with me.

100 See, for example, H. V. Blakeslee, 'Blood for cleansing', *IA*, 10:7 (1926). Stauffacher, however, thought that Africans had arrived at the idea that Communion wiped out sins from seeing whites whom they knew to be sinners partaking. Luise White has examined notions of blood and the Catholic Mass in a very different context. L. White, 'Vampire Priests in Central Africa: African debates about labor and religion in colonial northern Zambia', *Comparative Studies in Society and History*, 35 (1993), 746–72. See also Spear, *Mountain Farmers*, 68, 72–3 for conflicting missionary and Arusha notions of the meaning of blood, sacrifice and cleansing.

101 A Maasai teacher confessed to adultery and was barred from Communion as a result. The husband of the woman involved had disappeared, however, and she wanted a child, something that no reasonable man would or should refuse her. Shaffer, *Road to Kilimanjaro*, 46.

102 This was the *kidole* ('thumbprint'), an unfortunate association since other instruments of colonial power, *kipandes* and squatter contracts, were marked the same way. The AIM resolution of 29 May 1930 is quoted in Nixon to Leatherman, 26 Dec. 1940, AIMW.

103 The timing and the language of protest suggest communication with Kikuyuland, and to some extent both the missionaries and their converts read the situation in the light of

their knowledge of events elsewhere. There was also a substantial 'Kikuyu' element at Siyabei and close family links. Molonket's wife's family were among the leading protesters at Kijabe, for example. King, 'Molonket', 20; entry for 10 Feb. 1930, FSD; Florence Stauffacher to 'Dear Ones', 18 Sept. 1930, SP.

104 See generally, Strayer, *Making of Mission Communities*, Chapter 8 and Sandgren, *Christianity and the Kikuyu*, Chapters 4–5. The trajectory and outcome of the crisis at Siyabei better fits the experience of some CMS mission stations than it does the AIM's. As Strayer suggests, the variation in response argues against the view that the crisis was either 'political' or the product of deep religious differences.

105 Entries for 7 June, 31 July, 15 Aug. 1928, 6 June, 14 Aug. 1929, memo for Nov. 1929, FSD.

106 Entries for Feb., May, 20 Aug. and 1–2 Sept. 1930, FSD; Stauffacher to Campbell, 17 Sept. 1930, AIMBGW: 13/10. At least one girl, Noolmisheni, and her father were subjected to intimidation and enormous psychological pressure from both sides before agreeing to circumcision. More circumcisions took place in 1932 and 1933. Entries for 15–16 Aug. 1932, 22 June 1933, FSD.

107 Entries for 19–20 Sept. 1931, FSD. Ironically, at the moment when Stauffacher was asking his church elders to sign the 'card' in order to receive Communion, the Field Council, faced with disaster, had already abandoned the loyalty pledge and was considering relaxing its absolute ban on circumcision. Sandgren, *Christianity and the Kikuyu*, 94–5.

108 Shaffer to Campbell, 18 Jan. 1932, AIMBGW: 24/9. There are repeated references to attempts to come to terms by both sides – as well as walk-outs and denunciations. Stauffacher was willing to attend 'rebel' church services and to reopen the school. There were arguments about Communion (see above, pp. 196–8), and, in March 1931, 'young fellows' asked Stauffacher 'why he can't have fellowship with them and scolds all the time'. Downing to Shaffer, 11 June 1930, AIMK; entries for 7 April and 25 May 1930, memo for 1930, 15 March 1931, FSD.

109 In 1947, when the elders again resisted the imposition of a ban, they informed the Field Council that 'Mr Stauffacher had allowed them to do as they felt in the matter of circumcision...' Shaffer to Davis, 24 March 1947, AIMK.

110 For *kidole*, see p. 102 and fn. 102. Stauffacher was strongly opposed to making female circumcision illegal. He argued that African Christians did not object to church discipline, which they could take or leave, but would oppose any attempt by missions to make civil law – precisely what Arthur of the CSM and other missionaries hoped to achieve. While he shared the general mission assumption that opposition was 'anti-Christian' and was being fostered by the KCA for its own or 'Bolshevistic' ends, he was willing to admit that Africans did have genuine grievances which deserved expression. He deplored the coupling of religious and political issues, however, for which he held the missions partly to blame because they had not concentrated on evangelism: 'Politics and education only lead us deeper and deeper into hopeless trouble.' Stauffacher to Campbell, 25 June 1930, AIMBGW: 13/10. Shaffer shared his opinion and made it clear that he was not enforcing the ban. Shaffer to Campbell, 18 Jan. 1932, AIMBGW: 24/9; Shaffer, *Road to Kilimanjaro*, 103.

111 Letters to Campbell, 19 Nov. 1929, and 11 Feb., 23 April, 25 June, 17 Sept. 1930, AIMBGW: 13/10. Quotations taken from these letters.

112 See also pp. 95, 98–9 and fns 68, 88 above. The whole question requires more detailed and nuanced examination elsewhere, but see discussion and references in Hodgson, 'Engendered encounters' and F. Bowie, D. Kirkwood and S. Ardener (eds), *Women and Missions* (Providence, 1993), especially chapters by Kirkwood, Kanogo and Bowie. I am grateful to David Anderson and Leslie Patrick for discussing these matters with me.

113 Entries for 8–9 Feb. and 15 Dec. 1930, FSD; Florence Stauffacher to 'Dear Ones', 18 Sept. 1930, SP.

114 Entries for 27 Feb., 18 March, 18 June 1930, FSD.

115 With the exception of female circumcision, the revival of ear-piercing and removal of front teeth for boys, and a general relaxing of mission prohibitions on drinking and dancing, all of which could be seen as examples of a reaction to mission interference in private matters, the only evidence for the incorporation of any kind of traditional

practice comes in a single reference to 'sacrificing' honey beer. Stauffacher to Campbell, 23 April 1930, AIMBGW: 13/10; King, 'Molonket', 21, 24 but see also fn. 125 below). Nothing like the Kikuyu *arathi* emerged, and even the option of 'Christianized' initiation along the lines of the 'Kabare Experiment' was not explored, partly because the AIM ruled specifically against it, but also because the interests that promoted these initiatives elsewhere were either too weak or non-existent at Siyabei. For reasons that should be clear, Christianity at this time was not open to 'interaction', as Ranger puts it, with Maasai society. Sandgren, *Christianity and the Kikuyu*, Chapter 7; Strayer, *Making of Mission Communities*, 144–6; AIM resolution of 23 July 1931, quoted in Nixon to Leatherman, *op. cit.*; T. Ranger, 'Missionary adaptation of African religious institutions: the Masasi Case', in T. Ranger and I. Kimambo (eds), *The Historical Study of African Religion* (London, 1972), 247.

116 The elders had approached Stauffacher for advice and help in establishing their church. He listened, but Florence was scandalized: 'it gets me all worked up to think of the nerve they've got'. Entry for 19 Sept. 1930, FSD.

117 Entry for 11 Dec. 1929, FSD. Kuyioni was the son of an itinerant (Kikuyu?) healer or minor prophet who had attended school while working for the Shaffers. Milaon had come to the mission from Nakuru in search of an education. He and Sitoiya had no father living, while Kuyioni had been publicly disinherited. Siyabei interviews; Shaffer, *Road to Kilimanjaro*, 6–7.

118 Sandgren, *Christianity and the Kikuyu*, 78; Tignor, *Colonial Transformation*, 82–7. Surviving participants tended to structure their memories of the crisis in terms of age oppositions, but the sample at Siyabei is too small to draw more than very general inferences.

119 Here I disagree with King, who places dissatisfaction with mission education close to the centre of the crisis at Siyabei. While education was certainly a concern for some of the participants, the significance of arguments over school attendance seems to lie more in the fact that school and church were contested spaces. That this was literally the case was demonstrated during the negotiations with the DC when it emerged that the protesters were aware, probably through Mootian, who was working in the DC's office, that the mission property had never been properly surveyed and were ready to challenge the AIM title. King, 'Molonket', 17, 23; Stauffacher to Campbell, 11 Feb. 1930, AIMBGW: 13/10.

120 Older struggles over the control of the Bible and its multiple meanings remind us that to wrench religious and political inspiration apart is often to violate the integrity of historical experience. See, for example, C. Hill, *The English Bible and the Seventeenth-century Revolution* (London, 1993).

121 Stauffacher to Campbell, 11 Feb. 1930, *op. cit.*; Florence Stauffacher to 'Dear Ones', 1 May 1930, SP; entry for 15 Aug. 1932, FSD. It is perhaps going too far to see the Bible as the original 'hidden transcript'. See J. Scott, *Domination and the Arts of Resistance* (New Haven, 1990).

122 Stauffacher letter, nd, *IA*, 13:6 (1929); Stauffacher to Campbell, 25 June 1930, AIMBGW: 13/10. The New Testament translated into Maa by Stauffacher, Taki and others was available in part at Siyabei by 1924. AIM, *Annual Report* (1918–19), *IA*, 3:10 (1919); Stauffacher, *Faster Beats the Drum*, 125–6.

123 Many missionaries chose to emphasize instead the 'paganism' of the songs and activities surrounding circumcision and the health problems of the operation itself. Strayer, *Making of Mission Communities*, 137.

124 Florence Stauffacher to 'Dear Ones', 18 Sept. 1930, SP (emphasis in original).

125 Sandgren, *Christianity and the Kikuyu*, 74. The question of translation requires more study than it has received if we are to understand what the first Christians actually read. The original Maa version was found to contain errors, omissions and 'obscure passages' before it was revised in the 1940s. In the story of the Three Wise Men (*ilangeni*), for example, the Magi present Jesus with honey beer (*enaisho*), something approrpriate and ritually significant from a Maasai point of view but at odds with the church's ban on alcohol. In the revised version, *enaisho* was replaced by a literal, but meaningless to Maasai, rendering of 'gold, frankincense and myrrh'. Shaffer, *Road to Kilimanjaro*, 197, 200, 206. The shift from honey beer to gold, which also avoids any connection with the *laibons*, may indicate a hardening of the cultural boundaries in the name of accuracy in

translation. I have been unable to consult the original.

126 See P. Spencer, *The Maasai of Matapato* (Bloomington, 1988), Chapter 2 and 228–9. Circumcision generally took place immediately before marriage.

127 Shaffer, *Road to Kilimanjaro*, 7–10, 149–50. As late as 1935, however, Molonket was still attempting to persuade people to accept church marriage. Entry for 19 June 1935, FSD.

128 Memo for Feb. 1931, FSD; Florence Stauffacher to 'Dear Ones', 18 Sept. 1930, SP; Stauffacher to Campbell, 17 Sept.1930, AIMBGW: 13/10. Intimidation took other forms as well, but both Sitoiya and Kuyioni experienced major obstacles in their attempts to marry the daughters of Odupoi and Mpaayei respectively. Relations were inflamed by the fact that both girls had fled to their future husbands to avoid being married elsewhere, a serious affront to paternal authority attributed to mission interference.

129 MT/M/P29. Several of the early converts, including Molonket and Taki, had married Christian Kikuyu under mission auspices.

130 'Notes', *IA*, 26:1–2 (1942).

131 Hodgson, 'Engendered encounters'.

132 Ngong requires further study, but see Waller, 'Pastoral poverty'. Shaffer described Ngong as the 'cream of Masailand' as far as mission opportunities were concerned and lamented that the AIM had no effective presence there. Shaffer to Nixon, 2 June 1938, AIMK.

133 Neckebrouck, *Onzième Commandement*, 610–14. Neckebrouck compares four societies, Kikuyu, Chaga, Arusha and Maasai, but he entirely rules out both mission agency and Christianity itself (as opposed to a vague modernity), and fails to expand on what missions and their adherents lacked or failed to offer.

134 Paul Spencer has commented: 'To become a Maasai is to fit into a mould and to pass from one mould to another as the age-set spirals up to elderhood; and this extends to all facets of Maasai existence. To fail to fit into this mould … is to be outside the image of what is fitting for a Maasai'. P. Spencer, 'Becoming Maasai: being in time', in Spear and Waller (eds), *Being Maasai*, 156.

135 J. Galaty, 'Being "Maasai"; being "people of cattle": ethnic shifters in East Africa', *American Ethnologist*, 9 (1982), 1–20. When 'Kamuni' Kinana joined the Siyabei community, older residents advised him to turn his cash savings into stock, lest people should think him a pauper. MT/M/P11.

136 'Respect' (*enkanyit*) was the quality of proper behaviour which *murran* had to learn and which elders recognized in each other. Lack of 'respect' indicated a lack of appropriate socialization and suggested an affinity with non-Maasai, like 'Dorobo', who, Maasai felt, had no civilized society, no norms of behaviour and no sense of restraint. While poor men could still have 'respect', the very success of wealthy household heads testified to their moral worth. For a Christian view, see E. Hillman, *Toward an African Christianity* (New York, 1993), 54, 57.

137 For discussions of models of ethnicity in Maasai, see T. Spear, 'Introduction' and R. Waller, 'Conclusion', in Spear and Waller (eds), *Being Maasai*, 1–18, 290–302; D. L. Hodgson, 'The politics of gender, ethnicity and "development": images, interventions and the reconfiguration of Maasai identities' (PhD, Michigan, 1995), Chapters 3, 9.

138 Shaffer, *Road to Kilimanjaro*, 154–6, 46. Unsurprisingly, their staunchest female adherents were orphans like Kituruti, left at Lassit by an older brother, and women like Ngoto Mpaiyai, old, blind and beyond censure. Shaffer, letter, nd, 'Kituruti, a Masai girl', 'Notes', all in *IA*, 17:1–3 (1933), 20:7–9 (1936), 26:3–4 (1942). See also Hodgson, 'Engendered encounters' and A. Hastings, 'Were women a special case?', in Bowie, Kirkwood and Ardener (eds), *Women and Missions*, 109–25.

139 King, 'Maasai and protest', 133–4.

140 Some mission members or sometime members, like Oguyai ole Nanchiro, Christopher Tameno and Thomas Mootian, were members of the KCA and helped to form the Maasai Association, but they had wider personal networks which brought ideas and information in from outside. For a different assessment, see King, 'Maasai and protest', 125–33.

141 J. Lonsdale, 'The moral economy of Mau Mau: wealth, poverty and civic virtue in Kikuyu political thought', in B. Berman and J. Lonsdale (eds), *Unhappy Valley* (London, 1992), II:315–504. For another example, see John Peel on Yoruba, e.g. J. D. Y. Peel,

'The cultural work of Yoruba ethnogenesis', in E. Tonkin, M. Chapman & M. McDonald (eds), *History and Ethnicity* (London, 1989), 198–215 and *idem*, 'For who hath despised the day of small things? Missionary narratives and historical anthropology', *Comparative Studies in Society and History*, 37 (1995), 581–607.

142 King, 'Maasai and protest', 131. At a meeting held by Chief Masikonte to discuss a request that 'Kidole people' (i.e. those supporting the mission) be expelled, Stauffacher was able to deflect the attack by producing a leaked KCA document signed by 15 Maasai, including Molonket, Mootian and several government school teachers. The DC had not been interested, but the chief was, especially since three of his sons were signatories. He then ruled that they must give up the KCA or move away and suspended action against the mission. Stauffacher to Campbell, 25 June 1930, AIMBGW: 13/210, and FSD, entries for 13–14 April 1931 (dates as given).

143 See Waller, 'Acceptees and aliens', 242–6.

144 The mission itself seems first to have promoted an identification between the AIM and Maasai, but as a way of discouraging interlopers in their sphere – Shaffer to Nixon, 2 June 1938, AIMK. Much later, Steven (Sitoiya) Sankan, President of the Narok Court, an arbiter of custom, and an enthusiastic local historian, and John Tompo (Mpaayei's son), Makerere graduate and Secretary General of the Bible Society of Kenya, attempted in different ways to consolidate a Christian Maasai identity through writing history which evoked Maasai unity, and by presenting Molonket, the age-set spokesman rather than the outcast, as the 'Thorn Treader', the forerunner (and almost martyr) of modern Maasai. S. S. Sankan, *The Maasai* (Nairobi, nd); J. T. Mpaayei, *Inkuti Pukunot oolMaasai* (Oxford, 1954); MT/M/KE9 and interviews with J. T. Mpaayei cited in King, 'Molonket', 25 and Neckebrouck, *Onzième Commandement*, 593, 611. There are other similar history MSS in private hands.

145 See, for example, Headmaster, Loitokitok to Director of Education, 1 June 1938, KNA: PC/Ngong 1/17/1; Instructor, Ngong [Vet. Training School] to DC Kajiado, 25 April 1936, KNA: DC/Ngong 1/17/3; Waller, 'Uneconomic growth'.

146 Inspection Notes, Narok School, Sept. 1926, encl. in Director of Education to Principal, Narok School, 18 Oct. 1926 and minute by Director; Whitehouse, 'Memorandum on measures for increasing the popularity of the Masai schools', nd [1926?], both in KNA: Education Dept. Deposit I, file 152/26.

147 Government education was intended to control young men by taking them out of *manyattas* and into schools, and to break down 'conservatism' by creating a class of enterprising and commercially minded householders and herd owners who were, none the less, still firmly within the community. See Masai Province, *Annual Reports* (1924, 1930, 1936) and DC Ngong, 'Estimates for Kajiado School', 22 May 1926, Education Dept. *op. cit.*, file 419/26.

148 This is largely true of the older studies by Tignor, King (cited elsewhere), van Zwanenberg and Kitching, and, more recently, of Kituyi's work, where 'transformation' occurs *after* colonialism. R. M. A. van Zwanenberg with A. King, *An Economic History of Kenya and Uganda, 1800–1970* (London, 1975); G. Kitching, *Class and Economic Change in Kenya* (New Haven, 1980); M. Kituyi, *Becoming Kenyans* (Nairobi, 1990). See also Hodgson, 'Politics of gender, ethnicity and "development"', especially Chapters 4–5.

149 R. Waller and N. W. Sobania, 'Pastoralism in historical perspective', in E. Fratkin, K. A. Galvin and E. A. Roth (eds), *African Pastoralist Systems* (Boulder, 1994), 48–55; J. Lonsdale, '"Listen while I read": the orality of Christian literacy in the young Kenyatta's making of the Kikuyu', in L. de la Gorgendiere, K. King and S. Vaughan (eds), *Ethnicity in Africa* (Edinburgh, 1996), 17–53. I am grateful to John Lonsdale and Bruce Berman, who have generously shared their ideas with me.

150 See, for example, Strayer, *Making of Mission Communities* and M. Clough, *Fighting Two Sides* (Niwot, 1990). In an important sense, historians of Kenya have not yet fully escaped from *The Myth of 'Mau Mau'*, and the compelling logic and sophistication of *Unhappy Valley* (cited elsewhere) is likely to reinforce that bondage, although, by pushing the enquiry deeper into the community, it also offers an alternative. C. Rosberg and J. Nottingham, *The Myth of 'Mau Mau'* (New York, 1966).

151 An early critique of the connection made between 'religion and (elite) politics', and especially of the historiographical influence of mission centres of 'peculiar influence', is

125

in Ranger's introduction to Part Two of T. O. Ranger and J. Weller (eds), *Themes in the Christian History of Central Africa* (London, 1975), 92–4.

152 See, for example, C. Hoehler-Fatton, *Women of Fire and Spirit* (New York, 1996). Ranger's biography of the Samkanges, Zimbabwean *athomi par excellence*, occupies an interestingly ambiguous position here. It deals extensively with their (elite) politics and with their clashes with the mission hierarchy, but it also shows how they drew on Methodism and education consciously to create the model of an African middle-class family identity for themselves and others. T. O. Ranger, *Are We Not Also Men?* (London, 1995).

153 For contemporary developments in Tanzania, see Hodgson, 'Engendered encounters'. A study of church expansion in Kenya Maasailand, especially since the 1970s, is urgently required.

III

Conversion

&

Popular Evangelism

If the process of mission was complex, conversion was even more so, beset by the uncertainties of translating subtle religious concepts and cultural values across yawning cultural and linguistic divides. Missionaries, their beliefs, their social practices and their languages were all alien, and Africans made of them what they would. The gulf in Chaga was wide indeed, as Lema has shown, and it was only when local evangelists began to preach the Word and translate the Bible in familiar terms that the number of converts increased beyond the initial handful of social outcasts. And in Zaramo, according to Kimambo, the divide remained as long as the Lutheran mission continued to depend on non-Zaramo agents and languages.

The young were often the first to convert, drawn to the missionaries by their adolescence, curiosity and eye for new opportunities. While they lacked the social status, authority or commitment to entrenched values to be taken seriously by others at first, as Waller shows, in the long run, this would lead to an inversion of status as education, book learning and apparent poverty slowly supplanted experience, wisdom and wealth in cattle. While few took them seriously at first, then, the young catechists and evangelists would ultimately provide the cultural bridge the missionaries required as they translated the Gospel, interpreted the Word and preached it forcefully to their neighbours.

One sees this vividly in Smythe's account of Catholicism in Fipa, where the church rapidly became a church of children as parents willingly allowed their children to be baptized, even while they themselves resisted. Such forbearance, she notes, was probably due to the cultural tolerance and pragmatism of the missionaries, the congruence of Christianity and Fipa beliefs, the breakdown of royal authority and the priests' easy acceptance of their roles as fathers and patrons to their increasing families of children.

But such tolerance allowed Fipa to interpret the new faith for themselves, transforming both Catholicism and Fipa ideas in the process.

Maddox takes this analysis further by exploring in detail the ways a single Catholic priest, Father Stephen Mlundi, 'domesticated' the faith and incorporated Catholic religious categories into Gogo ones and vice versa. As the first ordained priest in the area, Fr Stephen was in a critical position to influence others, interpreting Catholicism for his fellow Gogo while at the same time negotiating between the colonial regime and his Italian colleagues.

Six

The Creation of a Catholic Fipa Society
Conversion in Nkansi District, Ufipa

KATHLEEN R. SMYTHE

Ufipa, in southwestern Tanzania, is often seen as a success story for the Catholic Church as it has one of the highest concentrations of Catholics in East Africa. If one examines the statistics, Fipa converted to Catholicism relatively soon after the arrival of the missionaries in 1888 and the vast majority of Fipa were Catholic by 1945. This chapter probes why the Catholic Church in Ufipa (and Nkansi District in particular) was so successful and the nature of its success.[1] Ufipa is also unusual because it was relatively isolated from most of the changes associated with colonialism, such as cash crop production, railway building, labour migration and settlement by Europeans, which often influenced conversion elsewhere.[2] Thus the impact of the colonial state cannot wholly account for conversion in Ufipa; one must look for other reasons to explain Fipa conversion to Christianity. Fipa did not convert simply to embrace a new world view or to become players in the changes brought on by colonialism, but instead they felt they were creating a new institution within Fipa society.[3]

The early success of the Catholic Church in Ufipa can be attributed to three factors that facilitated conversion. First, Nkansi royalty were receptive to the White Fathers' religious message. Second, their emphasis on conversion of children established a solid foundation for building a Christian society.[4] And, third, and most importantly, there was a significant congruence, both cultivated and innate, between the Catholic religion and the roles played by its missionaries in Ufipa, on one hand, and Fipa religion and culture on the other. This does not mean that conversion was a smooth process, however. The White Fathers did not find Fipa behaviour and practices beyond reproach. From the beginning, the missionaries worked actively to change some aspects of Fipa society. In some areas, especially those where European colonial officials held similar views, they were successful, but in others Fipa resolutely defied priestly regulations and warnings when they saw fit.

Conversion, then, was inherently dialectical in Ufipa. As the missionaries adapted to local culture, Fipa integrated the missionaries into their own cultural framework. Similarly, while the missionaries emphasized similarities between Catholicism and Fipa traditional religion, Fipa interpreted these religious and cultural messages as either corresponding or not corresponding to their own ideas about religion.

The Beginning of the Mission in Nkansi and Early Conversion of Royalty

My research was carried out in Nkansi District in Ufipa, and in the village of Chala, in particular.[5] Starting at Kirando on Lake Tanganyika in 1888, Chala was the eighth station built by the White Fathers in Ufipa. The missionaries' arrival there in 1912 was heralded by their calling for the elders of two former villages to come and form the new village of Chala.[6] The history of Chala, thus, cannot be separated from the history of the Catholic Church in the region.

Chala mission was founded by a French priest, Gauston Poultier, who is remembered to this day by elders in the Chala area for his role as founder of the mission and by many for his defection a decade or so later when he took a Fipa wife. After his departure from the society, he remained in the area and raised his children twenty miles south of Chala. His son, Michael, told me that Gauston only spoke Kifipa and Kiswahili at home, renouncing not only his native tongue but also most of his connections to his homeland. His defection was viewed with disdain by the rest of the missionaries, but, as time went by, priests visiting his village to lead mass or give catechism lessons stayed with him and made sure he was well cared for.[7] Gauston's unusual adoption of Fipa culture demonstrates, albeit at its extreme, the missionaries' willingness to adapt to Fipa ways, and the White Fathers' continued relations with Gauston reflect the relatively flexible attitude the missionaries showed to their would-be converts.[8]

White Father missionaries had first established themselves along northern Lake Tanganyika (at Karema in Ubende), where their energies were devoted to the freeing and conversion of slaves. Ubende proved a difficult place for conversion of the indigenous population, however, so the missionaries looked further south, to the Nkansi kingdom, where they were drawn to the *mwene* (king) as a means of developing a following among the local people.[9] The founder of the mission society believed the conversion of royalty was essential, as Roger Heremans notes:

> According to the desire of their founder, the White Fathers were forced to establish in Central Africa a Christian ruler. The instructions given by the Archbishop to the Fathers of the second caravan included a chapter entitled: 'The External Foundation of a Christian Kingdom'.

Based on historical events, Mgr Lavigerie noted that Christianity seemed to establish itself in a stable and general fashion, when it was officially adopted by the leaders of a country, who by their example and power, favored its diffusion. The priests came therefore, in their evangelical work, holding fully to this 'grand truth'.[10]

Locating and converting an African leader as a means of converting a large number of people was one of the ways they assured 'the cohesion of the tribes, peace, justice and the continual suppression of slavery', Heremans concludes.[11]

The White Fathers applied this strategy when they moved south along the lake to Ufipa proper. They first tried to win the support of the king of Nkansi, Mwene Kapuufi, with little success. Finally granted permission to build a station at Kirando in 1888, they were asked to leave a year later by the king. Some claim this was because Arab traders warned the king of the danger of having the missionaries in his land.[12] Alternatively, Willis argues that it was perhaps due to widespread resentment of the Germans, fuelled by the Abushiri revolt along the coast. Or perhaps Kapuufi, who had received gifts of gunpowder from the White Fathers to help fend off Kimalaunga from the southern part of Nkansi, resented a subsequent reduction in his gunpowder supply. There were also cultural reasons for disliking the missionaries. They 'attacked polygamy, they attacked fetishes, and at the level of the state attacked the custom of trial by poison ordeal which among other things served as a very important prerogative of chiefs'.[13]

After Kapuufi's successor, Msuulwa, allowed the White Fathers to return in 1892, however, they were able to establish better relations, and Mwene Kiatu received Holy Baptism at the mission of Kate in August 1909.[14] Kiatu's conversion reflects the complexity of the period. Mwene Kiatu (son of Kapuufi) came to power at a time when the authority of traditional leadership was beginning to weaken due to the presence of German colonial officials and Catholic missionaries. He was put in power by the Germans sometime after 1904, following manoeuvres by the Queen Mother and the Germans that resulted in the dethroning of his predecessor, Kapere (another son of Kapuufi). Mwene Kapere had been friendly to the missionaries, and this is one of the reasons the Queen Mother cited as making him unfit for the throne.[15]

In spite of the Queen Mother's opposition to the missionaries, however, Kiatu befriended the Catholic leaders and went to great lengths to create a royal Catholic village. At the beginning of the Kate mission diary in January 1909, the missionaries note that four members of his family were already Christian, and he and most of the remaining members of his family were already catechumens. Before his baptism, he assisted the priests with baptism ceremonies in Kate, and, six months after his baptism, all 300 houses of his village came to pray with him morning and evening. Five more of Kiatu's relatives were baptized in 1911, and later references depict him as zealously working as a catechist to convert as many more as possible.[16] In addition, two royal women, Adolphine Unda (the Queen Mother under Mwene Kapere) and Augustina Ngalu, became early members of a fledgeling congregation of sisters in the first decade of this century. Thus the missionaries succeeded in their first goal of obtaining royal converts, and the Catholic Church in Ufipa, especially on the plateau where the Kate and Chala missions were established, did not lack for official political support.

It is difficult to know how Fipa villagers perceived the king during the first decade or two of this century. While the missionaries emphasized the predatory nature of the *mwene*'s soldiers, the *rugaruga*, Fipa memories of Mwene Kapere (who ruled from 1932 to 1956) are of a distant ruler who travelled through his country once or twice a year to collect taxes and check on the welfare of his people. He was carried by porters in a royal chair and expected gifts of eggs, chickens and flour wherever he spent the night. We will probably never know how influential Kiatu's conversion was, but it seems probable, especially for those near Kate during the time of the grand celebration of his baptism, that they were favourably impressed by the royal conversion. Most importantly, Fipa must have been struck by the co-operation between Fipa leaders and missionaries.[17]

Royal support provided a foundation for Catholicism in a highly communal society. At the beginning of this century, Fipa lived in small settlements of individuals related either by birth or marriage. These villages are remembered as inhabited by members of one clan (*uluko*), though, as Willis notes, Fipa were fairly accepting of strangers or outsiders in their family units.[18] None the less, these small settlements provided close-knit communities for the people within them. Each settlement was connected to others by ties of blood or marriage, so that illness, death and marriage celebrations drew people from a number of different settlements together. Visiting between villages was common as a means of conveying messages, visiting relatives and seeking help for problems. Within a village of 20–30 houses, and maybe 100–150 people, there was little room for individual deviance.[19] People mention shame as a primary motivation for acting within established guidelines, and inappropriate behaviour was met by strict punishment, sometimes in front of the entire village community.[20] Some work activities and all holidays were celebrated as a community, further emphasizing the group rather than the individual. With such a heightened sense of community, official acceptance no doubt encouraged popular support for Catholicism.

Conversion of Children

While the White Fathers viewed royal support as essential, most of the mission stations were far from the home of the king, and so the missionaries pursued a second strategy focused on converting children around the mission stations. Examination of a diary of meetings held by the priests at Kirando in the late 1890s and early 1900s bears overwhelming confirmation of the attention paid to bringing children and youth to the Catholic religion. Approximately 90 per cent of the entries concern matters pertaining to children, their instruction and their induction into the Catholic Church. Whether to give gifts to attract children and how much to give were recurring debates in the early years. On 3 October 1895, a priest noted that the decision was made that children should receive a piece of cloth following two months of catechism classes.[21] In the early years, the missionaries also gave a piece of cloth to all those who received baptism and first communion. The entry for 5 July 1908 in Kate notes that the priests decided to distribute a small token to all the children at the beginning of class to reward their attendance. And, if a child attended all the lessons for the month, she received the equivalent of one pesa, with which she might be able to buy some school stationery or a piece of cloth.[22] For most of my Fipa informants, obtaining a piece of cloth (or, later, clothes) was important, as Western standards of dress increasingly became the norm. As a Kate diarist noted: 'Many of our Christians do not feel comfortable approaching the sacraments attired in animal skins. Sometimes some of them will lend each other their better clothes.'[23]

The priests employed less formal means of attracting converts as well. Many elderly men and women in Chala remember going to the mission as children, hoping to be given some oranges or bananas by the priests or to be allowed to scavenge for oranges that had fallen on the ground. They also told of organized scrambles for pins and other small trinkets, as Sister Oliva Nyaronga recalls:

We were going to play at the priests' and ask for oranges or steal them. We were taking them from the ground; there were many oranges. The water passed there, and the oranges were really sweet. Ah ah. When we saw them ... ah, childhood. Until you took the oranges from the ground. You ran and then the priest saw us. We took them from the ground; many of them had already rotted. We came to hide in the grass. When the time came for playing, we ate them.

The priest asked, 'Have you taken any oranges?'

'We took the ones from the ground.'

'OK.' Then he would say, 'Come here and line up to take the oranges from the ground.'

You could not take them from the tree or you would be beaten badly. There were many that would ripen and then fall to the ground. So we formed a line this way. And the priest would do this: 'One, two, three,' and he would blow the whistle. Run, fast, fast, very fast. If you were fast you would fill [a container]; many were falling; some were still fine, but some had already rotted. Ah ... we were really happy.... They were really making us happy.

Sometimes ... he [a priest] would have a package [of pins] like this.... He spilled them on the ground. Mama, mama, we were stepping on each other. We were taking them. Some got one, some got many; that was the way it was. And he did the same with beads. They really made us happy.... Children spent the day there.[24]

Such games became part of a systematic effort at attracting pre-school children to the mission. Both Chala and Kate also had a kindergarten, called *kafupe* ('the short one' in Kiswahili), where residents remember:

Before entering Standard I, there was a catechism class. They gave us guavas, bananas and lots of other things to make us happy. There were many things, little cars and little trains. There were many toys for children.... They helped us a lot and we really liked religion a lot.[25]

But it was not just the pins or fruit that were the draw. Many spoke also of enjoying the lessons and stories that the priests or sisters shared with them.

In addition, children were the focus of catechism classes run by male catechist teachers in every village. Catholic missions differed significantly from Protestant missions in that they rarely translated the Bible, but they did make the catechism available in the vernacular.[26] While Kifipa catechisms were initially employed,[27] priests and catechists who met to develop a new Kifipa catechism in 1915 were unable to agree on key religious concepts.[28] Later, the Bishop noted that the language question had long been a matter of discussion in the vicariate, and, while discussions continued, Kiswahili was used in the majority of the posts.[29] Not until Bishop Holmes-Siedle proposed in 1949 using Kifipa as much as possible for all religious purposes was a full Kifipa catechism developed.[30]

Whatever the language of the official catechism, most catechists taught village lessons in Kifipa, and people also learned some songs and prayers in Kifipa.[31] Kifipa was necessary because Kiswahili was hardly spoken in the area when the priests first arrived. What Fipa learned about Catholicism, then, was limited to the oral messages they received from the priests or catechists, and it is thus likely that both the catechists and parishioners' understanding of Catholicism was very limited for many years.

Catechists were usually married men whom the missionaries hand-picked, based on performance in catechism classes, attendance at mass and overall personality. Their choice also had to be approved by the villages in which the teachers were placed, thus demonstrating how the needs of both the Catholic priests and Fipa villagers were met.[32] Catechists were usually highly respected members of their community because of the knowledge they possessed, their service to the church and God,[33] and their age, which, according to Fipa custom, granted them status.[34]

As soon as possible after establishing a mission, White Fathers placed teachers of religion in as many neighbouring villages as possible.[35] These teachers were indispensable to the work of the Catholic Church because they had daily contact with the majority of parishioners whom the priests only reached four times a year. The quality and nature of these classes depended on the instructor's enthusiasm and training.[36] Most Fipa remembered the names of their catechist teachers, and praised their dedication and energetic teaching style. It was Fipa catechists who provided the crucial link between the foreign missionaries, with their Latin scriptures and mass, and Fipa villagers, with their own religious concerns and traditions.[37]

The village catechists proved very successful in producing Catholic converts. In the annual report of the Tanganyika mission for 1913–14, Mgr Lechaptois wrote:

> these schools are the biggest and best source of recruitment for our catechumens and our neophytes. I do not believe I am mistaken in saying that nine-tenths at least of our newly baptized Christians are from our schools.[38]

In addition to catechism, some pupils were given an extra hour of instruction by the catechists, during which the alphabet and some reading and writing were taught in Kiswahili. According to older Fipa, their parents distinguished between the catechism lessons, which taught religion, and the reading and writing lessons which followed. During the first few decades of this century, parents were unanimous in their approval of sending boys and girls to catechism lessons, but reading and writing were deemed inappropriate for almost all of their female children and some of their male children.[39] While parents were thus willing for their children to become Catholic, they were not always willing for them to become literate.[40]

This distinction between religious and secular learning differed profoundly from other areas of East Africa, where many sought out the European's religion to receive a Western education.[41] Fipa, by contrast, sought only religious knowledge, not a new way of life. Fipa reactions thus reveal the relatively slight colonial impact in the area and elders' attempts to lessen the impact of change brought by conversion to Catholicism.

The priests built dormitories (*baraza*) for boys at the mission stations to instil greater control over the daily activities of children. Boys were physically separated from their parents, lived near the priests, received lessons from them, worked for them and prayed with them. Boniface Songolo, born in 1934 in Kate, recalls that he grew up like a child in Europe because he was a *baraza* boy. He began his studies with the priests at the mission in Kate when he was five years old. He then spent two years there with eight to twelve other boys before going on to study at the 'seminary' in Karema. Classes there included geography, science, maths, Latin and Kiswahili. While it was called a seminary, it was more like an elementary school, albeit with a strong emphasis on Catholicism and learning the Latin mass. Songolo later became a Catholic priest.[42]

Many young people also worked at the mission station. Girls worked at the wheat milling machine in Chala for a month at a time.[43] Marta Kibelengi remembered coming from a village three miles away to help carry sand for the new sisters' building in Chala. She worked for a week and was given two pieces of cloth.[44] And some boys were specifically selected to lead the Latin response during mass every morning.[45]

The White Fathers thus expended much effort to convert children and youth through education, moral lessons, gifts and opportunities for work, and they received a generally enthusiastic response from Fipa in return. The positive response of Fipa children and their parents can best be understood by exploring Fipa views of the European missionaries. We cannot understand Fipa conversion solely on the basis of the ideas and strategies of the missionaries, but must also look at how Fipa viewed conversion. The context in which Fipa interpreted and appropriated Catholicism was an essential element in the conversion process.

The Cultural Context of Conversion

When elder Fipa in Nkansi are asked today what the early missionaries did to win converts, most respond that the priests coaxed or enticed them (Kiswahili: *kubembeleza*). This term, widely used to describe early conversions, is a self-conscious reminder that Fipa understood conversion as a reciprocal process. When Fipa say that the priests enticed them, they are expressing the strength of their own culture and the initial wariness with which they greeted the missionaries.

In presenting the new religion, missionaries emphasized the congruence between Fipa religion and Catholicism. Fipa had a complex religious belief system at the beginning of this century. As described by Fr Robert, a network of spiritual beings, including a monolithic god and a series of lesser deities and ancestral spirits were sought out in trees, rocks and ponds, and the main ritual entreaties and sacrifices were conducted at these locations.[46] Priests told Fipa who they found worshipping these natural objects that there was a God even greater than the ones they were worshipping. Missionaries thus did not openly condemn Fipa religion, but noted instead how their religion was similar, but superior.[47] When asked about the content of their lessons in religion, Fipa all began with the first question they were asked by their catechism teachers: 'Who created all this that you see about you?' The priests and teachers then noted that it made more sense to pray to the Creator than to the things He had created.

The priests then (and Fipa elders now) thus emphasized the similarities between Fipa religion and Catholicism. One elderly man likened the female and male leaders of Fipa worship ceremonies to priests and sisters of Catholic worship. Young male students learned in 'seminary' that Kifipa greetings were similar to parts of the liturgy in the Catholic Latin mass.[48] A man born in 1921 remarked that priests likened their ancestral spirits to the angels of the Catholic faith,[49] while another elderly resident of Chala noted that priests told them that the ancestral spirits were like the saints of the Catholic religion.[50] The similarity between Catholic saints and Fipa ancestors was made manifest by the Catholic baptismal requirement to take a Christian name chosen from a list of Catholic saints' names, thus echoing Fipa practice of choosing an ancestor's name for a newborn. In both cases, the saint or ancestor was believed to act in an intercessory manner between the Supreme Being and the individual.[51] As a result of such analogies, Fipa felt that Catholicism was similar to their own religion.[52]

Missionary priests recognized the strength of community in Fipa society and, in particular, the strength of the clan and family. For some Fipa, European missionaries became father figures. Luis Sigareti, an 80-year-old resident of Chala, studied in Catholic schools as a boy and worked for the White Fathers at their mission in Chala for many years. He was one of the boys who performed the Latin response to the mass; he herded the priests' goats; and he worked in their garden and kitchen. He studied for four years at Chala and then passed the test and was taken to Ujiji in 1926 to study at the seminary for another three years. After that, he joined a new organization of African monks and made a two-year commitment, but subsequently he became ill and returned home. When he returned to Chala, Bishop Joseph Birraux, who had been his instructor and whom Sigareti referred to as his 'father', told Sigareti to ask his birth father to look for a good girl for him to marry. He said the Bishop was interested in his marrying well so that he would not be a boy who slept with a number of women. Then, fifteen years later, Bishop Holmes-Siedle came to Sigareti and asked him for one of his children to become a sister, and Sigareti offered his oldest daughter.[53] It was common in the first part of this century for parents to encourage their children, especially their sons, to choose a spouse from a family they felt to be hard-working and healthy. The priest, then, took on the role of father in establishing what was essentially a marriage alliance between Sigareti's family and the Catholic Church. Sigareti was not alone in his affection for the White Fathers; many of the people I met in Nkansi District had such a personal relationship with one of the priests and remembered them for their gifts, education or support in deciding to become a priest or sister.[54]

Fipa also recall that the lessons, advice and morals espoused by the missionary priests were the very same ones they heard from their parents and grandparents at home.[55] In their roles as fathers and elders, European missionaries had the authority to dictate behaviour and to punish. Sister Oliva Nyaronga remembered that one of the priests who taught her catechism was particularly harsh. If he found a student talking during classes, he would throw the classroom keys at the child's forehead, often causing her to bleed. Other unacceptable behaviour was punished by severe beatings with a whip. When Oliva and her sister missed a lesson because they could not cross a swollen river between their home and the mission, they were beaten at the following lesson. Oliva told me that her parents did not protest at the harsh treatment meted out by the priests. On the contrary, parents were grateful to the priests for helping them raise their children.[56] The priests were likened to fathers who were often feared for their punishments. In their moral lessons and discipline, there was a sense that these foreigners reinforced the authority of the elders in the community. As one missionary noted:

> Our Christians have full confidence in us, and they demonstrate this well by continually making us the judges in all their disagreements and in telling us about all their small marriage quarrels. But, if there is a place where we feel truly their fathers it is at the confessional.[57]

Resolving marriage quarrels was traditionally a task carried out by Fipa elders. Thus the priests were acting as typical mediators, and, as indicated above, confession could be a very powerful tool of the missionaries. One Fipa girl spent several years contemplating joining the convent and ran away soon after what she described as an emotional experience at confession.[58]

Early White Fathers acted not only as fathers but also as political leaders and elders, establishing political alliances in order to further their religious cause. One elderly catechist recalled missionaries inviting the old men to the station on Sundays to drink beer with them.[59] Sometimes the missionaries maintained relationships with influential old men despite their refusal to be baptized.[60] In one case a man, living on an island near Kirando, established a relationship with the first missionaries in the area, who then left their books in his house between visits. His son said that, even after his father became Muslim, the missionaries continued to keep their books in his house and to rely on him as a contact.[61]

The giving of gifts was another way in which the missionaries imitated familiar Fipa social and political roles. Fipa kings, though theoretically responsible for distributing food in times of famine, were not noted for their generosity. The kings did, however, exchange gifts with the missionaries in order to establish alliances. By the time the White Fathers reached the plateau, Fipa had been exposed to German rulers as well, and German commanders had distributed cows to local-level representatives on their arrival.[62] It was in the distribution of meat that the missionaries' actions particularly resonated with Fipa villagers. A man at least 80 years old recalled the White Fathers in his village 20 miles south of Chala when he grew up. He said that the priests would go hunting and bring back meat for the villagers. Hunting was a very common activity in most places in Ufipa, and the meat obtained was always distributed within the village. Accordingly, the missionaries also distributed meat to all members of a village at the beginning. But after some time, he continued, the priests gave meat only to those people whom the catechist indicated had been praying faithfully.[63]

Missionaries also distributed salt to Fipa villagers. In the late nineteenth century, when a Fipa man travelled to a salt mine, he came back with enough for his own household use and for that of his relatives as well.[64] Heremans quotes Fr Dromaux's account of a meeting he conducted in 1884:

Twenty to thirty men or children grouped around me; some women listened at a distance. Silence was not achieved easily, but finally we began by all making the sign of the cross together. Sometimes I speak and sometimes I ask a question. One of the children whom I had instructed distributes salt and another distributes tobacco. He, who answers a questions, gets some salt taken with the point of a knife or he gets a leaf of tobacco. What remains of the salt and tobacco is distributed to all at the end – sometimes among quarrels.[65]

Undoubtedly, gifts were one of the reasons Fipa were attracted to the Christian message, especially in the early days when they had only a limited understanding of the Catholic religious message and were drawn by the missionaries' actions as much as by their words. Bertsch neatly summarizes the impact of gifts on Fipa:

The pagans could not understand why they should go to catechism classes for weeks and even months when they could be working their fields or having a good beer-party and relax. Why should they allow their children to go to learn to pray, instead of tending the goats and the cows? They needed more than just the promise of eternal life. In the beginning, in order to obtain the authorisation to open a school in the village, presents had to be offered to the chief and renewed from time to time. Since the country was rich in game and since most of the missionaries were good hunters, they used to distribute meat which did not cost them much effort or money. This was done at the Father's arrival in the district or sometime during his stay of one or two weeks.... On big feast days, salt and beans were distributed. These customs of the good old times were partly abandoned out of necessity during the war and later, and slowly disappeared thanks to the new mentality which little by little was bred into the Christian community.[66]

Whether Fipa priests took on the roles of father and community elder deliberately or inadvertently, the impact on Fipa was the same. Fipa elders must have seen the missionaries, in this sense at least, as their counterparts, espousing proper morality and taking care of the needs of the community. And Fipa youth were seen to benefit from the advice and guidance the priests provided to them at the mission dormitories and schools or to their specially chosen candidates for service in the Catholic Church.[67]

Fipa culture and Catholicism did not always neatly coincide, however. While the success of the Catholic Church in Ufipa attests to the fact that many Fipa embraced the tenets of Catholicism from its early days, many other Fipa still hold to beliefs and practices that predominated before the coming of the missionaries. White Fathers did not hesitate to discourage traditional Fipa magico-religious beliefs by destroying shrines and encouraging the destruction of 'witchcraft' medicines, but Fipa still attend shrines to ask for assistance from the spirits for activities such as hunting.[68] And, despite the missionaries' insistence that witchcraft does not exist, belief in it (though altered) is still strong.[69]

While missionary disdain for practices such as witchcraft is usually noted, not mentioned as often are missionary attacks on childhood institutions, which they felt were particularly immoral and which they made persistent efforts to change with little success. One such institution was the *intuli* (or *nsalo*), a house in one's parents' or grandparents' compound in which Fipa girls and boys slept until they married. Usually boys and girls did not occupy the same *intuli*. *Intuli* provided young people with some freedom and preserved the dignity of the parents as well, removing sexually mature boys and girls from the parents' home. The missionaries presumed that *intuli* were the sites of immoral liaisons between boys and girls, and they lamented the seeming lack of attention that parents paid to their children staying in them. As early as 1898, priests in Kirando complained that parents were lax in the morality of their children, especially girls, and they advocated abandonment of communal homes for girls.[70] They continued doing so for almost half a century, but it was not until 1947 that Bishop Holmes-Siedle publicly announced a campaign to do away with *nsalo*:

> All missionaries in the Fipa country were also unanimous in demanding the suppression of the 'insalo', or common dormitory. I accordingly preached on the subject in no uncertain terms in all the missions, and I now ask all missionaries to see that the decree suppressing these dormitories is carried out.

And two years later he noted that it was

> agreed that a good deal of immorality among young people is due to this institution which still remains from pagan days. As yet parents do very little to care for the moral well-being of their children. Missionaries should give instructions on the Catholic Family, and encourage the better type of people to build larger houses in which the family can be cared for and common prayers said, morning and evening....[71]

By the time Holmes-Siedle made these announcements, almost all Fipa were Catholic, so the Bishop was speaking not to would-be converts but to parishioners who he hoped would alter their behaviour. Several people I talked to remembered his preaching in particular. A 50-year-old worker at Chala mission recalled:

> First, it was a mixture, a mixture of boys and girls [in one *nsalo*] and this, to tell the truth for that time, did not bring any harm, but in Christianity it was seen as paganism.... The girls and boys got used to each other as a boy and his older sister. Perhaps a few created problems. But most of them respected each other enough to protect their respect.... They [the priests] believed that when a girl and boy sleep together that they are doing the marriage act.... After a while they [the priests] used the leaders in the church to try to get rid of boys and girls sleeping together.... The parents had to agree because ... any parent who refused to get rid of this practice was refused the sacraments.[72]

Frequently, the leaders of the church were the elders in the village so that their authority was respected by Fipa, no matter how serious their Catholic faith. Their participation in the campaign must have been significant. Instead of *intuli*, the missionaries encouraged the Fipa to build larger homes with additional rooms for their male and female children to sleep in. Today, there are only a few *intuli* left in Ufipa due, substantially, to the ongoing campaign of the church to eliminate them, but it has taken almost a hundred years to reach this point.[73]

The priests were also critical of the popular custom of dancing. Most evenings after dinner of millet *ugali* and beans or meat, teenagers met at at a local ground and danced. And, at weddings, the celebrants – young and old – stayed up all night to dance and drink. The noise and activity of these dances caught the attention of the priests early on, but they only started trying to restrict them in the 1930s.[74] And, in 1949, the priests moved the village in Chala farther away from the mission so that the drumming and dancing would not disturb them.

The noise, however, was only the tip of the iceberg. It was the immorality of the dances, especially the presumed sexual activity that followed in the *intuli*, that upset the missionaries most. So they started making attempts to stop dances they perceived as particularly lewd and to reduce the length of time spent dancing in the evening. Their tactics were never very successful, yet the priests continued them into the 1960s, at which time schoolteachers (many of them taught and trained in Catholic schools) joined the anti-dancing campaign. Several individuals remember the priests themselves coming into villages in the evening to observe what the youth were doing. An old man, who was a teenager in Kate in the 1930s, recalls priests making a rule that dancing was only allowed on Thursdays and Sundays, and then only until 9 pm. He also remembers priests coming into the village from the mission station and ordering their workers to steal drums from young people found dancing. But, he added, the priests' efforts were futile because they were young and would just make another drum.[75] An entry in the Kate mission diary for May 1944 notes that 20 young boys and girls from Pimbi (three hours from the station) were punished by a day of instruction for having joined a forbidden traditional dance. Still the dances did not stop. Father Lukewille remembers when he arrived in Chala in 1962 the priests required couples being wed in the Catholic Church to make a deposit at the mission that would be returned only if they did not dance all night.[76]

Obviously, dancing was very important to Fipa. There was little peer pressure (until the 1960s and 1970s when school activities provided an alternative to dancing) to cease dancing, as there was in the case of the *intuli*. Nor did the Catholic Church provide a reasonable alternative, especially in the case of weddings, the only social event at which dancing still occurs today.[77]

Becoming Catholic: Baptism and Spirituality

Thus, while most Fipa became Catholics, their conversion did not necessarily mean abandonment of familiar beliefs and practices. As elsewhere, Catholic missionaries made conversion relatively easy; baptism was all that was required to enlist on the rolls of the Catholic Church, and thus becoming a Catholic required little change in one's belief or practice.[78] The new religion appealed mainly to youth, however, while elders remained sceptical. Children (and a few adults) were drawn to the possibility of learning new things, and, perhaps, the personalities of the missionaries and catechists, but elders worried that their leadership and authority would be undermined by the missionaries and their church.

Catholic missionaries counted their success in numbers, most significantly the number of baptisms. According to Chala baptismal records, about 50 per cent of the baptisms between 1912 and 1916 were of elderly Fipa dangerously close to death. In this way, Fipa elders could satisfy the demands of the Catholic missionaries to become Catholic, and yet not abandon their own beliefs until the last moment. By 1922 (ten years after the founding of Chala mission), however, 85 per cent or more of those baptized were baptized within a year of their birth.[79] Neither the elderly nor the infants received much instruction before their baptism, so that the number of baptisms does not reflect the number of Fipa who had a deep belief in Catholic doctrine.

The priests faced little opposition to infant baptism. Since the second decade of this century, baptism has been a natural part of growing up for a majority of children, and non-Christian parents did not hesitate to bring their children for baptism in the Catholic Church. As a Fipa priest explained, an innocent child, one who did not yet know right and wrong, was eligible for baptism without any religious lessons. Once a child was old enough (twelve years of age) to know right and wrong, she or he was required to attend lessons before being baptized.[80] In the White Fathers' Annual Report of 1910–11, the entry on Kate notes:

> Parents, even polygamous ones in the neighboring villages, are not only not opposed to the conversion of their adult children but they ask instantly for the holy baptism for those who are still small and for those who are just born.[81]

The result was that Fipa society as a whole rapidly became at least nominally Catholic. In 1919–20, priests in Kirando noted that, of a population of 4,140, 2,086 were neophytes who were attending mass and catechism lessons. In 1923–4, missionaries in Kate noted that half the population was not yet Christian, but very few were opposed to the religion. In 1945–6, the Bishop noted that two-thirds of the population was Catholic and that the majority of the remaining third was located in areas not yet touched by the missionaries. The area of Nkansi kingdom would thus have been close to 100 per cent Catholic by then.

While the numbers are clear, it is not as clear *why* people joined the church. Early on, some believed baptism to be of medicinal or magical value.[82] Missionaries inadvertently encouraged this interpretation when, in their attempts to save as many souls as possible, they often baptized a person when he or she was ill. One man noted that the first convert in Chala was an adult woman who was in the middle of her studies to prepare for baptism when she became very ill. The priests responded by baptizing her prematurely.[83] Many elderly Fipa recall that, despite the regular attentions of priests and teachers of religion, their parents steadfastly refused to be baptized until the last moment. It was customary for the church leaders to visit the ailing and to encourage them to be baptized and choose a Christian name before their death. And many eventually agreed, possibly because they no longer saw any danger in gaining the blessing of the foreign religion and the medical benefits that it might confer.[84] Pius Mwanakulya, born in 1914, had lived and studied at the mission in Chala and tried to convince his father to convert with little success. The priests made repeated visits, but his father only relented and was baptized close to death.[85] Others related how they were baptized as small children only when they became ill. Another old man remembers that he was baptized as a small child even though his parents only agreed to be baptized themselves as they were dying. He recalls being a weak child and his parents baptized him early lest he die young, whereas all his other siblings were baptized as teenagers following catechism lessons.[86]

Thus, for a generation or two, older Fipa tended not to convert, but at the same time they were allowing their children to be baptized in ever larger numbers. Elderly Fipa men and women who were baptized as children, but whose parents remained unconverted until their death explained this seeming anomaly by saying that all the children were being baptized and that their parents often encouraged them.[87] One elderly Fipa woman explained: 'They [her parents] wanted me to get baptized because it was required.'[88] Obviously it was not required, but it seems there was a sense on the part of Fipa from early in this century that becoming Catholic was becoming a normal part of Fipa life, and therefore there was no reason to hesitate in following the priests' instructions and rites.

Perhaps, Fipa did explain the reason for early conversions to me but I, programmed to understand only instrumental reasons, could not make sense of their expressive ones. One older man in Chala tried to explain the conversion of his adult parents when Gauston Poultier came to the area in 1912:

> They [his parents] had a quick faith, yes. Others had doubts, but they saw this [religion] as a good thing, even though they did not know him [the missionary]. But his words were entering into us. It is good to follow it.... They saw themselves that this was a whole thing, a better thing.... So when the first ones saw that this thing had entered their heads they

saw that it was better to follow it.... Let's follow the way of these people [the missionaries].[89]

Maybe we cannot adequately explain intellectually the synergy of enthusiastic Catholic missionaries bringing a new religious message and Fipa willingness to learn and adopt it, but we can work harder to give such reasons more serious consideration.

Conclusion

The Catholic Church was successful in Nkansi District because its personnel and doctrines were flexible enough (or interpreted with enough flexibility) to allow Fipa to join without giving up beliefs and customs they held dear. For Fipa adults this was particularly important. Fipa children, with less of a stake in maintaining cultural norms and beliefs, responded to the missionaries' gifts, games, education and parenting. If one counts each person baptized as a Catholic, as the White Fathers did, new Catholics were able to convert without adopting all the missionaries' teachings or prescribed practices. Our discussion of dancing, *intuli* and witchcraft all indicate that Fipa Catholics often continued practising their own customs. Dancing as an evening activity for youth continued until the 1980s. And, though the policy against *intuli* was ultimately more successful, several people born in the 1950s and later reported sleeping in *intuli* before marriage. Fipa oral testimony attests to the fact that Fipa interpretations of Catholicism were not always in line with mission orthodoxy: viewing baptism as a curative, converting due to social or economic pressure, and selectively heeding warnings about participation in 'lewd' dances all underline this fact.

The result of this evangelization and conversion process has been the transformation of both Catholicism and Fipa society at the same time. As Sanneh argues, the strength of Christianity is that it is inherently translatable, so that peoples worldwide can understand the message. But, in the translation, meanings, symbols and leaders' roles all can be construed in unintended ways. Fipa society has also been transformed by Catholicism. There are hundreds of Fipa sisters and priests serving in Tanzania and Zambia currently. The education provided by the missionaries, while initially scorned, educated youth for careers and lifestyles quite different from those of their parents and grandparents. And, even though witchcraft, polygyny and immorality still exist, they are customs and ideas that are viewed with increasing disdain by many Fipa Catholics.

We have seen that Fipa saw in Catholicism and its proselytizers people and a religion that could be woven into the social fabric of their own society. This was due to the combination of a highly communal society, the early conversion of some Nkansi political leaders, a culture that assimilated many Catholic beliefs as well as its personnel, and the White

Fathers' own patience and cultural sensitivity. Intense contact with colonial officials or policies is not enough to explain the conversion of the Fipe, who were relatively isolated from the impact of colonialism elsewhere, and conversion in Ufipa was not closely associated with Western education or Western ways of life.

Notes

* This chapter is based on dissertation research carried out between September 1994 and May 1996. Dissertation research funding was provided by a Fulbright-Hays Doctoral Dissertation Grant, a Johann Jacobs Foundation Dissertation Grant and a grant from the Wenner-Gren Foundation. An earlier draft of this chapter was presented at a conference in Madison and has benefited from comments of the participants. In particular, Isaria Kimambo, Thomas Spear and Anne Lewinson were critical readers of earlier drafts.

1 Iliffe writes, 'The Fipa experienced early and unusually widespread conversion, a process which needs study but was possibly aided by village organisation, and emphasis on individuality and rationality, and experience of Islam without commitment to it.' John Iliffe, *A Modern History of Tanganyika* (Cambridge, 1979), 221. For examples of areas where the White Fathers initially did not meet with such success, see Brian Garvey, 'The development of the White Fathers' mission among the Bemba-speaking peoples, 1891–1964' (PhD, London, 1974) and Ian Linden, *Church and Revolution in Rwanda* (Manchester, 1977). These studies also emphasize how in each area White Fathers' personalities, local and territorial politics, and the presence of Muslims or Protestant missionaries played decisive roles in the tactics used by the Catholic missionaries. For example, the White Fathers were more high-handed in their rule making in Bemba than they were in Ufipa. And, in Rwanda, the White Fathers employed soldier-catechists to carry out their work far from the mission stations.

2 Ufipa is generally perceived as remote and backward. Until the early 1990s, the main road into the region from the south was in such bad shape that it took 1–2 days to travel 220 kilometres. Ufipa has never been carefully attended to by German, British or Tanzanian governments, either. Not until the late 1940s, for example, did the government begin building a few schools in Ufipa. Fipa informants bear out these general perceptions in their descriptions of the colonial period. Though they had some contact with colonial officials, or their representatives, when taxes needed to be collected or men recruited for the Second World War, most had much more contact with Catholic missionaries.

3 See Kathleen R. Smythe, 'Fipa childhood: White Fathers' missionaries and social change in Nkansi District, 1910–1980' (PhD, Madison, 1997). These are significant observations also because they differ from the common notion that during the colonial period there were two worlds colliding – that of colonial officials, missionaries and settlers and that of Africans. As others have recently noted, missionaries' agendas were not always parallel to those of the colonial powers or their officials. See Richard Gray, *Black Christians and White Missionaries* (New Haven, 1990), 59–60.

4 Iliffe, *Modern History*, 223, argues that most missionary societies tried to convert children first. Children usually were among the first converts, but missionaries often tried to reach families, heads of households or adults in their early proselytization. For example, see Dorothy Hodgson, 'Engendered encounters: men of the church and the "church of women" in Maasailand, Tanzania, 1950–1993', Workshop on African Expressions of Christianity, Madison, 1996.; Garvey, 'Development', 178.

5 Nkansi is the name for one of the two Fipa kingdoms which came to an end with independence in Tanzania. The current district was a natural choice for a research site because it is closely aligned with the old boundaries of the Nkansi kingdom, which was recognized as a political entity at least 200–450 years before independence in 1961. Roy G. Willis, *A State in the Making* (Bloomington, 1981), 64.

6 Chala was not a typical 'mission village' because Fipa in Chala were not living on mission land. The missionaries and Fipa together carved out a new settlement, each family claiming space for itself. Charles Lavigerie did not encourage his missionaries to create separate Christian villages. Birgitta Larsson, *Conversion to Greater Freedom?* (Uppsala, 1991), 23.

7 Tanzania National Archives (TNA) Acc. 159 16/15 Land: Rights of Occupancy (Long-Term) Namwele and Nkomolo.

8 He was not the only one to leave the mission society. A brother, Simon van Lankveld, later left the order and became a businessman in Ufipa. See Rev. F. Bertsch, *Notes on the History of Karema Diocese* (np, 1964), 48.

9 Anselm Tambila, 'A history of the Rukwa region (Tanzania) *c.* 1870–1940: aspects of economic and social change from pre-colonial to colonial times' (PhD, Hamburg, 1981), 98–109.

10 Roger Heremans, *Les Etablissements de l'Association Internationale Africaine au Lac Tanganika et les Pères Blancs: Mpala et Karema, 1877–1885* (Tervuren, 1966), 96. Hastings also notes this belief of Lavigerie's and describes it as anachronistic especially *vis-à-vis* the work of Protestant missions at the turn of the century. Adrian Hastings, *The Church in Africa, 1450–1950* (Oxford, 1994), 27.

11 Heremans, *Les Etablissements*, 97.

12 And the Arabs certainly had reason to dislike the missionaries' encroachment on their lands and trade. Tambila, 'History', 104.

13 Willis, *State*, 203; Tambila, 'History', 105; Mgr Lechaptois, *Aux Rives du Tanganyika* (Alger, 1932), 108; Sumbawanga District Book, Vol. II.

14 Sumbawanga Diocese, *History of Sumbawanga Diocese 1885–1985* (Peramiho, 1985). This event was very important to the missionaries and was well attended by German officials. Bertsch, *Notes*, 53. Father P. Boyer writes in the Annual Report of the Missionary Society of Africa 1908–9: 'En entrant dans sa nouvelle demeure, Kiatu a declaré énergiquement aux Grands du pays qu'ils ne devaient plus venir lui parler des coutumes anciennes, toutes plus ou moins superstitieuses. J'en ai fini avec elles, leur a-t-il dit, la loi de Jésus-Christ sera mon unique loi. Je reconnaitrai pour mes seuls vrais sujets et fidèles amis ceux qui me suivront dans le christianisme.' *Rapports Annuels (RA)* 1908–9, Vicariat du Tanganyika [Société des Missionaires d'Afrique (Pères Blancs)], White Fathers Regional House (WFRH), Nyegezi, Tanzania.

15 Sumbawanga District Book II; Lechaptois, *Aux Rives*, 66–7; Tambila, 'History', 132–4.

16 Kate Mission diaries, White Fathers Archives (WFA), Rome. See also *History of Sumbawanga Diocese*, 61–2.

17 Rev. Bertsch wrote of Kiatu's baptism: 'All the important people of the country were of course present, and during two days the great event was celebrated. The Commander of the *boma* of Bismarckburg had sent plenty of powder and the old muzzle-loaders let their big voices be heard to the great joy of the attendants.' *Notes*, 53.

18 Willis, *State*, 129.

19 A census done by the missionaries in Kate in 1912 revealed that there were 26–30 homes in each of the surrounding villages. Kate Mission Diary, WFA.

20 Some men and women recalled songs that were sung about a young person in their village who had been caught stealing or who had become pregnant outside wedlock. A middle-aged woman noted that a group of youth would sing the song in front of the wrongdoers' house and then circle the village singing it. Interview with MC, 14 April 1996, Chala.

21 Kirando Council Book, WFRH.

22 Kate Council Book, WFRH.

23 *RA*, 1916–17, Rapport du Kate, WFRH.

24 6 June 1995, Sumbawanga.

25 RK, 11 March 1996, Kate; also TY, 25 October 1995, Chala.

26 Lamin Sanneh, *Translating the Message* (Maryknoll, 1989), 3. A middle-aged man in Chala told me that the priests not only did not translate the Bible but forbade Fipa to read the Bible. Only the priests read it during mass. Unyese said at first that he never knew why they were not allowed to read the Bible, but later he informed me that the priests told people that they feared Fipa would rebel against Catholicism if they were able to read the Bible. EU, 7 November 1995, Chala.

27 In 1900, a missionary noted that a partial Kifipa catechism was in use in Kirando. Kirando Council Book, WFRH. See also Chala Mission Diary, 1913, WFA.

28 Kate Council Book, WFRH. There was no mention of the phrases or concepts that were particularly difficult to translate. It was not clear whether a Kifipa catechism ever emerged from these discussions. Based on my oral data, the answer was not until the late 1940s. Perhaps Swahili was easier to use in translation because it had already been used by other Catholic orders, such as the Holy Ghost Fathers. It seems the priests did use a catechism in Kikwa (a language spoken in the Rukwa valley). One Kifipa word that proved difficult was 'Father' because there is no word for father without a pronoun attached (i.e. my father, your father, etc.) in Kifipa. Eventually the Swahili word was settled upon, Chala Mission Diary, 1913, WFA.

29 *RA*, 1921–2, WFRH.

30 *The Link*, Karema Vicariate, No. 11, May 1949; No. 12, July 1949; No. 16, March 1950, WFRH.

31 Pius Mwanakulya, 27 November 1995, Milundikwa; NM, 5 September 1995, Chala. Apparently, singing was a very effective educational tool in the villages. Sr Irena Sokoni, 17 January 1996. See also Lechaptois, *Aux Rives*, 243, who refers to children singing the entire catechism.

32 BM, 16 February 1996, Isale; NM, 5 September 1995, Chala; DC, 10 July 1995, 21 September 1995, Chala; KM, 18 February 1996, Msilihofu; Roger Heremans, *Education dans les missions des Pères Blancs en Afrique Centrale* (Brussels, 1983), 324–5.

33 It could hardly be seen as wage labour since their pay was always quite low.

34 Low pay is noted in Karema Council Book, 9 August 1930 and *The Link*, No. 3, January 1948, WFRH. The prestige of the catechists is noted in *RA*,1946-47, WFRH.

35 In 1913 there were 18 catechists working in the villages surrounding Kate mission and two working in settlements around Chala. Five years later, Kate mission had 30 catechists and Chala had 35. *RA* 1912–13, Statistique du 30 Juin 1912 au 30 Juin 1913, Vicariat du Tanganyika, *RA* 1917–18; Statistique du 30 Juin 1917 au 30 Juin 1918, Vicariat du Tanganyika, WFRH.

36 How much training the early catechists received is difficult to determine. As early as 1895, there was a school for catechists, but it was not attended by all those who worked as teachers of religion in the villages, and many pupils selected for such training left before completing the course. Yet the number of catechists continued to increase. From 1913 to 1933 the catechist school in Zimba received a number of catechists for its three-year course. Since 1946, almost all catechists have attended a training course before beginning their work. Heremans, *Education*, 320–5; NM, 5 September 1995, Chala; BM, 16 February 1996, Isale; *History of Sumbawanga Diocese*, 40–2.

37 A diarist in Kirando noted in 1913 that without catechists the work of the mission would be impossible, *RA* 1912–13, WFRH.

38 *RA* 1912–13, Rapport General, Vicariat Apostolique du Tanganyika, WFRH.

39 According to one informant, the government officials in the late 1920s and early 1930s ordered all children to attend the reading and writing lessons. Sr Angelina Mwanauta, 19 March 1996, Sumbawanga.

40 KM, 21 January 1996, Chala; RK, 22 September 1995, Chala.

41 D. A. Low and J. M. Lonsdale, 'Introduction: towards the new order 1945–1963', in *History of East Africa* (Oxford, 1976), D. A. Low and Alison Smith (eds), III:32–5; Iliffe, *Modern History*, 216–36; Jean Comaroff and John Comaroff, *Of Revelation and Revolution* (Chicago, 1991), 233. See also Hodgson, 'Engendered encounters'.

42 Father Boniface Songolo, 15 March 1996, Kate; TS, 4 September 1995, Chala, informal conversation.

43 AK, 14 June 1995 Chala; MM, 15 May 1995, Chala.

44 15 September 1995, Chala.

45 Luis Sigareti, 14 June 1995, Chala.

46 R. P. J. M. Robert, *Croyances et coutumes magico-religieuses de Wafipa païens* (Tabora, 1949).

47 Iliffe noted that the missionaries in Ufipa systematically destroyed shrines and killed sacred pythons in the period before the First World War. *Modern History*, 219.

48 TS, 5 July 1995, Chala, informal conversation.

49 VD, 1 April 1996, Chala.

50 Luis Sigareti, 10 July 1995, Chala.

51 BY, 7 July 1995, Chala.

52 Other studies of Catholic conversion and evangelization also note the prominent place of the Virgin Mary in Catholicism as an aspect that was easily indigenized or inculturated. See Kassimir in this volume. Fipa did not mention this aspect as being significant, but Catholics honouring the Mother Mary fit neatly with Fipa notions of the primacy of parents, especially mothers, in a person's life. Recently, the Catholic church in Ufipa has come under attack from Protestants, new to the area, who claim that Catholics are worshipping idols when they pray to the Virgin. The most common Catholic response to this attack is that they are not worshipping idols, only putting the mother of Jesus in a place of honour in the church and worship service. This rebuttal, while not at all contradictory to Catholic theology, also reflects Fipa culture, where much emphasis is given to the role of parents in raising a child.

53 14 June 1995, Chala; 10 July 1995, Chala.

54 Sister Oliva Nyaronga, Sr Irena Sokoni, Pius Mwanakulya, and TS among others all discussed one or more priests as taking care of them as a parent would.

55 VB, 10 March 1996, Kate; HF, 11 March 1996; Kate; NC, 10 September 1995, Chala.

56 Sister Oliva Nyaronga, 9 June 1995, Sumbawanga.

57 *RA* 1912–13, Rapport du Karema, WFRH.

58 Sr Irena Sokoni, 17 January 1996, Chala.

59 This was despite the fact that the missionaries regularly preached against excessive use of millet beer. FN, 26 November 1995, Chala.

60 RK, 18 May 1995, Chala.

61 KK, 21 November 1995, Kirando.

62 NM, 5 September 1995, Chala.

63 NM, 21 July 1995, Chala; FN also recalled the missionaries regularly distributing meat to schoolchildren to take home to their parents, 26 November 1995.

64 Tambila, 'History', 34.

65 Heremans, *Les Etablissements*, 103. See also Bertsch, *Notes*, 72–3.

66 Bertsch, *Notes*, 72–3.

67 Not all elders were pleased with the active role priests took in the lives of some families. Sister Irena Sokoni's father and uncle reacted strongly against the Catholic missionaries when they feared that the priests wished their daughters to become sisters. 17 January 1996, Chala.

68 CK, 16 March 1996, Finda.

69 See Roy G. Willis, 'Changes in mystical concepts and practices among the Fipa', *Ethnology*, 7(1968), 139–57. One missionary lamented in 1948: 'Already all the small children have the fear of sorcery and believe that it is able to kill them even if the good Lord does not want it. Ah! If their parents instead of these hollow fears infused them with confidence in God!' *RA* 1947–8. Much has been written on the proliferation of witchcraft in sub-Saharan Africa despite the successes of Christian churches. A quest for healing not met by these churches as well as ongoing socal tensions are two key factors fuelling its continued existence. See Christopher Comoro and John Sivalon's chapter in this volume.

70 Kirando Council Book, WFRH.

71 *The Link*, No. 2, Nov. 1947; No. 13, Sept. 1949, WFRH.

72 NC, 25 February 1996, Chala.

73 Forced villagization in 1974–5 was the final factor contributing to reducing the number of *intuli*.

74 It is hard to note an exact date for these sorts of things because it appears individual priests emphasized restriction of certain activities while others did not. And the priests were moved from station to station frequently. Most of my older informants were in their teens in the 1930s and this could possibly account for my perception that the priests' attention to dancing started in the 1930s. But the mission diaries do not indicate concern about Fipa dancing until after the 1930s.

75 13 March 1996, Kate. Also RK, 25 January 1996, Chala; GS, 22 November 1995, Kirando; FN, 26 November 1995, Chala.

76 21 March 1996, Sumbawanga.

77 In 1958 the missionaries noted success in campaigning against 'night wedding dances',

but they were still occurring in Chala when I was doing fieldwork. *RA* 1957–58, WFRH.

78 See Gray, *Black Christians*, 51; Hastings, *The Church*, 323, 327.

79 A few notes about these statistics are in order. For 1912–16, the records were particularly incomplete so that in many cases the age of birth was not listed. I assumed that most of the 'unknown' birth dates were of older people because there were numerous entries each year indicating the birth year of the babies who were baptized. Some older Fipa also had years of birth supplied. For the years 1922 and beyond, I recorded only a small number of the hundreds of entries to establish average age at baptism and marriage. Many of the records throughout these years were incomplete and I did not use those. Statistics from the Annual Reports indicate that by the mid-1920s, in both Kate and Chala, more children were being baptized than adults.

80 Fr Bartolomeo Mwananjela, 11 April 1996, Chala.

81 *RA* 1910–11, Rapport du Kate.

82 Fipa elders had differing opinions on the efficacy of baptismal water as a curative. Some believed that it was a kind of medicine. Others noted (following the official church line) that it was simply water that had been blessed by the priest. In Fipa traditional belief, ponds of water were often considered to be occupied by deities and thus were sites of worship. Fipa also used water gathered from caves in special circumstances. So the idea of water as a religious and curative force was not new to the Fipa. Lechaptois, *Aux Rives*, 177, 194.

83 BY, 7 July 1995, Chala. Unfortunately, I did not ask the obvious follow-up question: 'Did she die anyway or live for a much longer period of time?'

84 *RA*, 1922–23, Rapport du Kirando.

85 Pius Mwanakulya, 29 November 1995, Milundikwa; 14 January 1996, Milundikwa.

86 AS, 25 November 1995, Chala.

87 The White Fathers noted in 1924 that Fipa did not want to die without baptism and usually gave their children permission to follow the religion, *RA* 1923–4.

88 IS, 7 July 1995, Chala.

89 BY, 7 July 1995, Chala. One of the missionaries in Bembaland wrote in 1927 that he believed 'the determining motives for conversion were the fear of God's justice, as taught in the sermons about the "four last things", and an intense desire for the life of grace as a means of escaping divine judgement'. Garvey, 'Development', 181.

Seven

The Church
& Cigogo

Father Stephen Mlundi
& Christianity in Central Tanzania

GREGORY H. MADDOX

The central challenge of this project is the attempt to take the faith of modern Tanzanians seriously. Religious change and motivations have too often been viewed either in instrumental (or functional) terms or as atavistic (almost psychological) responses to social change. For Tanzania, the spread of Christianity represents perhaps the most profound and far-reaching social and cultural change during the twentieth century. It marks and measures the transition to a modern world order. Yet this aspect has been little commented on by modern scholars.[1]

To help redress this lamentable lack of attention, this chapter examines the life story of one Christian from Ugogo in central Tanzania.[2] Father Stephen Mlundi was the first ordained Catholic priest in the region. His life and thought demonstrate the ways in which African Christians have domesticated their faith. This process linked African communities with broader institutions while maintaining strong indigenous continuities. Yet this process has also revealed new fissures. Father Stephen, for example, is a Catholic in a region were Anglicans dominate both numerically and socially. Likewise, Tanzania is a nation with many denominations and large Muslim communities. Father Stephen's life shows the connectedness that has emerged out of these changes.

This chapter will explore the process of the domestication of Christianity in the Gogo communities of central Tanzania through the life of Father Stephen Mlundi. It will begin with a discussion of the process of domestication and follow with a brief look at the earliest mission activities in the region. It will then pick up Father Stephen's narrative in the context of the expansion of Christianity in the region. It looks at the rivalry between Catholics and Anglicans in the region and examines the way in which Christianity became a part of the construction of identity both within Ugogo and in Tanganyika as a whole.

Domestication

Domestication was a multifaceted process, operating at both the individual and social levels. African converts to Christianity found ways to harmonize the tenets of their new faith with the evolving social situations they found themselves in. Converts and perhaps more importantly second- and third-generation Christians built institutions – churches – that linked individual believers and communities to the broader narrative of Christianity, while at the same time operating as powerful bureaucracies within colonial and national environments. Both faith and institutions were domesticated to the extent that Christians internalized their beliefs and changed their social practices to accommodate these beliefs. African Christianity (or more particularly Catholicism in Ugogo) is recognizable as Christianity yet remains distinctively African, born of both an international discourse and a local, Gogo, one.

Two elements here bear emphasis. First, domestication means not just the process of internalization and adaptation within any particular individual, but a process of social and cultural change. Missions almost always provided the original impetus, but in Ugogo, and in many other cases, discourses about Christianity rapidly became part of the local intellectual and cultural milieu.[3] As such, this process was never absolute. Mission Christianity with its outside origins created a tension within communities and individuals. Finally, domestication meant institution building and the situation of these institutions within a social order. Churches became power centres within local communities to which not everyone had access. They linked local communities with broader groups. They competed for power both within local communities and within broader colonial and national contexts.[4]

Although some of the most important early works on East African history recount the history of mission enterprise in the region, religious change has been largely ignored as a topic of scholarly enquiry over the last 30 years.[5] Later case studies in the Africanist mode tended to share with colonial social studies a search for a kind of authenticity that regarded the conversion of Africans to Christianity and the building of church structures as aberrations.[6] Questions of religious change, likewise, had no place, it seemed, in the political economy school of Tanzanian historiography that dominated the field after the mid-1970s.[7] More sophisticated analyses of religious change were thus few and far between.

T. O. Beidelman pioneered the field in *Colonial Evangelism*, but his work still operated within a dual framework that saw Christianity as fundamentally an alien imposition. For his analysis, the growing importance of the Anglican Church Missionary Society (CMS) in Ukaguru represented a graft onto the existing social order, with the deacon in Mamboya becoming an alternative ritual leader.[8] More recently Steven Feierman, Marcia Wright and Brigitta Larsson have sought to place the growth of Christianity within emerging colonial social orders in particular regions. While perhaps not as sophisticated as Wright's and Feierman's works, Larsson's work in particular shows the interaction between ideology, institutions and the colonial milieu as she charts the responses of different groups of women over the course of the colonial era in Buhaya.[9]

Most recent works of social history in Africa, however, have sought, in Feierman's terms, 'the end of universal narratives' and attempted to find authentic African voices untouched by outside epistemologies.[10] This concentration on the untranslatability of world views comes in response to the levelling effect of Africanist and radical scholarship, which concentrated on seeing Africans as part of new aggregations such as nations or classes. The emphasis on subjectivity, though, often ignores the interpenetration of Western and African interpretations. Too often this project continues the process that Mudimbe called separating the 'real African' from the 'Westernized African' and marginalizing the latter.[11]

It is at this point that a critical insight drawn from theological discourses illuminates both what many Christians see themselves as doing as well as broader processes of social and cultural change. African Christians see themselves as part of 'a world community in which the parts, in living tension with the aggregate whole, contextualize the universal truth of our equal, not to say mutual, proximity to one another and to God'.[12] A critical component here is the definition of the 'universal truth'.[13] While the Bible and the body of orthodox practice might seem self-evident as sources of that truth, the process of translation becomes one also of interpretation. In the last several decades theologians have debated the extent to which the revelation should be 'inculturated' into societies – that is, stripped of cultural baggage – and the extent to which God's message is 'incarnate' – that is, already apparent – within all human societies. Such arguments begin with revelation and debate the interpretation. Domestication means getting beyond the interpretations brought by missionaries to interpretations developed within particular African contexts.[14]

Yet the spread of Christianity cannot be seen as just an amplification of culture. Emphasizing the process of domestication within individual Africans and African communities does not mean ignoring the historical reality of the spread of Christianity in Tanzania. Despite the efforts of missionaries from the 1850s on, Africans did not convert to Christianity in large numbers until well after the beginning of colonial rule. A high degree of instrumentality guided the process of conversion. Likewise, while many if not most missionaries saw themselves as practising the religious equivalent of Indirect Rule, they proscribed important elements of African cultures and practices, interpreting them as anti-religious rather than as expressions of the search for the godly, so that becoming Christian always meant, in part, setting oneself off from inheritances of the past. Yet, whatever the motivations of any individual, Africans did not just follow European examples but also challenged Europeans for the control of their faith. In fact, most evangelization from the very earliest days was carried out by Africans.

Yet mission in Africa was politically the 'handmaiden' of colonialism and often reinforced obedience to the new colonial order. In 1904, for example, the Rev. A. Northwood preached a sermon to a conference of African teachers for the CMS in Mvumi in central Ugogo where he stressed the relationship of the believer to Jesus, the Master, as overseer, as teacher, as leader, as despot and as owner.[15] Conversion not only followed the flag, but the intensity of conversion varied directly with the political and economic changes of the colonial era. In Tanzania, given the near monopoly on education by the missions throughout the whole of the colonial era, conversion both became a path of social mobility and dominated the initial intellectual encounter with the West.

As Africans themselves moved to domesticate Christianity, however, they found in it, as other Africans would find in Islam, the intellectual means to attack the chains of mission paternalism.

Africans began earnestly to inquire into the Christian Scriptures, which missionaries had placed in their hands, to see where they had misunderstood the gospel. What they learned convinced them that mission as European cultural hegemony was a catastrophic departure from the Bible. They met the original irony with one of their own: they went on to claim the gospel, as the missionaries wished them to, but in turn insisted that missionary attitudes should continue to be scrutinized in its revealing light.[16]

It is just as obvious that the spread of Christianity came simultaneously with profound cultural changes within African communities. Yet, as Christianity became domesticated, Africans sought to define for themselves the balance between local continuity and global universality. A Tanzanian theologian puts it thus:

The Christian theologian will, when necessitated by his faith in Christ, choose to be the odd man out, to swim against the current of accepted cultural norms, when and if (and I mean literally only 'when and if') these clash headlong with his faith in Christ.[17]

Such a definition cuts both ways. African Christians also sought to mark their space clearly within their communities. They often sought outward and visible signs of their difference from their fellow Africans and from their past.

The domestication of Christianity for Tanzanians opened new worlds. It connected them to a universal narrative that they used to define their own cultural space both within Tanzania and in dialogue with the imperial milieu. It became not an opiate, but 'the heart of a heartless world'.

Father Stephen and the Spread of Christianity

Father Stephen Mlundi was elevated to the priesthood in the Catholic Church in 1944, becoming the first African from Ugogo to be ordained.

Born about 1910, during his long life he has served as a scholar, parish priest, administrator and political activist. I first met him in 1986, when he was in semi-retirement at St Peter's Cathedral in Dodoma. Over nine months we held a series of discussions on the history and culture of the people who call themselves Gogo. These dialogues shaped my understanding of the history of the region in a profound way. In 1993–4, I returned to Dodoma and held further discussions with Father Stephen about his own life, the growth of the Catholic Church in particular and Christianity in general in the region, and the nature of cultural change among the Gogo.[18]

In these discussions Father Stephen created a self-conscious narrative for me, an informed, interested outsider. An analysis of these discussions reveals the processes by which one African Christian, a man who answered his avocation, harmonized Christianity with a culturally specific version of Africanicity. Yet the narrative in these discussions is more than an individual statement. Father Stephen was and is a powerful symbol both for the Catholic Church and for the people of Ugogo. When I last saw him, preparations were under way for a large celebration of the fiftieth anniversary of his ordination. His own narrative is much more than one of conversion; it is one of dialectic. Just as his narrative is structured by his origin, his avocation and his life experiences, so his position allowed him to critically structure the discourses on those issues in the region and in Tanzania as a whole.

The CMS opened the first mission stations in Ugogo. It founded its first station at Mpwapwa in 1877, mostly as a way-station on the road to Buganda, but, until the imposition of effective German rule, the mission had little success in Ugogo. Most adherents at Mpwapwa were immigrants or freed slaves. While missionaries made trips further into Ugogo to the west, their first successful stations were in Ukaguru to the east. Conquests and pacification of the region did not themselves bring more converts. Numbers increased only after a series of disasters that began with an outbreak of rinderpest in the region in 1892, followed by a smallpox epidemic, then a famine remembered as *Magubike* in 1895, and finally Bushiri's revolt which briefly flared in the area. Before 1900 only in the area immediately outside Mpwapwa (although not in the town itself) were there many converts, but after 1900, the establishment of posts in central Ugogo at Mvumi and Buigiri greatly expanded the reach of the mission.[19]

The first Catholic missions did not arrive in the region until later. The Holy Ghost Fathers from Bagamoyo founded a mission in Kondoa in 1907 that also sent catechists into northern Ugogo. The most important Catholic influence, however, came from the south. In 1892, the German Benedictines of the St Ottilien Congregation had opened a mission at Tosamaganga in the hills overlooking the old Hehe capital of Kalenga, and from there made efforts to spread into Ugogo. The Germans, while committed to allowing missionaries of all nations to operate in German East Africa, actively sought to encourage German missions, both Protestant and Catholic. They had already asked the CMS to abandon their mission on Kilimanjaro as they saw it giving support to resistance. Conversely, CMS missionaries accused the German district officer of discouraging converts.[20]

The first Catholic mission station in Ugogo was founded in the southwest at Bihawana in 1909 by a Benedictine named Father Seiler. About 1910, the Catholic bishops of Bagamoyo and Dar es Salaam divided Ugogo along the recently completed Central Railway. As a result, in 1911 the White Fathers based in Tabora sent Father Caschy to found a mission in Bahi in the far west of the region in the Rift Valley. Once the Catholic Church had established a presence in Ugogo, the CMS mission reported hostility. Father Damm quickly expanded the work of the Benedictines from Bihawana. From Bahi, Father Ludwig went to the *watemi* of Ilundi and Ng'omvia and paid them 10 rupees to turn over buildings recently reserved for CMS teachers to Catholics. The CMS then sought an alliance with German Protestant missions and the intervention of the government. The colonial government, however, urged the parties to settle the matter themselves. A series of meetings between Bishop Peel of the CMS and both Catholic bishops resulted in a mad rush by each side to establish teachers in every major settlement in the region.[21] The Benedictines eventually established a short-lived station at Zanza near Mpwapwa.

The East Africa Campaign during the First World War greatly disrupted mission activity in the region. First, the Germans interned all mission personnel from Allied nations, including both CMS and Catholic missionaries. Then the invading Allies interned all the German personnel. During the war both Catholic and CMS missions continued to function under the leadership of African adherents. When the war ended and Tanganyika became a mandated territory, the Benedictines turned over their base at Tosamaganga to the Italian Consulata order, and in 1935 the Catholic missions of Ugogo and Kondoa were united into one prefecture under the direction of the Passionist Fathers from northern Italy.[22]

Conversion in Ugogo before the First World War remained relatively small-scale. The CMS had established important bases at Buigiri and Mvumi, and had begun to educate Africans for service in the colonial government at Mpwapwa. The Benedictines had established a large complex at Bihawana. While these areas and the men (and it was almost all men who operated in the public sphere) who received training at them became the nodes for a competitive transformation of Ugogo, Christianity remained an option only for the marginal and, in many cases, for outsiders. After the First World War, however, conversion became more general. The absolute chaos of the war years and the *Mtunya* famine that followed did much to disrupt the local social order.[23] Converts now came from all regions of Ugogo and from all levels of the older social order.

Father Stephen's conversion and early education exemplify these trends. In contrast to African CMS leaders, he always placed himself quite consciously within Gogo tradition. In several of our conversations he

7.1 *Bihawana Mission Church*

emphasized his status as a true Gogo, as opposed to people of 'slave' origin in the nineteenth century or immigrant origin in the twentieth who subsequently became Gogo.[24] Father Stephen was a member of the Wetumba clan, which claims origin in Hanang to the north and whose ancestors moved to Kibaya, Ukaguru to the east of Ugogo. His grandfather migrated to Mvumi, seat of the most powerful *mtemi* of the region, but in the late nineteenth century his father moved to Msangu in Mpwapwa District.[25]

Father Stephen placed such emphasis on his origins, I suspect, because he felt he had to answer charges that Christianity was an alien imposition as well as the de facto status of the Anglican Church as the 'national church' of Ugogo. The position of ritual authority in the region, the *mtemi*, had its most important function as propitiating the spirits in order to ensure adequate rainfall and harvests. Conversion thus threatened to disrupt the harmony necessary to ensure social survival. Mnyampala wrote a jeremiad claiming that *watemi* and elders resisted Christianity (and Islam) more than they did colonial rule.[26]

While Father Stephen claimed 'pure' Gogo origins, his father was apparently not very well off. Father Stephen's mother died when he was quite young, and his father never remarried. Father Stephen said his father devoted all his time to looking after his son, and he remembered his father strapping him to his back when he went to herd cattle. Father Stephen attended classes as a child in Msangu taught by a catechist. He said that many of his kinsmen had opposed his conversion, but his father had stood up for him. Later, when Father Stephen had an opportunity to attend secondary school in Bahi, some 200 miles to the west of his home, his father moved there to look after him despite initially objecting to Father Stephen beginning the process of taking vows.

Father Stephen's story corresponds with some of the general tendencies among the earliest converts. First, many early converts to Christianity came from groups marginalized within society. Father Stephen's emphasis on his origins, despite their humbleness, had a very specific political and religious context. He repeatedly stated to me that a significant portion of the catechists during the 1930s and 1940s came from slave origins. As a result, he claimed, many catechists faced severe problems. In a case from the 1940s, a catechist was assigned to a settlement with a considerable Catholic population. Within a few months, attendance at services dropped appreciably. Father Stephen enquired about the matter, and the senior elder of the settlement told him that they could not listen to the new catechist since he had formerly been a slave there. On another occasion, Father Stephen described how he had to intervene with missionaries to have a catechist moved from a village where he came from a dependent family. The catechist had given a potential convert sanctuary against a marriage to a man who already had a wife. Eventually, he claimed, the church no longer assigned catechists to areas from whence they came because of such problems.

Likewise, Father Stephen claimed that many of the men who received education during the colonial era were either of slave or immigrant origins. He claimed that chiefs would send boys who came from dependent households off to school at the request of the colonial government, claiming them as sons. This practice, which several other elders confirmed, had both practical and symbolic causes. At the practical level, ritual leaders wanted their heirs to learn the arts of statesmanship and rain making more than the new skills that came from education. At the symbolic level, the tie to the ritual territory, the *yisi*, meant that the departure of ritual leaders from their territories could bring destruction.[27]

These former 'slaves' then became Native Authority chiefs and, Father Stephen claimed, often married into the clan holding the ritual leadership of a territory.[28] Father Stephen dismissed the most important political family in the region, one that has provided a prime minister of Tanzania and a member of the first cabinet of the country at independence, as immigrants whose family only came to the region in the late nineteenth century.[29]

This charge, of course, reflects a lifetime of competition, but also cooperation, in religious and social spheres in the region. Father Stephen also commented on times he had worked with members of this family over the years in various projects, and once recounted how Job Lusinde, who did not spend a great deal of time in Dodoma, had stopped his car in the middle of the street in town to give Father Stephen a lift back to the cathedral. Gogo identity is and was open. All clans in Ugogo claim immigrant or non-Gogo autochthonous origins. Mnyampala described the process of becoming Gogo thus: 'Anyone who moves to Ugogo, pierces the ear, marks the forehead, and follows the customs and habits of Cigogo is then not called of another tribe but is an Mgogo.'[30] Father Stephen himself discussed with me the flexibility of Gogo identity. Yet in the colonial context, for very particular reasons, Father Stephen felt it necessary to assert his own authenticity.

After 1920, the Anglican CMS was seen as favoured by the new regime. The Germans had accused several CMS converts of aiding the Allied forces during the fighting in the region and imprisoned them.[31] In particular, they charged the young *mtemi* of Mvumi, Mazengo, where the largest CMS station in Ugogo was eventually located, with actively aiding the allied forces. He only escaped arrest, according to a well-known story, by hiding in the bush while his elders explained to German authorities that he had been killed by a lion.[32] By 1924, the senior British official in the region regarded him as the most effective political leader in the region, and Mazengo became a staunch patron of the CMS.[33] With the introduction of Indirect Rule in 1925, the British also attempted to replace non-local *karani* with locally educated men, the vast majority of whom came from the CMS, thus further strengthening the tie between the Anglican Church and the government.[34]

The second generation of Anglican leaders in the region also came from Mvumi and continued the dominance of the Diocese of Central Tanganyika (as it became known after the 1930s). Yohana Malecela, son of Maula, had immigrated to Mvumi from Uzigua as a rain maker. He came into the service of the *mtemi* of Mvumi under Mazengo's predecessor, Masenha. The disruptions of the 1890s sent him to Mpwapwa, where he became affiliated with the mission under Daulton.[35] He quickly became one of the first group of senior teachers under the CMS and, by 1902, he was stationed at Buigiri, where the Anglican Bishop of East Africa, Peel, wrote of him: 'Yohana, the senior teacher employed by Mr Daulton, is an uncommonly useful and whole-hearted Christian, pure in life, and earnest in keeping his household in the fear and love of God.'[36] As a sign of his devotion, and perhaps as a way of building a patronage network, he gave part of his own salary back to the mission to help support two other teachers at the station. He was considered a candidate for ordination in 1906, but a teachers' strike and then the First World War caused the CMS to put off the step of ordaining African clergy. He was later ordained in the first group of Anglican African clergy from Ugogo in 1924 and took up pastoral duties in the large mission establishment at Mvumi.[37]

The Senyagwa clan of the Malecelas became the most powerful clan in the region by the 1950s, backed in part by Mazengo. One son became a wealthy entrepreneur. Another, Petro Lusinde, continued his father's work as a teacher for the CMS. A grandson became the first person from the region to attend Makerere and then moved on to assume the leadership of the proto-nationalist movement in the region during the 1950s.[38] Another grandson eventually became prime minister. In particular, Job Lusinde became the dominant power broker in the region. Father Stephen claimed that they practised a sort of cultural hegemony by elevating Mvumi to the central place of Ugogo. He also charged that generally the Anglicans were not *safi*, 'clean', in their dealings with Catholics.

Catholic attitudes towards African clergy maintained a distinction between evangelist and clergy and sought to elevate Africans to the clergy. Catholic missionaries trained Africans as catechists at junior seminaries at Bihawana and Bahi. These were then sent to villages, often their own homes, to teach and preach under the supervision of the mission. The catechists would then recommend promising students for junior seminary, with a select few advancing to senior seminary and finally a small handful to full ordination.[39]

Catholic policy had encouraged the ordination of African clergy on the same level as European clergy since the nineteenth century. This policy meant that missionaries, at least nominally, searched for suitable candidates. However, it took the emergency of the war to bring about the ordination of African priests in German East Africa. The first Africans were ordained in Bukoba in 1917. After the war, responding in part to Benedict XV's *Maximum Illud* of 1919, which called for more indigenous clergy as well as cooperation between missionary orders, the various orders in Tanganyika operated several senior seminaries collectively. This bull both enjoined close cooperation between missionary organizations and stressed that African clergy were equal to missionary clergy and hence held to the same level of training. The seminaries in Tanganyika included Morogoro, Tosamaganga, Kipalapala (Tabora), Kibosho, Peramiho and Ntugama (Bukoba).[40]

Answering a vocation during the first half of the twentieth century required more than just an instrumental motivation. For both Protestants and Catholics, this choice involved much more than becoming an adherent. By the 1920s, converting to mission Christianity brought material and social benefits. The correlation between crises in Ugogo, whether food shortage or political or military crisis, and the number of 'readers' attracted to the churches is clear evidence of this aspect of conversion. Answering a vocation cut an individual off in important ways, however, both from the local community and from elements of the emerging colonial milieu – especially for Catholics, given the relatively close alliance between the CMS and the British administration.

These earliest church leaders, both Catholics and Protestants, carved out new positions for themselves. They became the critical vessels both for 'translating the message', thus defining ongoing cultural change in the communities of the region, and for challenging European cultural imperialism. This challenge, in turn, laid the groundwork for the political challenge to European rule. Yet the nature of both these challenges did not seek a return to an African essence but instead reflected an engagement with religious, cultural and political universalizing narratives. It also reflected the social position of individuals who self-consciously defined themselves as different from the communities from which they sprang. The CMS in Ugogo once held a conference to debate the 'forbiddances' that marked adherents. The list included dress as well prohibitions against visiting healers and the like. The Europeans had to block attempts by African representatives to add even more to an already exhaustive list.[41]

The process of ascending to the priesthood was a long and difficult one. At a personal level, it meant breaking with the norms of life in a region where kin networks were one of the primary defences against famine. Yet as individuals moved through the new hierarchies that churches created, they also became important sources of patronage and support in new arenas. Men like Father Stephen have become an integral part of such evolving family networks, and he retains close contacts with clan members and descendants of his father's sisters in Msangu.

Education under missionaries in preparation for the priesthood was difficult and not without tension. Father Stephen received his initial education from a catechist in his village. He then went to primary school in Mpwapwa. He passed into junior seminary at Bahi, when the White Fathers ran it, and eventually went to seminary at Kipalapala near Tabora, an institution founded by the White Fathers. He was ordained in 1944, part of a large number of priests ordained in the 1940s.[42]

Father Stephen served as a parish priest throughout the region. He served at Bihawana under the direction of an Italian Passionist named Father John. While there, he helped oversee a famine relief camp and handled all correspondence with the colonial government because he spoke and wrote English better than any of the missionaries. From this position, he began to take an active role in community affairs. Eventually, when the seat of the Diocese of Dodoma was moved from Bihawana to Dodoma, he became the parish priest in Dodoma.

As Father Stephen recalled his experiences within the church, he portrayed himself as the vocal critic of a dogmatic approach to Christianity. He told of the attempts by the church to prohibit converts from taking part in circumcision ceremonies, going so far as to expel from school boys who went through the rituals. Father Stephen instead argued for an approach that legitimized such ceremonies on the grounds that they made a person a Gogo, which was of critical importance, and not that they served as a rite of passage which could be coopted.

For Father Stephen this interpenetration between being Gogo and being Christian was a lived one. I once asked him about a practice called *chimehe*. During the 1920s, especially, colonial officials reported that people in Ugogo began to participate in what seems to have been a witch-finding movement. From *watemi* on, people drank blessed water provided by special diviners in an effort to ensure the coming of the rains. Colonial officials made much of prohibiting the practice, but Father Stephen commented enigmatically that in the past people had to be very careful in speaking to strangers, one did not know where harm lay, and then quickly changed the subject.[43] His own balancing reflected the larger tensions in the region. Several informants over the years said that the power that flowed from Mvumi came not just because of the establishment of the CMS mission there, but also because Mazengo retained the power to stop the rains. Such interpretations are not so much competing ones as intertwined.

Father Stephen always emphasized the variety of the Gogo experience. He once told me a story about a young couple whose marriage almost broke up because the groom expected the bride to finish the walls of their new *tembe*, as was done in his region of Ugogo, while the bride expected the groom to do it, as was done in her region. Yet I think Father Stephen was making the point that, in spite of these surface differences, people can live together. Mnyampala makes the same point when he writes that despite different dialects and customs 'all these together are Gogo; they are proud of their common land of Ugogo.... Remember that Ugogo is very big.... How can they be without different accents?'[44] I have often thought of Father Stephen's story (perhaps a theme in a sermon) as a catalyst for his own view of the church in Africa and, in a different context, as shaping my own views on the nature of Gogo identity.

Father Stephen's harshest critique of mission Christianity was that missionaries did not trust people to be true Christians.

> Missionaries brought their fights with them. They brought European Christianity both good and bad. All, however, attacked African culture. These were *shenzi*. People would wear medicines around their necks, and these the missionaries would condemn. Yet at the same time the Catholic Church gave out medals. The African could do nothing but become a European.... He had to speak English and attack other Africans as pagans. The missionaries made no effort to understand African culture and what it means.[45]

Even for him, the tension between being an African and being a Christian was difficult. He said that, to become a priest, one had to say he hated the things Europeans hated. He cited the example of a missionary preaching the evil of circumcision to a congregation, all whom were circumcised. He said people did not feel whole because they felt they had to lie to the missionaries. For him faith transcended the external forms but did not destroy them. To be a true Christian, one had to be whole.

Father Stephen here takes a defining motif in writing about African Christianity and turns it in on itself. From the very earliest days of missionary activity, many missionaries questioned the ability of Africans to internalize the message.[46] They even questioned their ability to understand the message, and often accused Africans of converting merely for material reasons. For some missionaries, the very drive to create rigid divides between converted and non-converted served as proof that Africans had not yet achieved the degree of faith necessary to live a Godly life without guidance. The emphasis on correctness of ritual and connectivity still draws remarks from some observers, although it is misleading in many respects. It reflects a power relationship that includes a strong cultural element. As one African theologian comments, 'awe of the white person and need for money'[47] continue to give foreign Christians an illusion of control.

Yet Father Stephen's faith was the central fact of his life, and he himself became an important icon in the region. On hearing that I knew Father Stephen, several Catholics, clergy and laymen, replied, 'He is father to us all.' At the same time, he was an outspoken radical on issues of current doctrine. He roundly condemned the Catholic ban on birth control, for example. Such frankness extended beyond matters of church doctrine; he also criticized both Ujamaa for its unreality and the subsequent liberalization policies of the government for promoting corruption. It was such outspokenness, perhaps, that prevented him from joining his age-mates in the church as the first generation of African prelates.

On Being Gogo and Christian

This chapter has argued that Christians in Ugogo, like Father Stephen, have domesticated their faith. That, rather than reinforcing an opposition between a 'new' faith and 'old' ways of life, has made the two indistinguish-able. This concept applies not just in the more specific arena of religious change, and it is more than a gloss on the theological discourse on 'inculturation'. This same phenomenon operates at a deep level in many African societies. Jan Vansina has written of Western Bantu-speaking cultures as culturally schizophrenic.[48] The old 'words' no longer explain the new 'things' and hence new orders of knowledge are not integrated with older ones but grafted onto them. Such a critique is also levelled at post-colonial proponents of hybridity; that in essence there is very little hybrid about them.

Sanneh has countered by stressing the historic ability of Christians to translate the message. In the case of the Christians in Dodoma, both Catholic and Protestants, the process of translating is I think beyond even Father Stephen's reading of it. Father Stephen himself has lived the praxis of translation, which, in part, means the connection of the particular com-munity's experience with a perceived universal. Although his own inter-pretations at times conflict with others, both within his community and within his church, there exists an orthopraxy, if not an orthodoxy, in both spheres.

Father Stephen, like many Christians in Africa, has defined in practice what African theologians have only theorized. For him the conflict is not between the message of Christianity and African culture but rather between the cultural imperialism of the mission enterprise and faith. Such seems to me to be the state of the practice of Christianity by many Africans.

The questions that remain about this translation in Tanzania are not so much those of West versus African and certainly not so much Christian versus Christian, but in a sense community versus nation and Muslim versus Christian. Father Stephen in some ways represents the community side of the equation. His concern for Gogoness, while casting Protestants as not true Gogo, meant for him that accepting Christianity does not mean giving up other forms of identity. In Tanzania, however, a variety of factors have tended to mute such divisions (certainly without silencing them totally), while creating new ones.

In one division, of course, the spread of Christianity played a key role. It wasn't just the colonial government that imposed Swahili as the language of administration on Tanganyika. Missions found it enormously more fruitful to concentrate on Swahili as the language of worship. While Bibles, other religious writings and primers were prepared in the Gogo language, Catholic missions in Gogo used Swahili from the first as the language of worship. The CMS mission, however, continued to use the Gogo language in worship in spite of the insistence of the German government after 1904 that Swahili become the language of education.

Likewise, in some places one church became a 'national' church while, conversely, denominational connections often cut across ethnic affiliation. Even though Protestant missions rarely 'poached' on each other's territory before the Second World War, ecumenical movements and formal cooperation linked believers. Although a division did emerge between Catholics and Protestants, such divisions themselves are more local than national, as Father Stephen's testimony shows. Because of all these linkages, independency movements never gained the prominence in the country that they did elsewhere in Africa.[49]

A more fundamental division, that between Christians and Muslims, runs through Tanzanian society. Even here, though, the fault line is not absolute. In essence, a sort of rough civil society has been created across much of Tanzania, one in which the project of conversion, translation and domestication has created connections at all levels of society. In a sense, then, conversion and the spread of Christianity are an important subset of the creation of this civil society, one that is resolutely non-partisan.[50] It has been more successful in connecting Christians of different communities and different denominations, but serious fault lines remain. As a result, religious radicalism, both Pentecostal movements and Islamic renewal movements, have tended to appeal to the socially alienated, with the Islamic version seemingly more political.

Such struggles both represent the external form of social cleavages and yet are about precisely the issues most precious to believers: whether the Son of God or Muhammad was the seal of the prophets. Likewise, the divisions in Ugogo reflect not just which mission got a teacher at which village, or which set of Christians got jobs with the Native Authority, but also an emerging tradition. Father Stephen, although not quite the mythic hunter so common in Ugogo clan origin traditions, shades into a culture hero, one who founds a new lineage while rooting himself in an older one.

Notes

* I would like to thank Father Stephen for allowing me to learn from him. I am also grateful to the Center for African Studies at the University of Florida for support during the writing of this chapter, and for the comments of Thomas Spear, Isaria N. Kimambo and the other participants in the conference.

1 See John Iliffe, *A Modern History of Tanganyika* (Cambridge, 1979) for one of the best examples of a general lack of attention to religious change.

2 Ugogo is the land of the Gogo people. I have retained the Bantu prefixes for the territory because it is common usage to do so in Tanzania. I have also retained the prefix 'Ci-' in the title. In the Gogo language, this prefix denotes both language and a general sense of attributes. Hence, Cigogo means, in this context, Gogoness.

3 My use of the concept draws on Antonio Gramsci's concept of hegemony. I have chosen to use the term 'domestication' to emphasize the indeterminate nature of the process. Indeed, as I argue below, within the colonial context, Christianity could become counter-hegemonic. See Q. Hoare and G. N. Smith (trans. & ed.), *Selections from the Prison Notebooks* (New York, 1971).

4 Although this chapter concerns 'mainstream' Christianity, separatist and theologically innovative movements also fit within this schema.

5 See Reginald Coupland, *The Exploitation of East Africa* (London, 1939); Roland Oliver, *The Missionary Factor in East Africa* (London, 1952); and Marcia Wright, *German Missions in Tanganyika 1891–1941* (Oxford, 1971). This obscurity at the academic level has partially been countered at the local level. Many dioceses, churches and denominations have sponsored local histories, and there are several broader church histories.

6 For a discussion of this topic more generally see Leroy Vail and Landeg White, *Power and the Praise Poem* (Charlottesville, 1991), 1–6.

7 I. N. Kimambo, *Three Decades of Historical Research at Dar es Salaam* (Dar es Salaam, 1993).

8 T. O. Beidelman, *Colonial Evangelism* (Bloomington, 1982).

9 Steven Feierman, *Peasant Intellectuals* (Madison, 1990); Marcia Wright, *Strategies of Slaves and Women* (New York, 1993); and Brigitta Larsson, *Conversion to Greater Freedom?* (Uppsala, 1991).

10 Steven Feierman, 'Africa in history: the end of universal narratives', in Gyan Prakash, (ed.), *After Colonialism* (Princeton, 1995), 40–65. See in particular his implicit contrast of 'purely African narratives' with Alex Kagame's and Rwabukumba's histories of Rwanda.

11 Mudimbe states that his work seeks 'rather than simply accept[ing] the authority of qualified representatives of African cultures, ... to study the theme of the foundations of discourse about Africa'. *The Invention of Africa* (Bloomington, 1988), xi.

12 Lamin Sanneh, *Translating the Message* (Maryknoll, 1989), 201–3.

13 John Parratt, *Reinventing Christianity* (Grand Rapids, 1995), 25–54. Among theologians there is an old debate over adaptation or inculturation of the Christian message.

14 See, in particular, Parratt, *Reinventing Christianity*, 30-40.

15 Church Missionary Society Archives (CMS), G3 A8/01 1904, 'Native Teachers' Conference', *Usagara and Ugogo Notes*, April 1904.

16 Sanneh, *Translating*, 163.

17 Laurenti Magesa, 'Authentic African Christianity', *African Ecclesiastical Review*, 37/4 (1995), 212.

18 Sadly, Father Mlundi died soon after, in late 1994.

19 Elisabeth Knox, *Signal on the Mountain* (Canberra, 1991), 122–5. The eastern side of the mission in Ukaguru had more early success.

20 Knox, *Signal*, 183–5; *Catholic Directory of Tanzania* (Tabora, 1988); and Lukas Malishi, *A History of the Catholic Church in Tanzania* (Peramiho, 1990), 20.

21 CMS, Usagara Letters, Minute, G. J. Manely, 5 December 1912, and T. B. R. Westgate, Buigiri to Manley, 27 Dec. 1912; see also Knox, *Signal*, 183–5.

22 S. Rweyemamu and T. Msambure, *The Catholic Church in Tanzania* (Peramiho, 1989), 10–15; and R. Ossola, *1919–1969, The Consolata Missionaries in the Diocese of Iringa and at Tosamaganga* (Iringa, 1969).

23 Gregory H. Maddox, '*Mtunya*: famine in Central Tanzania, 1917–1920', *Journal of African*

History, 31 (1990), 181–98.

24 See Mathais E. Mnyampala, *The Gogo: History, Customs, and Traditions* (Armonk, 1995), Gregory H. Maddox (ed. & trans.), for a discussion of the openness of Gogo identity. Mnyampala was almost an exact contemporary of Father Stephen, and Father Stephen said he was consulted by Mnyampala when he was writing his book.

25 Father Stephen was unclear where his grandfather had moved from. This story is a rather typical gloss of a clan origin story. There are at least three Wetumba or Itumba clans with many subclans; the term is used generally to denote the Gogo of the east. In the Gogo language the term is also used for the Kaguru people. Father Stephen went on to say that, in Hanag, the Wetumba had the same origins as clans among the Kimbu. He had met a Kamba from a Wetumba clan that also claimed origins in Hanag. See Peter Rigby, *Cattle and Kinship among the Gogo* (Ithaca, 1967), 312–13, and Mnyampala, *The Gogo*, 50–1.

26 Mnyampala, *The Gogo*, 117

27 Mnyampala, *The Gogo*, 118.

28 For discussions of the split that emerged in the region between the concept of *Mtemi we mvula* (rain chief) and *Mtemi we serikali* (government chief), see Rigby, *Cattle and Kinship*, 98 and Maddox, 'The ironies of *Historia, Mila na Desturi za Wagogo*' in Mnyampala, *The Gogo*, 21.

29 For a different version of this family's history, the Lusinde and Malacela family, see Ernest Kongola, *Historia mfupi ya Mbeya ya 'Wevunjiliza' toka 1688 mpaka 1986: 'Mbukwa Muhindi wa Cimambi'* (Dodoma, 1986), where Kongola emphasizes that they, like all clans in the region, have become Gogo. See also the interviews with Job Lusinde and Canon Lusinde, where these brothers discuss the migration of their grandfather to Ugogo, in Gregory H. Maddox, '"Leave, Wagogo! You have no food!": famine and survival in Ugogo, Central Tanzania 1916–1961' (PhD, Northwestern, 1988), Appendix.

30 Mnyampala, *The Gogo*, 13.

31 To this day the story of the imprisonment and ill-treatment of CMS teachers forms part of the lore of the Anglican church in the region. See Kongola, *Historia Mfupi ya Mbeya ya 'Wevunjiliza'*; Knox, *Signal*, 163; and I/33/53A Sahali.

32 See Paul White, *Doctor of Tanganyika* (Sydney, 1943) for an early published account of this story. See also I/17/14A-26A Chidoza etc. for an account from elders in Mvumi.

33 TNA 967.828 *Dodoma District Reports*, H. Hignell, Annual Report for 1924.

34 Mnyammpala, *The Gogo*, 49. Mnyampala was among the first Catholics to break into the civil service.

35 I/46/118A Lusinde.

36 CMS, G3 A8/01 1903, Bishop Peel, 'Notes on a Visit to Usagara and Ugogo', 6 Oct. 1903.

37 Knox, *Signal*, 102, 165.

38 It is interesting to note that the oldest of the third generation of this family, Naftali Lusinde, became a clergyman. Kongola, *Historia Mfupi ya Mbeya ya 'Wevunjiliza'*, 18/1-2.

39 This pattern is typical throughout the Catholic world. In Ugogo, the junior seminaries also served as secondary schools that trained teachers and others. In the 1940s, under the urging of the colonial government, the Passionists and the CMS jointly opened a secondary school at Kikuyu, outside Dodoma, known as Alliance Secondary School (today called Mazengo Secondary School). The CMS also operated secondary schools at Mvumi and Mpwapwa.

40 It is interesting to note that church publications generally do not mention prominent African clergy between the four ordained in 1917 and the large group ordained in the 1940s. The group ordained around 1943–4 included Laurian Cardinal Rgambwa and several others who eventually became Bishops. See Rweyemamu and Msambure, *Catholic Church in Tanzania*, 25.

41 Knox, *Signal*, 170–5.

42 Ossola, *Consolata Missionaries*; Malishi, *Catholic Church in Tanzania*.

43 Maddox, 'Leave, Wagogo!', 154–5.

44 Mnyampala, *The Gogo*, 51.

45 Interview, 15 May 1994.

46 Parratt, *Reinventing Christianity*, 14, quotes Desmond Tutu on Africans struggling with 'religious schizophrenia'.

47 Laurenti Magesa, 'The expatriate worker in Africa', *African Ecclesiastical Review*, 36/2 (1994), 96.

48 Jan Vansina, *Paths in the Rainforests* (Madison, 1990), 247.

49 There was a division from the Anglican Church in the western part of Ugogo, the Tanganyika African Church, that began in 1958. I have no details about it. See Knox, *Signal*, 154; David Barrett, *Schism and Renewal in Africa* (Nairobi, 1968).

50 Parratt, *Reinventing Christianity*, 117, discusses the work of the theologian E. Eboussi Boulaga on this issue.

IV

Struggles for Control

Given the colonial setting, linking economic exploitation with political repression and cultural arrogance under the rubric of the 'civilizing mission', it is not surprising that African converts soon came into conflict with missionaries over issues of religious leadership, interpretation and practice. The casual incorporation of European culture and superiority in mission Christianity was bound to offend many Africans, but African Christians soon came into their own as evangelists, teachers and translators, interpreting and appropriating the Word for themselves. As they did so, they increasingly bridled over missionary control of their faith and lives, leading to increasing struggles between missionaries and their erstwhile followers over Christian leadership, doctrines and practices, as Father Stephen's story shows so eloquently. Growing more self-confident in their faith, African catechists pushed for ordination, while parishioners resisted missionary attacks on their own practices and beliefs.

The struggles for control were manifested in a variety of ways. Sandgren's study of the African Brotherhood Church in Kenya is, in many ways, a classic study of African independency, as the new church fused cultural tolerance and African leadership into a strong cohesive body. The first Kamba were initially attracted to Christianity by the dynamic preaching and leadership of a young AIM missionary, George Rhoad, who was fluent in Kamba, intervened with the government on their behalf, helped people to build roads and schools, and encouraged Kamba to worship on their own by translating the New Testament into Kamba. Shunned by their neighbours, the missionaries and their converts formed a close community.

Kamba Christians soon grew disillusioned with the mission, however, as Rhoad left the field and his AIM colleagues became increasingly critical of Kamba polygamy, circumcision and other cultural practices; refused to

167

support Kamba wishes for education; and imposed increasing discipline on parishioners who resisted their control. The field became ripe for schism when Simeon Mulandi combined with Rhoad, now back in Kenya as an independent missionary, to establish a new mission in Nairobi among Kamba migrants. With its emphasis on cultural inclusivity, universal 'brotherhood' in Christ and education, Mulandi's African Brotherhood Church expanded quickly into the rural areas to become the dominant church in the area. Even more remarkable, however, was the ability of the new church to transcend the departure of its founder less than ten years after its origins. Independent churches were often dominated by the strong charismatic leadership of their founders, and they often failed when they departed or died, but the ABC proved unusually resilient under Mulandi's successors.

Omari's study of the recent emergence of the African Missionary Evangelical Church in Tanzania proceeds along similar lines, as Meru protested against external control and cultural intolerance to seek local control of their own church. What was different, however, was that the AMEC's struggle was with a national church that had been led by Africans for the previous 30 years. The dispute was unusually acrimonious, nevertheless, with periodic riots and killings over a period of several years while the secessionists warred with the leaders of the Northern Diocese of the Evangelical Lutheran Church in Tanzania and their supporters in Meru. The issues were not theological, for the secessionists remained orthodox Lutherans, or the product of a young and struggling church. The Lutheran Church was extremely well-established in Meru, and it was involved in all aspects of Meru life from the church itself, to schools, the cooperative, the development trust and the ruling party. That such a bitter struggle could engulf such an established, mature church leads Omari to conclude that the drive for the new church was part of a broader ethnic movement for local political, economic and social control. The schism thus echoes the earlier development of 'Ethiopian' churches against colonial authority, but now against the non-local leaders of their own national churches and government.

If Omari's study alerts us to the continuing potential for independency within today's national churches, Wamba-dia-Wamba's study of the Bundu dia Kongo (Kongo Church) introduces the potential of non-Christian cultural revival movements in response to political and religious corruption in contemporary Africa. Tracing the origins, theology and practices of the Kongo Church, Wamba senses the possibility of cultural renewal and emancipatory politics amid the devastation of contemporary Congo (ex-Zaire) in this new church that draws deeply on both Kongo and Christian roots, now so deeply intertwined that one can no longer consider African culture and Christianity as separate entities.

Eight

Kamba Christianity

From Africa Inland Mission to African Brotherhood Church

DAVID SANDGREN

Simeon Mulandi and a large group of organizers had planned the inaugural announcement of the new church carefully, making flags and banners to emphasize the festive occasion and choosing Kariokor, the largest African section of colonial Nairobi, for the announcement. But such an endeavour was politically risky in colonial Kenya, and, when the day came, none of the founding members appeared. Mulandi was not deterred, however.

> I delayed the announcement of the new church hoping that my friends would arrive as previously planned. As the minutes dragged on to half an hour and then an hour, I decided to go ahead on my own. I was sure that I would be arrested.... We opened with a hymn, 'Jesu Kwetu ni Rafiki', which means 'What a friend we have in Jesus'. And then something marvellous happened. Once we had started the song, many people drew near, even the policemen who were amongst us, just sang together. I announced that this occasion was the inauguration of the African Brotherhood Church, a church controlled and run by Africans for all people. Everyone, regardless of denomination, was welcome.

By this time quite a crowd had gathered. Mulandi preached for an hour and took up a collection to which even the police contributed.[1]

Such were the inauspicious beginnings of the African Brotherhood Church, a church that has subsequently grown to considerable importance among Kamba of Kenya with several hundred congregations, about one hundred African clergy and a church membership of more than 100,000. Indeed, Harold W. Turner has called it the 'best organized church in Kenya'.[2] Perhaps in recognition of these organizational qualities, the ABC was accepted as a member of the All-African Conference of Churches in 1966, one of only four independent churches so admitted.[3] Also in 1970, the World Council of Churches was sufficiently interested in the ABC to commission a survey of the church.[4] Thus by the 1970s the ABC had become a 'rightly respected member of the wider protestant family',[5] generally recognized for its stability, high-quality leadership and organization, and for its growing membership.

But how did such a successful African-led church come into being and what can its origins and early development tell us about the relationship between mission Christianity and African-directed churches? Furthermore, how and why did African Christians eventually come to realize that their own understandings of Christianity were often different from those of the missionaries? In cases where a new African church developed, what contributed most to its development – the vision articulated by its founder or the disenchantment with missions for not meeting local needs? Finally, did the African critique of missions eventually lead to protests and even rebellion against colonial authorities? Were African-led churches inherently political? In the discussion that follows, I will attempt to address these questions through the exploration of the following topics: the development of Christianity among Kamba by the Africa Inland Mission (AIM) and its influence on the origins and early history of the ABC; the AIM and British colonial government reactions to the ABC, especially concerning its possible connections with the 'Mau Mau' rebellion; and Simeon Mulandi's founding leadership and early departure from the ABC.

Simeon Mulandi's Vision of an African Church

All considerations of the ABC must start with Simeon Mulandi, its founder and early promoter. He was born in 1914 at Mukaa in southern Ukamba District, but spent most of his early years with his maternal uncle far to the north at Ngelani, on the edge of Kenya's White Highlands, and it was into this settler world that he ventured at the age of 10. He started as a seasonal labourer picking coffee and later went on to a succession of full-time labouring positions, eventually becoming a cook for his European employer.

During this time he was also attracted to a nearby Catholic school that offered night classes to local farm labourers like himself. Learning to read and write became a great ambition for Mulandi, and when his knowledge outstripped that of his African teachers, he and seven of his mates hired their own tutor, paying him out of their small salaries. Later Mulandi said that these were clearly the formative years in his life, when he gathered many diverse experiences, tested and challenged himself, and developed a love for learning.

It was also during the 1920s that he was challenged personally by Christianity. His first experience came when he talked to a fellow Kamba who was a Salvation Army evangelist. From this conversation and others, Mulandi later reported, 'I heard the call to become a minister.' The next year, 1929, he was accepted by the Salvation Army Officers Training

School in Nairobi. 'We studied Bible lessons all day,' he said, 'and at night we took up things like reading, writing and arithmetic.' He stayed for three years. Mulandi excelled in his studies and upon graduation was posted as a Salvation Army minister to Kakamega, in western Kenya, far from his Kamba home at Ngelani.

He threw himself into his work, and the Salvation Army was very pleased. He became a forceful and compelling preacher, compassionate and approachable by all people. He attracted people wherever he went, and the Salvation Army's work expanded accordingly. Mulandi was able to reach people and affect their lives. In appreciation, the Salvation Army promoted him to the rank of captain. Much later, when he resigned, they were reluctant to let him go and had nothing but good things to say about him.

In the midst of this outward activity and success, Mulandi began to lead a strong interior life. In 1935 he began to have dreams or visions.

> Sometimes they came to me at night, and other times it was as if I were in a trance. I could picture in my mind a new church building and new parishioners. They were in places that were familiar to me, like Ukambani and Mukaa and Ngelani. I sometimes could picture a long motorcade winding its way through the Kamba hills to the opening of some new school or new church.

Later, Mulandi and others maintained that these visions were predictions of the future, and that they all eventually came true, but, at the time, he was troubled and frightened. He told no one of his dreams at first, but eventually he sought guidance by writing to an old friend at Ngelani, Joshua Muoka. When he received no answer to his letter, he wrote again and, much to his relief, six months later his friend sent a short reply that went something like this: 'Thank you very much for your two letters, but I can't reply now. We are in the midst of very difficult times here, and everyone at Ngelani is suspected by the government.' Indeed, in 1938, Ngelani was the site of Kenya's largest peasant protest movement to date.[6] He wrote to another friend from Ngelani and elicited a similar response: 'Your ideas about starting a new church are good, but don't write to me again. Things here are too hot at the moment. Many people have been put in jail, and it is not possible to speak freely.' Mulandi was despondent. He felt compelled by his dreams to do something, and he was also anxious about what was going on in Ngelani 300 miles away.

Then, quite suddenly and without warning, the Salvation Army transferred him to the Kamba district of Machakos. Mulandi was ecstatic at this development and took it as confirmation that God was leading him in his work to establish a new church. When he arrived back home in 1939, he was 25 years old.

He immediately called together his two friends and a number of others to talk about starting a new church. Everybody thought it was a wonderful idea, but they were troubled by two things: first of all, what would the Europeans think about such an idea? Would the establishment of an

African church be interpreted as a political act, and the founders be criminally charged? And, second, how did one actually start a new church? To their knowledge, this had been done only once before, about ten years earlier by Kikuyu, and so they sent some people to Kikuyu to ask how they had started their church. The Kikuyu gave them some books, but they were not very helpful. What they had wanted was a how-to-do-it manual, but such a thing did not exist.

The difficulty of establishing an African church in a colonial society soon became apparent. Mulandi's energy, leadership and commitment, generated by his visions, were simply not sufficient to overcome the obstacles. Later Mulandi recalled, 'I knew that God was calling me to start a church, but the government could put you in jail if they didn't like you,' and two of the five people who were meeting secretly with him were put in jail subsequently. He continued, 'I didn't have degrees. I wasn't very educated. How do you stand up to the government?' He also was afraid that the Salvation Army would hear of his activities and fire him. Mulandi was then married and had five children: 'How was I going to support my family?'

So the group dispersed. Mulandi continued to work for the Salvation Army, and everyone remained quiet about the new church. Mulandi, however, could have no peace: 'I could not get rest in my mind or my soul,' and about eighteen months later he quit the Salvation Army. He confided in several other friends, most of whom thought he was crazy, and he didn't know what to do. The Kenya army was recruiting for the Second World War, and he tried to join, but on the day of his induction he was sick. He then arranged for a well-paid clerical position at the Kenya Meat Commission, just outside Nairobi, but, when he reported for his first day of work, he found they had hired someone else. He finally went back to Nairobi where he was hired as an evangelist by George Rhoad of the Gospel Furthering Fellowship (GFF).

The George Rhoad and Simeon Mulandi Collaboration

Rhoad had first come to Kenya in 1903 under the auspices of AIM, a non-denominational (though largely Baptist) American society that had worked among Kamba since 1895.[7] He had responded to the call for missionaries shortly after the founder of the AIM, Peter C. Scott, had died and the mission was on the verge of collapse. He came as an apprentice, first at Machakos and then at Kangundo, two established mission stations. He learned the Kamba language, gained experience in station management, and then in 1908 went to Mbooni to establish a new AIM station.

In the ensuing years, the Mbooni mission station took impressive shape under Rhoad's direction. Permanent housing was built, first of mud and wattle with thatched roofs, like the Kamba, and then in 1913 an enormous four-bedroom house, which Kamba regarded as a mansion. Kamba donated sun-dried bricks and the mission imported corrugated iron sheets for the roof. About the same time, Rhoad completed a 17-mile highway down Mbooni Hill and linked it to the main highway below that the government had built. This engineering feat endeared Rhoad to the local people; they could now use carts to transport their products to local markets.

Rhoad often helped people in other ways as well. Occasionally he intervened on behalf of Kamba in disputes with colonial chiefs. When government recruiters came to impress people into service as porters during the First World War, he sent them away. He was known as fair-minded, tough and fearless. People considered it a good thing to be his friend.[8] When Rhoad left for his first home leave in 1924, he was already a legend, larger than life and thought by some to be more powerful than the district commissioner.

Rhoad did not return to Kenya until 1936, and then it was as the director of his own maverick organization, the GFF. While on leave he had been suspended for having criticized shortcomings in the AIM leadership.[9]

Word of his activities began to appear in Machakos district administrative reports and correspondence. On 30 November 1937, the district commissioner for Machakos noted: 'Rhoad has applied for what he calls a kiwanzo – a house of prayer and a place of tarrying.'[10] He was turned down because the AIM already had a mission there, and the district commissioner didn't think the area needed another. Rhoad applied on at least three different occasions the following year for such houses of prayer. Perhaps he thought that by calling them houses of prayer instead of missions they would be approved, but he was turned down each time.[11]

The AIM, of course, was delighted because they saw Rhoad as a formidable rival. He had a large Kamba following, and considerable prestige. Among other things, he had translated the entire New Testament into Kamba before he left in 1924.[12] Then in 1938, at the height of the Ngelani protest movement, representatives of the Ukamba Members Association (UMA) asked Rhoad to offer a prayer at the beginning of a meeting between the protesters and the governor of Kenya. He refused, saying that Kamba were able to pray to God themselves and did not need to approach God through missionaries.[13] These words further endeared Rhoad to Kamba. It was this man whom Mulandi now went to work for.

It is possible that Rhoad saw Mulandi as a way to build up his own following among Kamba, perhaps even to gain access to areas that had been denied him formally. For Mulandi, Rhoad's pro-Kamba attitude provided, I suspect, a more propitious atmosphere in which he could think about and plan for his new church.

In the early 1940s, there were increasing numbers of Africans, like Kamba, going to work in Nairobi, and it was to these people that the GFF turned. Rhoad was careful not to give the appearance of competing with other missions because he did not want this niche in Nairobi to be taken away from him.[14] Kamba themselves had also established a number of self-help societies that met together to solve employment, housing and labour problems and to have contact with other Kamba. They immediately caught Mulandi's attention and he felt perhaps the prudent way to begin a new church was first to establish a Kamba society. He had plenty of contacts through Rhoad, and these Kamba societies might provide a nucleus for membership in his church.

In 1942 he started a new organization, the Akamba Christian Union.[15] Members met on Saturdays wherever they could, sometimes in social halls, sometimes even in Rhoad's GFF headquarters, unbeknownst to him. In a year it had a thousand members, and some even carried the association back to Machakos with them when they returned from working in Nairobi. At the end of 1944, Mulandi himself took a month's leave from the GFF and went back to Ukambani to follow up on this rural membership and to begin to lay the foundation for his new church there. Rhoad became increasingly suspicious of Mulandi's activities during this time and, when Mulandi returned to Nairobi, Rhoad confronted him and learned the situation was even worse than he had suspected. Mulandi said, 'I couldn't deny his accusations that I had formed a Kamba association and that most of his Gospel Furthering Fellowship members were now my people, part of this Akamba Christian Union.' In what must have been a tragic moment for Rhoad, he wailed at Mulandi, 'I gave you my sheep to tend, but instead of taking care of them, you stole them.' Though great credit goes to Mulandi for the skill – and guile – with which he piggybacked his new organization on the GFF, Rhoad himself helped contribute to Mulandi's success. He provided ample opportunities for Mulandi to continue to develop his leadership and organizational skills under the protective legitimacy of the GFF, and he encouraged Mulandi's progress. This was no small contribution when colonial society in Kenya continually under-valued and failed to acknowledge African leadership.

A month or so later, Mulandi announced the formation of his new church, the ABC, as we have seen, and, while no one showed up for the inaugural ceremony, the church went on to enjoy great success. Though Mulandi was both energetic and persistent in his attempts to launch his church, this accounts only in part for the readiness with which Kamba identified with his ideas and joined the ABC. To understand this, we must review their reception of the chief Protestant mission in Ukambani, the AIM. While the AIM was by no means a 'spent force' in Ukambani, it was increasingly seen by the Kamba as flawed, perhaps beyond repair.

The AIM in Kamba

For the first 20–25 years, the AIM enjoyed very cordial relations with Kamba. When the founder, Peter Scott, and his party of eight missionaries first arrived in 1895, they immediately set about establishing several stations on land given by local Kamba. The letters that filtered back to

AIM headquarters in Philadelphia were optimistic about the reception they had received and the possibility that Ukambani might become a base for a whole string of AIM stations stretching westwards across the Sudan and into West Africa.[16] Following Scott's death a year later, the mission managed to continue to recruit as missionaries young, energetic men and women very much like its founder. They were full of adventure and comfortable with the challenges of the rugged life on mission stations tucked away in the Kamba hills, two or three days' walk from the next mission station or government post. But they were also very much committed to the primary goal of the AIM, 'saving African souls'.[17]

It becomes clear from government records, however, that these missionaries were also products of their time, which, at the turn of the century, meant they were racist and ethnocentric. They frequently interfered in local affairs of which they showed little understanding and over which they held no jurisdiction. In one case an AIM missionary set himself up as a judge and pocketed the fees he levied against the alleged guilty party. In another case, several missionaries tried to expand their station by force so as to take in the only water supply for miles around. In both cases and several others, local colonial officials were in the rather ironic situation of defending the Kamba against missionaries rather than the other way around.[18]

Such incidents do not exhaust all those in which AIM missionaries breached accepted codes of social behaviour, but in focusing only on such activities we miss the fact that the missionaries often engaged Africans with their message of Christianity. Syo Myove, the first Christian woman at Mbooni, vividly recalled – 71 years later – her first encounters with Rhoad: 'They came riding on donkeys and pitched their tents on the top of Mbooni Hill, which was the place of *Ithembo*, a shrine for the spirits of the community, sacred, and certainly no place for foreigners.' She and some of her friends went to have a closer look at these new strangers. She was about 14 or 15 years old at the time, and these were the first white people she had seen.

> They were very frightening to look at; you could see right through them [blue veins on white skin gave the impression of looking into a person's body]. When we started to run away, Rhoad said to us in the Kamba language, 'Don't be afraid. I will give you the good news of Jesus.' We didn't stop but ran even faster, right through people's gardens and even thorn hedges. We couldn't get away from that 'good news' fast enough.

Later that evening, community elders came around to all those people who had seen Rhoad and smeared their eyes with animal fat. It was a cleansing ritual, used for people who had become impure. Syo Myove said that a diviner was also consulted, and he told the elders to kill a black sheep and sprinkle the blood everywhere the missionaries had walked.[19] Somewhat the same reaction was experienced at Kangundo, an earlier AIM station. There, near the end of the nineteenth century, the missionaries were greeted with a campaign for their removal organized by the area's religious personnel. Elijah Kamenzya, a lifelong resident of Kangundo explained:

> We were taught from a young age that when the missionaries first came here, their presence was not well received by the community. Many people were afraid that the spirits of the ancestors would be angry and so medicine was put all around their compound and on all footpaths where they were walking.[20]

Neither Mbooni nor Kangundo is an isolated example. Most AIM missionaries worked in difficult circumstances, and the people observing them clearly perceived them as a religious threat. Rhoad established Mbooni mission on a local religious site, and the gesture was not lost on the Kamba. They immediately purified anyone who came into contact with Rhoad, even consulting a diviner about what religious responses to take. The Kangundo missionaries elicited a similar response. Clearly, the missionaries were seen as a religious threat, and Kamba responded in kind.

But the missionaries' religious message was still heard by local people. In answer to the question of why she had become a Christian, Syo Myove said that it all started shortly after Rhoad settled at Mbooni. One day she brought him a load of firewood for which Rhoad paid local people. 'He looked at me, and said, "When the dead will be gathered, where will you be?"' She couldn't get that encounter out of her mind. Even later, when she expressed interest in attending church services, her husband beat her, and the community later shunned her and took steps to banish her from Mbooni Hill, she still said, 'I had to become a Christian or I would be lost to God.'[21]

Many other early Christians respond similarly. Ee Itumbuthi, from Mbooni, noted: 'The word of God entered me and I could not let it go.... God caught me, and I started composing songs of praise to God instead of songs for Kamba dancing.'[22] Elijah Mbusu expresses the same idea: 'When I became a Christian, the seed of the gospel was planted in me. I became a preacher straight away even while I was attending catechism class before baptism.'[23] Philip Mule of Mutitu was the oldest living Christian there, having first heard 'the Word' in 1910. He recalls:

> My mother died when she was giving birth to me. I was left only with my father who was taking care of me. While I was yet a boy, the missionaries came to my area and paid my father a visit. I think that they heard the news that there was a child here whose mother had died. They gave my father some cloth and I heard them telling him about someone called Jesus who loves and saves people. Shortly afterward my father died too and I went to live with a relative. While there, the missionaries visited again and they quoted to me John 3:16 what starts out, 'God so loves the world....' The verse pierced my heart; I wanted that God to love me too, so I started attending baptismal classes.[24]

The fact that Kamba heard and responded to a specifically religious message contradicts a large body of historical scholarship which stresses that Africans were attracted to Christianity for the practical benefits that it offered through literacy, access to Western medicine, and sometimes refuge from the harsher demands of colonial society such as forced labour, taxation and the oppressive authority of government chiefs.[25] Clearly, Africans responded to Christianity from a variety of motives, but these cases show the degree to which the missionaries also engaged Kamba with religious symbols and idioms, and Kamba responded accordingly.

These initial encounters produced an 'era of good feelings and harmony' between most missionaries and their early Kamba adherents. The missionaries depended on their followers for a host of station tasks, including the building of churches and schools, production of food, tutorials in the local language and customs, and eventually translating the scriptures. By 1915, the Rhoads and a team of Kamba adherents had managed to produce a Kamba translation of the Gospel of St Mark after collaborating closely for seven years.[26]

For their part, the first Christian enquirers also needed the missionaries. Just as Syo Myove was shunned by the community, adherents everywhere felt their community's wrath for what was considered deviant behaviour. As Simion Kiliku noted, '[You] could not be half-hearted about your Christianity because as soon as you set foot off the mission station, all the surrounding people called you a fool.'[27] Elijah Mbusu relates other aspects of community pressure and its outcome.

> When someone was going to be baptized, everyone came to the dam, including the non-Christians. As the person was led into the water for immersion, these people would begin to chant 'ni wai ma', which means, he is lost to us, or this person has now been contaminated beyond the point of reclamation.... I personally didn't have any second thoughts when this happened to me, but many people wavered when they heard the crowd shouting 'niwaima'.[28]

One person who did have second thoughts was Martha Muthembwa, who came to Mbooni mission from Kangundo.

> Many girls saw me coming to join them [at the mission hostel for girls] and they ran towards me and gave me a warm welcome. The reason why I came here was that at home I had been forced to marry a man not of my choice. My dowry had been paid but still that did not stop me from going to Mbooni.

Martha stayed for two years living in the girls' hostel, going to school and studying the catechism in preparation for baptism. But, on her baptismal day, her Kangundo relatives arrived and persuaded her to return home. 'At the time,' she said, 'I told people that I could not go through with my baptism because I was afraid of drowning while immersed. But everyone knew that it was because I feared my relatives.'[29]

The early missionaries and their adherents thus needed and depended on each other. They shared the crises in each other's lives, provided companionship during times of isolation, guided each other in the mysteries of each other's language and culture, often ate at the same table, and generally knew each other well. This relationship fostered a great deal of self-reliance among Kamba, and, while those at Mbooni occasionally called Rhoad 'father', missionary and adherent often worked together as equals.[30]

By the late 1920s, however, the harmony and equality between missionary and adherent had become seriously eroded. The circumstances of station life had changed significantly. On three of the four main Kamba stations, pioneering missionaries like George Rhoad had either retired, died or been shifted to newer, frontier posts. Only at Machakos did the AIM retain a seasoned and long-term missionary; Mukaa, Mbooni and Kangundo were all staffed with recent recruits. The new arrivals were not sufficiently fluent yet in Kamba, nor had they formed personal friendships with their adherents. Station life had changed too. The days of the isolated missionary were now past, and most AIM stations consisted of several mission families whose friendship with one another soon overtook that with Kamba friends. They became increasingly involved in administrative work as well, with a growing number of outstations, health clinics, printing operations, schools and dormitories to supervise. Their days were spent behind a desk working on the reports and budgets that a growing and better organized AIM bureaucracy demanded.[31] Less contact with Kamba resulted and, even when they did get off their stations, it was usually to go about their business by car. Seldom did they have opportunities to go on the walking tours of their areas that had characterized the early station experience.

The situation had changed for Kamba Christians as well. Many had left the central stations to become teachers and preachers in the outstation network that developed after the First World War. Others, like Ukuu Mukima, entered the cash economy as traders, using agricultural and business skills learned at the mission:

> Two years after I left the mission [Kangundo], I built my present house. I laid the bricks and baked them myself. I was the first person in Matingulu location to build a brick house.... I straightaway took to farming maize at the time. I employed some people to help me in my trade to Thika and Kabaa ... [and] with my profits I bought an iron plow and cultivator and used them on my farm. I also planted my crops in rows; soon my yields were the highest in the district and everyone came to see my farm.[32]

By the 1920s, Christian enquirers did not meet with the same community resistance that earlier adherents had, and therefore there was less need to reside within the protection of a central station community. While the Kamba community had not yet accepted Christianity, nor were there even large numbers of Kamba Christians, a general truce and sometimes co-operation had been established between Christians and their non-Christian neighbours. For instance, Christian marriage became increasingly common, and, while the non-Christian parents and relatives stayed away from the church ceremony, they did negotiate satisfactory bride wealth arrangements for their daughters. To facilitate such arrangements, missionaries occasionally participated in the negotiations and contributed to the dowry.[33]

The girls' hostel at Mbooni had also become less a refuge for Kamba fleeing from family or marriage difficulties and more a girls' dormitory for the school there. After 1930, there were no more recorded instances of angry parents demanding the return of their daughters. In sum, then, by the late 1920s, a period of coexistence and tolerance had developed between Christians and non-Christians; Kamba had acculturated to Christianity to some extent, and more peaceful relations reigned in the Kamba countryside. This *rapprochement* was taking place just at the time that the close and trusting relationship between the missionaries and their adherents were beginning to deteriorate.

Kamba Critique of the AIM

This deterioration was first visible in the area of education. To the AIM, education was a handmaiden to evangelism. Early missionaries at all AIM stations had used schools and the promise of literacy as a technique to reach Kamba with their gospel message. After Rhoad arrived at Mbooni, he lectured the elders of the area on the need to send their children to school. He backed up his appeal with the help of the DC, who also told people that education would serve them well in the colonial world of Kenya.[34] Others resorted to offering a cash payment or a gift of salt to encourage school attendance.[35] Over time, a set of AIM schools did arise, first on the four central stations, and then, by the late 1920s, through the network of outstations. Earlier Kamba hesitancy over the value of education had been replaced with enthusiasm, and the mission was increasingly hearing appeals from Kamba for more and better education.[36]

The system of finance within the AIM, whereby missionaries received stipends from individual congregations in the USA, did not easily permit the financing of this demand for more and larger schools. Furthermore, education as an end in itself was not compatible with the mission's belief that their primary responsibility was evangelism. Kamba began to hear AIM missionaries saying that 'money spent on schools was wasted' and 'we came to preach, not to teach'.[37] Accordingly, AIM schools at Kangundo, Mbooni and Mukaa were all closed in 1927. The mission said that, if local people wanted to pay their teachers' salaries and the general upkeep of the schools, that was fine, but the AIM would no longer finance them. Hoping that the AIM could be persuaded to change its mind later, the elders at Mukaa mission hired a teacher and paid his salary out of their own pockets. Guilding, the station superintendent, was furious, and he brought a case against them for insubordination, saying that all connection between education and the mission must be severed, including links with the local church hierarchy.[38] This was an over-reaction by Guilding, because the AIM had actually hoped that the indigenous church would assume responsibility for education, but for people in Mukaa it represented the growing insensitivity of the AIM to local needs.

In listening to people recount the closing of mission schools in other areas, one realizes that growing Kamba ill-feeling toward the AIM arose not so much because they had to assume responsibility for education as because of the way in which the AIM abruptly closed the schools. There had been little forewarning and no consultation, only the cessation of finances. As a result, all education stopped until local support or appeals to the government could be organized. In the case of Kangundo and Mbooni, schools remained closed for several years before alternative arrangements could be made. The lingering feeling was that the AIM did not have Kamba interests at heart.[39]

As serious as the schools issue was, the greatest strain on Kamba–AIM relations was mission discipline directed against Christians who continued to participate in aspects of Kamba culture. The first decades of mission activity had attracted young people, who often became station residents and almost adopted members of missionaries' families.[40] Though these early adherents reminisce now about how they occasionally stole off to attend local dances or undergo circumcision rites, their adaptation to Western culture often seemed to be complete.[41] But later, when these adherents returned to their home areas as adults, the pull to return to their culture become stronger. And as the mission established its network of out-stations in the 1920s and 1930s, all at some distance from the central station and often under the supervision of Kamba evangelists and teachers, a wider range of people was attracted to Christianity, and those baptized were often adults who were married and had families. As people living in the wider community and under little direct missionary influence and control, they were much freer to interpret Christianity within the context of their own values and beliefs.

To counteract what missionaries thought was an increasing trend among Kamba Christians toward continued practice of older customs, they developed a system of church discipline. At first, people known to have circumcised their sons or daughters, married according to Kamba custom, or even drunk beer were not allowed to lead prayer during church services.

> If such a person came to church and was known by people in the congregation to have committed these sins, they would be shouted down when they attempted to pray. I've witnessed many such cases when such people attempted to pray and they would be told to shut up. When this happened to Mathai [a neighbour], he just continued to pray, even asking that the person asking him to shut up be forgiven.[42]

When polygamists were baptized, they were given only limited church membership and permanently excluded from prayer or preaching. Kamba

Christians who took second wives were excluded in like manner.

Several informants from Kangundu reported that they were similarly disciplined, but not for practising Kamba customs. The Catholic school at Kabaa was close by, and, when the AIM closed all Kagundo area schools in 1927, several families transferred their children there. 'When I took my son to Kabaa, I was both "set aside" from fellowship and removed from my church elder's post.... Catholics were considered to be worthless people.'[43]

Church discipline was further refined to include its most intimidating instrument, the 'black chair'. Philip Mbole of Kikima explained:

> When one sinned, he was punished by being made to sit on a chair that was called the seat of shame that had been especially made higher than the others, painted black, and placed at the front [of the church] before all the others. The person would sit on this chair every Sunday, or when he came for other meetings, until the time allocated to him by the missionaries was over.[44]

There were actually several steps to this discipline. When people committed a 'sin', they first presented themselves to the church elders and missionaries to explain their errors. When known offenders did not come forward voluntarily, they might be accused by others and summoned to the meeting. After hearing their 'sins', the tribunal ordered public confession at the next Sunday service and sentenced the offender to so much time 'in the black chair'. Its word was final: 'No Christian could go against the council's judgment; it had to be accepted and you had to sit on the chair.'[45]

The emphasis was clearly on intimidation and humiliation. 'The offender sat there in front of everyone for many weeks and he had to look sorry for his mistakes.'[46] The person under discipline was even open to ridicule by the non-Christian community. Elijah Mbusu said that, before he became a Christian, he and his age-mates used to go to the AIM church at Mbooni, peek in through the open windows, and laugh at the person sitting on the black chair.[47] Whether the intended goal of church discipline was achieved – forcing people to ally themselves wholly with Western culture – or not is difficult to assess, but people felt shamed by the process. Informants remember that all AIM churches regularly had a number of people being disciplined at any given time well into the 1940s.[48]

If church discipline did not have its desired effect, some unintended effects can be noted. While never challenged directly, the 'black chair' and other forms of discipline caused many Kamba Christians to doubt the wisdom of the missionaries. Sometimes their judgements against people were arbitrary. Young people often found that simply being seen with a girl was considered sufficient evidence to convict one of fornication. This was especially the case if a person or a member of his or her family had previously been disciplined.[49]

Nor were the rules seen to be administered fairly. Simion Kiliku remembered with bitterness that, although he had been disciplined for sending a son to the Catholic school at Kabaa, when several church elders at Kangundo did the same several years later, no notice was taken of their action.[50] All Christians also noted that racial distinctions affected the awarding of discipline. Syo Myove, who had observed activities at Mbooni mission since 1913, had this to say:

> Whites never sat in that black chair and I never saw them publicly repent for their sins. They wanted us to think that they were very holy and devoid of any sin. Just because they brought us the 'good news' doesn't mean that they could not sin.[51]

Still others began to doubt the theological validity of insisting that people confess their sins publicly and then be punished for them. With the New Testament available in Kamba by 1920, Kamba were able to assess missionary decisions for themselves.[52]

> Gradually people came to learn that God is the only judge over people and that once one has repented, then it is between him and God. You can see that these people [the council] were condemning him and that was the work only of God.[53]

Another Kamba Christian came to similar conclusions:

> This punishment or judgment wasn't justified according to the words of God because we read: 'If we confess our sins God is quick to act and has the right to forgive us.' So, according to the scriptures, once one falls into sin and repents, then the Lord forgives him. God, who is full of mercy, receives and welcomes the sinner again to serve him. God never counts our sins.[54]

Several other consequences resulted from church discipline. Many Kamba stopped volunteering their confession of wrongdoing to the church council. 'Many just kept quiet over their sins.... In fear of being taken forward to the black chair to be shamed, many Christians became deceitful; they led a sinful life but admitted to nothing.'[55] Others took more drastic action. Some simply stopped going to church regularly. Others left Christianity altogether. And many left the AIM and looked for alternative church affiliation. Elijah Kamenzya talks about what he did: 'When the Salvation Army came to Kangundo area in 1935, I joined with them; there was no black chair in that church. I stayed with them for more than ten years.'[56] For Simion Kiliku, the solution to his disenchantment with the AIM after being disciplined for sending his son to the Catholic school at Kabaa was to abjure membership in any church.

> It was at this time that the Salvation Army came to Tala and I went all the way there for services. I never, however, became a member of that church but just attended services there. I counted myself more a 'free' Christian, not officially a member of any church.[57]

Other AIM drop-outs joined the Seventh Day Adventists, and a few even attended Catholic services nearby. For the most part, however, most

Kamba Christians kept their AIM affiliation and did not let their growing disenchantment with the mission show, waiting and hoping for something better.

ABC Beginnings

Though Kamba had numerous grievances against the AIM and were thus ready to hear Mulandi's message of a new African-run church, they were slow to join his ABC. As the original Nairobi group of stalwarts returned to their home areas in Ukambani, they talked to their neighbours and friends about the ABC. Several of these first crusaders of the ABC describe the tactics for attracting members:

> Those of us 'free Christians' at Kangundo rejoiced at hearing about the ABC. We took it upon ourselves to spread the word about this new church. We preached the whole day and the next too, and the next week and still the next one after that. With time women started coming and then their children. We sat under the trees at Kathithyamaa market or spent the day at the river where women were drawing water and children were playing. We did everything we could to persuade people to join [the ABC]. At first we met for services in people's houses. It took some time before we had enough people to build a church; we contributed money for the nails and cut down trees for the construction.[58]

The Salvation Army at Tala and Mbilini even permitted ABC 'information' meetings to be held in their churches, though this was not at all typical.[59]

While it took several years before the ABC had a network of churches among the Kamba, their schools met with instant success. A number of files in the Kenya National Archives are filled with ABC applications for school plots all over the district, applications sometimes made long after the schools had been started. A number of letters were exchanged between the Machakos district commissioner and Mulandi about what the commissioner called this 'back door method' of getting into the district, applying only after the school had been there for a year or two. But the commissioner grudgingly approved them because he knew the government could not meet the Kamba demand for education, and the AIM record for doing so was very poor.[60] So a number of Kamba joined the ABC as a means of fulfilling their educational needs, and Mulandi's schools became very popular.

Initial Kamba caution about joining the ABC was largely the result of the acrimony between the AIM and the first proponents of the ABC. The AIM viewed Mulandi and his church as malcontents out to destroy the AIM.[61] They told their congregations to avoid these 'evil' people, their leader and the organization. At both Kangundo and Machakos, whole Sunday sermons were taken up with the idea that people who associated with the ABC could not be considered Christians.[62] Clearly, the AIM identified Mulandi and his church as rivals to be thwarted at every turn. Mulandi, in an uncharacteristically sharp letter, demanded that the AIM station superintendent at Machakos stop repeating false rumours about him. He ended his letter by saying, 'if everyone behaved as you have, Satan would [be able to] carry out his work among us to the destruction of God's work'.[63] Other letters give further examples of mission ill will. In one case, an AIM adherent sat on the local education board and consistently vetoed all ABC applications for schools in that part of Ukambani.[64] In another, the local government chief harassed ABC evangelists and members.[65] The AIM grudge against the ABC was still visible in the mid-1960s, when the AIM rudely refused to sponsor the ABC for membership in the National Christian Council of Kenya, even though the ABC had become a well-established church in Kenya with a membership of 25,000 or more.[66]

The mission was correct in identifying the ABC as a threat to their long-established work in Ukambani. The first centres established by the ABC were immediately adjacent to the oldest AIM stations at such places as Mbooni, Kangundo, Mukaa and Machakos, and large numbers of AIM Christians crossed over to Mulandi's church. Sometimes AIM church elders became interested in the ABC and began to talk among themselves. On hearing this, the AIM missionary would call them in, tell them that they would be stricken from the church's rolls if they continued to talk about the ABC, and inform them they would probably go to hell as well. Following such threats, the elders often crossed over and joined the local ABC church. To a considerable extent then, the AIM interpreted the ABC as a divisive secessionist movement. To them the ABC was anti-mission, and they rightly interpreted its growth and development as a criticism of them.

The ABC was also a reaction to the AIM's policy of valuing education only in its service to evangelism. The small, thatched one- and two-room schools, where Bible lessons dominated the curriculum, might have been adequate for the first adherents, but, by the 1940s, Kamba wanted more; they wanted a literary education, and they wanted it taught in English.[67] This was much more than the AIM was prepared to offer and, as we have seen, they had withdrawn financing from many of their schools. When Mulandi opened schools under ABC auspices, then, Kamba were attracted, and ABC schools immediately grew into a large educational network for the church. The opening of a divinity Bible school at Mitaboni in 1950 and the subsequent ability to secure training for some of its pastors at St Paul's United Theological College at Limuru, as well as colleges and universities abroad, were received with immense popularity.

Finally, and most clearly, the emergence of the ABC was a reaction to alienation created by the AIM's attitude toward Kamba culture. Mulandi himself commented on this: 'To conform to all the missionary teachings forced one to become unAfrican. To be a Christian in the AIM and other missions meant that you always had to be apologizing for being an African.'

All informants were adamant on this point, that the European-led churches made little attempt to understand Kamba traditions. Their idea of a good Christian was someone who broke all his or her ties with African traditions, and this alienated many people. The example cited most often by informants was polygamy. All felt that some consideration had to be given to Christian enquirers who had more than one wife. The AIM acted, they said, as if they didn't even know the Kamba practised polygamy. Was it not possible for such people both to be loyal to their traditions and to be good Christians too? The AIM thought not, with the result that the 'Good News' to polygamists became bad news. They would not be accepted into the church unless they disposed of all but their first wife.

Another source of dispute was the AIM's insistence that couples, upon becoming Christians, had to be remarried in church before being legitimately considered husband and wife. Syo Myove was baffled about this need to be remarried. She had a running battle over the issue with several missionaries at Mbooni, starting with Rhoad. She argued, 'Either you're married or you're not. Everyone knows that I've been married to Myove for my whole life. How is a wedding in church between two already married people going to change anything?' But finally, in her old age, she consented, and in the early 1960s was remarried, but she was still clucking about it in 1979 when I talked with her.[68] In contrast, the missionary Mrs Schellenberg, who had coaxed Syo Myove into a church wedding fifteen years earlier and who helped translate for me that day, continued to express satisfaction over her accomplishment. Following the interview, she said to me in the car on the way back to Machakos, 'Oh, David, I wish you could have seen that wedding. It was so beautiful to see those two old sinners married.'[69] Such sentiments irritated Syo Myove and many other Kamba Christians, even when uttered by a respected missionary like Mrs Schellenberg.

Church discipline also alienated many people, as we have seen. Mulandi said that by the 1940s there were so many people under church discipline that they were becoming increasingly alienated from Christianity. They were, to use his words, 'left out in the cold, like sheep without a shepherd. They were people, according to the AIM, who were not considered fit for church membership.' He felt an enormous burden to reach such people.

The birth of the ABC can be seen, then, as a reaction to the missionary atmosphere in which Kamba lived. But to view it only as an agency of protest against the AIM or as an organization involved in mobilizing people for nationalistic purposes is to underestimate the church and its members. Surely its remarkable growth in the last 50 years cannot only be attributed to people continuing to flee the AIM, a mission that has now surrendered authority to its national and African-led church, the Africa Inland Church (AIC). What political motivation can there be now for joining the ABC, when Kenya has been an independent country since 1963? Indeed, the very notion of the ABC as an independent church is largely redundant in the 1990s, since, as religious scholar Andrew Walls states, 'Nowadays most

African churches are independent in the sense that their leadership is African, their ministry overwhelmingly African and missionary direction minimal.'[70]

The ABC as a 'Political' Church

While the AIM failed to stem the tide to the ABC, it was the colonial government's suspicion that caused the most concern among Kamba enquirers of the ABC. Initially the government had no evidence of ABC wrongdoing, but, in a colonial environment as politicized as Kenya's, it presumed the church to be politically motivated by the simple fact that it was initiated and run by Africans. Its independence from recognized and approved mainline mission churches made it automatically suspect in the government's view. Indeed, the government, like the AIM, immediately came to the conclusion that the ABC was directed against them. So, at the very outset, the ABC was presumed to be nationalistic and anti-government.

One piece of evidence that seems to establish a connection between the ABC and Kenya nationalism was its association with the insurgent forces that came to be known as 'Mau Mau'. The official government report of the rebellion, written after it ended in 1960, asserts that, after Kikuyu, it was Kamba who were most heavily involved in the rebellion, and several Kamba areas participated in oath taking, Ngelani among them.[71]

While ABC members admit to some nationalist and anti-government links, their interpretation of the church's role differs from that of the government or AIM. For some, the church was simply an opportunity to do something on their own and claim credit for it. Simion Kiliku explains:

> We had a chance to stand up and start our own church. I was convinced that this salvation for Africans was good because we could show everyone in Kenya [meaning whites] that we could preach the gospel just like anyone else.[72]

To Simion Kiliku, the ABC, then, was an opportunity for Africans to demonstrate their equality with Europeans. In answer to a question as to whether the ABC was political, John Kivati, an early leader and the ABC's first treasurer, responds:

> Many people like teachers and clerks, people who were politically aware, were among the first to join ABC. But they didn't talk politics in the church; nobody wanted politics in the church, and these people didn't join the ABC on political grounds. They joined it because it was a church run by Africans for Africans.[73]

One of the first ABC churches to grow very quickly was at Mitaboni. This was Mulandi's home area and it is natural to assume that he attracted a strong response there. But there was a political connection too, as Nathan Ngala, Bishop of the ABC, explains:

Initially, our greatest response was from Mitaboni. Our chairman [Mulandi] was from there and he had many followers. But an even greater reason was that Mitaboni had been the headquarters of the organization[74] that had been protesting for cattle; those who had belonged to it could see the reason for our church very clearly when it came. They joined because they knew how to be independent.[75]

The argument, then, is that an African-led church was attractive to politically aware people, but that did not make the church political of itself.

Some evidence, however, does link the ABC to the Kikuyu Independent Schools Association (KISA). KISA had initiated and maintained a network of several dozen schools in the Kikuyu area north of Ukambani for more than 15 years. After the Second World War, it participated in the rural radicalism taking place in Kikuyu by allowing its schools to be used as political meeting places.[76] It was this organization to which Mulandi allied the ABC in 1950. In a short time there were five KISA schools under ABC management, the flagship institution being at Kathithymaa. Teacher recruitment was assisted by KISA, and Kamba were guaranteed access to Githunguri Teacher Training College, a KISA institution in Kiambu.[77] According to the Machakos District Education Office, these schools refused government grants-in-aid and relied entirely on KISA funding.[78] A KISA pamphlet published about 1952 claimed ABC-affiliated schools as their own.[79]

Oath taking against the colonial government as a sign of unity with the insurgent forces of Mau Mau apparently took place at the ABC school at Kathithymaa. Chief Ukuu Mukima had suspected this for some time, and he attempted to halt Kamba participation by force:

> I asked people to stop completely their involvement in Mau Mau business [oath taking]. They refused. I then forced as many as I could find at Ngelani to come to a certain meeting. There I made them take one of the most serious Kamba oaths against participation in Mau Mau.[80]

The government decided to take its own action as well, and a short time later, in October 1952, the police raided Kathithymaa school and detained several teachers, members of the school committee, and John Kivati, its chairman and treasurer. He was charged with being the chief administrator of Mau Mau oaths in the area and generally someone who was working to overthrow the colonial government by force.[81] What was most damning to the ABC was the fact that Kivati was closely tied to it, not only as a member of the church and director and treasurer of some of its schools, but also as a personal friend and confidant of Mulandi.[82]

These revelations fuelled further attacks on the church by its critics. In some areas of Ukambani, the ABC was publicly called the 'Mau Mau church'. Samuel Mangaya, an observer of these events and later an ABC pastor, comments:

> Even though these were difficult times for the ABC, when the AIM

missionaries at Kangundo and Machakos were spreading tales that the whole church was just a front for Mau Mau, we persevered because we knew that it wasn't true. We were a Christian church following God.[83]

The government ultimately came to a similar conclusion. No other schools or churches were closed, and no more ABC members were detained. The one exception was in nearby Kitui district where a government chief and AIM elder managed to close down all ABC churches until 1960 on the pretext that they were involved in Mau Mau. The fact that the AIM absorbed these churches as their own prompted quite a controversy when the ABC was permitted to reestablish its work in the district after 1960. The AIM did not wish to give up the church buildings and the ABC, and large numbers of local ABC members, claimed them as their own.[84]

In sum, then, while the ABC can be seen as a reaction to the colonial circumstances in which Kamba lived, it was not overtly political. While some members of the church were politically as well as spiritually aware, and they clearly were interested in carrying out both political and religious activity through their membership in the ABC, to label it the 'Mau Mau church' seems more a reflection of the AIM's effort to discredit the ABC than an accurate description of the ABC itself. Evidence of this can be seen in the fact that Willington Mulwa, one of the ABC teachers employed at the Kathithymaa school that the government closed, later became headmaster of the AIM high school at Kangundo and eventually president of the mission-created Africa Inland Church (AIC).[85]

The Appeal of the African Brotherhood Church

The appeal of the ABC, then, must be seen in its efforts to meet people's needs. First was its inclusiveness and friendliness. From the beginning Mulandi said that the ABC was open to all, regardless of ethnicity, denomination or status. It was a place free from rivalry, a place where people were accepted regardless of their ideas, their practices or their short-comings. And, even to this day, the ABC has a reputation for being open to everyone. All are welcome at their services, and one will always be dealt with politely. So-called 'backsliders in the faith' are quietly visited by neighbours, friends and church elders, and are earnestly persuaded to return to fellowship, but there is no public confession or punishment, no refusal of communion, no excommunication.[86]

The ABC also promotes unity and fellowship among themselves and projects this image to the public in general. Barrett highlights this characteristic as common among many independent churches: '*Philadelphia* or brotherly love is seen as the Christian version of African traditional values of corporate life, community, group solidarity, hospitality and the like.'[87] The concept is embodied in the word 'Brotherhood' in the church's name.

The church's promise of unity and fellowship met a strong need among

Kamba that was not being met through the former structures of society embodied in clans, lineage and extended families as colonial and missionary forces diminished the effectiveness of these communities and occasionally destroyed them. Colonial economics, with its emphasis on European plantations and export commodities, took men and boys, and occasionally women, away from their homes for long periods of time for contract labour. Mission-sponsored Western education and colonial society created a new elite of educated people no longer comfortable in traditional society, and yet also alienated from their new-found status and residence.

Unity and fellowship were also directed against the competitive nature of denominationalism that existed in Ukambani. The AIM taught that Catholics were not true Christians. One AIM prayer letter records: 'We learned that Satan is not inactive in our locality for those with false ways have crept in ... all over there are reports of the deadly work of the Romanists....'[88] By contrast an ABC pastor notes:

> Brotherhood means that you can't snatch away Christians from other denominations.... If people join ABC from other denominations, no backbiting is permitted. It would be like biting yourself since we are all part of God's big family.... ABC wants to unite Kamba Christians.... Christianity in Ukambani is like a large extended family. Some belong to the family as Catholics, Salvation Army, AIM, and so on. In the past, none of these would pray or even eat together; there was much enmity and divisiveness. The ABC says that we are all part of the family of God and therefore there should be unity.[89]

There are a number of indications that the idea of unity has been put into practice. Father John O'Mahon, a Catholic priest from the Mbitini area of Ukambani, said in 1979 that the ABC stress on unity and fellowship among all Christians had certainly promoted ecumenism in his area. Most of the parishes in which he served were situated in communities with several other churches, the ABC among them.

> I have been surprised and pleased at the harmony with which all of these churches work together. They regularly visit the sick, share in joint services and generally tackle community problems together. The ABC has given good leadership and a good example in this regard.[90]

There is another indication that the ABC actively promotes harmony and unity among its members and that they live peacefully with the results. By the 1970s, perhaps earlier, a few members of the ABC had switched to other denominations, usually for the sake of convenience. Perhaps the best example is J. M. Kyoyo, who left the AIM as an adult in 1946 to join Mulandi's new church, eventually becoming a pastor who took the church to many remote areas of Ukambani. Then, upon retirement in 1975, he rejoined the AIC, where he regularly officiates, because that was the church closest to his home. Even upon close questioning in 1979, when I interviewed him, I could uncover no other motive than convenience. Neither he nor his close friends, most of whom were ABC members, thought this switch was remarkable.[91] *Philadelphia* is more than just an attractive concept to the ABC, but a goal that has been realized in its dealings with other churches. In particular, the acrimony that characterized its early relations with the AIM seems to be no longer present.

But there is a strength and determination for success in the ABC that is visible even beyond their central ideas of unity and brotherhood. It is perhaps most apparent in the continued smooth running of the church, despite the change of leadership that took place before the church was a decade old. In 1950, Mulandi allegedly impregnated a woman and then later took her as a second wife. Mulandi's assistants, who had begun to act as a church council, confronted him with the impropriety of his actions, saying that, while polygamy was no reason for exclusion from membership in the ABC, his actions had been sinful and were not appropriate for the head of the church. Mulandi agreed and resigned his post in April 1951. But a year later, after some reflection and the encouragement of his friends at Ngelani, especially John Kivati, he returned to the council and asked Nathan Ngala, his former assistant and now the head of the church, to be restored as head. There followed an acrimonious exchange of letters between both Mulandi and Ngala and Mulandi and the local district commissioner. To Ngala he wrote:

> Take note that I am the founder of ABC and you are just employed as an evangelist. You have no rank whatsoever of working under the name ABC... My letter [of resignation] is hereby cancelled and I am from this date forth the Founder and Minister in Charge of ABC.[92]

Two weeks later, Ngala answered Mulandi saying that his resignation was the appropriate course of action and that he should not change his mind:

> It is good for you to retire because of your sins: fornication with a sick young girl entrusted to you ... which you denied for four months, then admitted. Since then, you have gone with prostitutes.... You are destroying the work of ABC and its peace.[93]

Within the same week, Mulandi received a final letter from the DC, to whom he had repeatedly written to approve his return to ABC. The DC did not mince his words:

> Please note that until such time as any change is made in the ABC constitution, the Rev. Nathan Ngala will continue to be regarded as the Minister-in-Charge by myself and other Departments in Machakos district. The kind of unilateral action you are at present taking cannot possibly be recognized by any responsible body, and I must warn you that if you continue to act in this way you are likely to cause harm to the ABC, whose interests, I know you have very much at heart.[94]

No answer to these letters is recorded, and apparently Mulandi departed without pursuing his case further to work for ten years as a foreman on a succession of European farms. Then in 1962, a young ABC pastor located Mulandi and persuaded him to return to the ABC. As J. M. Kyoyo recalls:

> I found Mulandi at the Anglo-French sisal estate at Thika. At this time, he had married five wives, three of whom were still alive.... After supper, we talked late into the night about how all the good that he had done in starting the ABC would be gone unless he reformed his life, stopped drinking and marrying more wives.... From that day, Mulandi repented and I prayed with him.[95]

Ngala, then Bishop of the ABC, did not welcome Mulandi back, nor did he give him a post in the church as Kyoyo had hoped. In response, Mulandi started the Church of the East African Society (CEAS) on a piece of land at Tala donated by his old friend, John Kivati. Mulandi built his new church to nearly a dozen congregations, and a number of ABC members in the Tala area joined him, but in 1967 he was persuaded by Kyoyo to lead the churches back into the ABC, which he did. He did not interfere in ABC operations after that, and is said to have died in the mid-1970s.[96]

How does one explain why Mulandi should let the ABC slip away from his grasp, not once but twice, without a fight? Often the founders of independent churches have retained tight control of their creations, and competition over leadership has frequently resulted in splits among potential claimants. But the ABC has remained whole. Twice within fifteen years Mulandi departed without seriously contesting the leadership or fracturing the church. The answer to this problem that is most generous to Mulandi suggests that he avoided this course of action simply because he did not want to split the church. Both Ngala and the Machakos DC in their letters appealed to his sense of what was right and suggested that his quiet departure would be best for the welfare of the whole Church. Many people within the ABC reinforce this view by generally stating that Mulandi always sought what was good for the Church, and that he sacrificed his leadership ambitions for the sake of the Church.[97] By contrast, Bishop Ngala takes a less sympathetic view. When asked in 1979 why Mulandi left, he said that Mulandi was simply embarrassed about his sexual misconduct.[98]

There is a ring of truth to each of these views regarding Mulandi's departure. He appears to have been gentle and earnest in his endeavours with people throughout his life. Neither his correspondence nor his actions reveal an ego in need of constant gratification that might have prevented him from giving up his leadership without a fight. But several other factors were also relevant. Mulandi's strengths were clearly as a preacher, not as an administrator. All who knew him were attracted to his preaching. The Salvation Army, his first mission employer, sent him on preaching tours to western Kenya and promoted him because of his success there. Informants report that AIM adherents regularly left the comfort of their churches to listen to Mulandi in the open air. Years later, when he came out of retirement to create the CEAS, he drew crowds outside even in bad weather.

His style was simple, direct and spellbinding.[99] Even George Rhoad, who had a great reputation as a preacher himself, respected Mulandi's preaching skills.[100]

But, while dynamic preaching helped establish the ABC and attract its first members, the Church's rapid growth increasingly placed demands on his administrative skills as well. Soon there were schools and churches to organize, permits to obtain from the government for plots of land, new clergy to recruit and train, finances to raise and bills to pay. Mulandi is not remembered for his organizational ability, and apparently many of these duties were handed over to his assistant, Ngala. Ngala also coordinated the informal council of elders that advised Mulandi and occasionally acted on his behalf in official matters with the government.[101] He also supervised the building and administration of the divinity school at Mitaboni.[102]

Mulandi was clearly not in charge of all aspects of the ABC. He actually reported in another letter to Ngala that he had had a dream, which he interpreted as coming from God, in which he was advised to leave the ABC and move on to other pursuits.[103] Perhaps the dream indicated some level of recognition that he was not quite up to the job and that Ngala had the ABC organization well in hand. This certainly seems to be the case in the late 1960s, when Mulandi gave up his CEAS churches to Ngala without a struggle.

Another factor that helps explain Mulandi's departure from ABC leadership concerns the church's link with political activities, especially during the period just before the Emergency was declared in 1952. Mulandi was clearly aware of the appeal that an African church, independent from any mission, would have for politically aware Kamba. It is widely believed by Kamba that Mulandi purposely chose to announce the beginning of the ABC at the very site in Nairobi where Ukamba Members Association (UMA) leaders had been arrested in 1940.[104] Ngelani, the most militant area during the 1936–7 Kamba cattle protest and the organizational headquarters of the UMA, was also the site of the first ABC congregation in Ukambani. The connections between the ABC and the now illegal UMA did not escape the government's notice either; informers regularly reported on ABC activities.[105]

But it was the ABC's independent schools that could have landed Mulandi in the most trouble. In the months just before the declaration of the Emergency in October, a number of these schools were used for oath giving and money raising. And some teachers and students joined the insurgent forces forming in Kenya's forests during this time. Though there is no direct evidence available, Mulandi's hasty departure from his post at this very time may indicate his recognition of his vulnerability of being implicated in these anti-government activities. As Minister-in-Charge of ABC, he might well have thought that he would be held responsible for the behaviour of his associates, like John Kivati, and the activities taking place on ABC premises. As a result, he could have thought that his resignation from the ABC and exit from Ukambani was a prudent action to take.

The details of Mulandi's activities are worth pursuing because they demonstrate the strength of the ABC. Even though the ABC's origins and early development clearly reflected Mulandi's vision, leadership and hard work, the church was able to transcend his personal involvement when he left in 1951 and again in 1967. The appeal of Mulandi's message and the church he founded was clearly greater than that of the founder, and the Kamba need for a church of their own was stronger than their need for a single and continuous leader. Expressed another way, Mulandi's vision of a church run by Africans, independent from mission control, had mobilized commitment on such a large scale that, when Mulandi resigned the church, it remained faithful to its original purpose.

Notes

1 William B. Anderson, 'Feeling after God', unpublished manuscript, n.d. Unless otherwise cited, the material concerning Simeon Mulandi and the beginnings of the African Brotherhood Church comes from oral evidence collected by myself in 1979 or by others at an earlier time. My own interviews concerning this topic are the following: James Kyoyo, 26 June, 15 July and 20 July 1979; Bishop Nathan K. Ngala, 30 May and 25 June 1979; Wilson Musyoka Mbelenzi, 1 June 1979. Since Simeon Mulandi was no longer living in 1979, I am indebted to William Anderson, tutor at St Paul's Theological College, Limuru, Kenya, who shared with me the interviews that one of his students had conducted with Mulandi: Simeon Mulandi, interviewed by Jasper Kioko, 15, 16, 17 December 1969.
2 Harold W. Turner, *Religious Innovation in Africa* (Boston, 1979), 185.
3 David B. Barrett, in *Encyclopedia Dictionary of Religion* (Washington, 1979), Paul Kevin Mecgher *et al.*, (eds), A-E:65.
4 'The African Brotherhood Church', *Ecumenical Review*, 24 (1972), 145–9.
5 Adrian Hastings, *A History of African Christianity 1950–1975* (Cambridge, 1979), 255.
6 Jeremy R. Newman, *Ukamba Members Association* (Nairobi, 1974).
7 This entire section on George Rhoad is based upon the reading of his personal file at AIM headquarters. George Rhoad and GFF Files, AIM Archives (AIM), Billy Graham Center, Wheaton College, Wheaton, IL.
8 Syo Myove, 8 August 1979.
9 Minutes of the Committee of Direction, December 1, 1925, GFF File, AIM.
10 George Rhoad to District Commissioner, Machakos, 30 November 1937, 'Land For Missions, 1929–1948', DC/MKS 17/4, Kenya National Archives (KNA).
11 District Commissioner, Machakos, to Provincial Commissioner, Nyeri, 28 June 1938, 'Land For Missions, 1929-1948', DC/MKS 17/4, KNA.
12 Geraldine E. Coldham (compiler), *A Bibliography of Scriptures in African Languages* (London, 1966), 269.
13 F. A. Okwemba, 'The foundation and development of the African Brotherhood Church' unpublished manuscript, nd.
14 Kenya Missionary Council to Colonial Secretary, Secretariat, Nairobi, 17 February 1937, 'Land For Missions, 1929–1948', DC/MKS 17/4, KNA.
15 District Commissioner, Nairobi to Criminal Investigation Department, Nairobi, 9 September 1943, 'Native Associations, 1938–1950', PC/CP 8/5/4, KNA.
16 In the first issues of this AIM journal, long sections are devoted to the establishment of the mission in East Africa. *Hearing and Doing*, 1895–1900.
17 For a fuller description of AIM doctrine, see Richard Waller, Chapter 5 in this volume, and David Sandgren, *Christianity and the Kikuyu* (New York, 1989), 17–25.
18 Machakos Political Record Book II, PC/CP 1/3/2, KNA.

19 Syo Myove, 22 June 1979.
20 Elijah Kamenzya, 21 August 1979.
21 Syo Myove, 8 August 1979.
22 Ee Itumbuthi, 12 July 1979.
23 Elijah Mbusu, 22 August 1979.
24 Philip Mule, 23 August 1979.
25 For example, see Frederick Welbourn, *East African Christian* (London, 1965); Marshall Murphee, *Christianity and the Shona* (London, 1969); Robert Strayer, *The Making of Mission Communities in East Africa* (London, 1978).
26 Unfortunately, unknown to them, J. L. Kraft had made a Kamba translation of the same gospel in 1850. Coldham, *Bibliography of Scriptures*, 268–9.
27 Simion Kiliku, 21 August 1979.
28 Elijah Mbusu, 22 August 1979.
29 Martha Muthembwa, 14 August 1979.
30 Philip Mule, 23 August 1979.
31 By the late 1920s not only had the volume of mission correspondence accelerated, but reminders from headquarters for overdue reports had started to become more frequent too.
32 Ukuu Mukima, 11 August 1979.
33 Martha Muthembwa, 14 August 1979.
34 John Muthembwa, 14 August 1979.
35 J. Forbes Munro, *Colonial Rule and the Kamba* (Oxford, 1975), 107; John Muthenbwa, 14 August 1979.
36 A number of informants said that after the First World War it was common on preaching tours to outlying areas to encounter requests for schools even before the need for a church was spoken about. Ee Itumbuthi, 13 August 1979; Aarun Kivuva, 20 August 1979; Joel Mulwa, 14 August 1979.
37 Aarun Kivuva, 20 August 1979.
38 Nathan Ngala, 25 June 1979.
39 Aarun Kivuva, 20 August 1979.
40 One informant described Chief Kala, raised at the AIM station at Kijabe and the first Christian chief of Kangundo, as 'one of those old Christians who believed in himself pure of Kamba traditions'. Simion Kiliku, 16 August 1979.
41 Ee Itumbuthi, 16 August 1979; Syo Myove, 16 August 1979.
42 Simion Kiliju, 21 August 1979.
43 Elijah Kamenzya, 24 August 1979. See also Simion Kiliku, 21 August 1979.
44 Philip Mule, 23 August 1979.
45 Ee Itumbuthi, 16 August 1979.
46 *Ibid.*
47 Elijah Mbusu, 22 August 1979.
48 John Taylor in his study of the Ganda church notes a similar phenomenon. *Growth of the Church in Buganda* (London, 1958), 97.
49 Nathan Ngala, 25 June 1979.
50 Simion Kiliku, 21 August 1979.
51 Syo Myove, 16 August 1979.
52 Coldham, *Bibliography of Scriptures*, 269.
53 Syo Myove, 16 August 1979.
54 Ee Itumbuthi, 16 August 1979.
55 *Ibid.*
56 Elijah Kamenzya, 21 August 1979.
57 Simion Kiliku, 28 August 1979.
58 Simion Kiliku, 21 August 1979.
59 *Ibid.*
60 See especially Simeon Mulandi to District Commissioner, Machakos, 28 April 1945, 14 July 1945, 24 October 1945, 3 April 1947, 9 May 1947, 'Land For Missions, 1929–1948', DC/MKS 17/4, KNA.
61 Linell Davis, 20 February 1974. I wish to thank J. Newman for kindly allowing me to read and use this interview and the one with John Kivati cited below.

62 Samuel Mangaya, 11 July 1979.
63 Simeon Mulandi to Nixon, Superintendent AIM, Machakos, 29 February 1945, Letter File No. 1, ABC Archives (ABC), Mitaboni, Kenya.
64 Kitui African District Council Minutes, 1 May 1952, KNA.
65 Simeon Mulandi to District Commissioner, Kitui, 17 February 1948, Letter File No. 1, ABC.
66 Mrs. Schellenberg, 22 June 1979; NCCK to Bishop N. Ngala 19 February 1966, Letter File No. 2, ABC.
67 African Inland Missions/Kangundo to District Commissioner, Machakos, 24 July 1945, 'Land for Missions, 1937–1951', DC/MKS 17/8, KNA.
68 Syo Myove, 22 June 1979.
69 Mrs Schellenberg, 22 June 1979.
70 Andrew Walls, 'The Anabaptists in Africa: the challenge of the African Independent Churches', *Occasional Bulletin of Missionary Research*, 3 (April 1979), 49.
71 Corfield, F. D. *Historical Survey of The Origins and Growth of Mau Mau* (London, 1960), 204.
72 19 February 1966, Letter File No. 2, ABC.
73 John M. Kivati, 10 December 1973.
74 This was the Ukamba Members Association, begun in 1937 to protest against the colonial government's plan of forced destocking of the Kamba District. For a full account, see Newman, *Ukamba Members Association*.
75 Nathan Ngala, 25 June 1979.
76 Carl Rosberg and John Nottingham, *The Myth of 'Mau Mau'*, (New York, 1966), Chapter 7.
77 Chief Savano, 15 August 1979.
78 Machakos District Annual Report, 1951, DC/MKS, 1/130, KNA.
79 D. M. Kiragu, *Kiria Giatumire Independent Igie* (Independent Church Origins) (Nairobi, nd).
80 Ukuu Mukima, 11 August 1979.
81 Machakos District Annual Report, 1952, KC/MKS 1/1/30, KNA.
82 John Kivati, 10 December 1973.
83 Samuel Mangaya, 11 July 1979.
84 *Ibid.*
85 John Kivati, 10 December 1973.
86 Unless otherwise cited, the last section of this chapter is based upon interviews with Bishop N. K. Ngala, 30 May and 25 June 1979.
87 David B. Barrett, *Schism and Renewal in Africa* (Nairobi, 1968), 168.
88 Bulletin No. 3, October 1936, Prayer Letter File, AIM.
89 Samuel Mangaya, 11 July 1979.
90 Fr John O'Mahon, 17 July 1979.
91 J. M. Kyoyo, 26 June 1979.
92 Samuel Mangaya, 11 July 1979.
93 J. M. Kyoyo, 26 June 1979.
94 DC/MKS to S. Mulandi, 16 September 1952, DC/KTI/3/7/25, KNA.
95 J. M. Kyoyo, 26 June 1979.
96 *Ibid.*
97 James Kyoyo, 15 July 1979.
98 Nathan Ngala, 30 May 1979.
99 P. E. N. Hellsten, 'African Brotherhood Church and its role in social and religious change: preliminary reach findings of field research in Kenya, June–July 1969', translated from Swedish by Maud Andersson, 1996, 76.
100 James Kyoyo, 15 July 1979.
101 ABC to D.C. Machakos, 1 August 1949, DC/MKS/2/17/4, KNA.
102 Nathan Ngala, 30 May 1979.
103 Mulandi to ABC Council, 22 June 1951, DC/KTI/3/7/25, KNA.
104 Hellsten, 'African Brotherhood Church', 31.
105 Director of Security to Chief Secretary, MAA 2/122 1943-58, KNA.

Nine

The Making
of an Independent Church
The Case of the African Missionary
Evangelical Church among the Meru of Tanzania

C. K. OMARI

Independent church movements have existed in Africa for over a century now. The pioneering work of Bengt Sundkler in southern Africa opened the door for many other works on the subject, and his focus on the independent churches as rebellions against the dominance of missionary churches and the impact of 'racial discrimination upon the life of the Christian Church' has strongly influenced succeeding studies.[1] Later studies of the subject, however, have focused more on local African elements. David Barrett's analysis of six thousand independent churches throughout Africa, focused on local churches, leadership and liturgical practices in addition to mission ones, sought to identify the independent churches with their tribal contexts on the basis that 'the tribe has been for centuries past and to a large degree is still today the main social, psychological, economic and even governmental reality' for these churches.[2] In this respect, the study of independent churches reveals much about the indigenous identities, beliefs and practices among these churches, such as their use of local languages in the Bible, hymns, prayers, worship and communication in general. Furthermore, cultural traits and practices used by traditional religions have been adopted and become part of Christian worship. Barrett's conclusion that 'the background conceptive factors of independency are largely unchanged by the coming to power of Africans in church or state' may be challenged, however, when we examine local church schisms and breakaway churches whose theological or ethnic backgrounds are the same as those of the churches which they have left.[3]

This chapter examines the recent emergence of just such an independent church, the African Missionary Evangelical Church (AMEC), among Lutherans in the Meru area of Tanzania, and it shows how new, non-traditional factors and actors were involved in the making of an independent church. The Evangelical Lutheran Church in Tanzania

196

(ELCT) is the second largest Christian body in the country, with a member-ship of over two million followers.[4] It has also been, since the 1960s, a national church, and thus the break was from an African church under local leadership, unlike earlier schisms from mission-led churches.

Furthermore, while some analysts, like Mbiti, see the development of independent churches as part of the development of the African Church and African theology,[5] the AMEC claims to be orthodox Lutheran and thus heir to its mission and national forerunners. To what then can we attribute this schism from an African church by a theologically orthodox successor?

Some studies of church conflicts leading to the emergence of indepen-dent churches do not take into account the historical socio-political dynamics that led to schism. A recent paper by Catherine Baroin, for example, analyses the Meru crisis as if it were solely a contemporary political issue.[6] Unless the history of the Christian church among the Meru and the people's resistance is analysed and understood in its socio-cultural and socio-political context, the impression one gets is that the AMEC started in the 1990s as a result of multi-party politics in Tanzania.

The Meru Background

The Meru of Tanzania are a Bantu-speaking people who live on the southeastern slopes of Mount Meru.[7] All Meru speak the same language, a West Kilimanjaro dialect of Chaga, with whom some Meru claim a common origin. Structurally, Meru are a conglomeration of small migra-tory groups who settled on Meru over the past 200–300 years. Social organization was based on a segmentary lineage system with a recognized head (*mangi*) and clan leaders (*vashili va utwari*), selected by the clan members, who allocated land and mediated disputes among clan members. Meetings took place under a *mringaringa* tree, where important matters related to political, social and economic affairs were discussed and resolved. Once an issue had been discussed and resolved at the *mringaringa*, the resolutions were respected and implemented by the people concerned.

The Struggle for a Separate Diocese

The Lutheran Church was introduced into Meru in 1896 by two Leipzig missionaries, Karl Segebrock and Ewald Ovir. Both men were killed in Akeri on 19 October 1889 by Meru and Arusha warriors who, it is claimed, identified them with the German colonialists who came to take their country.[8] In 1902 two other missionaries from the Leipzig mission society were sent to Meru to reestablish the Church.[9] This time they established a mission station at Nkoaranga, and over the years the church has grown into the dominant church in the area with 65,912 adherents, or some 60 per cent of all Meru.[10]

The idea of creating a separate Meru diocese first emerged in the late 1960s, when Pare and Arusha suggested dividing the existing Northern Diocese of the newly independent ELCT into a number of smaller dioceses on the grounds that the single diocese was too big and cumbersome to administer. At the same time, however, the new dioceses would be established along ethnic lines according to the ethnic boundaries followed by the local churches. After some debate, new dioceses were recognized in Arusha and Pare in 1972, but Meru chose to remain within the existing Northern Diocese instead of forming its own separate diocese or joining the new Arusha one, also on Mount Meru.[11] The argument advanced by Meru church leaders at the time was that Meru would benefit from the experience of the districts on Kilimanjaro if they remained within the Northern Diocese.

Meru supporters of a separate diocese, however, claimed that Meru church leaders also feared losing their leadership posts. Thus, whenever the idea of forming a separate diocese was brought up, they failed to include it on the agenda at Meru District council meetings, and so the suggestion to form a separate Meru diocese was never formally discussed at church headquarters in Moshi. While this indicated a weakness of local church leadership, supporters also asserted that local church leaders were acting with the blessing of the diocesan headquarters at Moshi for their own ends, an allegation denied by the diocesan leadership. Nevertheless, the separatist movement was promoted more by lay people than by pastors, as pastors feared being disowned by the church as had happened in Arusha.

Supporters of a separate diocese also claimed that the diocesan leadership transferred Meru pastors who supported them to other parts of the diocese while appointing local pastors favourable to the leadership. Rev. Urio, for example, was transferred to Mwika Bible School after his return from studies abroad in 1968, while Rev. Ngira and Rev. Nassari, both pro-diocesan leaders, were appointed to Meru. From the diocesan point of view, the transfers were simply normal administrative procedures; all pastors in the diocese were allocated centrally, and thus, it was argued, the transfer of Rev. Urio was made according to existing procedures to better utilize human resources.

Nevertheless, the issue of a separate diocese continued to be debated through the 1970s and 1980s. Meru began to build a new headquarters costing 25 million Tanzanian shillings for the future diocese in 1975, and the issue continued to be raised at Meru District council meetings throughout the 1980s.[12] The most serious charges by the secessionists alleged that the diocesan leadership was dominated by Chaga who discriminated against Meru by channelling church resources to Kilimanjaro and refusing to allow Meru to choose their own church structure and leadership.[13]

The demand to establish a separate diocese increased in the late 1980s as Meru complained that the diocese failed to support education in Meru, and Meru began to build new secondary schools in Nkoaranga and Engare Nanyuki on their own. In 1988, Rev. Erasto Ngira was reelected as the head of the Meru District. Vowing that the district would not become a separate diocese as long as he was in power, Ngira so irritated many of the laymen that they began to seek a more effective way to make their voices heard.[14] A series of meetings and consultations with the district and diocese councils took place to try to resolve the issue, but, as discussions and consultations dragged on, lay people became increasingly impatient and intolerant of the leadership. The struggle for a new diocese was becoming a volcano that could erupt at any time.

In an effort to resolve the issue, Rev. Nassari, the new district pastor, and another pastor sought the advice of Jackson Kaaya in November 1989. Kaaya was not only a representative of the Meru District of the Lutheran Church on the Northern Diocese Church Council, but also served as chairman of the Meru Social Development Trust (MESODET) and was regional chairman of the ruling party, Chama cha Mapinduzi (CCM). He was thus an influential person in the church, the government and the community, and the pastors hoped he would play an important role in the search for the solution of the issue. Kaaya, in turn, sought advice from Mr Urassa, the secretary of MESODET, an influential person in the Meru Cooperative Union, and a fellow member of the Northern Diocese church council representing Meru District.

The discussions were soon disrupted, however, by a dispute over the use of alcohol at weddings and other church-related social gatherings. Such use was common throughout Meru and Kilimanjaro, but a new diocesan by-law banned the practice as contrary to Christian morals. Thus, after Kaaya served alcohol at his son's wedding in 1990, the diocesan leadership removed him from both the district and diocese councils. Kaaya took this as an attack on Meru culture and further evidence of diocesan discrimination against Meru. While the church tolerated the use of alcohol on Kilimanjaro and Chaga pastors openly blessed foreign hard liquor at family ceremonies, he claimed, Meru were punished for serving locally brewed alcohol. In the process, Kaaya joined the ranks of supporters of a separate diocese in which Meru cultural practices, including serving alcohol, would be respected.

Kaaya then called a meeting of lay people on 29 September 1990 to discuss why church membership was dwindling. The meeting concluded that the problem was caused by the advent of new Pentecostal and separatist churches in the district which took members away from the Lutheran church. The church was not meeting the needs of the people, they thought, because it had not allowed them to choose their own leadership and had mishandled the long-standing issue of establishing a separate diocese.

A subsequent meeting was called on 3 October 1990 by MESODET at Makumira Secondary School to discuss the formation of a new diocese. Attended by 36 people, the meeting concluded that a new diocese, called the Mount Meru Diocese, should be inaugurated by 1 January 1991. Further, the meeting agreed to ask the Meru District head to call a district church general meeting on 18 or 19 October to discuss the issue of forming a new diocese, and a delegation of prominent church, MESODET and cooperative leaders was named to take the letter to the district church leader. The delegation, consisting of Godfrey Ngumuo (Makumira), Akundaeli Nanyaro (King'ori), Yesaya R. Kaaya (Akeri) and Unambwe M. Sumari (Karangai), was received by Pastor Nassari, and they all knelt and prayed for the proposed district general meeting.[15]

Rev. Nassari then went to the diocesan headquarters in Moshi to ask permission to hold the special district general meeting as proposed by the lay people. When he announced that the meeting was to discuss the formation of a separate diocese, however, the diocesan leadership refused to grant permission, and he was told to go back and tell the people that the request to hold a special meeting would not be granted.[16] He then returned home and wrote to all Lutheran congregations in Meru District informing them that the Makumira meeting held on 3 October had been illegal and that no further meetings of such a nature should be held.

Ignoring the letter, lay people met under Jackson Kaaya's leadership at Makumira Secondary School to discuss the formation of the diocese further. This time, all district pastors were invited to attend, but Nassari wrote to the pastors ordering them not to attend the lay meeting and calling them to a district meeting on the same day. Lay initiatives for the formation of a new diocese were thus disowned by the church leaders, further alienating the secessionists from the leadership. Over one hundred people attended the Makumira meeting, including two pastors — one of whom, Rev. E. Issangya, led the opening prayer. While the delegates were informed that the meeting was not recognized by the church leadership, they nevertheless decided to proceed with drafting a constitution and pursuing government registration for the new diocese.[17]

The meeting also decided to send another delegation to the Meru District leadership to discuss the ongoing process. The delegation met twice with the district leadership, but the leadership insisted that the meetings were illegal, and they failed to agree on the establishment of a separate diocese. The lay people then formed another delegation of prominent Meru lay people, including Japhet Kirilo, Emmanuel Nko, Yakobo Nyari, John Issangya and Emmanuel Sarayo, to meet with Bishop Kweka in Moshi. Bishop Kweka was absent from his office when they arrived, however, which the secessionists interpreted as a deliberate move to continue to deny their freedom to choose their own leadership and church structure.[18] The delegation then resolved to forge ahead with the idea of forming a separate diocese that would remain within the ELCT and would continue to follow fundamental Lutheran doctrine such as the Apostle's Creed, the Nicene Creed and the unaltered Augsburg Confession. Church life and ethics would be sustained and places of worship would be respected. The proposed diocese would thus be no different from other dioceses within the ELCT.[19]

A tug of war between the church leadership and lay people continued

until the new diocese was registered. MESODET became the organizational rallying point for the new diocese, as Kaaya and Urassa called a
number of meetings to develop the new constitution. A special meeting on
19 November then approved the constitution of the new diocese, to be
called the Mount Meru Diocese. Rev. Issangya was nominated as pastor-
in-charge, while Kaaya became chairperson and Urassa secretary; these
three then went to Dar es Salaam to register the new diocese with the
Ministry of Home Affairs.

The government officially registered the new Mount Meru Diocese on
15 December 1990 and ceremoniously handed the certificate to the
delegates two days later. The delegates immediately telephoned their fellow
members in Meru and told them to hold a special worship service to
celebrate the event. The local government feared that this would provoke
a clash between Mount Meru's adherents and those remaining loyal to the
old Meru District, however, and banned the meeting, but the new
diocese's supporters conducted a Christian procession through Meru
country, none the less, and held a special worship meeting at Usa River
on 1 January 1991 to inaugurate the new Mount Meru Diocese.[20] Among
those who attended the inauguration of the new diocese were the Roman
Catholic Bishop of Arusha and Rev. Tomito of the Arusha Diocese of the
ELCT.

The Responses of the
Evangelical Lutheran Church in Tanzania

The splinter group had made a bold move. The leadership of the Lutheran
Church was furious and immediately took steps to block the development
of the new diocese. From late 1988, when the idea of creating a separate
diocese had first reached the headquarters of the Northern Diocese of the
ELCT in Moshi, the church leadership insisted that the request had to
follow proper procedures. Further, they denied the allegations made by the
lay leaders that Meru were dominated by the Chaga leadership, and they
produced statistics to show that developmental resources within the diocese
were distributed fairly between Chaga and Meru.[21]

A letter from Bishop Kweka, dated 27 December 1990, regarding the
MESODET meeting on 3 October, set out the Northern Diocese's case.
The church had its own procedures for establishing a new diocese, Kweka
argued, and lay people were attempting to force the diocese to accept
decisions made by others without the church's participation. Communication should be established between the lay movement and the church
leadership, and, in any case, both Mr Kaaya and Mr Urassa, as members
of the diocese council, had had ample opportunity to present the issue in
appropriate settings, and both had been absent from the meeting on 25
October when the Meru issue was discussed.[22] Finally, Kweka stated
categorically that the Church did not forbid people from forming a new

diocese, but procedures had to be adhered to before permission could be granted.

Once the supporters of the new diocese gained government registration, however, the issue became a national one, and the leaders of the Northern Diocese appealed to the ELCT and the government for assistance. A delegation consisting of Bishop Kweka, Mr Mwenegoha (General Secretary of the ELCT) and Rev. Nassari went to Dar es Salaam to seek an audience with government officials to discuss the issue of the registration of the new diocese. The delegation stated categorically that the Mount Meru Diocese was registered illegally because it had not followed established church procedures. The government subsequently revoked the new diocese's registration on 16 February 1991, and it ordered the leaders of the Mount Meru Diocese to return the certificate.[23] In the meantime, the head of the ELCT, Rev. Shebastian Kolowa, went to Usa River on 25 January 1991 and, in a speech to a special gathering of Meru, stressed the importance of maintaining peace and of following proper procedures in establishing a new diocese. The ELCT also appointed a special committee of prominent church leaders from Protestant churches throughout Tanzania to probe the issue and report back to it.[24] The committee took its mandate seriously, and it travelled around Meru listening to Meru complaints before concluding that the Mount Meru Diocese was, indeed, illegal.

The ELCT then took disciplinary action against a number of individuals who had supported the formation of the new diocese. One of them was the Rev. Bumija Mshana, an instructor at Makumira Theological College near Arusha, who had sympathized with the Meru secessionists and helped them train new evangelists and pastors at special short courses to replace those who had remained with the Northern Diocese.[25] His service at Makumira was terminated. Some media people working with the church were also relieved of their duties, including Nichi Lyimo, an announcer with Radio Sauti ya Injili, a Lutheran radio station, and Ms Gelege, the editor of the Christian Council of Tanzania newsletter. Lyimo had sent information concerning the Meru church crisis to the BBC, while Gelege had written an editorial sympathetic to the movement.[26]

The Entanglement of the Government of Tanzania

Following the government's revocation of the new Mount Meru Diocese's registration in February 1991, violent clashes broke out throughout Meru between supporters of the new and old dioceses, and Kaaya and his committee went to see the prime minister, Mr Malecella. According to Ms Nditi, a former district commissioner, the government had no intention of interfering in the religious conflicts in Meru, but it had to because clashes between the two groups had already claimed a number of lives and resulted in the destruction of property worth millions of Tanzanian shillings.[27] The government then appointed its own commission late in 1991 to go around Meru probing the issue while preaching peace among the Meru people. The commission consisted of prominent politicians from throughout Tanzania and delivered its report eight months later.[28] In the meantime, the Minister for Home Affairs, Mr Mrema, speaking at the general meeting of the ELCT Central Kilimanjaro District at Masoka, cautioned the people on the danger of religious conflict in a speech widely interpreted as favouring the Northern Diocese's stand.[29]

The commission's report, submitted to both the government and the Lutheran Church, was not received favourably by the Northern Diocese of the Lutheran Church, however, since it was thought to favour the Mount Meru group.[30] The bishops of the ELCT responded by writing an open letter to the prime minister accusing the government of mishandling the issue and asking Christians to pray for Mr Malecella.[31] In the church's view, the government favoured Kaaya and his group because Kaaya occupied a high position in the ruling party. The church leadership then sought an audience with President Mwinyi to inform him about the situation and encourage him to find a permanent solution.[32] In response, the president urged the delegation and the Meru people to restore peace. No one should try to frustrate the efforts of the government to resolve the issue, he said, and no one should humiliate others or prevent them from worshipping in their own ways. Finally, he asked the two groups to exercise tolerance to end the clashes, which had already had devastating effects, and said that proper procedures should be followed in establishing a new diocese.

The Birth of the Meru Diocese of the ELCT

While the ELCT was pursuing efforts in early 1991 to block the registration of the Mount Meru Diocese, the Northern Diocese of the ELCT was also working on procedures for the Meru people to have their own diocese within the church. Thus, on 2 April 1991, the Meru District church executive committee asked the Northern Diocese to allow the district to become a separate diocese and, on 2 May 1991, the Northern Diocese's executive council acceded to the request and forwarded it to ELCT headquarters for a final decision. On 28 August 1991, the ELCT executive council formally accepted the Northern Diocese's request that Meru District be elevated to a diocese within the ELCT. The new diocese, which was to be named Meru Diocese, would have 80,000 adherents, 40 pastors, 10 deacons and more than 100 evangelists.

Adherents of the earlier Mount Meru Diocese, however, vowed to oppose the new official diocese, and when ELCT delegates met on 18 March 1992 at Usa River to approve the new constitution and elect the bishop, riots broke out, one person was killed, numerous others were hurt, and the army's Field Force Unit was called in to disperse the demonstrators.

Clashes between adherents of the two groups continued throughout Meru during April and May, during which many more people were killed and there was wide-scale destruction of property.

The new Meru Diocese was finally inaugurated officially and the Rt Rev. Akyoo consecrated as its first Bishop on 1 June 1992 amidst continuing fear of violence. The ceremony was held under tight security, with state security forces occupying the church and surrounding compound. The ceremony was attended by high government officials, including the regional commissioner, the district commissioner and the new regional CCM chairman, and hopes ran high that the inauguration of the new diocese would put an end to the crisis. But Bishop Akyoo was seen by the Mount Meru group as a representative of the Northern Diocese leadership, and they continued to oppose him.

The Secession Process
and Government Involvement

While the leadership of the new Meru Diocese was celebrating, the lay leaders of the Mount Meru movement were making their own plans to establish a new church, and, two days after the government approved the registration of the new diocese on 24 July 1992, it also approved the registration of the Mount Meru Church as a full-fledged church. Such an action by the government puzzled the ELCT leadership, and they could not understand why the government had reissued the group's certificate after having revoked it seventeen months previously. The subsequent admission by the Kilimanjaro regional commissioner, Samuel Sitta, perhaps reflecting the government position on the Meru Church crisis and acknowledging that the handling of the religious conflicts in Meru reflected laxity on the part of the government, only increased their concerns.[33]

At this point Mrema was entrusted by the government with the responsibility of handling the festering Meru issue. Coming from Kilimanjaro, Mrema was more acceptable to the Lutheran Church leadership than the Prime Minister, who was believed to favour the Kaaya faction on the basis of long friendship and political alliances. Mrema's handling of the crisis brought widespread approval in government and church circles for his apparent success in resolving the conflict, and President Mwinyi subsequently promoted him to Deputy Prime Minister, but Mrema's apparent bias towards the church leadership offended the secessionists.[34]

Mrema started by arranging meetings with people throughout Meru to talk with them about the crisis. He was told at numerous places he visited that people favouring the Northern Diocese were not wanted in Meru and that, as long as the leadership of the new Meru Diocese received their orders from Moshi, it would not be respected. In the process, however, he revealed that he was not in favour of issuing the second certificate to the

Mount Meru Diocese (now Church), and he criticized the process by which his own ministry had granted it, thus contradicting the government's stand and offending the Mount Meru group.

Nevertheless, Mrema persisted and thought that the best way to solve the problem was for the two sides to meet and resolve the issue for the betterment of Meru people and society at large. He suggested that the two existing church constitutions be presented to a special meeting for discussion with a view to forming a new committee that would write a new constitution acceptable to both sides. Meetings held between the two groups in January 1993 agreed that Mrema should introduce Bishop Akyoo to all the congregations throughout Meru, and that the Bishop would then sit down with lay people to nominate those who would sit on the new committee. Mrema had his own ideas of who should serve on the committee, however, and, when he announced his choices over Radio Tanzania, the Mount Meru group interpreted his selection as a unilateral act favouring the ELCT position.

Finally, Mrema announced that the Meru Diocese was the only legal Lutheran church structure in Meru and that the Mount Meru Church had ceased to exist. While he made it clear that the state apparatus would protect everyone without discrimination, he also cautioned that anyone continuing to follow the Mount Meru Church would be dealt with accordingly. As the violence continued into early 1993, the state dealt with the Mount Meru group ruthlessly; further meetings were banned, and Kaaya, Urassa and Mshana were all arrested.

The Mount Meru followers then established a new meeting place in the Pentecostal church at Sakila. While district authorities told the Pentecostal church leaders not to allow the new members to worship on their premises, the Pentecostals rejected the government's demand on the ground that these were God's people who wanted to worship in their own way, and they did not see why they should not be allowed to worship in the house of God.[35]

The Mount Meru group thus continued to function and, on 29 December 1993, it ordained twelve evangelists as pastors. At the same time, they began to work secretly to produce a new constitution and organize themselves into a new church, the African Missionary Evangelical Church (AMEC), with their own bishop. The new church was eventually registered by the government on 6 June 1995, claiming to have 33 congregations and 70,000 followers, and it is now building its own churches throughout Meru.[36]

Conclusion and General Interpretation

The vehemence of the advocates of a separate diocese and the violence their demands provoked was unprecedented in Tanzania; the conflict drew in leading figures from the churches and government to attempt to reconcile the two sides. In spite of the Northern Diocese's eventual concession of a separate diocese and government repression, the separatists rejected all compromise, eventually founding their own independent 'Lutheran' church, the AMEC, outside the ranks of the ELCT. Such extraordinary events must have had extraordinary causes, and yet it is difficult to see what those were.

In retrospect, the advocates of the separate Mount Meru diocese cited a number of issues behind their appeal. First, every church district within the Northern Diocese was supposed to remit 25 per cent of its income to the diocesan headquarters in Moshi as part of its contribution to the cost of running the diocese. The secessionists argued that these monies would be better utilized within the district, and hence they needed to create their own diocese. Second, they believed that there was an uneven provision of social services within the diocese, favouring districts on Kilimanjaro over those elsewhere.[37] Third, they believed that by electing their own leadership they could correct this imbalance and bring more social services to the Meru people. Fourth, they wanted more pastors from their own people to take care of their growing church membership. Since the training and placement of the pastors was centrally controlled, people in Meru thought by having their own diocese they could alleviate the problem. Finally, they wanted to have their pastors trained like their counterparts in other districts in the Northern Diocese of the Lutheran Church of Tanzania.

These issues thus ostensibly revolved around local control of the church, its budget and its personnel. As the most prominent institution in Meru, the Lutheran church was deeply embedded in all aspects of Meru life, including not only the church's own buildings, schools and medical facilities, but also the local cooperative, the development trust (MESODET) and the ruling party (CCM). What was at stake, then, was not simply control of their religious destiny, but of their social, economic and political destinies as well. All these institutions were important organs in the struggle for the new diocese and church. They expanded the issues and mobilized people to support the case for forming an independent diocese.[38]

Implicit in their appeal for local control was also a demand that Meru, not Chaga from Kilimanjaro, control their own institutions, and Meru ethnicity was evoked in support of their claims. It is claimed, for example, that some of the secessionists' meetings during the crisis were held around the same *mringaringa* tree used in olden days to sustain unity and identity among the people, thus asserting their roles as ethnic leaders, roles they had lost in the political sphere.

One of the issues reported to have triggered off the Meru church crisis was the diocese's banning the use of alcohol in any Christian festival. Claiming that serving alcohol was an important part of Meru culture, Meru objected to the ban. Further, they criticized the application of the ban as discriminatory. While local brew was generally forbidden in Christian festivals, many pastors and church leaders on Kilimanjaro blessed imported liquor at family festivals of influential people. While the issue of serving alcohol at family festivals was probably not the central issue of the crisis, it was used to heighten Meru cultural consciousness and to justify Meru resistance against external authority.

Meru thus felt discriminated against and so sought to become independent of the Northern Diocese. But they did not wish to break with Lutheranism. That is why the AMEC pledged to remain Lutheran, as shown in the basic teachings of the church in Appendix I.[39] At the same time, the Northern Diocese was facing increasing internal resistance from the growing number of independent prayer groups that rejected the current church leadership as well as from followers abandoning it for newer fundamentalist and Pentecostal churches.

In an earlier study of church leadership, I associated the emerging episcopacy system among Tanzanian Lutherans with a rise of ethnic leadership.[40] In the absence of traditional ethnic leadership, abolished by the government in the 1960s, the office of bishop has replaced that of the secular leader among some ethnic groups.[41] Given that the dioceses of the ELCT are established according to ethnic boundaries, following earlier missionary policy, the ethnic bishop becomes a natural 'tribal' leader. A demand for a separate diocese among the Meru people by the lay people thus accorded with this process.

What emerges, therefore, is that the demands of the Mount Meru group for their own diocese was a way of voicing their need for ethnic independence and freedom. This idea was echoed by Ole Tomito:

If one dominant community is oppressing other communities through the existing leadership, there must be dissent – whether we like it or not, dissenting Christians in Meru have not rebelled against God – to reject repressive leadership is an act of liberation.[42]

At the same time, the splinter group promises to remain true Lutherans, but outside the ELCT. Conversely, the leadership of the ELCT, the official Lutheran Church in Tanzania, has excommunicated the splinter group and has rejected the AMEC as a Lutheran church.

From the foregoing discussions, a number of conclusions can be drawn. First, lay people dominated the movement for an independent diocese and leadership. Thus there was a split between them and the church leadership over issues of power, freedom, culture and ethnic identity. Second, there was a chance for reconciliation between the concerned parties from the beginning of the crisis had the leadership of the Church agreed to sit down earlier and discuss the process of establishing a separate diocese.

The making of an independent church in Meru was thus more a socio-political process than a theological one. People wanted to have their own church structure and leadership where they could have access to power and share resources as a group. The issue can also be looked at as socio-cultural resistance to outside dominance, as Meru sought to preserve their identity by choosing their own leaders and having a say on church structure and church leadership. In this sense, there was little difference between the making of an independent church during the colonial period and the present.[43] Power, authority and dominance all played important roles.

The struggle for independency within the African church was thus not limited to colonial times, but continues today. As the churches grow and expand as a result of both missionary activities and natural growth, local identities based on ethnic loyalties can be used to rally people behind the issue of establishing separate dioceses or church groups.

Appendix 1

Basic Teachings of the AMEC

TRANSLATED BY THE AUTHOR FROM KISWAHILI

The Lutheran Church confesses and upholds the doctrine of the Trinity, that is God, the Father, the Son and Holy Spirit, Amen.

1. It bases its teachings on fundamentalism.
2. It respects the Word of God as obtained in the Old Testament and New Testament in its totality; the Bible is the Word of God from the first verse in the Old Testament to the last verse in the New Testament. There is no word of prophets or Jesus' disciples; all is the word of God. God used the prophets and Jesus' disciples with the Holy Spirit to be pens in writing all that was intended to be written down.
3. The word of God in the Bible has the whole power to guide the Church, to nurture and to teach it, to enlighten it in its meeting's decisions, to strengthen it and develop it spiritually. The Church will be under the guidance of the word always in humbleness.
4. This Church (AMEC) accepts wholeheartedly all the universal church creeds, which are:
   Apostles' Creed
   Nicene Creed
   Athanasius Creed
5. This Church (AMEC) receives with pleasure and respect:

(a) the unaltered Augsburg Confession as the basis of teachings as laid down by Dr Martin Luther;

(b) the Small and Large Catechisms of Luther as the basis of our teachings;

(c) the Book of Concord, which has the teachings of Dr Martin Luther; these are accepted and trusted as true interpretation of the Word of God.

6. This church which is under the guidance of the Word of God and the leadership of Holy Spirit, does not ordain women into the priesthood. To do so as others are doing is to go against the Word of God because JESUS CHRIST himself, the Lord of the Church, did not do so in choosing his first disciples: Mk. 3:19–23, Mt. 28:16–20. There were no women among them. The same with St Paul in his writings: 1Tim. 2:8–14, 1Cor.14:34–38; 11:3–10. On the basis of the word of God this Church ordains men only for the holy work of pastor.

7. All Church leaders, that is Bishops and all Pastors, are servants of the Church of Christ and not rulers of the Church as it is observed among others.

8. The congregation has the authority on implementing the process and growth of services within the congregation and outside it.

9. The Ministry of the Pastor of this Church will be responsible in the proclamation of the Gospel and to show to the people the love of Christ to all the people.

10. This Church as a Lutheran Church will administer wholeheartedly the teachings of the Lutheran Church without allowing, either openly or secretly, other teachings to become mixed in.

11. This Church will follow its worship services with spirituality on the basis of the principles of the Lutheran Church.

12. This Church will cooperate with the worldwide Lutheran family who have not altered the word of God or Lutheran teachings as stated in Nos 3, 6 and 10 above.

13. This Church will have a Bishop who will be in charge of the Church overall. In other areas of the Church, like Districts of the Church, there will be District Bishops whose power and authority are the same as those of the Church Bishop, only that they are limited by geographical area. The District Bishops will be elected among the ordained Pastors in the area (The Pastors will be responsible in electing the District Bishop.) The Bishop will serve in all areas (of the Church). The minimum age for being selected as Bishop is 50 years old. The Bishop elect will serve for a maximum of six years for two terms only.

14. The Executive Secretary and the District or Zonal posts will be held by ordained pastors. The officer will be nominated by the Executive Council of the Church and will be confirmed by the General Assembly of the Church.

15. The Treasurer may be a pastor or a lay person with knowledge in financial matters. He must hold a degree in finance-related studies.

16. The Church will have sisterhood services whose responsibility will be to look after the congregations, schools, hospitals and dispensaries, etc.
17. The Church will have Diocanic services which will be led by males [brothers] to take care of the various church projects and buildings/ constructions in the church.
18. The Church will serve all the people who have been baptized and have been confirmed through the WORD and SACRAMENT.
19. Only ordained pastors will serve all sacraments of this Church.
20. To withdraw from the Church membership or excommunication. The Church does not excommunicate or withdraw a person from the Church membership but the individual excommunicates or withdraws him/her self from the church. The church will conduct funeral services for those outside the church membership without any condemnation, leaving the whole issue in the hands of God. In any funeral services the target is for those who are alive and not the dead.
21. This Church will instruct its members to use a sign of a cross like true Lutherans, following the guidelines by Dr Martin Luther.

Notes

1 Bengt G. M. Sundkler, *Bantu Prophets in South Africa* (London, 1948), 17. For later studies, see, for example, C. G. Baeta, *Prophetism in Ghana* (London, 1962); Benjamin C. Ray, *African Religions* (Englewood Cliffs, 1976).
2 David B. Barrett, *Schism and Renewal in Africa* (Nairobi, 1968), 3, 7, 44.
3 Barrett, *Schism and Renewal*, 277.
4 The Evangelical Lutheran Church in Tanzania consists of 20 autonomous dioceses from differing missionary backgrounds. The main missionary societies which started missions in Tanzania were all German, including the Leipzig mission in northern Tanzania, the Bethel mission in the northeastern and western areas, and the Berlin (I, II and III) missions in eastern and southern areas. After the First World War, other missionary societies, such as the Augustana, Swedish, Danish, Finnish and Norwegian missions, started working in the country.
5 John S. Mbiti, *Bible and Theology in African Christianity* (Nairobi, 1986).
6 Catherine Baroin, 'Religious conflict in 1990–1993 among the Rwa: secession in a Lutheran diocese in northern Tanzania', *African Affairs*, 95 (1996), 529–54. See also Sally Falk Moore, 'Post-socialist micro-politics: Kilimanjaro, 1993', *Africa*, 96 (1996), 587–606.
7 For more on Meru, see: Thomas Spear, *Mountain Farmers* (Oxford, 1997); Paul Purritt, 'The Meru of Tanzania: a study of their social and political organisation' (PhD, Illinois, 1970); C. T. S. Nasari, 'The history of the Lutheran Church among the Meru (Warwa) of Tanzania' (B. D., Makumira, 1980).
8 Spear, *Mountain Farmers*, 61–74; A. S. Mbise, 'The evangelist: Matayo Leveriya Kaaya', in *Modern Tanzanians* (Nairobi, 1973), John Iliffe (ed.), 27–41; Sally Falk Moore and Paul Puritt, *The Chagga and Meru of Tanzania* (London, 1977); Thomas Spear (ed.), *Evangelisch-Lutherisches Missionsblatt* (Madison, 1995); B. Kaaya, 'The planting of Christianity in Meru: its conflicts and similarities with the traditional culture of the Wameru' (Fieldwork Report, Diploma in Theology, Makerere, 1978).
9 Spear, *Evangelisch-Lutherisches Missionsblatt*.
10 Nasari, 'History of the Lutheran Church'; 'Kanisa la Kiinjili la Kilutheri la Tanzania', Kalenda, Arusha 1996; Puritt, 'Meru of Tanzania'; Spear, *Evangelisch-Lutherisches*

Missionsblatt; Moore and Puritt, *Chagga and Meru*. My own estimates based on the available church statistics.

11 Martha Mandao and C. Omari, *Hayati Askofu Stefano Ruben Moshi* (Moshi, 1994).

12 According to Ms S. Nditi and Mr G. Ngomuo, in separate interviews on 5 October 1995, the Christians of the Meru Lutheran Church had anticipated the decision to be allowed to have a separate diocese and hence were constructing a new building to house the proposed new diocese headquarters. Lay people in general did not see the reason why it took so long to make such a decision.

13 See the letter, 'The truth about the Meru church crisis', from the ELCT, Arusha dismissing such a claim.

14 Interview with Mr Pallangyo, 5 October 1995, echoing the views of the Mount Meru group.

15 Ms Nditi, 5 October 1995.

16 Mr Pallangyo, 6 October 1995 and Mr Ngomuo and Ms Nditi, 5 October 1995.

17 Normally in Tanzania, all religious groups and associations are treated as NGOs and hence have to be registered with the appropriate ministry, in this case, the Ministry of Home Affairs.

18 Minutes of various meetings deposited at Makumira Theological College Library speak bitterly of the church leadership. Similar criticisms of the leadership style of the church were raised in my own discussion with a group of lay people from the Mount Meru group on the evening of 6 October 1995 at Usa River.

19 See the draft of the Creed or doctrinal basis of their church in Appendix I.

20 Various minutes at Makumira Theological College Library archives report on this occassion.

21 ELCT, 'The truth about the Meru church crisis'.

22 According to standing Church orders, any issue requiring a discussion and decision at diocesan level had to be sent to the diocesan office as an agenda item by the district church office showing exactly the minutes of the church district assembly meeting where the issue was discussed and resolved.

23 See letter of the Acting Administrator General of the Trustees, 19 February 1991, Ref. No. ADG/1/984/11, addressed to Advocate Lebulu in Arusha.

24 Participants on the committee included Yohana Wavenza of the Moravian Church, Methusela Nyagwasa of the Africa Inland Church, S. Chiwanga of the Anglican Church and S. Mushemba of the Lutheran Church.

25 Following the secession, the new diocese had only two pastors and 12 evangelists, most of them from the Northern Diocese of the ELCT.

26 *Lengo*, 219 (April 1991).

27 Interview with Ms Nditi, 6 October 1995. The properties were estimated at Tshs 75 million. The number of the people who died in the various clashes varies depending on the source of information. The best estimate, after comparing different notes, stands at 20 persons.

28 Members of the commission included Mr Mwakangale, Mbeya regional commissioner and head of the commission; Mr Budadi, Mwanza; Mr Semkiwa, Tanga; Mr Ndejembi, Dodoma; and Mr Meita, secretary to the commission.

29 Mr Mrema, a member of the Roman Catholic Church in Kilimanjaro, had been briefed about the issue by the pro-Northern Diocese leadership. *Daily News*, 18 January 1992.

30 *Business Times*, 18 December 1992.

31 *Business Times*, 18 December 1992, 25 December 1992.

32 *Daily News*, 24 April 1992.

33 As reported by the Evangelical Lutheran Church of Tanzania, 30 July 1992.

34 According to Ms Nditi, not only Mrema was promoted in this case; other security officers who were working in the area during the crisis were promoted as well.

35 Conversation with a focus group of Pentecostal Church members at Usa River, 7 October 1995.

36 The AMEC now has members as far away as Dar es Salaam. It leans towards a movement rather than a structured church.

37 AMEC minutes deposited at Makumira Theological College Library archives show that the institutions were distributed fairly.

38 Although this episode could also be linked with the development of civil society in Tanzania following liberalization, the issues started in the late 1960s, and thus the movement has to be understood within the Meru socio-cultural and socio-political context.

39 For example, in the case of ordination of women, the North-Western Diocese of the Evangelical Lutheran Church in Tanzania does not allow women to be ordained as pastors, though the Lutheran church as a whole has accepted the practice of ordaining women into priesthood.

40 C. K. Omari 'Episcopacy: a sociological trend in the Lutheran Church in Tanzania', *Africa Theological Journal*, 16 (1987), 4–12.

41 C. K. Omari, 'The management of tribal and religious diversity in Tanzania', in G. V. Mmari and C. Legum (eds), *Mwalimu* (London, 1995), 23–31.

42 As quoted in the *All African Press*, 10 June 1990.

43 See, for example, T. O. Ranger, *The African Churches in Tanzania* (Nairobi, 1969); Adrian Hastings, *A History of African Christianity* (London, 1979); F. B. Welbourn, *East African Rebels* (London, 1961); F. B. Welbourn and B. A. Ogot, *A Place to Feel at Home* (London, 1966).

Ten

Bundu dia Kongo

A Kongolese
Fundamentalist Religious Movement

ERNEST WAMBA-DIA-WAMBA

Until recently, Zaire (now the Democratic Republic of the Congo) was passing through a critical period of existential despair, as human instincts for survival confronted genuine spiritual anxiety and led to religious fanaticism.[1] Even well-known agents of the repressive state apparatus, such as Ngbanda, the special adviser to the former president for security matters, and Bolozi, the vicious former director of military intelligence, have become leaders of prayer circles. Ideologues of the Second Republic appealed to religious institutions and expectations to plead for forgiveness and reconciliation (regardless of truth) to forestall popular vengeance against them. Some claimed that Zaireans faced difficult conditions because they had sinned and should thus ask for forgiveness as a solution to the curse. Solicited by political power, organized religion moved from anti-communist ideological support for the Mobutuist regime to ideological opposition to a radical break from the Second Republic. Radical elements of the lower clergy such as the Groupe Amos constituted an exception.[2]

In the context of the Cold War, which forced Zaire onto the side of the West, Congo/Zaire has suffered from a triple determination:

- The production, dissemination and advocacy of knowledge has been conducted on the assumption that knowledge came only from outside the lived experiences of the masses of the Congolese/Zairean people.
- Political leaders and leadership (including religious leadership) are seen to originate and be legitimated from outside the people's control.
- The management of the economy (i.e. development rather than self-development, which was eliminated during the Atlantic slave trade) is conceptualized or regulated through World Bank/IMF prescriptive guidelines known as conditionalities.

Organized knowledge centres around the paradigms of 'technology

213

transfer' and the 'discovery' syndrome (in which almost nothing is known unless a Westerner discovers it).[3] Human development is viewed as the formation of 'sophisticated catechists' whose principal function is to spread ideas originating from elsewhere among the people. Indigenous religious awakening is seen in the same way. As Mudimbe says:

> Missionary speech is always predetermined, pre-regulated, let us say colonized.... This is God's desire for the conversion of the world.... This means, at least, that the missionary does not enter into dialogue with pagans ... but must impose the law of God that he incarnates....[4]

Pagans can only aspire to syncretism and not real religious thinking, creations or inventions. This can be extended to other heroes of an outward-looking epistemology, including the explorer, the ethnologist or 'applied anthropologist', the developmentalist-cum-consultant, and to some extent the African priest and pastor.[5] In a situation of hybridity, in which colonized people have ceased to be conversant with their 'traditional' culture but are not yet fully conversant with 'modern' culture, a loss of cultural identity and external spiritual guidance are prevalent. It is quite revealing that the catastrophic outcome of the last 'development decade', for example, has brought the contradictory notion of the 'cultural dimension of development' to the fore. Is it not a fact that a particular development culture is disorganizing, destroying or reordering other cultures?[6] Even the so-called participatory research problematic, intended to dethrone the oppression of outside knowledge/faith/truth bearers, seems to have failed. This is also reflected in constant attempts at indigenizing the religious element.

Single-party state authoritarianism in Zaire was followed by a disastrous never-ending transition to democracy. The state, whose political prescriptions were closely linked to Cold War logic, collapsed. Rampant systematic corruption promoted 'negative values' (*anti-valeurs*) at the expense of positive ones.[7] The opportunistic call for 'authenticity' to deal with the situation proved to be a tragic farce. The intellectual or mental worker, in almost all sectors, tended to function through a number of sub-paradigms which include:

- Consciencism, i.e. consciousness-raising or the spreading of knowledge, truth or faith as a form of consciousness to the masses of people. This creates catechists of different degrees of sophistication out of intellectuals. The most remote ones from the masses of people and those most separated from nature seem to be the most affected. The desire to return to cultural sources is felt intensely.[8]
- 'Fusion of Marxism and masses in liberation movements', i.e. an adoption of Marxism as technology or ideology, often without a ready-made environment for its germination.
- Use of European languages as marks of civilization, education or development. As Ne Muanda Nsemi notes, Kongo intellectuals have

become 'militants of *Francophonie* and *Lusophonie*'.[9] Education has become more mechanical, providing more titles than real preparation or initiation to relevant modes of living. It appears that the possibility of active thought, beyond a simple reproduction of foreign gods by sophisticated catechists – in other words, the possibility of a culture of African self-mastery leading to cultural regeneration, similar to the regeneration of 'Mother Earth' after she has been ecologically devastated by capitalism, and not to a simple return to past cultural traditions – has taken place through religious movements. Some peasant movements, for example, have produced ancestrally rooted religious leaders. Movements of cultural revival have also brought to the fore new expressions of Christianity.

Movements that had a relatively strong sustainable impact, such as Kimbanguism and Matsouaism (despite its lack of a hierarchical organizational structure), were based on a cultural rethinking of self-mastery, of self-identity or of one's faith. 'People think and thought is a relationship to reality.'[10] It is on this basis that we can discover certain forms of thought active in certain movements which explicitly propose, among other things, theories and practices of cultural change. In an epoch of democratization, knowledge process and spiritual process have to be democratized as well.

In the Kongo cultural area, politically dominated and increasingly invaded by Lingala culture, intense feelings of 'marginalization' and 'loss of cultural identity' emerged.[11] Catholic, Protestant and even Kimbanguist institutions had become drawn into the system of clientelist autocracy – stimulated by what Bishop Mansengwo Pasinya has termed 'President Mobutu's proverbial largesse'.[12] The Kimbanguist church, under Diangienda, a friend and ally of President Mobutu, was drawn into the regime, while the Protestant L'Eglise du Christ au Zaire (ECZ), under Bishop Bokeleale, an admirer of Mobutu, became more autocratic, suspending certain dispositions of the by-laws regulating the presidential mandate, for example. Religious sects and new churches, both indigenous and foreign, were on the rise.

Bundu dia Kongo

It is in this context that one can understand the visionary call 'to regenerate Kongo culture' Ne Muanda Nsemi claims to have received from Nzambi Mpungu. My research on emancipatory politics in Africa led me to be interested in the Bundu dia Kongo (Kongo Church) movement as it advocates a politics of cultural emancipation.[13] This chapter is an introductory study. Although I have met with Ne Muanda Nsemi and one of his associates and have attended two of his religious services, I have not had access to the basic book, *Makongo*, which is available only to *maziku* leaders, or to a number of Ne Muanda Nsemi's more than 150 publications. Nor has the BDK been studied by others. With the exception of a few Protestant churches that have been affected by the Kongo Church's activities, other churches have not reacted openly, and state reactions to the BDK have been sporadic. The intellectual community in Zaire has not yet come to terms with the BDK either. Yet Kongo intellectuals, in the main, have been very sympathetic to the movement, and the accusation of mystification, made by one or two scholars against Ne Muanda Nsemi's work, has not been based on thorough study. Prescriptive thought cannot be evaluated as if it were scientific (descriptive).[14]

Ne Muanda Nsemi Ne Makandala: Founder and Leader of the BDK

Ne Muanda Nsemi[15] (née Badiengisa Zakalia) was born in Mongo Luwala, on the border with Congo-Brazzaville, among the Manianga, a sub-group of the Bakongo. His early studies were done at the former Svenska Mission Forbundet (SMF) at Kingoyi, and he grew up as a Protestant. He later studied mathematics, physics and chemistry at the National University of Zaire (UNAZA, Polytechnique Faculty) and is now employed as a Senior Chemist at Mama Yemo hospital. Unlike Simon Kimbangu, who also attended Protestant (Baptist Mission Society) schools before receiving his visionary call, Ne Muanda Nsemi was not oriented towards a religious career, was never very religious and never trained as a catechist.

Nevertheless, Ne Muanda Nsemi claims to have received a call and a vision while still a student at the university in 1969. He described to me what must have been a very vivid and frightening experience. Asked to complete the mission that Simon Kimbangu was unable to accomplish, he was selected by Ne Muanda Kongo (Nzambi/God) to rescue Kimbangu's work, which had deviated from the correct path, and thus to give new life to and regenerate Africa generally. A giant 'person' who takes care of Kongo affairs in heaven was telling him that he must lead God's people through the Kongo initiatic path (*voie initiatique Kongolaise*) or life style (*bukongo*). The Kongo cultural tradition was selected as the principal axis of universal religion adapted to the negro mentality. Kongo religion was to be the soul of a negro-African renaissance.

With his background in mathematics, physics and chemistry, and little interest in religion, Ne Muanda Nsemi felt he was unqualified to take up the challenge and respond to the call. It took him seventeen years of doubt, hesitation and opposition before he accepted the mission. Finally in 1986, he created the Bundu dia Kongo[16] as a spiritual school, an academy of sciences and a religious training party, all in one. Its main objective was to provide ethical and political training for future leaders of Africa. The BDK's mission targets the whole world; it must, however, start by bringing order to Kongo Central before moving on to Kongo Dianene, to Central Africa, to Africa, and lastly to the world.

In 1989 he started to write a sacred book, *Makongo* (also called *Makaba*), as a working instrument for the believers of Kongo religion. This book is conceived as the equivalent of the Christian Bible, the Jewish Torah, the Islamic Koran, the Nihongi and the Bhagavad Gita. The *Makongo* was presented to the public on 30 August 1992. I attended, by invitation, this important ceremony. Ne Muanda Nsemi is a remarkable person, and he has a profound understanding of Kongo culture and the Kikongo language. His sermons are stimulating learning experiences to those conversant with the language. His vast programme for the development of Kongo culture, in just a few years, has already started bearing fruit.

According to Ne Muanda Nsemi, a fundamental church is characterized by a special message contained in its sacred book. There are thus three fundamental churches in Zaire: the Christian church with its Bible, the Islamic church with its Koran, and the Bundu dia Kongo with its *Makongo/Makaba*.[17] While claiming to have received the materials of the sacred book through visions, he does not claim the former to be God's dictation. The BDK promotes a message rooted in and drawn from the negro-African spiritual heritage. Past messengers, sent by Nzambi a Mpungu to the negro-African people, such as Vita Kimpa and Simon Kimbangu, have been pioneers of that message. As a promoter of this message in the present epoch, Ne Muanda Nsemi considers himself a *nlongi a Kongo ne makandala*, an instructor of religious leaders and political leaders and the spiritual leader of the Kongo state. He understands his main task as *vutukisa va fulu kia nzitusu lusansu ye ndinga Kikongo* ('rehabilitating or regenerating Kongo culture and the Kikongo language').[18]

The BDK Organizational Structure

The Bundu dia Kongo has no churches. General conferences, such as the *lukutukunu lua nsikumusu* (awakening conference) or the anniversary of Vita Kimpa's birthday, are held in public places, such as la Salle du Zoo and Palais du Peuple. Converts to Kongo religion are organized around a *zikwa* or *ziku* (plural: *mazikwa/maziku*), each of which has its own *mfumu'a zikwa* (*zikwa* chief). By 1994, there were 500 *mazikwa* with close to 50,000 members. Each country in which the BDK has members has a national executive committee of the BDK in charge of the BDK programme in that country. There is an international executive committee at the world level that is responsible for the elaboration of the general BDK programme. Thematic general assemblies of BDK followers meet, from time to time, as required by circumstances.

Each *zikwa* chief is also called a *nlongi*, or teacher. The supreme chief of the BDK, Ne Muanda Nsemi, is also called *Ne Makandala*. His role is to educate, to advise and to foresee and forestall future risks for 'the greatest good of Africa'. He is responsible for Kongo spirituality (*kinzambi kia Kongo*) in this epoch when the Bakongo are still enslaved. There is thus no Mani Kongo (supreme political chief), but there may be future periods in which there will be a Mani Kongo ne Makandala in charge of both politics (*kimayala*) and spirituality, a king and first priest of *bukongo* (Kongo path to spiritual and material fulfilment).

Mbanza Kongo, in northern Angola, the former capital city of the Kongo Kingdom, is seen as the sacred city of the BDK, the equivalent of Jerusalem for Jews or Mecca for Muslims. It is seen as the reflection on Earth of the Kongo temple, *kinlongo kia Kongo*, located in the centre of the sun. All *mazikwa* are directly linked spiritually to the Kongo temple.

The BDK doctrine is expressed through the trinity, *Muntu i mpeve, muela ye nitu*.[19] A person is composed of a spirit, a soul and a body. The trinity is reflected by the three primordial ancestors of the Bakongo: Nkulu Nsaku na Vunda, the first ancestor, who was given responsibility for spirituality, divinity and holiness; Nkulu Mpanzu, the primordial blacksmith who was in charge of knowledge; and Nkulu Nzinga, the primordial supreme political chief who was given responsibility for political power. God is also seen to be composed of *zola* (love), *ngangu* (wisdom) and *lendo* (power). There are also three holy 'Beings' in the Heavens: Ne Kongo Kalunga, God as Love; Ne Mbumba, God as Wisdom; and Ne Mpungu Tulendo, God as Power. BDK activities are also organized according to the trinity: those concerning spirituality constitute the *Kinlongo kia Kongo*; those related to knowledge fall in the *Lusanga lua Kongo* (Kongo Academy of Sciences); and those related to political power constitute *Kimayala kia Kongo*.

Nlongi'a Kongo Ne Makandala is assisted in his work by those in charge of these three institutions. As *mfumu'a mayala*, *mfumu'a kinlongo* and *mfumu'a lusanga lua Kongo*, Nlongi'a Kongo Ne Makandala acts as supreme leader and takes care of spirituality, political power and scientifico-technological knowledge or principles (*minsiku*). It is only in special circumstances, such as the present epoch, that one person is required to do all three. There were epochs in which such a person was a woman. Specialized schools are also organized by the Bundu dia Kongo. There are some people who are now studying *Kimayala* to become political leaders in eight years or so.

The Message of the Bundu dia Kongo

The message of the BDK is contained in its sacred book, *Makongo* or *Makaba*. Initially distributed only through *mazikwa* due to financial limitations, one had to be a member of a *ziku* to have access to it, and now it is only available to BDK members who have gained real insights from the publications and teachings of the BDK. I thus could not obtain a copy, though Ne Muanda Nsemi told me that this decision may change in the future. I did see the book when it was first presented to the public, but I was only able to read a few paragraphs.

Ne Muanda Nsemi is very much aware of this limitation and he makes sure to include the BDK message in almost every publication. *Bibila dia Kongo* (1992) is a brief presentation of *Makongo*. *Makaba 118* (1994) is a portion of the sacred book. The on-going series *Bukongo* (I have seen four volumes) and *Mayala* (24 parts projected; I have seen five) explicate different aspects of the message. While the publications in French are simplified, those in Kikongo are more profound and require more concentration to grasp the message. While there are a lot of *recoupements* in the publications, one needs to read all of the basic doctrinal texts to have an understanding of the consistency of the BDK message. Publications made in response to 'provocations' from Protestant Christians especially tend to generate misinterpretations as they are read without the necessary knowledge of the basic texts.[20] The lesson drawn by Ne Muanda Nsemi from his exchanges with Protestants is 'their pastors don't know their own Bible very well'. Having established this fact, he has decided not to react to their 'provocations' any more. What follows is a simplified introduction, based on the limited number of texts at my disposal, of the basic message of the Bundu dia Kongo.

Tata Nzambi'a Mpungu (Our Father, the Omnipotent God) created multiple groups (*makanda*) of people. Each people has its own spirit mediums (*bisimbi*), its ancestors (*bakulu*), its country, its culture (*lusansu*) and its religion (*kinzambi*), which came from the prophecies and teachings of the messengers (*ntumwa*) God sent to each group. The holy writings of a people contain the sacred law of its ancestors, of its spirit mediums or guardians of its country, and of God. The sacred book of holy writings must contain the history (*kinkulu*) of the people of that *kanda*, their culture, and the prophecies made by the messengers sent to them. Religion is the core of the culture of a people; it must be consistent with and rooted in that culture and must reflect the history of their struggles, suffering, miseries or triumphs. A foreign religion that is inconsistent with a people's history, their ancestors and their messengers' teachings represents spiritual enslavement of that people. The Kongo people, under the influence of 'colonial religion', are thus an 'enslaved people', or *bena kunsia kinkole*. Spiritual liberation can only be achieved by breaking with such a foreign religion and returning to one's own.

At each critical moment in the history of a people, God sends a messenger, a teacher or a prophet for the awakening and salvation (*mpulusu*) of the people. From Moses to Jesus Christ, for example, many prophets arose amidst critical circumstances in the Jewish tradition. The history of *Bena Kongo* (Bakongo) has a similar long list of messengers, prophets (*ngunza*) and teachers sent by God to the Kongolese people. These include: Kimosi (1217), Katumi (1230), Funza and Muanda Munana (1300–69), Buela Muanda (1457), Makoko (1654), the priest Lubeladio (1665), Vita Kimpa (1702), Ne Buta (1910), Ne Mbianda Ngunga (1914), Simon Kimbangu (1921), Andre Matsoua (1926–42), Matai Muanda (1933), Mpadi (1939) and Ne Muanda Nsemi (1969–present).[21]

Kongo religion builds on, and is consistent with, the origins of the Bakongo, their history and their culture (*bukongo*). Kongo mythical origins credit Nimi and Ngunu as the original ancestors who gave birth to three children: Nsaku, Mpanzu and Nzinga. The Bakongo are descendants of these three. The number three reflects the trinitarian character of God as love (*zola*), as intelligence/wisdom (*ngangu*) and as power (*lendo* or *tulendo*). Accordingly, the three names of God are: Ne Kongo Kalunga (Over-flowing Love), Ne Mbumba or Ne Nsemi (Creator) and Ne Mpungu Tulendo (The Most Powerful). The same trinitarian character is reflected in God's spirit, *muanda Kongo* or *mpeve ya zola* (God's spirit of love), *muanda mbumba/muanda nsemi* (God's spirit of intelligence) and *muanda mpungu* (God's spirit of power). These forms of God's spirit are incarnated in the country's *bisimbi bia nsi*. It is clear, for example, that, as leader of the BDK, Ne Muanda Nsemi incarnates God's spirit of intelligence.

The whole organization and functioning of Kongo culture and history are expressed in similar terms. The person and personality are similarly marked by a trinity of body (*nsuni*), desire (*ngunda za ntima*) and thought (*ngindu za ntu*), an outcome of the material world, the world of desire and the world of thought.

Similarly, Kongo religion is the religion of the ancestor Nsaku (the primordial prophet), of the ancestor Mpanzu (the primordial blacksmith or creative intelligence) and of the ancestor Nzinga (the primordial king or political leader). Nsaku was a religious leader associated with divinity or religiosity (*kinzambi*) and was given the task of spiritually training God's people. The ultimate objective of the people is spiritual evolution or development. Nsaku was responsible for the spiritual training of political leaders and was the guarantor of just politics in the country. The country, thanks to his vision, was ruled according to the sacred law. Ancestor Nzinga, also called Na Luyalu (Mister/Madam Politics), was given the tasks of good governance; of combating injustice, disorder and vices; and of ruling the country according to the sacred law. Ancestor Mpanzu, or Na Mazayu (Mister/Madam science), was entrusted with creative intelligence to produce the products required by people's material life.

> *Na Kinzambi, Na Mayala et Na Mazayu sont les trois grands fils de Dieu que le Dieu Muanda Kongo envoie à l'Humanité terrestre pour venir éclairer et guider les fils des hommes sur le chemin du bien-être spirituel et matériel. Ensemble, ces trois grands Fils de Dieu sont La Lumière du Monde.*[22]

(Mister Religion, Mister Politics and Mister Sciences are three great sons of God that God sent to the Earthly Humanity to give light to and guide sons of men on the path to spiritual and material well-being. Together, those three great sons of God constitute the Light of the world.)

Bundu dia Kongo is the union of all that the three primordial ancestors represent; it is an articulation of religion, science and politics under the determination of religion. Religion ethically guides politics which guides science so that it may serve the greatest number of people. The believers of Kongo religion are thus grouped into three groups: *kabu dia kinlongo* (the group of spirituality), *kabu dia mayala* (the group of politics) and *kabu dia mazayu* (the academy of sciences).

That is a very condensed summary of the BDK message. The understanding of it is made somewhat difficult by its constant use of esoteric language. The Kongo kingdom was a variant of a tribute-paying social formation with an unstable elective system of succession. These formations usually have a systematic cosmogonic ideology with its related intellectuals. In this particular case, four initiation schools formed those intellectuals: *kinkimba* (for cosmological world view), *lemba* (for law), *kimpasi* (for medicine?) and *bwelo* (for the military?). The basic principle (*nkingu*) was that 'everything relates to everything else'. In the absence of writing, a graphic system of symbolics, composed of colours (black representing life; red, power or maturation; white, decline and death; and yellow, knowledge – *kala*, *tukula*, *mpemba* and *musoni*), drawings and analogies drawn from life processes, was used. Because of this limitation, it was difficult to conceptualize and transmit cosmological thought without some changes. There is a range of variations on key issues or on the elements that are emphasized. The BDK leader puts emphasis on the trinity rather than the quadrinodality of life stages (to be born, to grow to maturity, to decline and die, and to grow in the ancestral world and be born again) emphasized by Fukiau kia Bunseki, for example.[23] Drawing on the long tradition of fusion or selected integration of Kongo religion with Christianity, Ne Muanda Nsemi seems to trinitize everything and trinitarian manifestations in everyday life, such as the three stones on which food for life is cooked, are emphasized.

Historical Background

Kongo religion, as developed by Ne Muanda Nsemi, is rooted in Kongolese cultural history. Even the songs (*Nkunga mia Bundu dia Kongo*) are, for the most part, praises to past prophets (such as Simon Kimbangu and Vita Kimpa) or educators, and they voice meditations on the historical predicament of the Kongolese people. From the late fifteenth century this cultural history included elements of Christianity. The Bakongo have thus had contact with Christianity for over 400 years. Kongolese cultural history has been marked by missionary activities, episodic resistance against Christianity and relapses into variants of Kongolese traditional religion, attempts at Africanizing Christianity at both royal and popular levels as well as Christianizing Kongo *kinzambi*, and prophetic visionary religious upsurges. The issue has ceased to be that of opposing Christianity and traditional *kinzambi per se*, but has become that of spirituality as a cultural feature of cultural resistance or accommodation in various historical and critical contexts. Christian elements and Kongolese elements are articulated or disarticulated depending on visions or calls made by leaders and cultural perceptions of the tasks and possibilities at hand.

The constant cultural pursuit of *kinenga kia nsi* (politico-religious-knowledge balance) is mediated through cultural history. There is thus a sense of cumulative cultural reaffirmation throughout successive historical conjunctures as fixed, among other means, by proverbs. Depending on the 'tasks' of the conjuncture, politics or religion is emphasized in the articulation of politics, religion and knowledge. Simon Kimbangu's main teaching, 'Nobody can be truly Christian unless politically free', reflected colonial circumstances. Ngunzists Mpadi and Mbumba emphasized spirituality. A rich literature on this history exists, but it is often confused by different authors, depending on their mastery of the Kikongo language and their selection of informants.

Ne Muanda Nsemi's *L'Histoire du Kongo Central* is a brief chronological background, highlighting political and religious events, for Kongo religion. It is sad, though, that technico-scientific events are not chronicled; the scientific dimension of Kongo religion inaugurated by Mpanzu is not given the attention it deserves while it is implied in the very conception of the religion. While the lists of kings and prophets, messengers and teachers are provided, no list of pioneers of the Academy of Science is provided. Ne Muanda Nsemi stated that he is still working on this aspect. His approach is first to develop scientific Kikongo before writing about the tradition of *Mazayu* among the Bakongo.[24]

Because of the historical conception of Ne Muanda Nsemi, according to which history is made by gods or spirits (*les génies superviseurs*) and people, Kongo historical chronology starts with spiritual and heavenly actors and events. Ne Muanda Nsemi conceives of himself not as an ordinary historian, capable of grasping only the visible causes of events, but as a great initiated (*grand initié*), inspired and intuitive writer who is capable of grasping and revealing the invisible and profound causes of events. The last word in the making of history belongs to the supervising geniuses. According to this conception of history, the religious dimension becomes the key to historical dynamics. This may explain why a people's history is inseparable from its traditional religion, its language and its culture. The historical trajectory is thus determined by the spiritual evolution of man. For man was said to be placed on this Earth to accomplish his spiritual evolution towards becoming a man-god, a divinity, acting on Earth to create a spiritual and material civilization worthy of God's descendants or true sons of Ne Kongo. Here the BDK departs fundamentally from the Christian notion of the status of man's life on Earth. There is a sense in which Kongo culture entertains the notion that spirits, ancestors and God intervene in human actions and the crucial importance of qualitative living on Earth.

Even the name 'Kongo' is grasped in its complex historical etymology. God, in His trinity, was known as Ne Mbumba, Ne Kongo Kalunga and Ne Mpungu. So 'Kongo' is first of all the name of the God of love and wisdom that sustains the visible and invisible universe. 'Kongo' is also the magical circle, the rainbow which accompanies the process of self-creation of the universe. 'Kongo' is also a cosmic and universal name denoting the great God Kongo Kalunga whose energy dominates the solar system. 'Kongo' is a name that belongs to all heavenly and earthly humanity; as such it is the solar system and beyond. 'Kongo' is the name of the whole black race of the World, as it was the name of the solar religion of ancient Egypt. 'Kongo' is the name of the kingdom founded in Central Africa by the great initiates originating from ancient Egypt. In brief, Ne Muanda Nsemi claims that, according to the Bakongo initiates, 'Kongo' is the name of the God of love, wisdom and unity. It assembles people, protects them and keeps them. It incarnates God's love, religion, spirituality, the colour blue, the circle and the primordial ancestor Nsaku.

The first part of the history of Kongo Central up to 1482, as told by the leader of the BDK, is difficult to evaluate as there are no other written sources. It does seem to have some similarities with Jewish religious history. The Bakongo are also said to be an elected people whose main task is to liberate negro-African people from continuous enslavement. As presented, the historical trajectory of the Bakongo is spiritually guided by a protracted coming of messengers or teachers. Ignoring the latter's teachings brought about, each time, misery and suffering.

Upsurges of creative politics in the Kongo area were often preceded by a spiritualist movement. The Ngunzist movement, from the 1930s and the 1950s, taking off from Simon Kimbangu, eventually led to the emergence of the Alliance of the Bakongo–ABAKO. A cultural awakening was called forth. Cultural forms of keeping records – coded memories, visions (*kimona meso*), visitations by ancestors and cultural capacity of invocation of ancestral presence, or the *zumbu dia nlongo* (sacred forest) – help visualize the forgotten past. Enslavement also means the promotion of structures or institutions that blocked the capacity to recall the liberating past. To erase visions made possible by Kimbangu's teachings, the L'Eglise du Christ au Congo par le prophète Simon Kimbangu was erected by Kimbangu's children, colonially educated in Catholicism, to coopt the Kimbanguist movement and to promote a Kimbanguism without Kimbangu's visionary message. A family-based personality cult was emphasized. Surviving close collaborators of Kimbangu distanced themselves from that Kimbanguist church. Embarrassing witnesses such as Emmanuel Bamba had to be eliminated.

After the disintegration of ABAKO politics, due to the cultural uprootedness of its leadership, the Kongo community was unable to organize itself on that basis. Spirituality again will prepare the community for a new political regeneration. One hears people claim: '*Tulendo wuna kwiza bonso bwenina nsilulu*' ('The powerful one will rise according to the prophecy'). Ne Muanda Nsemi, or the Creative Spirit, first received his call in 1969. This was the year that Fukiau published his *Cosmogonie Kongo* and *Imeni (Enough is Enough)*, which partly triggered the movement for cultural regeneration or authenticity.[25] The regime in place mystified and coopted it through the so-called 'Recourse to Authenticity', and Bakongo started distancing themselves from support of the Mobutu regime. The massacre of university students, including some brilliant Bakongo (like Pierre Bayenekene), certainly affected Ne Muanda Nsemi, then a univesity student. As in the past, in a situation of sharp cultural crisis, a prophetic personality emerges: 'In conditions of social urgency, God always sends a messenger.' Anyone who knows the language well and goes through BDK publications will understand the claims that Christianity, or the 'colonial church', has tended to destroy, rather than build on, Kongo culture.

The socio-political impact of this movement should not be evaluated on the basis of its theological limitations or controversies (such as the status accorded to Jesus Christ as a messenger sent to the Jewish people and not as a saviour of all humanity, putting an end to the coming of prophets). The cultural creativity provoked by the publications, actions, deeds and sermons of the BDK inspires a lot of people. The cultural behaviour of BDK followers, consistent with Kongo cultural values, inspires others to take the movement seriously. Serious problems are explained by the creative use of Kongo cultural traditions. A short proverb, such as *'mfuka ni kinkole'* ('debt is slavery') explains the country's debt burden. The cultural foundations of politics and the cultural implications of a possible future federal republic are made clear.

Despite its conciliatory tendency, the BDK is in favour neither of the regime nor of the opposition; the pivotal position of religion in the articulation of religion, politics and science may not leave any room for multi-party politics. How the group of politics, *Kabu dia Mayala*, will be organized in this epoch has not been clearly elaborated in the publications I read. But it would appear that it will be based on the paradigm of *mika ma mbwa: vumbukila kumosi ye lambimina kumosi* (the dog's hairs rise together and lie down together), the paradigm of unity without division or competition.[26] Politics determined by religion suffers from this fundamental constraint. Cultural nationalist politics is also marked by this sort of limitation.

I attended the ceremony of *lukutukunu lwa nsikumusu*, held on 4 August 1996. While the ceremony formally appeared Christian, its content was very different and very close to people's daily preoccupations. Let me give some high points of the ceremony to illustrate the point. The protocol was impeccable. The selection of songs was in line with requirements of preparations for spiritual and political liberation. The first song emphasized how the Kongo people have become enslaved and how thinking only of oneself (*kimonokwami*) divides them and is one of the leading causes of bad deeds (*mavanga mamvualangani*). The second song, entitled *Mbanza Kongo*, explained how the city was destroyed and exhorted people to rebuild it to fulfil their promises. The third, *Kanda dia Kongo*, was more a performance than a song and described what has happened to the Kongo people under imposed cultural alienation in which 'they want us to be like them'. The fourth song of invocation was an engaging prayer for liberation, requesting God to give the people '*mwind'aku watukienzula*' (His enlightening lamp).

Before giving the sermon, Ne Muanda Nsemi had to identify himself fully by his name, parents and clan (*luvila*). The theme of the sermon was: 'God cannot transform the country if those who live in it don't change their mentalities and thinking'. Appropriate verses from *Makongo* were read, such as '*Kadi ngindu I ngudi yibutanga kimpwanza ye kinkole vava ntoto. Kesa mu nzila Kongo kafwiti toma sadila ngindu zandi bwambote*' ('Thought is the main source of liberation or enslavement on Earth. A militant in the Kongo path must use wisely her/his thought'). It was a very clear philosophical analysis clarifying the relationship between thinking (*ngindu*), speaking (*mpova*) and acting (*mavanga*) in one's personal behaviour.[27] Concrete examples were given from daily life, and both spiritual and political liberation were discussed. The sermon was followed by various group (*bilombo*) songs, which were prescriptive declarations.

The ceremony continued with 'concluding remarks' specifically related to the three basic groups of religion, politics and science. These concerned what the Kongo should do in this period of transition to 'democracy' and how they should prepare themselves for that transition. The idea of a regional socio-economic conference was launched. The ceremony ended with the song '*Kongo dia Bakongo difwiti vutuka*' ('The Kongo of Bakongo Must Come Back'). Even prayers had a triple content: spiritual, political and 'scientific'. Prescriptions concerning the preparation through transformation of modes of living for spiritual liberation – *bukongo* – were differentiated from those concerning the preparation for political liberation (*kesa mu kinsuni*).

Bundu dia Kongo
and Emancipatory Politics in Zaire

As mentioned earlier, I came into contact with this cultural movement while studying modes of emancipatory politics in Congo/Zaire. The BDK's main concern is the social transformation, through cultural regeneration, of African societies. Emancipatory politics, in its modern sense, is politics on condition.[28] This means that politics is of the order of phenomena of consciousness in the sense of the expression 'revolutionary consciousness'. It is a break with 'spontaneousness', daily activities, routine-based attitudes or submissive accommodating consciousness. Emancipatory politics is an active prescriptive relationship with reality and not a reflection or representation in consciousness of invariant structures of society (the economy, the state, etc.). As such, it is a creative invention. The active realization that the existing state of affairs does not have to remain so because it is so is of the order of politics. Despite Ne Muanda Nsemi's visionary claim subordinating politics to religion, politics as invention traverses his doctrine. One does not need to be religious to appreciate the thesis of emancipatory politics under the condition of a cultural break with alienating Western culture. The notion that religion is the core of every culture may not be universally upheld by militants of the culturalist mode of politics.

In fact, each mode of emancipatory politics has its own forms of organization that give consistency to political consciousness; the Marxist vanguard party was the necessary form of organization of revolutionary politics for Lenin, for example. What we may call 'universal *ziku*' could be seen as the form of organization of the BDK regenerative cultural politics. It is very clear also that the BDK continues the Kimbanguist conception of politics summarized by Kimbangu's 'civilization of the Congolese by the Congolese for the Congolese' and 'the right of direct contact with God without missionary intermediaries' (that is, politics under the condition of complete subjective independence). Once again, one has the feeling that spiritual liberation requires political liberation. The fact that the sub-thesis of 'scientifico-technological liberation' remains undeveloped makes the thesis of the articulation between religion, politics and science under the determination of religion less certain.

Conclusion

Despite the reservations one may have as to the historical authenticity of some of the claims made – and this is no different from any religion – the Bundu dya Kongo has given rise to a major cultural revival in the Kongo cultural area. The Kikongo language is being developed. A scientific lexicon is being developed. The *Makongo* is a much more familiar cultural history to a Mukongo than is the Biblical Old Testament.

Zaire now has about 400 registered political parties. Even though the BDK does not function as a political party itself, there is no party, as far as I know, that is as clear as the BDK regarding the type of society to build, how to do so and where to find the building materials. They are all interested only in obtaining state positions through either elections or clientelism ('consensus').[29] The emphasis on 'mystic elements', on the 'uniqueness' of Bakongo people and culture and on unity for unity's sake constitutes the main limitations of the BDK conception of emancipatory politics. This is reflected in the way, for example, that Kongo history excludes common people's voices, and institutions such as the palaver are not given their due place in the experiences of the Bakongo. This particular institution is the key to an internal critical assessment of Kongo culture itself.

This is a short study of the BDK cultural movement; more research and access to the movement publications are needed to make a more thorough analysis of its message, practices and impact on Zairean society generally. It is, for example, reported that the Mongo elite met and raised funds to request Mongo intellectuals to develop Mongo culture along the lines developed by Ne Muanda Nsemi for Kongo culture. I met and interviewed Ne Muanda Nsemi and had a number of discussion sessions with one of his collaborators, a medical doctor. Nevertheless, this is still not enough to gain sufficient knowledge of the movement or to be able to make a critical assessment of it. And comparisons with other similar movements, such as L'Eglise des Prophètes Africains, a Protestant sect in the Luba area, would have shed some light on the current circumstances in Zairean society that serve as fertile grounds for movements of this type.[30]

Notes

* The first draft of this chapter was presented at the Conference on 'African Expressions of Christianity' at the University of Wisconsin, Madison, 23–27 August 1996. My thanks to the organizers for having invited me and given me funds to partially finance the research for this chapter.
1 This question is touched on in Rene Devisch, 'Frenzy, violence, and ethical renewal in Kinshasa', *Public Culture*, 7 (1995), 593–629.
2 Groupe Amos was one of the most active Christian groups militating for radical change of Zairean society. It was a co-organizer of the 16 February 1992 Christians' March for the reopening of the national conference.
3 Jacques Depelchin, *Silences in African History*, forthcoming.
4 Valentine Y. Mudimbe, *The Invention of Africa* (Bloomington, 1988), 47–8.
5 Ernest Wamba-dia-Wamba, 'Mfunu wa Zinsonokono za Kikulu: Vonza Kilendele kala vo kikulu kia Dibundu mu konso Kimvuka ka kiena Kiasonomako', unpublished MS, 1996.
6 Marie-Dominique Perrot, 'The "cultural dimension of development": a new gadget', *EADI Journal*, special edition, forthcoming.
7 David Gould, *Bureaucratic Corruption and Underdevelopment in the Third World* (New York, 1980).
8 Amilcar Cabral, *Return to the Source* (New York, 1979).
9 Ne Muanda Nsemi, *Le Kikongo et l'enseignement* (Kinshasa, 1994), 2.
10 Sylvain Lazarus, *Anthropologie du nom* (Paris, 1996), 17.
11 A seminar was organized by the Evangelical Church Community on the theme, 'Loss of cultural identity among the Bakongo' in 1995.
12 An observation made in a speech at the Sovereign National Conference, 1992.
13 Ernest Wamba-dia-Wamba, 'Africa in search of a new mode of politics', in U. Himmelstrand *et al.* (eds), *African Perspectives on Development* (London, 1994), 249–61; *idem*, 'Democracy, multipartism and emancipative politics in Africa: the case of Zaire', *Africa Development*, 18 (1993), 95–118.
14 Lazarus, *Anthropologie du nom*, 19. The distinction between prescriptive and descriptive thought is the distinction between political work and scientific work. Politics works with enunciations rather that proofs. Political enunciations are confronted with other political enunciations.
15 *Ne* is an abbreviated form of *muene*, a title of respect; *muanda* means 'spirit' and *nsemi*, 'creator'. Ne Muanda Nsemi thus refers to the spirit of creativity.
16 'Bundu' comes from the Kikongo verb *bunda*, 'to add' or 'bring together'; thus *bundu* means an 'assembly', 'crowd', 'community' or, by extension, 'church'. Bundu dia Kongo thus means 'a community of believers in Kongo culture and religion'.
17 According to Ne Muanda Nsemi, the BDK is a fundamental or fundamentalist church in two senses of the word: first, he was first asked to rescue the fundamental work of Kimbangu from the deviations of his children, as noted above. But he also seeks to restore Kongo culture and religion by returning them to their foundations, with the ultimate goal of restoring the Kongo Kingdom.

18 Ne Muanda Nsemi, *Makaba 118* (Kinshasa, 1995); *idem, Connaître Bundu dia Kongo* (Kinshasa, 1996).
19 Ne Muanda Nsemi, *Mayala*, 5 vols (Kinshasa, 1995–6).
20 He said this to the author in a discussion, August 1996.
21 Ne Muanda Nsemi, *L'Histoire du Congo Central* (Kinshasa, 1990). Ne Muanda Nsemi attributes the names and dates of the prophets to visionary revelations.
22 Ne Muanda Nsemi, *La Spécificité de la religion Kongo* (Kinshasa, 1992), 6.
23 Fukiau kia Bunseki, *Self-Healing Power and Therapy* (New York, 1991); *idem,* 'Ntangu-Tandu-Kolo: The Bantu-Kongo concept of time', in J. K. Adjaye (ed.), *Time in the Black Experience* (Westport, 1994), 17–34; *idem,* 'Mukuku Matatu', unpublished MS, 1983; *idem, The African Book Without Title* (Cambridge, 1980); *idem, Nkongo ye Nza Yakunzungidila: Cosmogonie Kongo* (Kinshasa, 1969).
24 Ne Muanda Nsemi has already published a number of books on the issue, e.g. *Le Kikongo et la science* (Kinshasa, 1991); *Le Kikongo et la science nucléaire* (Kinshasa, 1994).
25 See fn. 23.
26 This was also the unifying slogan of the Alliance of the Bakongo (ABAKO) as a political party struggling for political independence (1956–60).
27 This topic is further analysed in Ne Muanda Nsemi, *Soba Ngindu* (Kinshasa, 1995).
28 Wamba-dia-Wamba, 'Africa in search of a new mode of politics'; *idem,* 'Democracy, multi-partism and emancipative politics'.
29 Ne Muanda Nsemi has written on current issues from which other parties shy away, e.g. *Les Africains sans papiers* (Kinshasa, 1996), on immigration problems in Europe; *Le Problème Hutu et Tutsi* (Kinshasa, 1996); *Les Frontières coloniales* (Kinshasa, 1996).
30 Pius Ngandu Nkashama, *L'Eglise des Prophètes Africains* (Paris, 1991); *idem, Eglises nouvelles et mouvements religieux* (Paris, 1990).

V

Charismatic Prophecy
&
Healing

Struggles for control, both political and theological, characterized all
missions, and in extreme cases often led to schism, as we have seen in the
preceding studies by Sandgren and Omari. Bengt Sundkler has classified
the independent churches that resulted from these struggles into two types:
Ethiopian and Zionist. Ethiopian churches resulted primarily from
leadership struggles within the missions, and they largely retained the
theology and practices of their mission forebears while coming under
African leadership. Both the Kamba Brotherhood Church (Sandgren) and
African Missionary Evangelical Church (Omari) are independent churches
of this type. Zionist churches, on the other hand, were usually the
outgrowth of charismatic movements, in which African prophets
communed with God and founded their own churches, often based on
Biblical beliefs, African religiosity and the practice of charismatic gifts.[1]

Both of these types of churches emerged in Central Kenya in the late
1920s and 1930s as a result of the female circumcision crisis, becoming
known as the *Aregi* ('Those who Refused' to take loyalty oaths to the
missions) and *Arathi* ('People of the Spirit') or *Aroti* ('Dreamers'),
respectively. While *Aregi* subsequently formed their own churches cast in
the mission mould – the African Orthodox Church and the African
Independent Pentecostal Church – *Arathi* developed a profusion of
charismatic and millenarian churches, all of which evoked the power of the
Holy Spirit to heal, drive out witchcraft and cleanse the land of pollution.[2]

The theology of such Zionist churches is not well known, however, as
a result of which many scholars have considered them as either atavistic or
syncretistic religions drawing primarily on their African roots. Zionists
themselves, however, are disdainful of both the established Christian
churches and local traditions, while asserting a firm Biblical basis for their
own prophecies, beliefs and practices, as Francis Githieya shows in his

229

perceptive study here of Arathi theology. Drawing on the vernacular Kikuyu Bible, Arathi rooted their own beliefs in God and the Holy Spirit; their election by God as a chosen people; their concepts of purity and impurity; and their faith in dreams, prophecy, healing and the coming end of the world firmly in the Old and New Testaments. Like many other Zionists, they see themselves as true Christians, born of Biblical prophecy and free of the accumulated errors of the established churches.[3]

Notes

1   Bengt Sundkler, *Bantu Prophets in South Africa* (London, 1948).
2   David Sandgren, *Christianity and the Kikuyu* (New York, 1989), especially Chapters 5–7.
3   Revivalists and popular Catholics also share many of these views, as seen in the studies by Kassimir, Comoro and Sivalon, and Mlahagwa to follow.

Eleven

✠✠✠✠✠✠✠✠✠✠

The Church
of the Holy Spirit
Biblical Beliefs & Practices
of the Arathi of Kenya, 1926–50

FRANCIS KIMANI GITHIEYA

The Arathi was an indigenous African spirit church movement that emerged in Central Kenya in the mid-1920s.[1] Since Arathi have a belief system that stresses ritual, spirits, possession, prayer, healing, dreams and prophecy, many scholars argue that its cosmology is more African than Christian. Such a cosmology, they argue, is incompatible with biblical Christianity, despite popular attempts to blend Arathi beliefs with the Christian faith, and it is therefore 'pagan'.[2]

Such explanations, however, are one-sided. They highlight the Arathi African heritage while ignoring the fact that the Bible was of enormous importance for the early Arathi church. The Bible functioned as the church's primary source for theological reflection, and it profoundly influenced the formation of early Arathi vocabulary, including the term 'Roho' (Holy Spirit) that most Arathi use to designate themselves as a community in the power of the Spirit. As the early Arathi community began to proselytize, it also used the Bible as a means of communicating its message to other Africans. And the Bible provided Arathi with a principled basis for rejecting any teachings that they could not reconcile with the gospel of Jesus Christ, including the theology of the mission churches, which, early Arathi felt, encouraged Africans to be content with their servile condition, as well as Gikuyu (or Kikuyu) beliefs in ancestral spirits, which Arathi argued were incompatible with their biblical understanding of the Holy Spirit. The Bible thus functioned as a double-edged sword for Arathi, allowing them to critique both Western and Gikuyu beliefs. It was also the critical tool by which Arathi appropriated some biblical concepts and blended them with African concepts in a new and different context to make Christianity a truly African religion. For this reason the beliefs of the early Arathi cannot be understood or adequately explained apart from both their biblical and African contexts.

231

If we wish to locate Arathi theology, then, we must first trace their beliefs in God, election, holiness (purity and impurity), the Holy Spirit, dreams, prophecy, healing and eschatology back to their Old and New Testament sources. Since early Arathi also drew on Gikuyu beliefs, we must also attempt to identify Gikuyu concepts and teachings that early Arathi used in their desire to bring the Christian message to their converts.

Origins of the Early Arathi Movement in Kenya

Although the origins of the Arathi movement are traceable to the cultural and religious crises of the late 1920s in central Kenya, it did not result from a break with the mission churches. Rather, its origins were connected with itinerant prophetic figures, such as Joseph Ng'ang'a and Musa Thuo, who claimed divine calling to their ministry.[3]

Joseph Ng'ang'a was born at Ng'enda in Kiambu District in the 1900s. Though he received a minimal education at the Gospel Mission station at Kambui, he was not baptized, and there is no evidence that he ever joined a mission church. His religious and prophetic experiences date from 1926, when he had a dramatic experience after a bout of drunkenness, after which he became ill for several days. During his illness, he was amazed one night when he heard someone calling him in a dream by a new baptismal name, Joseph. The voice identified itself as God and called him to a prophetic ministry. It also declared His intention to form a new community of Arathi (similar to Israel in the Old Testament), a community that was to be separate from both Gikuyu society and that of the Europeans. The voice also called Ng'ang'a to preach the Gospel and reveal God's intention of destroying the Europeans, who had colonized Gikuyu and taken away their land.

Following this experience, Ng'ang'a went into seclusion for three years, during which he abstained from normal life and devoted himself to prayer, reading the Bible and fasting. When he reemerged in 1929, he quickly gained a reputation as a pious person and began to gather a group of followers around him. Most of his followers, drawn from missions in northern Kiambu, were easily identified by their long white robes, their emphasis on the work of the Holy Spirit, and their millenarian beliefs that God was going to usher in a new age among the Gikuyu.

Ng'ang'a's group was not the only spirit group to develop in central Kenya at the time. The same year he started in Kiambu, a similar movement appeared in Gakarara, in southern Murang'a, led by Musa Thuo. Thuo was born about 1900 in Gatanga location of Murang'a District. He received a fourth-grade education at the Africa Inland Mission (AIM) at Githumu, and during his stay at the mission he became a Christian and was baptized. In 1921, Thuo left the AIM and joined a group of dissidents, under the leadership of Daudi Maina Kiragu, who had separated from the AIM over the issues of education and African leadership. In 1926, however,

Thuo began having intense dreams and visionary experiences that were at variance with the beliefs and practices of the larger group. He also experienced God calling him to preach so that people would repent of their sins and be saved. Soon after, Thuo, like Ng'ang'a, started preaching in neighbouring villages and gathering his own following.[4]

Arathi Appropriation of the Christian Bible

The early Arathi did not ground their teachings on pre-existing Gikuyu beliefs or on the existing structures and beliefs of Western mission churches but on the newly translated Gikuyu versions of the Christian scriptures.[5] Arathi were unshakeably convinced that the Bible was the Word of God (*kiugo kia Ngai*) and, as such, constituted the complete and definitive revelation of God's Word to Arathi and through them to the rest of humanity.

As God's revelation, the Bible was the absolute and infallible rule of faith and practice for Arathi. Arathi turned to the Bible for inspiration, for their values, for religious instruction, for exhortation, and for the structure and nature of the church they sought to establish. The Bible was thus regarded as the principal source for Arathi theology.

This is illustrated by Joseph Ng'ang'a's devotion to prayer and the study of the scriptures during the first three years of his ministry. He was convinced that the Bible spoke of a faith unlike that practised in the mission churches, who had hidden the true meaning of the scriptures from their African converts.

Prior to the translation of the scriptures into Gikuyu in the 1920s, only missionaries and a few select elite catechists had access to them. They alone could read the Bible in English or in Swahili, and they alone had contemporary methods of Biblical study and interpretation. The translation of the Bible into Gikuyu, however, placed Ng'ang'a and other Arathi on what they believed was an equal footing with the missions in understanding and interpreting the Bible.[6] For Arathi, then, the key to unlocking the truth of the scriptures came not from the mission churches but through their own study of the scriptures as illuminated by their experience of the Holy Spirit. This is why Ng'ang'a went into seclusion to seek guidance from the Holy Spirit in his interpretation of the scriptures. And within the Arathi church much emphasis was put on the study of the scriptures and regular Bible study sessions. Arathi were also expected to bring the Bible to worship services and to read and quote from it as required.

Knowledge of the scriptures, they believed, would help correct theological irregularities within mission Christianity. The Bible contained references to Gikuyu beliefs and practices, such as circumcision, with which Arathi were familiar but which the missions either condemned or prohibited. It also included detailed prescriptions and taboos (*thahu*) necessary to attain purity that the missions ignored. And it described sacred rites and ritual prohibitions (*migiro*) neglected by the missions. In addition, the Bible portrayed the Israelites as the chosen people of God. Since Arathi faced opposition and persecution from both the mission churches and the colonial establishment, they came to see the liberation of the Israelites from Egyptian bondage as exemplifying God's power to liberate the oppressed. Just as God had liberated Israel from Egyptian bondage, so would He liberate them from colonial oppression.

The Arathi Concept of God

Arathi found many religious ideas in the Bible with which they were already familiar, one of which was the Old Testament concept of God. The Old Testament, like Gikuyu religion, depicted a supreme monotheistic God (Ngai).[7] In both, God was an invisible creator and sustainer of the universe; He gave people land as their inheritance; He welcomed burnt offerings and sacrifices; and His presence was connected with a great mountain – Mount Sinai for the Israelites and Mount Kenya for Gikuyu. Thus, Old Testament ideas of God resonated with Gikuyu ones, such that early Arathi did not think of themselves as embracing a 'new' God. For them, the God of the Old Testament was also the Ngai of the Gikuyu people.

There were also differences, however, that caused a paradigmatic shift in the Arathi conception of God. One was God's involvement with Israel as depicted in the Old Testament. In Gikuyu religion, there were no stories of God's involvement in the day-to-day affairs of the people. In fact, Gikuyu believed that one does not pester God (*Ngai ndagiagiaguo*), but Arathi found many stories in the Christian scriptures of a God who actively intervened in human history. Both the exodus and the advent of Christ were important incidents that revealed God's involvement with humanity, manifesting its liberation, its redemption and the beginning of a new community. Arathi thus believed that God intervened in human history to save people from sin and liberate them from oppression, made possible because Arathi, like the Israelites, were a chosen people.[8]

Divine Election and Conversion

Arathi's ideas of election and conversion were conjoined. Arathi regarded themselves as God's chosen people, an 'elect' constituted by God through the Spirit after delivering them from the oppression and paternalism of the mission churches. Arathi found confirmation for this belief in the similarities between their own experiences and those of the Israelites in the Old Testament. Just as God had elected the Israelites as a people by calling Abraham to be their father, delivering them from bondage, and giving them the laws in the Pentateuch, so He elected the Arathi as a special people when He constituted the first Arathi church and gave it the laws in the Bible for guidance.

While divine election implied the work of God, who chose and reconstituted a new people out of the old, it also involved human responsibility. According to Arathi, when God called them from the larger Gikuyu society, they were required to make both 'social' and 'theological' turns, or conversions, in order to be worthy of the God who had chosen them. Socially, they had to leave their next of kin and join their religious brethren, thus transferring their loyalties and sense of belonging from one set of social relations to another. Simultaneously, they were also required to make a theological transformation in which they transferred their loyalties from Gikuyu deities to the Biblical God.

In traditional Gikuyu society, social relations were defined in terms of two interrelated organizing principles: agnatic kinship (*mbari*) and age-sets (*rika*). Agnatic kinship, the most elementary form of Gikuyu social organization, consisted of patrilineal kin, often composed of the oldest surviving male in a group, his wife or wives, and their children and grandchildren. Age-sets, by contrast, consisted of groups of people who had been initiated into adulthood together. Through them, people from different sections of Gikuyu society came together irrespective of their local associations. The age-set system was the most cohesive in bonding members of the larger ethnic group together. Though Arathi did not deny they were Gikuyu, they denied that their community was based on either blood relations or age-sets. Rather, it was a community of Christian brothers and sisters who patterned their lives after the early apostolic church. Its primary point of reference was not the kin group or the age-set, but the Christian community.

The social relocation of Arathi from Gikuyu social relations to Christian ones also had theological implications. Although Arathi did not regard conversion as an act of turning to a different God, they did see it as a thoroughgoing change in religious allegiance. Arathi loyalty was to their God, a God who required them to live a different kind of life from that of the rest of Gikuyu society. They were expected to be worthy of the God who had called them and to be virtuous in terms not of the norms of Gikuyu society but of the laws of God as found in the Pentateuch.

Arathi conversion ritualized their separation from Gikuyu society and their incorporation in a new Christian community in a variety of ways. New converts were required to wash the whole body in order to cleanse them of the perceived impurities of Gikuyu society and purify them for the community of the Arathi. After washing, converts were endowed with a new set of white clothes, symbolizing their new state, and given extensive instruction in the laws of purity and impurity that Arathi observed.

Laws of Purity and Impurity

Early Arathi regarded the laws of the Pentateuch as divine commands that mandated the fundamental duties of people to God, to their neighbours and to themselves. These were not the mere folkways or mores of a people, but the commands of God without which no individual or community could rise to the moral level God required of humanity. And, since they were God's revelation, Arathi were required to adhere to their moral and ritual requirements as literally as possible in order to attain purity and righteousness.[9]

Arathi laws and prohibitions can be classified into two categories. The first included 'internal' prohibitions aimed at maintaining both personal purity and the sacredness of their place of worship. The second category included 'external' prohibitions aimed at maintaining the purity of Arathi in a hostile and impure external environment.[10]

Within the internal category, Arathi took their rules from the Pentateuch, which they viewed as prerequisites for attaining personal purity and participating in public worship. They were to avoid contact with bodily discharges, such as female menstruation or male nocturnal emissions, and were forbidden from coming into contact with a woman immediately after childbirth. They had to keep the Sabbath holy by not performing any work: they were not to make a fire or cook, get food from the market or the garden, or walk or travel except to go to church. Other prohibitions included rules against eating pork, rabbit, camel, blood or animals strangled according to Gikuyu tradition. Arathi should not cut their hair or beard, drink any alcoholic beverages or commit adultery.

Violating these prohibitions was believed to lead to *thahu*, or a state of ritual contamination.[11] In wider Gikuyu society, *thahu* referred to a state of ritual uncleanness brought on by acts that breached Gikuyu ritual and moral rules. To remove *thahu*, a *mundu mugo* (diviner) performed sacrifices in conjunction with the council of elders.[12] For Arathi, however, *thahu* was not primarily caused by breaching Gikuyu moral codes, but by breaking divine laws, producing a state in which one became unacceptable to God. Similarly, *thahu* could not be removed by a traditional priest or diviner, but only by the cleansing blood of Jesus Christ or by undertaking certain sacred rites prescribed by Arathi. While Arathi held that one was only temporarily impure and could restore fellowship with God after most transgressions, they made an exception when it came to adultery or illicit sex. Arathi regarded those who violated these prohibitions as threatening the purity of all. Incapable of repentance or purification, they were expelled from the movement.

The second category of Arathi prohibitions concerned their relationships with mission and Gikuyu society. Arathi held that those outside the movement were perpetually in a state of *thahu* because they participated in religious rituals that rendered them impure as far as Arathi were concerned. In contrast, those within the Arathi community were thought to be ritually clean or in the process of becoming so. To maintain their purity, Arathi developed a series of prohibitions to protect them against possible contamination by outsiders. Arathi were not to come into physical contact with non-Arathi, and thus they could not shake hands with non-Arathi or mingle with them. Arathi were not to eat in public places, where they might come in contact with prohibited foods or foods that were not prepared properly. And they had to wear white clothes as a sign of their holiness and as a way of distinguishing them from the rest of society.

The Holy Spirit

Although Arathi held to Old Testament laws, they also regarded theirs as a Christian church. One of their most distinctive beliefs was that their church was possessed by the power of the Holy Spirit, a belief based on II Corinthians 13:14 and Philippians 2:1, where Paul describes the Church as the fellowship of the Holy Spirit (*koinonia tou hagiou pneumatos*). According to Murray, when Arathi are asked to what Church they belong, most respond that they belong to Kanitha wa Roho – the Church of the Holy Spirit.[13]

Arathi ideas about spirits were dualistic, divided between the Holy Spirit (a good spirit) and the spirit of error (a bad spirit).[14] The spirit of error manifested itself in false teachings, such as the paternalistic teachings of mission churches or colonial views of oppression. It also manifested itself in Gikuyu religious teachings and practices, which Arathi regarded as ritually impure. The bad spirit caused evil, unholy or ungodly things to happen, and it was manifested in social divisions, judgement, pride and boasting, while the Holy Spirit brought power and renewal to the life of believers.

This was a central Arathi belief. Arathi believed that Christian life arises out of the Holy Spirit (John 3:58), since it is the Holy Spirit who convicts people of sin and enables them to turn in repentance and faith to Jesus Christ. In addition, the Holy Spirit teaches people about God, so that in knowing God they become God's people. The Church of Christ, Arathi were convinced, extends to all those whom the Holy Spirit has called, for the Holy Spirit is He who builds the people of God into the Church of God and hence confirms that they are the Children of God (Romans 8:14, Acts 2:44–7).

In addition to being regarded as the source of unity and fellowship within the church, the Holy Spirit was also held to be the power that empowers and preserves the church. This empowerment, Arathi contended, derives from receiving 'baptism in the Holy Spirit', which brings 'a special sense of God's reality in their lives. It involved a deep sense of joy and peace.'[15] As at Pentecost, such baptism was often followed by signs and wonders, particularly prophecy, speaking in tongues, dreams, visions and healing (Acts 2:4, 10:46, 19:6). In addition, the Holy Spirit gives the Church its basic structure, calling some to be prophets, others to be evangelists, and others to be pastors and teachers (Ephesians 4:11, Acts 2:1).

Prophets and Prophecy

Arathi also regard themselves as a community of prophets. According to Sandgren, the term *arathi* (prophets) was the earliest term Arathi used to identify themselves.[16] And, from the beginning, Arathi claimed that they were a prophetic community, such as that spoken of by Joel, a community empowered by the Holy Spirit that can prophesy, experience visions and dream (Joel 1:28–9).

In claiming to be prophets, however, Arathi were not introducing something new to Gikuyu society. In pre-Christian Gikuyu society, prophetic figures were also referred to as *arathi*. Unlike the Arathi church, where prophecy devolved upon all those on whom the Spirit had been poured, however, the traditional office was limited to a few people drawn from the council of elders. Unlike diviners, who underwent special training and used oracles to interpret messages, prophets were believed to receive their messages directly from Ngai, either through dreams or by being possessed by ancestral spirits. When so possessed, they went into a trance and were able to interpret the word of Ngai and to predict future events. A good example of such a prophet was the legendary Mugo Kibiro, a pre-Christian prophet who predicted the coming of the Europeans and warned Gikuyu of the implications of their presence. Thus pre-Christian Gikuyu, like Arathi, believed that spirits give utterance to prophets in a way that enabled them to predict the future.

Although traditional prophets and Arathi shared the name *arathi* as well as the belief that spirits could give utterance to a prophet, there were important differences between the two. In traditional Gikuyu society, prophecy was limited to a few individuals drawn from the council of elders. Typically male, prophets also served as seers, diviners and mediums. Prophets in traditional society thus comprised an exclusive class of male specialists. In contrast, Arathi prophecy was not limited to a few professionals. Nor was it limited to men, but included all those upon whom the spirit of God had descended.

The two concepts of prophecy also differed regarding the source of prophecy. In traditional society, prophets were regarded as mediums through whom ancestral spirits conveyed the will of Ngai. Arathi also believed that a spirit could give utterance through a prophet, but the voice was exclusively that of the Holy Spirit, or God.

A final contrast between the two concepts was the nature of the message conveyed by prophets. According to Arathi, a prophet spoke the Word of God as it was revealed to him or her by the Holy Spirit. Like the Old Testament prophets, whose prophecies were influenced by the exilic (587–516BCE) and post-exilic (516–250 BCE) times in which they lived, early Arathi prophecies highlighted the problems Gikuyu faced from the missions and colonial rulers. On occasion, early Arathi prophets also castigated their own community for failing to observe certain legal precepts, but they usually attacked the injustices of colonial rule. The prominence of spiritual messages against colonial oppression is what differentiated Arathi messages from those of the pre-Christian Gikuyu prophets. While Arathi castigated the colonial establishment for oppressing Africans, traditional prophets tended to warn that European invasion and presence were inevitable and that it would be suicidal to resist them. Thus, while Arathi raised a militant if not a radical voice, traditional prophets advocated caution in the face of colonial power.

Eschatological Beliefs

Eschatology was central to Arathi belief. The earliest Arathi believed that God had called them to tell other Africans that redemption was close at hand. They were convinced that God was going to free Africans from British oppression by ushering in a golden age during which the chosen would be blessed with abundance and the wicked overthrown. The messages of Joseph Ng'ang'a, for instance, spoke of 'God freeing the Gikuyu from the colonial rulers'.[17] He argued that Gikuyu had suffered abuse, humiliation and loss of their land from Europeans, but a time would come when God was going to free Africans by 'sweeping the Europeans aside and ushering in a Gikuyu golden age'.

Arathi disputed the exact time when this would come to pass. Some never gave a date, but believed that it would take place after a big earthquake. Others believed that the end would come after a 'big yawning pit' appeared outside Nairobi that would swallow first the governor and then all the other Europeans. Still others attempted to date the coming end more precisely. According to Sandgren, some Arathi believed that the world would end in 1931.[18] To these Arathi, the presence of God's Spirit among God's people was a sign of the last days. This new age, they believed, would free Gikuyu of their oppression and enable them to be masters of their own destiny.

Although many early Arathi messages emphasized the coming of a new age, subsequent teaching about it developed in two directions. Ng'ang'a, who died in 1934 after a confrontation with colonial officials, envisioned a new Gikuyu community without Europeans. This new society would be based neither on older Gikuyu tradition nor on newer Western ones, however, but on God's law as conveyed in the Old Testament. According to many informants, Ng'ang'a believed that Old Testament law played a crucial role in the life of Israel. It established the code of conduct for all Israelites; it expressed the relations between members of the ruling class and the less powerful; it gave expression to the obligation of just and righteous behaviour; and it expressed God's will for the community. Without it, people would not be able to achieve what God required of them.

As Arathi awaited the coming of the Gikuyu golden age, some continued to see such millenarian messages as a solution to Gikuyu political problems.

Others, however, merged these eschatological ideas with a new message that foresaw a martial figure who would lead Gikuyu against the British. One such prophet was Musa Thuo. According to contemporary colonial documents, Thuo admonished people to repent of their sins, 'for the Kingdom of God was coming', and he led his followers in prayer for Gikuyu deliverance from colonialism.[19] But he also encouraged Arathi to join the Kikuyu Central Association (KCA), a political organization that protested against colonial land alienation, low wages, the colour bar and taxes.

The sources do not reveal why Thuo encouraged his followers to combine both divine and political solutions to colonial problems, but what is clear is that millennial expectations had failed to alter the political situation in Kenya. Many Arathi had expected a rebirth of Gikuyu society, inspired and empowered by God's Spirit and law, between 1931 and 1935. The fact that the world had not ended may thus have led Thuo and others to revitalize the church while also pursuing other means of bringing about the liberation of the Gikuyu. To revive the church, Thuo called all the Arathi groups to his Kaguthi home in 1933, admonishing them to systematize their beliefs and organize a church similar to that called for in Ng'ang'a's messages.[20] Thus, while Thuo had started his career preaching imminent redemption, he began to modify his message as the days of the anticipated end passed. It was in this context that he encouraged his followers to join the KCA, though the majority of Arathi refused in accord with Ng'ang'a's admonitions that religion and politics belonged to different realms. One had its origins in God, while the other had its origins in human existence, and the two should never be mixed.

Faith and Healing

From their formative years, Arathi stressed supernatural healing practices by looking to the work of Jesus Christ in the New Testament for guidance and instruction. The New Testament contains many references to Christ's ministry to the sick; to his curing people of blindness, paralysis, demon possession, leprosy, fever, haemorrhaging, deafness and epilepsy; and to his raising people from the dead. These convinced Arathi that Christ was concerned with the well-being of the total person, the body, the mind and the soul. Nothing was more indicative of Jesus' concern for the total human being than Luke 4:18–19, where Jesus declares that the Spirit of God is upon him to preach the good news to the poor, set at liberty those who are oppressed, give sight to the blind, and proclaim the acceptable year of the Lord. Since Jesus' power to conquer illness (and evil) came from God through the Holy Spirit and Jesus' disciples also possessed such power, it followed that Arathi in the power of the Spirit also had such power.

Jesus' method of healing, however, was not to be confused with medical methods introduced by the mission churches or with those previously practised in Gikuyu society. Most mission churches introduced medical centres where people were treated with Western medicines. Arathi, however, rejected these methods on the basis that Jesus cured exclusively by speech, by touch or by anointing with saliva. Since Jesus' method did not involve physicians or medicines, therefore, Arathi were also prohibited from seeking Western methods of healing.

Arathi were also forbidden from appealing to traditional Gikuyu methods of healing. In pre-Christian Gikuyu society, illness was thought to be caused by spiritual powers (*ngoma*) that maliciously afflicted human beings with various diseases. Their most common agents were either witches (*arogi*), who attacked others out of malice, or ancestral spirits, who sought to avenge wrongs done to them by the living. Sick people then sought cures from diviners, who either countered a witch's attack or diagnosed and appeased the anxiety of the spirits. In Arathi thought, however, spirits were divided between good and bad spirits. The bad spirit was identified in many Arathi songs with Satan. Since Satan was also the source of moral evil, Arathi thought that illness was caused by Satan and not by Gikuyu *ngoma* or ancestral spirits.

Traditional Gikuyu believed that in order for a patient to be healed, the besieging powers of the *ngoma* must be controlled by a diviner or healer. Such healers, they believed, had power over the spirits that caused the disease. Healers either prescribed herbal medicines or resorted to their own spiritual forces. But both these methods were forbidden by Arathi. Early Arathi had destroyed their charms, herbs, amulets and talismans; disavowed faith in the ancestral spirits; and insisted on prayer and the laying on of hands as the only acceptable healing methods, for these were the methods Jesus had used, and they were the only ones sanctioned by the Bible.

Conclusion

This study has examined the beliefs and practices of Arathi in order to determine their primary source. Throughout the study we have pointed out various ways in which early Arathi drew their primary beliefs from Christian scriptures. The translation of the Bible into Gikuyu provided Arathi with the means of legitimating their existence as a church, as well as the language to reject certain beliefs and practices from both Gikuyu and Western Christian traditions. Though Arathi accepted the whole Bible as authoritative, they drew most of their beliefs from the Old Testament. It was from the Old Testament that Arathi developed the idea that they were chosen by God for a special purpose. The term they used to describe this experience was *athure*, 'the chosen ones' – or, in theological terms, 'the elect'. Arathi believed that God had chosen them after delivering them from sin and oppression by the colonial establishment. Since deliverance from sin and oppression entailed a paradigm shift in a person's life, Arathi believed that divine election was linked with conversion. Election was the objective way God called a human being, while conversion was the human response. For Arathi, conversion followed election. One was able to turn to God only after God had elected one.

Conversion was both social and theological. Socially, it meant separation from larger Gikuyu or African society and incorporation in another set of social relations. Theologically, it meant their religious orientation was also changed. Conversion rituals initiated these transformations. First, converts were washed to cleanse them of the impurities of the larger Gikuyu community and purify them for their new lives as Arathi. After washing, as we have seen, converts were given new white clothes and turbans, thus symbolizing their new lives as believers.

After conversion, Arathi were required to follow strict rules of purity. Although many Arathi laws, together with the related concept of *thahu*, were also found in Gikuyu traditional beliefs and practices, Arathi theology differed from that of traditional society. According to Arathi, their laws were more than mere Gikuyu customs; they were the commands of God, found in the New and Old Testaments. From the Pentateuch, in particular, Arathi adopted Jewish ritual laws. They believed that the moral injunctions found in the Pentateuch summed up their duties to God, to each other and to the whole of humanity. These laws, therefore, constituted eternal and universal rules for the fulfilment of an individual and society. This belief that Arathi laws had a universal value distinguished them from those of the larger Gikuyu society, laws that Arathi believed were local.

Christian scriptures were thus the ultimate source of Arathi beliefs and practices. It is from the Bible that Arathi drew their ideas about God, the Holy Spirit, the church, prophecy, purity and impurity, and healing. These are just a few examples. The study of Arathi beliefs and practices is relatively new and identification of all its theological sources is provisional and unfinished. There is therefore a critical need to do more work in this area.

Notes

1 The name *arathi* means prophets in Gikuyu. Arathi are also known locally by a variety of names: Aroti (dreamers), Akurinu (a term whose meaning is not clear, but perhaps is derived from the term *mukurinu*, who is the saviour), Andu aa Iremba (turban people), Kanitha wa Roho (Church of the Holy Spirit) and Waru wa Mungu (People of God). See David Sandgren, *Christianity and the Kikuyu: Religious Divisions and Social Conflict* (New York, 1989), 121; Jocelyn Murray, 'The Kikuyu spirit churches', *Journal of Religion in Africa*, 5 (1974), 199–200.
2 D. H. Rawcliffe, *The Struggle for Kenya* (London, 1954), 27–35. See also, Robert Buijtenhuijs, *Essays on Mau Mau* (Leiden, 1982), 123–4; Garhardus C. Oosthuizen, *Post-Christianity in Africa* (London, 1968), 45–52.

3 Much of the data concerning Arathi origins comes from oral sources, primarily from oral interviews that I conducted in Kenya in 1988. The original texts of the interviews are preserved and available for consultation. In addition, Jocelyn Murray and David Sandgren kindly allowed me to use their interviews and research materials. Their work has greatly enriched mine.

4 For the growth and development of the Arathi movement, see Francis K. Githieya, *The Freedom of the Spirit: African Indigenous Churches in Kenya* (Atlanta, 1997), 93–150; Sandgren, *Christianity and the Kikuyu*, 121.

5 See Murray, 'Kikuyu spirit churches', 202–4. For translations of the Bible into Gikuyu, see Jocelyn Murray, 'Production of Christian literature', in David B. Barrett *et al.* (eds), *Kenya Churches Handbook* (Kisumu, 1973), 93–9. See also, David B. Barrett, *Schism and Renewal in Africa* (Nairobi, 1968), 127–34, where he argues that one of the main causes of the emergence of African independent churches was the translation of the scriptures into the vernacular.

6 Oral evidence: Samuel Chegge, Daudi Daniel Nduti and Josephat Mwangi, 10 August 1988, Nyahururu.

7 Samuel G. Kibicho, 'The interaction of the traditional Kikuyu concept of God with the biblical concept', *Cahiers des Religions Africaines*, 2 (1968), 223–38.

8 Oral evidence: John Chegge, Daudi Daniel Nduti and Josphat Mwangi, 10 August 1988, Nyahururu.

9 See John Chegge, 'Hadithi ya Kanisa ya Roho Mtakatifu' ['The history of the spirit churches'] (unpublished MS, Nyahururu, nd), 1; Murray, 'Kikuyu spirit churches', 203–5.

10 See Sandgren, *Christianity and the Kikuyu*, 161–74; Francis K. Githieya, 'The new people of God: the Christian community in the African Orthodox Church (Karing'a) and the Arathi (Gikuyu Spirit Churches)' (PhD, Emory University, 1992), 228. –

11 See Sandgren, *Christianity and the Kikuyu*, 161–74; Githieya, 'New people of God', 228; Murray, 'Kikuyu spirit churches', 228–9; Mary Douglas, *Purity and Danger* (New York, 1966).

12 Samuel Kibicho, 'The Kikuyu conception of God: its continuity into the Christian era' (PhD, Vanderbilt University, 1972), 32.

13 Murray, 'Kikuyu spirit churches', 201.

14 Sandgren, *Christianity and the Kikuyu*, 170–1.

15 *Ibid.*

16 *Ibid.*, 121.

17 *Ibid.*, 124.

18 *Ibid.*

19 KNA: DC/FH/2/1/4 Documents 1/15 and 1/18.

20 Sandgren, *Christianity and the Kikuyu*, 126.

VI

Protestant Revival
&
Popular Catholicism

While independent Christian churches have received considerable scholarly attention, including the preceding studies by Sandgren and Githieya, the frequent struggles for control taking place within the mission (and now national) churches have received much less attention, as Omari demonstrates.[1] And yet most ex-mission churches are now independent national churches, and African Christianity today offers a plethora of vibrant new religious movements within and outside the historical churches, many of which stress prophecy and spiritual gifts that challenge the authority of the established churches.

Historically, such movements within the Catholic Church have often been referred to as 'popular' or 'folk' Catholicism, and they have a long history in Europe, Latin America and elsewhere. They were also imported into Africa by European priests, often drawn from rural backgrounds in France, Quebec and elsewhere, where they provided an instrumental dimension usually lacking in twentieth-century Catholicism or Protestantism. These movements were then eagerly taken up by Africans disturbed by the epistemological gap between their own worldly spiritual concerns and the other-worldly ones of the missionaries. But such movements could be dangerous, granting religious authority to lay people or to individual priests that challenged the ultimate authority of the church.

Kassimir's chapter on popular Catholicism in Uganda is a fascinating study of the church's attempts to control such movements through sponsoring 'official' popular movements while seeking to proscribe truly 'popular' ones that challenged its *raison d'église*. Unlike the Protestant churches, the Catholic Church understood Africans' concerns with the power of the spirit world in everyday life and sought to channel them into acceptable forms through such organizations as the Legion of Mary or the canonization of the Uganda martyrs. When African followers strayed

245

beyond the realms of acceptable orthodoxy and authority to receive Marian visions themselves or to exorcise evil spirits and heal in the name of the martyrs, however, the church hierarchy proscribed them, driving them out of the church and beyond their control. As a result of the increasing weakness of 'official' movements sponsored by the church, however, genuinely popular movements have flourished outside the bounds of the church to address people's continuing concerns with sickness, witchcraft and possession by spirits. A church that has been committed since Vatican II to the 'inculturation' of its practices and beliefs with African culture thus finds itself ironically powerless to incorporate local religious concerns into Catholic practice and organization.

In their chapter Comoro and Sivalon take up the similar case of a Catholic priest in Tanzania who has embarked on his own prophetic ministry. Appealing to the intercession of Mary, Fr Nkwera addresses popular concerns over spirituality, sickness, poverty and political corruption through stirring religious services, communal prayer, healing and mutual assistance. Attributing the ills of contemporary society to the presence of the devil, he calls his followers to spiritual and social communion to overcome their problems. As he has done so, however, Nkwera's Marian Faith Healing Ministry has come under increasing attack from the Catholic bishops, who see his practices as unorthodox, his followers as disruptive and his ministry as a challenge to their own religious authority. In response, Nkwera and his followers see themselves as a devotional community within the Catholic Church and Catholic traditions, and bemoan the church's denial of the sacraments to them as further evidence of Satan's power. In calling the church back to its spiritual foundations, they see themselves as a reform or revival movement within the church. While Nkwera's beliefs and practices may resonate with African spiritual concerns, Comoro and Sivalon conclude that the beliefs and practices of his ministry are based on traditional Catholic rites and beliefs and thus represent an authentic African interpretation of Catholicism. Their conclusions thus parallel Githieya's earlier regarding the biblical basis of the Arathi in Kenya.

Revival movements have long characterized Protestant missions and churches throughout eastern Africa as well. Starting with the East African Revival (Balokole) in the late nineteenth century, revival movements have flowed periodically through Protestant mission churches, regardless of denomination. Characterized by the formation of prayer groups within individual churches, members met nightly in fervent prayer to address their concerns with sickness and the prevalence of evil in the world. In the process, they threatened to split their churches by challenging the spirituality, faith and leadership of their pastors and fellow parishioners alike. Revival groups thus tended to exist independently – both theologically and organizationally – of the churches in which their members continued to participate. As a result, they were frequently opposed by both missionaries and African church leaders until such opposition threatened the very survival of many of the churches, but today many African church leaders are themselves active members of the revival movement.

As the movement has continued to grow from the 1970s, significant changes have occurred in Protestant churches across Tanzania, as Mlahagwa, a prominent revivalist himself, shows. Protestant church practice is expanding to embrace charismatic practices of speaking in tongues, prophecy and healing, encouraged in turn by the development of large inter-denominational crusades led by lay evangelists and preachers. When these practices come under attack from church authorities, members form new Pentecostal churches, which are also spreading rapidly, but increasingly revivalists are also finding comfort in fellowships within their own churches. What is unique about the fellowship movement is that such groups exist independently of the churches in which they are housed. They have their own organization and frequently include members from other churches, including Catholic ones. Outside the individual fellowships, however, no wider organization exists that knits either them or the periodic crusades into an established group. They thus represent a genuinely popular movement, spread by example and drawing sustenance from the convictions of their members. As in Fr Nkwera's Marian Faith Healing Ministry, members pray for each other, cast out spirits, heal the sick and support one another in their daily lives, providing mutual spiritual and social support.

The dramatic rise of new Christian movements in African today certainly echoes the earlier struggles that gave rise to widespread independency in Africa, and these movements continue to challenge the leaders, doctrines and practices of the established churches, now largely under African leadership. They also continue to reflect Africans' beliefs in the spiritual foundations of daily events, as people struggle daily with political corruption, economic impoverishment, social malaise and ill health. In many ways, then, they continue to reflect and draw on specifically African spiritual concerns and traditions. In other ways, however, the appeals of popular Catholicism and Protestant revival in Africa parallel the dramatic spread of popular, evangelical and charismatic movements throughout the world.

Are these movements, then, simply further extensions of Christian movements elsewhere, or do they represent, in the terms used by Comoro and Sivalon, an authentic African interpretation of Christianity? Given the deep roots Christianity has sunk in African soil over more than a century, during which Africans have interpreted and appropriated the Word for themselves, the popular roots of these movements outside the established churches, and the degree to which such movements resonate with and address specific African spiritual concerns, they must be seen as genuinely African movements, but they draw on the rich traditions of Christianity to interpret them in new lights. They are, then, both African *and* Christian, as Africans interpret their faith in terms of their own conditions and context.

---

1 David Barrett's comprehensive study of independent churches stresses the prevalence of endemic struggles within the mission/national churches themselves. *Schism and Renewal in Africa* (Nairobi, 1968).

Twelve

The Politics of Popular Catholicism
in Uganda

RONALD KASSIMIR

Interviewer: Would you say the church has grown numerically during your period?
Archbishop Wamala: Physically and numerically the church has grown. It is the Lord who can judge the quality.[1]

The growing church in Uganda has produced very good, good, mediocre and indifferent Christians. Some are very zealous, active and convinced, others are convinced but inactive, others are critical and active, others are critical but inactive and again others simply constitute numbers for statistics. The phenomenon is not a specifically Ugandan one but a universal phenomenon. However there are certainly some aspects of it which are specifically Ugandan.[2]

These two statements, by Archbishop Wamala and Ugandan theologian Charles Ssemuju, resonate with trends in the anthropology and sociology of religion that emphasize the plurality of meanings that members of a religious denomination may hold regarding their faith.[3] In a recent study of American Catholicism, Gene Burns states: 'to understand what Catholicism really is socially and historically, we must study its divergent interpretations'.[4] In this chapter, I adopt this conceptualization of Catholicism and, following Ssemuju, reflect on both its universal aspects and those 'which are specifically Ugandan'. In particular, I address the activities of some Catholic Ugandans whose interpretations of their faith go beyond the basic sacramental system of universal Catholicism and lead them to public and organized expressions that sometimes take them outside the bounds of officially acceptable Catholic practice. It is when this extra-sacramental, public and organized expression of religiosity explicitly or implicitly calls into question the bases of authority within the church that I refer to it as 'popular religion'.

It is necessary, however, to qualify Ssemuju's comprehensive list of 'categories of Catholics', because Ugandan Catholics are not evenly distributed across his categories. Indeed, a high percentage of Ugandan Catholics fall into three of Ssemuju's categories: convinced and inactive, critical and inactive, or 'simply constituting numbers for statistics'.[5] The operative term in all these categories is 'inactive'. As I define it here, inactive means not that most Catholics do not attend mass or participate occasionally in the most important events of the church calendar. Rather, it means that most Catholics are not actively involved in Catholic lay associations or other public expressions of their faith,[6] while many are active in private expressions of spirituality – outside church-approved idioms – that are officially considered highly questionable or condemned. And some 'inactive' Catholics have been actively involved in public and organized expressions of religiosity that challenge institutional norms and power.[7]

This may be changing, however. The last ten years have produced a wide range of popular religious expressions and mobilization with strong lay Catholic (and sometimes clerical) participation. This recent rise of popular religiosity is evidence of the church's reluctance and/or incapacity to incorporate widely held spiritual concerns into officially acceptable practices in spite of the fact that such incorporation was adopted explicitly by the church through its theology of 'inculturation', which became a prominent feature of African Catholic discourse after the Second Vatican Council (1962–5).[8]

Vatican II advanced inculturation as an evangelization strategy in non-Western contexts that seeks to find points of accommodation between indigenous cultures and Christian discourse, symbols and practices. Implemented from the top down, inculturation in Uganda on the whole has failed to create a 'new' Catholicism comprised of 'active' church members, which is reflected in the dearth of officially legitimated extra-sacramental practices and associations with popular appeal. At the same time, the possibilities for a bottom-up inculturation that includes space for lay religious charisma or for the most pressing spiritual interests of many Catholics (especially healing and protection from witchcraft) have not been realized. What I argue is that the political and cultural context of Ugandan Catholicism, and the historical legacy of church formation[9] – the ways in which relationships of power and authority were constructed between clergy and laity – have sown the seeds of contemporary popular religious movements and made the internal reforms that might incorporate these movements difficult to implement.

A radical growth in the public expression of popular religion in Uganda has taken place since the coming to power of the National Resistance Movement (NRM) in 1986. The near monopoly of the Roman Catholic and Anglican churches is being shaken both by new missionary movements (inspired and often financed by American fundamentalist Christian groups) and by the growth of independent or heterodox religious groups.[10] The most dramatic was the Holy Spirit Movement of Alice Lakwena, a young woman from Acholiland in Northern Uganda who, shortly after her conversion to Catholicism in the mid-1980s, became possessed by the spirit Lakwena, who gave her powers to heal and find witches. The spirit eventually instructed her to lead her followers in a war against the NRM shortly after its successful guerrilla struggle ended in 1986.[11] Recently, under the name of the Lord's Resistance Army, remnants of Lakwena's movement have continued to cause major security problems in the north. While it is impossible to know the degree to which Catholics have participated in Lakwena's movement and its offshoots, Acholiland has one of the highest percentages of baptized Catholics of any region of Uganda.[12]

Within the Catholic Church, popular religious expressions have also been on the rise. There has been a surge in the apparitions of the Virgin Mary in parts of southern Uganda in recent years. In one area, Rakai in southern Buganda, the apparition was connected with miracle cures of AIDS and other diseases. While members of a local religious order (the Banyakaroli) and a few priests sought to establish the site as a shrine, officials from Masaka Diocese either played down the affair or declared it a sham. Two priests in Ankole also claimed to have been visited by Mary, who instructed them to redirect the church towards the ultramontane position of the excommunicated Archbishop Lefebvre. And in Masaka a man claiming to have had Marian visions began his own movement (Byonzira Monks Ggye – or the Monastic Army of the Rejected), which opened group homes for children, whom many in the region believed had been abducted.

Other forms of popular religiosity have also emerged. Catholic groups in Kampala and Toro in western Uganda devoted to the Uganda Martyrs have been holding exorcism sessions led by lay people. Similarly, in Toro and neighbouring Bunyoro, a former Catholic catechist and composer of hymns – Dosteo Bisaaka – established a popular independent movement based on exorcism and witchcraft eradication. None of these expressions were initiated or organized officially by the church. In at least two cases, movement leaders openly challenged or rejected church authority, and both their movements were shut down by the government in 1991 under pressure from Catholic officials. It is difficult to claim unequivocally that such examples of religious innovation were not as pervasive in Uganda prior to 1985, given the situation in the country and the paucity of available information, but many Ugandans to whom I spoke during my research claim that the level of such activities, and especially the extent of their public organization, is unprecedented.[13]

At the same time as Ugandan Catholics were increasingly participating in independent movements or non-approved religious practices, the older organizational mechanisms established by the church to nurture extra-sacramental religious practice were becoming moribund. In addition, newer innovations such as small Christian communities (modelled in part on the basic Christian communities of Latin America) failed to take hold.

The decline of the older associations, such as the Legion of Mary, was not caused by the rise of the new popular religious movements, since it had begun several decades earlier. Rather, it was the decline of these associations that, in conjunction with broader socio-political changes, contributed to the creation of space for the new expressions. Combined with recent competition from evangelical churches, the atrophy of lay associations and rise of new popular movements could thus be construed as the beginning of a breakdown of the hegemonic equilibrium that the Catholic and Anglican churches attained in Uganda from the late nineteenth century.[14]

The Political Context
of Popular Religious Movements

> Messianism and miracles often find space in an ambiguous climate of truce and dissatisfaction, of outward peace and latent conflict, in which no equilibrium ever is definitive or stable.[15]

The dominance of the Anglican and Catholic missions in Uganda, and their competitive and often antagonistic relationship, has been the subject of a rich historiographic literature.[16] From their first arrival at the court of Buganda in the late 1870s, the two missions brought the rivalry and mutual prejudices of their mother churches from Europe to East Africa. When the British made Buganda a protectorate in 1894, the Anglican mission attained quasi-establishment status. Chiefships under indirect rule were parcelled out according to religious denomination, with the most going to followers of the Anglican Church Missionary Society (CMS) and the remainder divided among Catholics and Muslims. This model was emulated in other parts of what became the Uganda Protectorate as the British extended their rule to new territories. While the Catholic mission was allowed to remain in Uganda under the norms of religious liberty agreed to by the major colonial powers, all the rulers in Uganda's western kingdoms converted to Anglicanism and most of their chiefs (and those in the non-kingdom territories as well) were, or became, Anglicans.[17]

As this pattern was reproduced in succeeding generations, the Catholic mission and many of its followers developed a deeply held grievance at what they perceived as official discrimination, particularly since Catholics outnumbered Anglicans in most parts of the protectorate. This grievance was a major factor in the formation of the Democratic Party (DP), most of whose important leaders were Catholics, in the mid-1950s. And, with the introduction of electoral competition, party support in many districts was seen as strongly correlated with religious denomination; Catholics supported the DP, while Protestants voted for the Uganda People's Congress (UPC).[18]

While the colonial state structured opportunities for power and social mobility in a manner that favoured Anglicans, it also helped to minimize competition from indigenous religious organizations or from other Christian missions in ways that benefited both the Catholic and Anglican churches. From the start, colonial officials and local governments either encouraged or countenanced attacks on indigenous shrines and religious practitioners undertaken by chiefs or catechists of the two major missions. And colonial forces themselves ferociously suppressed the allegedly 'atavistic' Nyabingi cult in southwestern Uganda in the 1910s.

Fearing that greater religious pluralism was bad for political stability, colonial officials also generally opposed the entry of new missions into Uganda, especially those whose charismatic practices were perceived as providing the seeds for independency and protest. When several new Protestant groups began exploring the possibility of working in Uganda in the late 1950s, the Permanent Secretary of the Ministry of Social Services issued a memorandum to his field staff on 'New Missions'. He warned that 'small missionary sects' tend to peter out and their followers then begin their own movements:

> experience in some territories has been that in a short time the breakaway Church becomes anti-Government and subversive.... It is also relevant that the two main Christian Missions have extended their coverage to almost every part of the Protectorate, and that except for those Africans who are Muslims, the great majority professes to be Anglicans or Catholics. A new mission could only therefore succeed by dividing the existing Churches and creating another body from converts from one or the other. This is not thought to be at all a desirable development.[19]

Thus, the delegitimizing of non-Christian (and non-Islamic) religious practice, combined with the discouraging of new Christian missions, permitted little space for the public expression of religiosity outside the two mainstream denominations. Finally, the intense competition for members and political power between followers of the Anglican and Catholic churches and their mutually privileged position provided incentives to Ugandans to be affiliated with one of the two mainstream churches.[20]

The lack of space for religious expressions outside the two main missions continued in the independence period. Under Idi Amin's rule, all religious denominations other than Anglican, Catholic and Muslim were banned. During the regimes of Amin (1971–9) and Obote II (1980–85), almost any form of new social organization, whatever its goals, was likely to be suppressed by the state. And the leaders of the National Resistance Army (NRA), while fighting a guerrilla war against the Obote II regime, were themselves hostile to popular beliefs and practices.[21] In the context of extreme political oppression, the Catholic Church became an important component of the survival strategies of its members, who were thus unlikely to provoke the opprobrium of church leaders, whatever the content of their private beliefs and practices.

In the much more open political climate of Uganda after 1985, however, the possibility of groups publicly practising and even recruiting is far greater, and Catholics' dependence on their church has lessened. Perhaps counter-intuitive to the idea that religious movements accelerate at moments of the breakdown of political order, the restoration of some semblance of order in Uganda has correlated with the rise of new movements or the 'going public' of existing ones. At least, this seems true in southern Uganda where the NRM has its strongest base of support. In the north, disorder reigned in the first years of the NRM regime, and it was there that Lakwena's Holy Spirit Movement evolved into violent opposition to the government. But, generally, the allowance of a public sphere under the NRM, despite the regime's ambivalence toward popular religious expression, has both permitted the influx of new Christian missions and emboldened indigenous religious movements.[22]

The Deep Structure of Spiritual Power

In addition to the shifting political context, broad changes in local under-standings of spiritual power in everyday life in Uganda undergird the content of popular religion and its public expression. Virtually all of the movements mentioned above have expressed themselves in a Christian idiom of one sort or another. For example, Lakwena's movement was called the Holy Spirit Movement, and, since her mysterious departure from Uganda into a refugee camp in Kenya, some of her followers have continued under names such as the Uganda People's Christian Democratic Army and the Lord's Resistance Army. Bisaaka's group in Toro is called the Holy Quaternity Movement, and it explicitly incorporates Catholic elements in its rituals. Thus, with a few isolated exceptions, religious discourse and practice in Uganda are infused with Christian language and concerns. Indeed, pre-Christian and Christian ideas intertwine to the point where sorting between the two becomes an increasingly arbitrary exercise. Thus, whether or not Christian discourse and symbols are hegemonic in Uganda, they have penetrated the religious consciousness of even those people the churches would consider the most wayward. But this 'cognitive' syncretism has not found a space within official Catholic structures.

The historical process which unfolded in the kingdom of Toro is instructive. As elsewhere, Catholic missionaries sought to transform Toro culture. While rarely successful on their own terms, they did introduce three new elements into Toro religious life: (1) a new institutional arrangement assigning explicitly defined statuses and roles (clergy and laity) for a new cult (Catholicism); (2) a new 'religious benefit' (salvation) as well as the means of achieving it (the sacraments);[23] and (3) a new set of spirits (the Holy Trinity, Mary and the saints). While the first two had no local correlates, the introduction of new spirits was more easily incorporated.[24] Indeed, the focus of the dominant religious cult in western Uganda on the *bacwezi* spirits was predicated upon a myth of conquest by an external group who became the objects of the cult. Thus, the incorporation of Christian spirits was facilitated by the power and 'otherness' of the missionaries themselves. At the same time, non-Christian spirits from outside the region proliferated during the colonial period.[25]

Church evangelical strategies influenced this tendency to absorb outside spirits in both intended and unintended ways. Catholic missionaries understood that Batoro did not necessarily perceive that they were making a choice between old and new rituals and spirits, and they adopted three different stances to handle the situation. They told Batoro either that their spirits did not exist – pointing out that existing spirits (especially ancestor spirits and a remote creator spirit called *Ruhanga*) were either proto-Christian or the actual Christian spirits themselves – or that Toro spirits (especially the *bacwezi*) were manifestations of Satan and that the new Christian spirits were ultimately more powerful. Different groups within Toro Catholicism tended toward one or another of these interpretations, with the latter ultimately gaining the greatest currency. Initially, this version – that Toro's *bacwezi* spirits and other spirits were evil – was reworked so that local spirits maintained their basically amoral character in regard to certain life-cycle experiences and in their use as remedies for misfortune. But, over time, the moralization of the spirit world gained a stronger hold in popular consciousness. The spirits most prone to being re-defined as evil were those involved in sorcery, especially newer spirits whose origins were from outside the region.[26]

Throughout the colonial period, church officials employed a number of criteria to categorize the majority of non-Westernized Catholics. They labelled as 'convinced' Catholics those who accepted local spirits as evil, burned their shrines and stopped attending their rites; who acknowledged the primacy of salvation and the sacraments; and who relied on the power of the Christian God (with the assistance of other Christian spirits – the Virgin Mary and the saints) to fight the evil consequences of local spirits. Conversely, those who accepted the autonomous power of the Christian spirits and the value of salvation and the sacraments, but not their total hegemony over the whole of the spiritual world, were considered 'Sunday-goers' or 'inactive' Catholics. Unhappily for the missionaries (as well as for Toro priests today), the majority of Catholics fell into the second category.

This categorization of church members took place in the context of the vigorous suppression by Christian chiefs and catechists of the public and organized expression of local religion, especially the *bacwezi* cults. The extensive mobility and internal migration of the Batoro, which made clan organization increasingly diffuse, also weakened the pull of the cults in the countryside.[27] Over time, as more and more Batoro adopted (nominally, at least) Christianity and the cults were increasingly driven underground, socialization into these cults, as well as the veneration of the ancestors, weakened. Sorcery, or at least the perception of it, greatly expanded, so that elements of mediumship and possession which were part of the response to sorcery persisted.[28]

To summarize, the moralization of the spirit world has been, in some ways, the greatest influence of the missionizing project in Uganda. But this moralization occurred without diminishing ontological beliefs regarding the plurality of spirits. In theory, the Catholic Church was well placed to capitalize on the persistent perception of a world filled with spirits, as the Virgin Mary and the saints in Catholic practice might have provided a means for a powerful syncretism within a Catholic symbolic and institutional frame. But in practice this has not happened in Ugandan Catholicism to any degree. Within a new political context, this situation has created the space for the new expressions of popular religion described earlier. It has also given the church a legacy of weak mechanisms to incorporate, rather than ignore, condemn or suppress, these popular expressions.

Popular Catholic Religiosity in Comparative Perspective

Notions of popular religion as they have been applied to Africa by 'secular' scholars have focused mainly on neo-traditional or Christian separatist movements. Far less attention has been paid to popular religion within the mainstream churches of mission origin, especially Catholic .[29] In the study of popular religion as applied to Christian Europe, the use of the concept presupposes a formal body of church doctrine, ritual and practice against which popular religion is counterposed, often in very stark terms. While the concept has been applied to all religions, 'popular religion' is historically rooted in the practice of Roman Catholicism as it evolved in Europe and established itself in the non-Western world since the church has been so explicit in elaborating and codifying its religious system.[30]

As an analytical construct, popular religion has three basic variants: (1) popular religion as belonging to a particular social group, or the dominated classes; (2) popular religion as deviations from a canonical set of beliefs, symbols and practices; and (3) popular religion as a rejection of the authority of designated religious specialists and the institution they represent. Recent studies of Latin American Catholicism often stress the first definition – religion of the dominated – but perhaps this stems from a conflation of the specific meaning of the term 'the popular' in Latin America with its use in 'popular' religion.[31] It is useful mainly for suggesting an elective affinity between the more general position of individuals and classes in the structure of power and religious practice. The second and third definitions are more important, precisely because the church construes them as mutually constitutive. In other words, official Catholic belief and practice is constructed as inseparable from the hegemonic role of the institution and its representatives.[32]

Evidence of this assertion can be found in the institution's own practice: a fairly wide range of tolerance of 'misinterpretations' of doctrine exists, which in some contexts are either accommodated or dealt with through catechism and pedagogy, but in others are suppressed when those beliefs take autonomous organizational form or deny clerical authority. Analytically, this can be dealt with best by getting away from the dichotomous formulation of 'official' and 'popular' and introducing an intermediate category, which I will, somewhat clumsily, call 'official-popular'. This seems necessary in the case of Catholicism because many aspects of what is called 'popular religion' – for example, saint or Marian devotion – are openly tolerated or even encouraged by church officials, as shown by the attempts of Christian missionaries to organize devotional cults in Uganda such as the Legion of Mary.[33]

The idea of 'official-popular' religion is related to what is often called 'folk Catholicism' in Latin America and Europe. As John Ingham notes in the case of rural Mexico:

> the church had a history of making concessions to local cultures as a matter of missionary expediency.... When local customs were not encouraged and even canonized, they were often tolerated. As missionaries accepted and accommodated local custom, the orthodox ritual and the received supernatural pantheon of the church were affected. The company of saints replaced and assimilated tribal and clan gods, acquiring in the process their associations with meteorological phenomena, agricultural fertility and healing.... The Catholic worldview was able to assimilate not only some of the content of indigenous religion but also its underlying structure.[34]

Given the church's limited capacity for coercion or persuasion, I see 'official-popular' or folk Catholicism as a level of 'acceptable ambiguity' towards everyday practice. To be sure, the missionary church impressed upon the laity the need for a proper interpretation of 'official-popular' symbols and practices – to venerate, not worship, Mary or a saint; or to ask for their intercession and prayer, not for the delivery of worldly desires. But the degree of tolerance of this ambiguity was quite large as long as the devotion did not diminish the sacramental commitments of Catholic practice controlled by the clergy and the laity did not exercise their own spiritual authority or act as a medium without the direction or approval of the institution. Once the boundaries of the 'official-popular' were transgressed, however, claims of institutional monopoly were also breached and church officials sought to suppress popular expressions of faith.

The post-Vatican II church introduced innovations such as a more participatory liturgy and the use of vernacular languages and indigenous music that aimed to transform the church's approach to these issues, especially in the young churches of Africa. Yet, in spite of repeated calls for inculturation, few strategies for more culturally specific forms of 'official-popular' practice have been implemented effectively in Uganda or elsewhere in Africa.[35]

This is not to say that Catholic missionaries made no attempt to establish a space for 'official-popular' religion. White Fathers in Toro stressed the importance of the Virgin Mary as well as certain saints from the outset, especially the Uganda Martyrs. Catholics were instructed to celebrate their saint's day (having taken their names at baptism). This was not merely a cynical strategy on the part of the missionaries; the White Fathers were themselves devoted to the Virgin Mary, and they saw such devotions and their organized expression among the laity as integral to their own faith as well as to the success of their enterprise.

In the inter-war period, the Toro mission initiated pietistic lay groups: the Legion of Mary, the Purgatory Movement, the Sacred Heart of Jesus and various saint cults. Introduced from the top, however, such 'official-popular' movements were relatively uninterested in assimilating local religious ideas and practices, as shown by the suppression of the *bacwezi* cults, the labelling of most indigenous spirits as evil, and the avoidance of Christian spiritual strategies for dealing with healing and witchcraft. In early modern Europe, pre-existing shrines to local saints were formally incorporated and controlled by the church while at the same time the primacy of the sacraments in Catholic religious life was promulgated.[36] In Latin America, confraternities and other social institutions resulted from the absorption of pre-Christian symbols and modes of sociality.[37] While such syncretic forms came to be regarded by secularists and even some clergy as 'superstition', the key point is that they were 'Catholic superstition'. As John Ingham argues:

> Elements of pre-hispanic religion persist – indeed, they do so to an extraordinary degree – but ... they express rather than contradict the Catholic worldview.[38]

By contrast, the degree of syncretism and assimilation in Ugandan Catholicism was less thorough, and the imported religious system and local notions and practices of spirituality have not (yet) become interwoven to the point where a vigorous folk Catholicism can 'express rather than contradict a Catholic worldview'. This does not mean that Christian discourse and symbols are not pervasive in Uganda or that some kind of 'cognitive' syncretism has not taken place for many Ugandans, but it does mean that, where it has occurred, it often does not express a Catholic worldview. In general, the Ugandan church lacks both the ideologies and organizational mechanisms to create an acceptably ambiguous realm of folk Catholicism. Thus, the recent movements constitute 'popular' rather than 'folk' religious expressions: they contradict Catholic doctrine and/or the institution's monopoly of charisma (as perceived by church officials) rather than reflect it.

The Legion of Mary

The Legion of Mary is an important example of the church's failure to institutionalize 'official-popular' belief and practice. The Legion was the exemplary Catholic lay association throughout colonial Uganda and the most pervasive mode of organized lay life outside the daily purview of the church, especially in rural communities. The church relied on Legion members as dependable loyalists at a time when social changes and perceived political discrimination against Catholics generated anxiety among the clergy about the status of the faith among its educated elites and its constituency of peasants.

The Legion of Mary combines a devotional cult to the Virgin Mary with a variety of outreach activities: visiting the sick, teaching the catechism and counselling 'backsliders'. Throughout Uganda, the Marian cult had an immediate appeal.[39] The Catholic tradition of the veneration and inter-cession of Mary and the saints corresponded with pre-Christian appeals and sacrifices to ancestor spirits and local spirit cults. There were important differences between the two, however. First, missionaries succeeded in instilling recognition and adoration for Jesus and Mary without eradicating beliefs in pre-Christian spirits responsible for misfortune. Those devoted to Mary could thus appeal to her to resolve problems caused by these spirits. While the missionaries hoped that devotion to Mary would be a stepping stone to a more direct relationship to God, the theological distinctions between veneration and worship may have been lost on early converts to the faith. This phenomenon was no stranger to the Catholic Church elsewhere in the world, however, and it might have been an acceptable compromise if it had meant that Legionnaires refrained from traditional ritual practices and reliance on witchdoctors.

Over time, the church developed a formal structure for the Legion in which local groups were federated to parish and diocesan bodies controlled by the clergy and lay elites in order to monitor the groups and to prevent serious deviations from Catholic dogma. It was largely successful, if success can be measured by the absence of Marian apparitions.[40] However, officials in Toro's Fort Portal Diocese in the 1960s observed changes in the membership of the Legion with some dismay, as the social base had become overwhelmingly rural, relatively uneducated women. As Father (later Bishop) Serapio Magambo, the Director of the Lay Apostolate in Fort Portal Diocese, noted in his report on the lay apostolate for 1966:

> The Legion of Mary virtually a reserve for old and uneducated women is doing quite well.... 'Educated' people have, as far as I have been able to assess, abandoned the whole movement. The Legion of Mary, the unreformable reformer, should I think go in for a bit of *aggiornamento* if it is to attract and retain the elite of ... this Fort Portal Diocese.[41]

The term *aggiornamento* was taken directly from the recently concluded Second Vatican Council. Used to describe reforms needed in the church worldwide, it literally means 'a bringing up to date'. However, during the ensuing period of social and political upheaval in Uganda, the Legion did not undergo such a revitalization. While its grassroots structure remains, it has failed to attract the elite, young people, and especially males. It remains a visible but increasingly marginal form of lay apostolate, still respected for its outreach work and piety but seen as hopelessly old-fashioned by the young, and too simple and 'peasant-like' by the educated.

Yet, while the Legion had become marginal to most lay Catholics by the 1980s, visions of the Virgin Mary began appearing in several rural parts of Uganda.[42] In its report on the state of the Diocese to the Vatican submitted in 1986, Bishop Magambo wrote:

> There is also the problem of break-away Christian religions mush-rooming in Fort Portal. Disgruntled Christians entice our people with miracle cures. Others, mostly Catholic, pretend to have visions of a dubious kind and disturb the simple. There have been three places like that in the diocese. We have consistently preached and taught people to be careful and have courageously opposed all pretensions to see visions, knowing that they are not authentic.[43]

In the same year, the Diocese distributed a letter to parish priests condemning a young Rwandan woman living in Buganda, who claimed to have visions of Mary, as a sham and mentally unstable.[44] By the early 1990s several reports of Marian visions circulated throughout Uganda. While none of the more popular ones occurred in Fort Portal Diocese, many Batoro knew of them and some visited the places where the apparitions occurred. These unofficial pilgrimages were officially discouraged by the Ugandan hierarchy.

While Magambo had indicated in 1966 that the form and content of the Legion of Mary were in need of reform, he clearly did not have messages from the Virgin in mind. Yet these visions, having been largely denounced by church leaders, have not reinvigorated the Legion. Thus, perhaps the most efficacious organizational mechanism for imbuing lay membership with intensive commitment has atrophied. The Legion no longer serves as a means of channelling Catholics, especially younger ones, into lay religious groups which the church can monitor and control. 'Official-popular' space was emptying, leaving even more room for the expression of extra-sacramental and non-orthodox religiosity.[45]

The Uganda Martyrs

Uganda is rare among African Catholic churches in that it has its own homegrown saints – the Uganda Martyrs. The Ugandan church has turned to developing devotional groups dedicated to the Uganda Martyrs to deepen the appeal of 'official-popular' symbols more broadly among the Catholic masses. The Martyrs have been promoted by the church as a model of Catholic religiosity and loyalty since their execution by the Ganda king, Mwanga, in 1886. In 1964, the year of their canonization, the church stepped up its campaign to organize lay groups devoted to the first modern-day indigenous African saints.[46]

Their canonization coincided with the Second Vatican Council, and soon after African theologians engaged the question of how the Catholic tradition of saint veneration could be inculturated with local perceptions of the spirit world and ancestor veneration via an extended image of kinship.[47] In a pastoral letter, 'Celebrating Our Ancestors in the Faith', Uganda's Catholic Bishops wrote:

> While we rejoice in the human qualities of the Martyrs, we are equally proud to recognise in them our ancestors in the faith. For us Africans, the dead, those who have gone before us, have a special part to play in our lives. In our devotion to the Martyrs, we see this traditional belief of ours taken up and purified, so that we can truly say that it is from their blood that we have been born anew in the faith.[48]

While the bishops clearly portrayed the Martyrs as ancestors, their reference to 'purification' indicated their concern that aspects of 'traditional' ancestor worship were inherently non-Christian and thus must be excised for a proper correspondence to be made between the ancestors and the Martyrs. In the past, mission Catholicism had attacked ancestor veneration unambiguously. While after the Second Vatican Council the Ugandan church was more open to certain indigenous customs, the Martyrs were promoted, like other saints, as vessels for prayer to the Christian high God. A key element of ancestor veneration – as an explanation of and a practical response to misfortune – was thus not included in the way connections were to be drawn. In any event, rituals of ancestor veneration were relatively marginal to 'neo-traditional' practice in many parts of Uganda by the 1980s, ironically due in part to Christianization.[49]

Groups devoted to the Martyrs (*bakaiso* in Rutoro) in Toro have existed for several decades, although they have never approached the membership levels of the Legion of Mary. Fort Portal Diocese concentrated especially on the one Uganda martyr who hailed from Toro – St Adolphus – and his birthplace at Katoosa in Mwenge county was designated as a shrine. The emphasis on Katoosa grew as the canonization approached. In a letter to the White Fathers headquarters in Rome, the Diocesan Chancellor wrote:

> A sub-committee of the diocesan Toro and Bunyoro Deaneries has been formed to prepare plans of action toward the materialization of the shrine at Katosa. We are selling the idea of the Martyrdom and the Saints by radio speeches, newspaper articles, Bishop's pastoral letters read in all churches, and we intend to start pilgrimages to the site of the future shrine without delay. We are still fighting for land titles, then a temporary cross will be erected and we wish to bring our people there to start prayers in view of the Canonization.[50]

An indigenous priest, Fr Hilario, was put in charge of building the shrine. Fort Portal Diocese also began organizing yearly pilgrimages, emulating the much larger pilgrimage to the main site of the Martyrs' execution at Namugongo in Buganda.[51]

Efforts at cultivating a lay movement devoted to the Martyrs have had meagre results, however. The lay association devoted to the Uganda Martyrs had only twenty members for all of Katoosa parish in 1990.[52] Most parish-based *bakaiso* groups have a small membership, which, like the Legion of Mary, consists mostly of elderly women. Other Catholics, however, are devoted to the Martyrs and invoke them in their prayers. In interviews, group members and others gave responses similar to that of a man who claimed: 'Whatever I ask them, they do it for me.' Such a pragmatic orientation is common throughout the Catholic world, and one of the acceptable ambiguities of 'official-popular' religion, but, in this case, it has not led to organized lay practices.

The possibilities for change are not absent, however. When I arrived in Fort Portal in 1989, for example, the *bakaiso* group of Virika parish had around 30 members, the majority being older women living near the parish. But, by May 1991, several hundred people of all ages crowded into McCauley Hall, the auditorium of the diocese, for a group meeting. What had happened? In July of 1990, Virika parish received a visitor, Vincent Mfumbo, who had for the previous few years been holding exorcism sessions in Kampala at the site of the execution of another of the Uganda Martyrs, St Jean-Marie Muzeeyi.[53] Mfumbo had come to Toro to spread his message that evil spirits, sent by the Devil, were the cause of much disease and anti-social behaviour in Uganda, and that God had empowered Mfumbo to exorcise them with the assistance of the Virgin Mary and the Uganda Martyrs. Witches were sometimes seen to be possessed by such evil spirits, who then attacked the innocent to cause misfortune. At Virika, Mfumbo met with the parish's *bakaiso* group, and the meeting went on into the night, filled with the reciting of the rosary, the singing of hymns and the casting out of spirits.[54]

One of those who attended was Lawrence Kasaija, a Mutoro in his mid-30s who had been suffering from a series of debilitating and unusual physical problems.[55] Through prayer and the laying on of hands, Mfumbo was able to exorcise the spirit attacking Kasaija. Kasaija then began visiting Kampala to search for work and to attend more sessions at the shrine of St Jean Marie Muzeeyi. Within six months, Kasaija believed that he had received the power to heal, and he and fellow members of the Virika group began meeting in people's homes, where he prayed over the possessed, laid on hands and commanded evil spirits 'in the name of Jesus Christ' to go out.[56]

When the parish priest at Virika heard about the group's exorcism practices, he invited Kasaija to hold a meeting at McCauley Hall after high mass.[57] A series of hymns, including one honouring the Uganda Martyrs, was sung. Then the rosary was recited while those wishing to be 'prayed for' knelt on the floor of the hall in front of Kasaija. Praying softly, he laid hands on various parts of the head and chest, often rocking the head slowly back and forth. Over the course of an hour, evil spirits were exorcised, with some of the possessed speaking in tongues or in the voices of the possessing spirit.[58]

At this and a subsequent meeting at McCauley Hall on Pentecost Sunday, the diocese sent a team of observers, led by the parish priest and a young cleric, Fr Pascal, who had taken a strong interest in spiritual healing. On the whole, diocesan officials felt it was better to monitor the group and judge whether their practices were genuinely 'Christian' rather than to ban it immediately and risk losing the loyalty of what, in a few months, had become the fastest-growing lay movement in the diocese.

Like Mfumbo, Kasaija claimed that he would stop his exorcisms if the hierarchy instructed him to do so. Both were strongly aware of the politics of popular religion in the Ugandan church and emphasized that it was the power of Christ through the agency of the Holy Spirit that chased out evil spirits. They themselves were only vessels, and the rosary, the Virgin Mary and the Uganda Martyrs interceded without autonomous power. Using the metaphor of a pipe, Kasaija noted: 'But it's the water we need to drink, and water passes through that pipe. I'm like a pipe, and Jesus Christ is like water.'[59]

The vast majority of the people that Kasaija healed were women, including many young ones. Women are seen both as dominating the practice of witchcraft in Toro and as its most frequent victims.[60] Those attending the exorcism sessions brought witchcraft items, called *mahembe*, as well as items to protect against sorcery, which were typically burned on the spot. Some Catholics were very dubious of these exorcisms, and a lay leader of the diocese referred to Mfumbo as a 'pagan Christian'. Yet, for many church members, the 'official-popular' religion negotiated between them and the church was insufficient, especially in a context where witchcraft was perceived as rampant. The space for lay people like Kasaija to take on such charismatic roles was made possible, in part, by the reluctance of priests to incorporate exorcism into their ministry.[61] Their watchful approach to Kasaija and his group thus stems from a fear of the *public* expression of lay charisma without institutional mediation.

The Holy Quaternity Movement

While the *bakaiso* group professes unambiguous loyalty to the Catholic hierarchy and seeks its approval, other Catholics have created or joined organizations outside the church to find space for practices that the church does not provide. The most notable of such groups is the Holy Quaternity Movement, officially called the Itambiro Ly'Omukama Ruhanga Owamahe Goona Association (the Meeting of the Lord God of All Forces).[62] Founded by Dosteo Bisaaka, a former Catholic catechist, the Holy Quaternity Movement centres on exorcism and witchcraft eradication. Its origins go back to the early 1980s, when Bisaaka claims that he became possessed by the spirit Obwosobozi, the spirit of power or force. His following has expanded rapidly since a relative calm came to western Uganda in 1986 with the rise to power of the NRM. Although Bisaaka and his followers duly registered with the government in 1988, the group was prohibited from practising by the NRM in October 1989, and Bisaaka himself was detained briefly. After a period in 1990–1 when the ban was not enforced, the group was formally outlawed in October 1991.[63] The mainstream churches in both Toro and Bunyoro had been pressuring the NRM government for several years to shut Bisaaka down.[64]

Bisaaka was born in 1931, and for most of his life he served the Catholic Church as a teacher, catechist and composer of some of the most popular Runyoro/Rutoro hymns. As such, he had been a well-known figure in Catholic circles in Bunyoro and Toro for many years, but the journalist George Kawule noted that Bisaaka harboured 'disappointment with the catholic leadership ... for the little importance they attached to his contribution and dedication to the church'.[65] Bisaaka's followers claim that he was not motivated by resentment, however, but had received from God the power to heal and cast out evil spirits. Bisaaka claims to have been taken up to heaven by God himself in 1983, when he was told that the spirit Obwosobozi, the fourth member of the Holy Trinity (or Holy Quaternity), had possessed him and given him the power to defeat evil spirits with the assistance of an army of angels.[66]

An important theme of Bisaaka's is that the plurality of religions in the world has been a disservice to God and has allowed evil to flourish. Traditional religion and all its spirits are considered evil, and Christianity has been ineffective. The churches are seen as a necessary phase of religious evolution now made superfluous by the presence of Obwosobozi on earth. While the Son of God and the Holy Spirit exist in heaven, it is the Spirit of Power which is the active spiritual and moral agent in the world, and Bisaaka is its human medium.

While Bisaaka's followers (*abaikiriza*) claim that their groups had been established throughout Uganda, the vast majority of *matambiro* (plural of *itambiro*) were located near Bisaaka's home in southern Bunyoro and in eastern Toro among Runyoro/Rutoro speakers. Membership was drawn from all the existing religious organizations in the region, with some observers claiming that Catholics were represented disproportionately. Bisaaka's following expanded through the appointment of *abahereza* (literally 'servers') in many rural and peri-urban centres in Bunyoro and Toro. The *abahereza*, mostly men but some women, are former clients who have been healed, learned Bisaaka's teachings, and been 'ordained' formally by Bisaaka personally through touching them on the head, thus mimicking Catholic practices. Once ordained, the *abahereza* establish *matambiro* at their homes, where they hold meetings three times monthly. They have the authority to cast out spirits simply by invoking the name of Obwosobozi. There appears to be no hierarchy among the *abahereza*. Each is personally responsible to Bisaaka and each *itambiro* is an autonomous unit.

Confession is an important aspect of the healing process in Bisaaka's group, and here the linkage to Catholicism is clear. Prior to entering an *itambiro*, first-time participants must write down (or have written down for them by the *abahereza*) all the evil deeds they have committed in their lives. These written confessions are then brought to Bisaaka on a regular basis. Bisaaka reads them, knowing intuitively whether they are accurate and complete, and then sends word to the *abahereza*, giving them permission to heal or exorcise. Confession, which within the Catholic Church ritually cleanses the believer to receive Holy Communion, here serves to prepare one to receive the power of Obwosobozi, and it confers membership in the group as an *omuikiriza* (singular of *abaikiriza*).

A revised version of the Lord's Prayer figures prominently in the *itambiro* exorcism ritual.[67] In Bisaaka's version, the words are changed to eliminate any separation between heaven and earth. Thus, 'Our Father, Who art in heaven, Hallowed be Thy name, Thy kingdom come, Thy will be done' becomes 'Our Father, Who art here, Hallowed be Thy name, Thy kingdom has come, Thy will is done'.

Through the use of the Lord's Prayer, the transformation of the Holy Trinity to the Holy Quaternity, the 'ordaining' of *abahereza*, and the importance of confession, Bisaaka has appropriated Catholic symbols that are familiar to most Batoro.[68] From the point of view of the church, however, these appropriations are utter blasphemy, and the church has reacted to Bisaaka's movement with a heavy hand. Fort Portal Diocese excommunicated Catholics who attended meetings at the *matambiro* and ruled that a six-month period of new catechism was required for those seeking to return to the fold.[69] While the church excommunicated Catholics who followed Bisaaka, however, it is unclear whether those excommunicated considered themselves as having left the church, and some continued going to mass. While such religious straddling is common in Toro Catholicism, the crucial difference here is that Catholics publicly participated in the rites of what church officials perceived as a rival religious organization. They thus felt that several thousand members of the dioceses of Fort Portal and Hoima had 'defected' from the church, and, as one Bisaaka follower cynically added, from 'their tithes'.

The attitudes of lay Catholics who do not follow Bisaaka are mixed. Church loyalists unambiguously opposed him and appeared happy with the government's decision to ban the group. I heard a few rumours of clashes between Catholics and *abaikiriza* in villages in northeast Mwenge and of a priest burning down an *itambiro* with the assistance of some parishioners. Many Catholics, however, are less sure, suspicious of Bisaaka's motives and fearful of his power, but grateful that the level of witchcraft has decreased in areas where *matambiro* have been functioning.[70]

If the Uganda Martyrs *bakaiso* group is negotiating the limits of 'official-popular' Catholicism, Bisaaka and his *abaikiriza* have, in the eyes of the church, crossed the line. The Catholic Church, with the power of the state on its side, has put a halt indefinitely to his movement, but popular concerns about healing, possession and witchcraft that fed Bisaaka's movement are not likely to disappear. Church leaders and Bisaaka followers tell different stories about whether Bisaaka jumped or was pushed from the arms of the church. Fr Pascal, who was assigned by the diocese to look into Bisaaka's activities, claims that church leaders tried to convince Bisaaka to remain within the fold, but *public* enactment of lay religious charisma and independent control of 'religious benefits' were bound to be strongly opposed by the institution and its representatives.

In principle, Fort Portal Diocese had other options to deal with new competition. It could have engaged in pro-active and intensive evangelization to head off Catholic participation in the movement. Part of this effort could have involved the clergy performing exorcisms to show that the power of Obwosobozi was no match for the Holy Spirit, in spite of Bisaaka's claims. Alternatively, it could have shown indifference, either by publicly stating that those Catholics who went to Bisaaka helped separate the Christian wheat from the pagan chaff, or by simply ignoring him entirely. None of these strategies were attempted, however. Evangelization was not an option because the church lacked the mechanisms such as mobilized and loyal lay associations to make it succeed. Exorcism was not pursued because most priests were reluctant to perform it, and it could open the way to legitimating lay charisma, as with the *bakaiso*. Doing nothing was not an option because of the threat to the institution's authority and the public challenge to the status and honour of church officials by a former layman.[71]

The state of officially constituted lay groups in the church thus had a double effect. Their weakness provided a ready-made constituency for Bisaaka's movement. And, without the means to coopt the movement through its own popular groups, church officials felt that they had no option but to try to shut it down.[72]

Conclusion

The case of Bisaaka is not entirely unique. At virtually the same time, the Monastic Army of the Rejected, founded in 1988 by the visionary Anatole Ssentamu in 1988 (himself a follower of Mary Naiga, who claimed to have been visited by the Virgin in 1985), also drew the attention of both church and government officials, and it was banned within weeks of the Holy Quaternity Movement.

Fr Charles Ssemuju, identified as a supporter of the Monastic Army in a newspaper article on the movement, is one of the few voices within the Ugandan church calling for a radical accommodation with popular beliefs about the power of the spirit world in everyday life.[73] In his article 'Categories of Catholics', he criticizes the church for ignoring issues such as polygamy and witchcraft. Regarding witchcraft, he writes:

> Whether we like it or not we may not realistically deny the existence of this satanic world. I do admit that anyone who wants to be modern tries

his best to deny the existence of such a world – I hope sincerely! – and then does so as if all this is petty superstition. But can we build on this self-deception?[74]

Ssemuju's controversial stance is at odds with most of his clerical colleagues, at least in their public statements if perhaps less so in their private beliefs. In response to questions about the Monastic Army, Bishop Henry Sentovu said, 'Our target is not the extraordinary but the day-to-day life of joys and sorrows.'[75] The problem for the church, however, is that a number of its followers see the joys and sorrows of everyday life as inextricably linked to the 'extraordinary' presence of the spirit world. Whether or not such numbers are increasing, the number of Catholics who pursue this link in a public and organized manner has been on the rise since the mid-1980s.

The dominant view among church officials is that such extraordinary concerns are the result of ignorance or psychological problems and are to be remedied by education and pastoral care, rather than a readjustment of church policies toward the spiritual world. The view of the NRM and Uganda's secular press is even more vehement in seeing popular religious expressions as evidence of backwardness and in depicting charismatic individuals as money-hungry charlatans. A *New Vision* reporter exemplified this view in a report on the Monastic Army:

> If therefore you are keen on becoming a millionaire overnight, agitate yourself like one possessed, yell at the top of your voice that, there and then, you are seeing the Blessed Virgin Mary. Within moments you will have hundreds of believers at your beck and call....[76]

Many Ugandans, however, see no necessary contradiction between the alleged greed of visionaries and the reality of their spiritual power. Indeed, as in the Bisaaka case, many Catholics who do not follow such individuals see the new wealth of charismatic virtuosi as dependent on both the gullibility of their followers *and* the genuine power they possess. They remain loyal to the church in part because they see this power as used in the service of Satan. While church officials at times make a similar claim, they mostly emphasize the greed of leaders and the naivety of followers because, at least in part, this stance denies that lay people have access to unmediated spiritual power.

Thus, an ideology both modernist and paternalist has impeded internal reform and diluted most attempts at 'inculturation' despite the vast amount of attention paid to this topic in the past two decades by Ugandan clerics, theologians and lay intellectuals. Indeed, most of the research theses produced by seminarians at the national seminary in Katigondo are on the theme of lay religiosity, and they bemoan the failure to establish religious practice that is both popular and identifiably Catholic. In a sense, what these Catholic intellectuals define as the problem is the extent of religious practice outside Catholic bounds, as opposed to elements of 'traditional religion' *within* Catholic practice. It is the latter, here labelled 'official-popular' religious practice, that is seen as in short supply.

But the limits to internal church reform are not just a question of ideology.[77] Equally if not more important are institutional interests and the strategies to achieve them, what the sociologist John Coleman calls *raison d'église*:

> the fundamental religious commitments and organizational slant which set parameters on the church's range of flexibility and adaptability in political situations.... The mission of the church and its message (its social teaching) is progressive and bold in support of the poor, open in its sense of a range of allies. But sometimes the church follows a logic of maintenance of the organization rather more than its logic of mission.[78]

As several observers have pointed out, many African Catholic churches, especially the Ugandan church, maintain a pre-Vatican II ethos and mode of operation.[79] Operating until lately in a highly insecure context, *raison d'église* shapes the church's orientation and ways of implementing reform. Ironically, the pursuit of institutional interests through the logic of maintenance helps to explain the lack of implementation of inculturation reforms that might incorporate popular lay religiosity. The Ugandan church's attachment to its hierocratic structure, which insists on a monopoly of the distribution of religious benefits, is very much in place. Such an approach continues to encourage lay religiosity without lay charisma, since the latter implies access to religious benefits without institutional intermediation.

As with all Catholic churches, the Ugandan church's claim to monopoly is compromised in practice by tolerating and sometimes introducing devotional groups among the laity which allow individuals more direct contact with spiritual beings and an associational life outside the immediate control of the clergy. The church tolerates (in part because it cannot control) a variety of interpretations, but it is far less tolerant when spirits (including even the Holy Spirit) are invoked by the laity, openly and publicly, to use their power to intervene in the world, even when the intention is to combat evil. This is because, on one level, such practices *publicly* raise religious benefits other than salvation and the sacraments to an unacceptably high status and, on another, *publicly* enact the limits of the institution's claimed monopoly of religious charisma.

Thus *raison d'église* has shaped the church's initial relationship with popular religiosity, its current ambivalence toward such expressions and its inability to transform itself in the face of new circumstances.[80] Institutions, and especially highly formalized and bureaucratized ones, do not change easily. Lacking competition from more charismatic religious groups in the colonial era, the Ugandan church was not pushed into developing accommodations with local religious concerns that might have produced a folk Catholicism capable of assimilating these concerns into Catholic practice and organization. Not only did this help to create the context for new popular expressions, it also left the church particularly ill-disposed to respond to them. In a sense, it is not only institutional interest, but also institutional capacity and institutional momentum that has guided the church's response. While the majority of Ugandan Catholics in the 1990s remain 'loyal', and even those who engage in popular practices often seek to maintain a link with the institution, the strength of this loyalty and the nature of institutional linkages are coming more and more into question.

Notes

* The fieldwork on which this chapter is based was carried out between 1989 and 1991. It was assisted by a Fulbright-Hays Dissertation Fellowship from the United States Department of Education and by a grant from the Joint Committee on African Studies of the Social Science Research Council and the American Council of Learned Societies from funds provided by the Rockefeller Foundation and the William and Flora Hewlett Foundation. I wish to thank the participants in the Madison workshop for their feedback and Thomas Spear for his detailed substantive and editorial comments.

1 Cited in Nathan B. Matovu, *Mityana Bishops* (np, nd), 9. The interview was conducted when Wamala, recently appointed Cardinal by Pope John Paul II, was leaving the office of Bishop of Kiyinda-Mityana Diocese after being appointed as Archbishop Co-adjutor of Kampala Archdiocese.

2 Charles Ssemuju, 'Categories of Catholics', in J. M. Waliggo and M. D. Byabazaire (eds), *Rethinking the Mission of the Church in Africa* (Kisubi, 1989), 65.

3 For an excellent recent example in West African Islam, see Adeline Masquelier, 'Identity, alterity and ambiguity in a Nigerien community: competing definitions of "true" Islam', in Richard Werbner and T. O. Ranger (eds), *Postcolonial Identities in Africa* (London, 1996), 222–44.

4 Gene Burns, *The Frontiers of Catholicism* (Berkeley, 1994), 16.

5 This statement is a generalization based on field research carried out during 1989–91, and it certainly reflects the perception of a wide range of both clergy and laity. It is also reflected in Cardinal Wamala's statement in which he makes a distinction between the quantity of church members and the quality of their faith.

6 For example, the festivals and confraternities of European and Latin American Catholicism.

7 Perhaps they constitute a category not included in Ssemuju's list, 'unconvinced but active'.

8 See, among many examples, J. M. Waliggo *et al.*, *Inculturation* (Kampala, 1986).

9 See Ronald Kassimir, 'The social power of religious organization: the Catholic Church in Uganda 1955–1991' (PhD, Chicago, 1996).

10 Here I focus mainly on independent movements that have included Catholic participation and activity by Catholics that, while not breaking from the church, are seen as undesirable and perhaps heretical by the institution. New evangelical churches are also gaining members in Uganda, although they are largely an urban phenomenon.

11 See Tim Allen, 'Understanding Alice: Uganda's Holy Spirit movement in context', *Africa*, 61 (1991), 370–99, and the two articles by Heike Behrend, 'Is Alice Lakwena a witch: the Holy Spirit movement and its fight against evil in the north', in H. B. Hansen and M. Twaddle (eds), *Changing Uganda* (London, 1991), 162–77, and 'The Holy Spirit movement and the forces of nature in the north of Uganda 1985–1987', in H. B. Hansen and M. Twaddle (eds), *Religion and Politics in East Africa* (London, 1995), 59–71.

12 According to a recent publication of the Uganda Catholic Secretariat, Catholics comprise over 60 per cent of the two administrative districts that encompass Acholiland, which is served by the Diocese of Gulu. Only the Diocese of Masaka in southern Buganda has a higher percentage of Catholics, according to the Secretariat's statistics, in Uganda

Catholic Secretariat, *The Catholic Directory of Uganda* (Kisubi, 1992).

13 In an article on the Monastic Army in Masaka, reporter John Tibemanya of the government-owned daily *New Vision* mentioned a sighting of the Virgin Mary in Masaka in the late 1960s. 'Dark side of Masaka cult revealed', *New Vision* (23 October 1991).

14 I leave out of this discussion the situation among adherents of Islam, although the older Islamic organizations are also experiencing pressures of fragmentation in the current period.

15 This quotation, from Giovanni Levi's discussion of the context within which an exorcism movement arose in seventeenth-century Italy, rings true in the Ugandan case. See his *Inheriting Power* (Chicago, 1988), 157.

16 Among many works, see Deogratias M. Byabazaire, *The Contribution of the Christian Churches to the Development of Western Uganda 1894–1974* (Frankfurt am Main, 1979); Holger Bernt Hansen, *Mission, Church and State in a Colonial Setting* (London, 1984); D. A. Low, *Buganda in Modern History* (London, 1971); J. A. Rowe, 'The purge of Christians at Mwanga's court', *Journal of African History*, 5 (1964), 55–72; Michael Twaddle, 'The emergence of politico-religious groupings in late nineteenth-century Uganda', *Journal of African History*, 29 (1988), 81–92; John Mary Waliggo, 'The Catholic Church in the Buddu Province of Buganda, 1879–1925' (DPhil, Cambridge, 1976); Frederick Welbourn, *Religion and Politics in Uganda 1952–1962* (Nairobi, 1965); and C. C. Wrigley, 'The Christian Revolution in Uganda', *Comparative Studies in Society and History*, 2 (1959), 33–48.

17 Hansen, *Mission, Church and State*, Chapters 3–8.

18 As I have argued elsewhere, the social bases of these antagonisms have dissipated in contemporary Uganda, and the Anglican–Catholic divide is no longer an especially salient political cleavage. See Kassimir, 'Social power of religious organization'; *idem*, 'Ambiguous institution: the Catholic Church and the reconstruction of Uganda', in L. Villalón and P. Huxtable (eds), *The African State at a Critical Juncture: Between Disintegration and Reconfiguration* (Boulder, 1998).

19 The memo concludes with a reference to the US-based Baptist Missionary Society: 'I am to say that Government Officers should be instructed to give this mission no encouragement.' All quotations from Confidential Circular issued by R. A. Malyn, PS, Ministry of Social Services, 30 May 1957 (Entebbe Archives).

20 I discuss this in detail in Kassimir, 'Social power of religious organization'.

21 In a 1991 speech, President Yoweri Museveni recounts an incident that occurred while he was leading his guerrilla army in the Luwero Triangle. When several peasant soldiers claimed that they were protected from bullets by carrying reeds into battle, the NRA leadership responded, saying anyone who even spoke of carrying reeds would be shot by firing squad: 'We said we would give him his reed, let him perform his ceremonies and shoot him to see whether or not his reed would protect him. That was the end of the reed theory in our army....' Yoweri Museveni, *What Is Africa's Problem?* (Kampala, 1992), 116.

22 The NRM itself has been wary of this activity, leading it to limit access of the new religious missions to Ugandan television and occasionally banning new groups. In 1989, the regime reversed itself more than once on whether it would allow people to visit the farm of an elderly Buganda woman who claimed that dirt from her land, when ingested, would cure AIDS.

23 This terminology reflects Max Weber's definition of a hierocracy, which he modelled on the Roman Catholic Church, as an organization that monopolizes the distribution of religious benefits or the means of salvation. Max Weber, *Economy and Society* (Berkeley, 1978), G. Roth and C. Wittich (eds), II:1158–211.

24 On the organization of pre-Christian religion in western Uganda, see Iris Berger, *Religion and Resistance: East African Kingdoms in the Precolonial Period* (Tervuren, 1981).

25 See John Beattie, 'Sorcery in Bunyoro', in *Witchcraft and Sorcery in East Africa* (London, 1963), J. Middleton and E. H. Winter (eds), 27–55; *idem*, 'Spirit mediumship in Bunyoro', in *Spirit Mediumship and Society in Africa* (London, 1969), J. Beattie and J. Middleton (eds), 159–70.

26 One example is *kifaaro* spirits, believed to have come from neighbouring Buganda. These spirits, noted by Beattie ('Spirit mediumship', 169) during the 1950s, are still seen as pervasive and dangerous in contemporary western Uganda. See also John Akiiki Kahimbaara, 'Some traditional beliefs of the Batooro', *Occasional Research Papers in African*

Traditional Religion and Philosophy, 29 (1974), 281.

27 See Sandra Hoover, 'Social stratification in Toro: a study in social change' (PhD, Indiana, 1978).
28 See Beattie, 'Spirit mediumship'.
29 This is not a minor gap in empirical knowledge, given the greater number of Christians in most African countries who belong to these churches. There are many theological works on this topic, although few based on extensive field research. I must frankly confess that I have not surveyed extensively studies published in French.
30 For two relatively recent anthropological explorations of the concept in Western Europe, see Eric R. Wolf (ed.), *Religious Regimes and State Formation* (Albany, 1991), and Ellen Badone (ed.), *Religious Orthodoxy and Popular Faith in European Society* (Princeton, 1990). Particularly because of its origins, distinguishing normative from analytical uses of 'popular religion' is a somewhat precarious exercise. See Thomas A. Kselman, 'Ambiguity and assumption in the concept of popular religion', in *Religion and Political Conflict in Latin America* (Chapel Hill, 1986), Daniel H. Levine (ed.), 24–41.
31 For a discussion of the specific meaning of the term *lo popular*, see Daniel H. Levine, 'Popular groups, popular culture and popular religion', *Comparative Studies in Society and History*, 32 (1990), 718–19. In his study of religious change in Latin American Catholicism, *Popular Voices in Latin American Catholicism* (Princeton, 1992), Chapters 5–6, Levine examines transformations in the form and content of popular Catholicism as related to participation in basic Christian communities. His findings include: (1) a shift away from 'traditional' popular religious practices (e.g. saint veneration) to more orthodox, rationalist and sacramental ones; and (2) a shift away from reliance on the institution as an intermediary both with God and with other Catholics. For my purposes, it is only the second finding that qualifies these practices as 'popular' religion. Regarding the first finding, Levine rightly contends that popular religion is not static, that it has its own internal dynamism, but in order to render a definition of the term useful in the Ugandan context, a change toward orthodoxy here is considered as a move away from what I call popular religion.
32 In a sense, the acceptance of the institutional role is more determinant since it defines legitimate belief and practice. Kselman writes that, during the Counter-Reformation's attempts to 'channel' as well as control popular religion, the church was suspicious of any group unwilling 'to accept that the Catholic clergy were exclusively endowed with the ability to act as mediators between the supernatural and natural'. 'Ambivalence and assumption', 26–7.
33 John M. Ingham writes, 'local religion in sixteenth-century Spain had heterodox elements, often with the approval of clergy'. *Mary, Michael and Lucifer* (Austin, 1986), 8.
34 Ingham, *Mary, Michael and Lucifer*, 8–9.
35 Ironically, some older Catholics accuse post-Vatican II priests of 'dis-enchanting' the Catholic faith by shifting from the more mysterious Latin mass to local languages. More generally, Waliggo writes that modern priests are accused of weakening Christian substitutes for the deep-rooted traditional rites:
    > The practice of blessing pregnant and newly delivered women is disappearing, the use of holy water to dispel evil forces is declining, and the popularity of religious processions is withering away. The vacuum created by the removal of Christian substitutes, old Catholics argue, has been to the advantage of traditional religion.

    John Mary Waliggo, 'Ganda traditional religion and Catholicism in Buganda, 1948–1975', in Edward Fasholé-Luke *et al.* (eds), *Christianity in Independent Africa* (Bloomington, 1978), 420.
36 See the essays in Stephen Wilson (ed.), *Saints and Their Cults* (Cambridge, 1983).
37 One other feature shared by European and Latin American Catholicism but largely missing in Africa is the competition from religious orders to regular clergy and the diocesan structures. In the former case, this competition between the two types of clergy for followers and legitimacy often provoked greater compromises with 'heterodox' lay practices. See, for example, the essays by Mart Bax, 'Religious regimes and state-formation: toward a research perspective' and 'Marian apparitions in Medjugorje: rivalling religious regimes and state-formation in Yugoslavia', in Wolf (ed.), *Religious Regimes*, 7–27, 29–53.
38 Ingham, *Mary, Michael and Lucifer*, 1. Elsewhere, he states: '[while] significant elements of

the deep structure of the pre-Hispanic world view persist in present-day beliefs and practices, they are embedded in, and subordinated to, Catholic beliefs and symbols' (180).

39 In Buganda, Waliggo attributes this to its resonance with the Ganda Queen Mother, a figure of respect among Baganda. See Waliggo, 'The Catholic Church'. I have no hard evidence for this in Toro, although the Queen Mother held a similar position in the traditions of the Bunyoro kingdom that Toro replicated after its secession in the early nineteenth century.

40 At least, there seems to be no record of them in the annual reports of the White Fathers throughout the colonial period.

41 Note the contradiction within these few sentences: the Legion of Mary 'is doing quite well', yet is 'unreformable' and has been abandoned by educated people. Reflected in this statement were church concerns that educated and influential Catholics lacked an appealing form of associational life and were thereby open to secularizing influences.

42 It would be interesting to know if the increasing number of Catholic elites making pilgrimages to Lourdes and Fatima, as well as greater knowledge of these shrines among the laity, is connected to the rise of apparitions in recent years.

43 Diocese of Fort Portal, 'Quinquennial Report 1981–1986', 5.

44 The letter, which I found in a file in Katoosa parish, read in part: 'We have considered her a cheat. One day she crushed ticks in her mouth in order to claim afterwards that the Host which she had just received had been miraculously shedding blood. You can see, Your Excellency, that this trick is a truly unworthy act of profanation. It simply shows that the girl wanted to appear as a very special person, the object of a Eucharistic miracle.... This girl is a fraud, without honesty and certainly with neither a right intention nor a good life'. Monsignor J. B. Gahamanyi, Bishop of Butare (Rwanda), to Monsignor Ssekamanya, Auxiliary Bishop of Kampala, 27 August 1986.

45 Most of the other pietistic lay groups are also in decline. These include groups devoted to saints, the Sacred Heart of Jesus, and the Purgatory Movement. The latter is dedicated to prayer for the souls of the recently departed and resonates, at least superficially, with traditional notions of ancestor veneration. Interestingly, the most popular of the devotional cults, beside the Legion of Mary, is that of St Jude Taddeo, which was begun in Uganda by a Ganda priest and spread rapidly without official church promotion. A White Father described the cult as 'satisfying a need for religiosity. But it needs follow-up, and pastoral care' (Interview, June 1990, Kasese). I take the last statement as warning against the cult's tendency to go beyond the bounds of acceptable popular practice.

46 I have written elsewhere on the efforts of the church to construct the Martyrs as a national symbol of Ugandan Catholic identity. The results of this effort have been mixed. On one hand, the Martyrs are typically represented and widely perceived not simply as exemplary Catholics, but as models of moral agency in the face of tyranny, and their virtues are extolled by secular politicians as well as church officials. On the other hand, the nationalizing of the Martyrs is partial, as the context of the martyrdom was limited to the Buganda kingdom and almost all the Martyrs were themselves Baganda. See Ronald Kassimir, 'Complex martyrs: symbols of Catholic Church formation and political differentiation in Uganda', *African Affairs*, 90 (1991), 357–82.

47 See, especially, the work of Charles Nyamiti, *Christ as Our Ancestor* (Gweru, 1984) and 'Uganda martyrs: ancestors to all mankind', *African Christian Studies*, 2 (1986), 41–66. Some inculturation literature implies that Catholicism, with its emphasis on intermediary spirits such as Mary and the saints, so central to European popular religion, has a natural affinity in appealing to Africans. Although writing on a different theme (Dinka creation myths), Lienhardt nicely problematizes the assumption of such parallels:

> Although such correspondences might appear advantageous for those wishing to persuade the Dinka to accept the Christian version, they could also appear simply as alternative and foreign versions of religious truths already familiar on their own terms to the Dinka, and unlike the Christian version, intimately connected to their own way of life.

Godfrey Lienhardt, 'The Dinka and Catholicism', in J. Davis (ed.), *Religious Organization and Religious Experience* (London, 1982), 83.

48 *Celebrating Our Ancestors in the Faith* (Kisubi, 1984), 8. The letter was part of the preparation for the centenary of the martyrdom.

49 This varies, of course, depending on the specific customs and histories of specific groups. Beattie claims that Nyoro (and Toro) traditional religion 'does not centre on an ancestral cult' ('Spirit mediumship', 159) while A. B. T. Byaruhanga-Akiiki, *Religion in Bunyoro* (Nairobi, 1982), sees ancestors as more important to religious practice. While there was a strong belief in the spirits of dead ancestors among many I interviewed in the course of my research, few claimed that they engaged in any specific or regular ritual practice addressed to the ancestors. As mentioned, the vast majority of spiritual explanations for misfortune centred on witchcraft and spirits that originated from outside Toro.

50 Uganda Martyrs file, Fort Portal Diocese Archives, letter dated 21 February 1964.

51 The 1990 pilgrimage in Katoosa was a festive occasion, attracting thousands of Catholics who trekked from Fort Portal and from as far away as Bugombwa parish on the slopes of the Ruwenzoris, over 50 miles away. For most participants, however, the pilgrimage and celebration was more of a social occasion than a devotional one. Indeed, only a small percentage were within earshot of the official proceedings and sermons.

52 Interview with Katoosa catechist, Teopista Mbabazi Aheembwa Abwoli, 31 May 1990. Another informant also mentioned that the dedication to the Martyrs is not as strong around the parish as in other parts of the diocese, and that, while 'the shrine has become popular', local people 'are not very devoted'. Interview with Consolata Hambere Atwoki, Katoosa, 7 June 1990. This distinction between popularity and devotion indicates that, for many, the shrine and the pilgrimage are valued mostly as a site for social interaction.

53 Mfumbo's activities were chronicled in a Kampala-based magazine, *The Exposure*, 28 (November 1989). I wish to thank the magazine's editor, Henry Mirima, for introducing me to Mfumbo.

54 One diocesan official claimed that he did not know the nature of Mfumbo's visit, and indeed a letter was sent out to *bakaiso* groups following the visit announcing that he was not to be invited back to Fort Portal.

55 All of what follows is based on interviews with Kasaija (24 May 1991) and other members of the Virika *bakaiso* group.

56 When interviewed, Lawrence mentioned that, when a child, he had wanted to join the seminary and become a priest, but (for unspecified reasons) it did not work out. When Serapio Magambo was named the first Mutoro bishop in 1969, Lawrence remarked: 'I promised my grandmother that I would soon become a bishop.' As an adult, Lawrence tried to join the Bannakaroli Brothers, a Buganda-based Catholic confraternity devoted to St Charles Lwanga, but he was rejected. Thus, the acquisition of the power of healing could be seen as the fulfilment of a lifelong goal to obtain religious charisma within the Catholic Church.

57 The enactment of the exorcism ritual was in most ways identical to Mfumbo's in Kampala. I attended several of Mfumbo's sessions in Kampala in 1990–1. I also attended the Virika session led by Kasaija on 19 May 1991.

58 The actual response varied from person to person. Some remained on their knees, and began to pray after Kasaija had moved on. Others went limp and softly collapsed to the ground, lying on their stomach or side as Kasaija continued praying, touching their side or legs. Others who collapsed then became violent, kicking and speaking in voices not their own, sometimes listing the evil things they had done or the names of people they had bewitched or killed. Some of those seemingly possessed began reacting before Kasaija even approached them, wildly shaking or vibrating, and speaking in the voice of the spirit possessing them. These people, after Kasaija had commanded the demon to leave them, remained lying on the ground for a long period, and some continued shaking and muttering softly.

59 Interestingly, Lawrence's job at the time was managing the laying of culverts for a new road.

60 The gendered dimension of witchcraft, and its implication in gender-based power struggles is common throughout contemporary Africa, as discussed in several of the essays in J. Comaroff and J. L. Comaroff (eds) *Modernity and its Malcontents* (Chicago, 1993).

61 But to say reluctance is not quite right, as for most (but not all) priests, given their training and the example of the missionaries, it would not occur to them in the first place. In addition, clergy are aware of cases like Archbishop Milingo of Zambia, who was recalled to Rome in 1982 for psychological tests after performing faith-healing and exorcisms. See

Gerrie Ter Haar, *Spirit of Africa* (Trenton, 1992). I should add, however, that several older Catholics related to me that a few White Fathers would perform exorcisms on a very occasional basis.

62 *Itambiro* in Toro literally means 'enclosure' and is the name for the ritual space marked off with a reed fence where the followers of Bisaaka hold their meetings.

63 Apparently, this was not publicly announced until the government daily *New Vision* reported it as a front page article on 16 December 1991. This was the first time the movement had ever been mentioned in the national press. The newspaper story referred to a Ministry of Internal Affairs investigation into the group that noted: 'Although the association was properly registered, it was not registered as a religious organization.' I want to thank Heike Behrend and Mikael Karlstrom, who both sent me copies of the *New Vision* article. In addition to the story, the newspaper included an extended feature on Bisaaka by George Kawule based on an interview with him ('Kagadi religious sect banned'). Most of the information in Kawule's piece accords with interviews I conducted with several of Bisaaka's followers throughout 1990–1. I should add that, when I went to his home in southern Bunyoro in March 1991, Bisaaka refused to see me out of fear of drawing attention to himself.

64 Kawule reports that in his interview Bisaaka 'singled out the Catholic church as his major persecutors' ('Kagadi religious sect'). When President Museveni visited southern Bunyoro in October 1989, he received reports that Bisaaka and his 'priests' were preventing people from going to hospitals to get medical treatment. Shortly afterwards, Uganda Radio announced that Bisaaka and his followers were not allowed to hold public meetings. A government investigation recently claimed that the groups were sowing discord in local communities.

65 In the interview with Kawule, however, Bisaaka claims that Hoima Diocese gave him several awards and gifts for his musical contributions.

66 These experiences, and many others, are recounted in a book Bisaaka distributes only to his followers, *Okwahukana Kuhoireho*, or *Disunity Has Ended*, which is used as a sacred text. *New Vision* reports the title of the book as *The Book of the God of Oneness*. *Obwosobozi* is also the word Batoro use for electricity. I might add that Bisaaka's terminology – forces, power, army – may have reminded the government of Lakwena's Holy Spirit Movement and that this was another reason for his banning.

67 I attended one such meeting at an *itambiro* in northeastern Toro in February 1991. The actual sessions of healing and exorcism resemble in many ways those for the Uganda Martyrs group, but with some important differences. The reactions of those possessed tend to become more violent when the *abahereza* approach them. The *abahereza* simply prayed over them, rarely laying on hands. Clients began by lying on the ground, and some suddenly leapt up and tried to run out of the *itambiro* in fear of the power of Obwosobozi. They were chased down and grabbed by 'guards', usually young men under the authority of the *abahereza*.

68 One other Christian element is prominent. When discussing the group's persecution, Bisaaka's followers cite biblical analogies, especially Christ's treatment by the Romans and the Pharisees. Thus, like the Jewish priests who tried to stop Jesus, present-day Christian leaders are trying to block God's latest message and messenger.

69 It should be added, however, that the six-month probation for return to the church was not a very stiff penalty, chosen as much to permit a relatively easy return for those who strayed as a threat to others who might consider participating in the Holy Quaternity Movement.

70 At least, many people I interviewed had this perception.

71 Rumours circulated widely throughout Toro that Fort Portal Bishop Magambo's stroke in 1989 was caused by Bisaaka through ritual means.

72 The NRM government had its own reasons for shutting down Bisaaka. While the official justification was that Bisaaka's followers were not seeking medical treatment for religious reasons, the experience of Lakwena's Holy Spirit Movement, still operating in northern Uganda, was no doubt on their minds. The NRM's highly rationalist discourse, which often described not just Uganda but Ugandans as backward, predisposed it to suspect any movement based on spirit possession. Finally, the Catholic Diocese of Fort Portal was a strong supporter of the NRM, and it is likely that their close ties facilitated the state's

definitive action.
73 Tibemanya, 'Dark side'.
74 Ssemuju, 'Categories of Catholics', 69.
75 Tibemanya, 'Dark side'.
76 *Ibid.*
77 Indeed, some priests may privately share some of their parishioners' beliefs in the power of non-Christian spirits and witchcraft while largely ignoring these issues in their public practice. Elsewhere, I have discussed one other relatively new religious movement within the church which has the active participation of some members of the clergy, the Catholic Charismatic Renewal Movement. See Kassimir, 'The social power of religious organization', Chapter 5.
78 John A. Coleman, '*Raison d'église*: organizational imperatives of the church in the political order', in J. K. Hadden and A. Shupe (eds), *Secularization and Fundamentalism Reconsidered* (New York, 1989), III:273.
79 See, for example, Adrian Hastings, *African Catholicism* (London, 1989).
80 The international dimension of *raison d'église*, while I have not focused on it here, is obviously not insignificant. Indeed, African Catholic leaders are aware of the fate of Archbishop Emmanuel Milingo of Zambia, who was removed from his position by the Vatican for performing exorcisms. Ironically, he was permitted to perform healing rites in Rome, with the implication that what was safe for the church in Italy might be deeply corrosive in Africa. More generally, the papacy of John Paul II, with its renewed emphasis on orthodoxy after the *aggiornamento* of Vatican II, is not a propitious time for African priests to display charisma autonomous from the Holy See.

Thirteen

✝✝✝✝✝✝✝✝✝✝

The Marian Faith Healing Ministry

An African Expression of Popular Catholicism in Tanzania

CHRISTOPHER COMORO & JOHN SIVALON

My name is Helena. My husband, who was a civil servant, died about seven years ago and left me with two children. I have been struggling on my own all these years to care for myself and my children. I am a secretary/typist with a monthly salary of Tshs 25,000 [$40]. I always tried to solve my own problems, but I was always bothered by high blood pressure and my low income and wondering where the next meal was going to come from.

One of my neighbours kept talking about 'Mary's Grace', and about miracles that she had witnessed at Fr Nkwera's services. So I decided that maybe by praying to Mary she would give me the means to solve my problems and get a better life. Now, I devote most of my free time to the group's activities. By praying, I feel close to God and feel the assistance of the 'Mother of God'.

My problems have diminished and even my income has increased. People in the group have given me part-time work typing for them, and people outside the group now see that they can trust me as a faithful person so they too give me their work to do. You have to trust in God and God will help. Most of the *wanamaombi* [petitioners] have been helped and had their problems solved. Because of this I see no reason to leave this group no matter what the bishops say.

It is hard for strangers to Tanzania to conceive how difficult life is for a person like Helena. According to recent World Bank development indicators, Tanzania is rated as the second poorest country in the world.[1] Between 1980 and 1993, the GNP per capita registered an annual average growth of 0.1 per cent. During the same period the inflation rate soared to an annual average rate of 24.3 per cent. In 1993, one study found that a household income of Tshs 54,950 was necessary to maintain a household at the poverty line defined in minimum daily calorific requirements.[2] This

275

means that Helena's basic salary was half of what was required just to reach a minimum level of simply surviving. Helena is not an exception. The same study indicated that 35 per cent of non-Dar es Salaam urban households, 27 per cent of Dar es Salaam households, and 60 per cent of Tanzanian rural households are in the same position. The seriousness of this situation is further highlighted by a dramatic drop in life expectancy in Tanzania, from a high of 54 years in 1988 to 49 for men and 50 for women in 1993.[3]

In this situation of hardship, people have developed various coping strategies. Helena is one of a number of people throughout Tanzania, mainly Roman Catholics, who have joined a group known as the Marian Faith Healing Ministry. This is a group who are followers of a healer priest named Fr Felician Nkwera. They have a strong devotion to Mary the Blessed Mother, which is expressed through a number of traditional Roman Catholic pietistic practices. Popularly, they are called *wanamaombi* (petitioners).

As Helena indicates, this group has had an unsettled relationship with the Roman Catholic hierarchy in Tanzania since its beginnings, and in recent years those relationships have deteriorated dramatically. In June 1991, the Roman Catholic Archbishop of Dar es Salaam Archdiocese, Polycarp Pengo, ordered that all members of the Marian Faith Healing Ministry (MFHM) be denied the sacraments, including a Catholic Church burial, and that they should remove themselves from any leadership positions at the sub-parish, parish and diocesan levels. This was the last in a long line of measures taken by Roman Catholic Church officials of Dar es Salaam against this group of Catholics.

Prior to this, the group was insulted from the pulpit and accused of fanaticism and fundamentalism. Some followers were physically beaten in church when they knelt down to receive Holy Communion. Now, some parishes have even denied the followers entrance into their church compounds. According to archdiocesan officials, the followers of the group have a 'holier than thou' attitude. Church officials claim that the followers of Nkwera portray their way as the only Roman Catholic way and judge others to be not Roman Catholic because they don't kneel to receive communion, don't receive it on the tongue, or don't have an adequate appreciation of the Blessed Mother and the Holy Eucharist. Church officials add that the followers are disruptive of church services and threaten the unity of the church by their disobedience of the archbishop and the majority of the priests of the archdiocese.

This chapter attempts to understand this group with two primary questions in mind: (1) Is it Roman Catholic? and (2) Is it popular? A number of commentators claim that the attractiveness of a group like the Marian Faith Healing Ministry is its incorporation of African culture and beliefs.[4] Some would even say that groups like this are more African than Roman Catholic. While a critique of this sort is often heard among church officials, Nkwera and the followers of the movement describe themselves as a devotional group within the Roman Catholic Church. They claim to have no intention of becoming an independent church and their cosmology is a traditional Roman Catholic cosmology, though it includes an explanatory element that has been lost in most modern European secularized Christian expressions. Within this explanatory component, there are many elements, like the stress on the devil, fallen angels and evil spirits, that resonate with African cultures.

Furthermore, commentators have indicated that the healing ministry is an example of the Africanization of Christianity specifically in terms of the meaning of salvation.[5] They claim that Africans are attracted to this concept in some Christian expressions because it is a part of their own culture. This study found though that, while many people joined the group because of this, it was not the only reason given, and even those who gave it as their first reason indicated a change in their attitudes as they became more involved in the group. Rather, many cited the dominant reason for their joining the group and remaining in it was the attraction of traditional Roman Catholic prayer life, which made it easier for them to praise and worship God. The conclusions of this study thus support the claim that this is a Roman Catholic group with a traditional Roman Catholic cosmology that resonates much more with the African cultures of its followers than do Western expressions of Christianity.

In terms of whether or not it is popular, we define popular as those sectors or strata of societies which do not enjoy much wealth, status or power, and which are perceived as part of the common people in their milieu. Thus 'popular Catholicism' includes those beliefs, symbols and practices followed by Roman Catholics of the above identified sectors of societies. As Kassimir notes in this volume:

> As an analytical construct, popular religion has three basic variants: (1) popular religion as belonging to a particular social group, or the dominated classes; (2) popular religion as deviations from a canonical set of beliefs, symbols and practices; and (3) popular religion as a rejection of the authority of designated religious specialists and the institution they represent.[6]

It is the thesis of this chapter that 'popular religion' includes all three of these elements, and that the Marian Faith Healing Ministry is 'popular' in all senses. First, it is an expression of the dominated, especially in its heavy stress on nationalism and on Tanzania's marginal status in the global politico-economic system. We found that the followers, while comprising a mixed group in terms of class, gender and ethnicity, showed a strong correlation between class and how they perceived their membership in the group. Second, the MFHM is popular in the sense of reviving traditional practices and beliefs of Roman Catholicism against the dominant secularized explanations of mission Roman Catholicism. Finally, it is popular in that it rejects accepted Roman Catholic authority placed in religious officials.

In Chapter 12, Kassimir further differentiates between 'official-popular' and 'popular', depending on whether such groups are sponsored by the church or not. While the followers of the Marian Faith Healing Ministry claim to be an 'official-popular' Catholic devotional group under the aegis of the church, they are being forced into becoming a 'popular' one because of conflict with the hierarchy. The source of the conflict appears to be centred around the rejection of church authority. This is an implicit rejection based on the strong belief in private revelation. Yet Nkwera continues to petition the hierarchy formally to recognize and bless his ministry.

History and Development

The Marian Faith Healing Ministry has a long history of development that is closely associated with the personal career of Father Felician V. Nkwera. Fr Nkwera was born into a large Catholic family in Iringa. His father was a catechist and strong supporter of the church. Shortly after his ordination in 1968, Nkwera experienced the central feature of his life that has set him apart from others in his priestly career. One morning after mass he heard the words:

> Felician my son, I am the Heavenly Mother speaking. I have chosen you to help my children who I will bring to you. You will pray over them and through your prayers God will heal them, and through your prayers they will receive my assistance. I will continue to enlighten you about this work as days go by.[7]

From that day on, Nkwera (called the 'Servant of God' within the ministry) has dedicated himself to praying for the sick, healing them and receiving private revelations and apparitions from the Blessed Mother which guide his work and teaching.

In 1973, after graduating with a BA, he was posted to government service in Tabora as a school inspector. With permission from the Archbishop of Tabora, Mark Mihayo, Nkwera organized prayer services for the sick on both an individual and a group basis. In 1974, however, Archbishop Mihayo reversed his decision and ordered Nkwera to stop his services of healing and exorcisms.

After quietly continuing his ministry, Nkwera formally requested recognition for his work from the Tanzania Episcopal Conference in 1977. The bishops replied that they were unable to grant blanket permission, but that all bishops were free to invite Nkwera to perform healing services in their respective dioceses. Thus, the initial response by the national church was sceptical and cautious. From 1977 to 1980, bishops from seven dioceses – Dar es Salaam, Morogoro, Mwanza, Musoma, Same, Bukoba and Mbeya – all agreed to Nkwera's prayer services. While during this time very little formal organization surrounded the ministry, he had begun to develop particular centres, often at the homes of followers, for the ministry in Tabora and the above-mentioned dioceses, and assistants began to work with him.

Conflict and hostility within the clergy continued to grow during this period. Finally, in 1980, the Tanzanian Episcopal Conference ordered Nkwera to stop performing his healing services. Against this order, Nkwera continued his healing ministry, especially in Dar es Salaam. Just prior to and including the 'Special Marian Year' of 1987–8 announced by Pope John Paul II, the Marian Faith Healing Ministry experienced a joyful period of peace and growth. During this period the ministry received special blessings from the Blessed Mother. These included divine working tools and symbols in the form of special holy water, special consecrated hosts and a holy ring.[8] Finally, Fr Nkwera was suspended by his Ordinary, the Bishop of Njombe, and ordered back to his diocese in 1990 as a result of the growth of the movement in Dar es Salaam and the ensuing conflict that arose between the clergy of the archdiocese and the followers of his ministry.

As part of his duties as a civil servant in the Ministry of Education, Nkwera has spent much time in Dar es Salaam. In 1976, he attended the ideological programme at Kivukoni, the Ideological College of TANU/CCM. From 1986 to 1989, he studied for his MA at the University of Dar es Salaam. It was during these years that the ministry took root and prospered in the archdiocese. Beginning with home-based services, Marian Faith Healing Centres were built eventually in Kibaha and Riverside. In 1987, Nkwera formally installed four assistants (*watendakazi*) who had the same charisms as Fr Nkwera in terms of healing, apparitions and private revelations. The four were Eledina Ntandu (Dina), Venant Pelekamoyo (now deceased), Agnes Biseko Nyamburi and Adelphina Magessa.[9]

Agnes and Adelphina are no longer active in the ministry, having sided with the archbishop of Dar es Salaam when he banned the ministry and all involved in it. Kalemera terms their defection the 'Oysterbay Demon's Resolution', after a group of leaders of the *wanamaombi* met with the seer Adelphina at the home of Salvatory Mosha, general manager of a major public corporation, in Oysterbay. After praying together, the Blessed Mother began to speak:

> A few days back, I gave you my message to suspend the Faith Healing Ministry.... I passed this message to my seer Agnes, saying that you should not perform my work in public. Rather you should pray only for those patients who come privately to your homes.... If you want peace with your Church leaders, then obey them.... Obey them, counsel them; tell them with humility what they should do and pray for them.[10]

Subsequently, the leaders broke with Fr Nkwera and the ministry.

The leaders of the breakaway group were known as *walezi* (guardians) within the Marian Faith Healing Ministry. The guardians claimed they had been directed by the Blessed Mother that the seers should be answerable to them, but Nkwera countered that this message had come from the devil.

He refused to listen to the guardians, who eventually wrote a letter of apology to the archbishop and ceased their involvement in the Marian Faith Healing Ministry. Many others also left the Marian Faith Healing Ministry because of the struggle between church officials and the ministry or because their families put pressure on them to maintain good relations with the church. Some, however, claimed that they left after they saw no perceptible improvement in their own personal problems or simply because they didn't have the time to participate in all the services and activities of the ministry.

As noted earlier, this chapter attempts to understand the Marian Faith Healing Ministry with two specific questions in mind: Is it Roman Catholic? And is it 'popular'? The sections that follow are related to these questions. First, we discuss the beliefs and rituals of the ministry to assess its religious claims. Then we look at who are the followers of this ministry, and how they are helped by being members. Finally, in terms of social transformation, what, if any, contribution does this ministry make?

Beliefs and Practices

Wanamaombi have a deep belief and dedication to Nkwera as the centre of the ministry. They believe that he receives direct revelations from the Blessed Mother, and that through her intercessions he has the power to heal. Through a series of apparitions and private revelations, the Blessed Mother has emphasized ten basic messages to the *wanamaombi*.

1 Repent and pray with your whole heart, the entire Fatima Rosary and the rosary of the seven dolours.

2 Pray for sinners, for the souls in purgatory and infants who die without baptism.

3 Pray for world peace and a deep faith in God.

4 Pray for the church and her leaders; pray for the *watendakazi* and all the Marian children with weak faith.

5 Keep God's commandments, especially the sixth and ninth that are most violated today. Abandon all superstitions and symbols of superstitions. Be humble and avoid hypocrisy.

6 Faithfully observe the first Thursday, Friday and Saturday of the month in honour of the Holy Eucharist, the Sacred Heart of Jesus and the Immaculate Heart of Mary by fasting and attending the Holy Eucharist.

7 Observe prayer vigils on every first Saturday of the month for reparation and to console the sorrowful and Immaculate Heart of Mary.

8 Daily perform acts of charity and always remember to offer your sufferings to the glory of God.

9 Catholics who are not barred should receive Holy Communion in a state of sanctifying grace, i.e. confess your sins well and then kneel and receive the Holy Eucharist on the tongue.

10 Do not segregate one another on the basis of religion, but each one should strive to marry or to be married to a member of one's religion and denomination in order to perpetuate peace in the family and deep faith in God.[11]

The central ritual of the group is the all-night vigil that takes place on the first Saturday of every month. This service begins at about 10 pm and closes at about 6.30 am, so that people can go to their respective parishes for Sunday mass. Estimates of the congregation at these vigils average 2,000 people; officials of the ministry claim that membership nationally is over 14,000 people, however, including those with casual contact.

The vigil is divided into four major sections. The first is the opening, which includes an entrance procession, introduction and evening prayers from the Catholic 'Liturgy of the Hours'. The procession includes the choir, servers, a sister helper, Nkwera and his assistant. Strikingly, there is little distinctive liturgical dress. Fr Nkwera wears a simple Kaunda suit (short sleeved African suit) with Roman collar. Sister and the assistant wear normal street attire. They process from the rear of the centre, which is roofed but open on the sides. The service is led from a sanctuary with an altar, a small shrine to the Blessed Mother, a podium to the front and a large container of water to the rear on the right side. The congregation have their own books and photocopied sheets with the liturgy of the hours and a schedule of the service.

The second section would ordinarily be the liturgy of the Holy Eucharist, but, since the suspension of Nkwera, it is similar to the Catholic 'Sunday Service without a Priest'. This includes a Liturgy of the Word, including a lengthy homily; prayers of the faithful; and Liturgy of Thanksgiving for the institution of the Blessed Sacrament and its adoration. Father's homilies vary, but usually during the homily one or two people begin speaking out or shouting. This is understood by the followers as the devil speaking through them. It often turns into a dialogue between Father and the devil, with Father commanding the devil to be silent. Nkwera has also explained that at these moments the power of God can move the devil to reveal some truths about its strategy and struggle with God here on earth. As a group, the followers of the Marian Faith Healing Ministry express a deep devotion to the Holy Eucharist. They resent deeply the archbishop's ban on their receiving the Eucharist and Father's suspension from celebrating it for them. Their devotion is shown during the adoration of the Blessed Sacrament when a 'special host from heaven' is displayed in a monstrance on the altar. At one service, a follower took me to a particular corner of the centre to see how the host glowed like no other host, proving God's special presence.

The third section is dedicated to prayers of exorcism and healing. Once again the prayers of this section are taken directly from the Latin ritual, with some in Latin and some in Swahili. There is a general blessing through the sprinkling of holy water throughout the congregation. This is followed with the special healing rite for those possessed. This includes a generous washing with water and laying on of hands. For the washing and laying on of hands, people line up. There are leaders present to control the line and comfort the ones who begin to throw themselves around and onto the ground. Women helpers take special care to wrap sheets of cloth around the women in the line to maintain a degree of modesty as they writhe and struggle with the demons within. While this is going on, the rest of the congregation, which is the vast majority of the people, continue with the praying of the rosary, songs and adoration of the Blessed Sacrament.

The majority of those prayed over are women; when asked why, some people denied this was so. Others claimed that it was because the majority of the followers were women. Some, including some leaders of the group, said this was how it has always been since Adam and Eve. Finally, in a subsequent focus group discussion, women explained:

> Life is difficult and is especially difficult for women. We have to struggle against all odds to survive. That struggle opens us up to all forms of temptations and makes us especially vulnerable to the devil as our strength begins to lessen.[12]

Members of a male focus group added:

> Women are more vulnerable to attacks by the devil because the devil knows that mothers are the pillars of the family. If he can take over the mother, the devil knows that he has taken over the whole family.[13]

The final section of the vigil is a time of testimony when a few individuals witness to the healing they have experienced. They are usually people who have suffered for a long time with a physical ailment and who have sought treatment at various health facilities without success. But, when they were prayed over by either of the healers, they experienced a miraculous cure. This period is followed by announcements and directions that come to the group through the various seers, morning prayers from the 'Liturgy of the Hours', and then a closing procession.

The vigil is well coordinated and professionally done. The choir sings a variety of songs in both Latin and Swahili that are appropriate to the various sections of the vigil. Most songs are known well by the general congregation, which allows for a great deal of participation and life throughout the vigil. This makes the vigil an enjoyable service and, while most people expect the service to be too long, because of its structure and liveliness it passes very quickly. A number of our research assistants expressed their own enjoyment of the service, especially the singing, and wished to join.

Besides the vigil, the ministry has a variety of other identifying characteristics and beliefs. First, it stresses that Holy Communion should be received kneeling and only on the tongue out of respect for the sacredness of the Sacrament. Secondly, many remove their shoes when they enter the healing centre and their parish churches. Thirdly, many have a shrine to the Blessed Mother in their homes, and many wear the rosary around their necks. They believe that they have been given a special holy water which is a mixture of our Lord's blood and water from his side and the tears of the Blessed Virgin Mary, shed out of concern for her suffering 'sons and daughters on earth'. This water is used in a variety of ways. In the service itself, people were observed drinking the water. Others filled bottles to take home. In subsequent interviews, followers said they added a small amount of the water to their cooking and sprinkled themselves and their houses with it as protection against the devil and as medicine for the sick. They also claim to have been given three consecrated hosts from heaven. These are said to be signs of Our Lord's presence as healer in the Marian Faith Healing Ministry, even in times of conflict with church officials.

The ministry also has shorter services three times a week. In addition, they meet in small neighbourhood gatherings and are organized with a general council and a small central committee at the national level. While Nkwera is the central figure, the other seers also have a special voice in matters, and there are a number of lay leaders who have had a great deal of leadership experience within the archdiocesan structure before they were banned by church officials. This experience is evident in how well organized the liturgies are, but also in other community activities like visiting the sick, attending funerals and wakes, and protecting themselves as an organization.

Problem Solving

Who are the followers?

As part of our research, we conducted a survey of 132 respondents. This was not a random sample, from which statistical inferences can be drawn, but it does give some indication on a broader level of who the followers of this group are and why they joined.[14] This is an extremely mixed group with no clear-cut class, gender or status make-up. As can be seen, the survey sample is almost evenly split between women and men. It includes people who are highly educated as well as those with only primary education or less, and it is evenly split in terms of age.

Table 13.1 *Education & Gender of Respondents*

Education: Gender	Tertiary	Secondary	Primary	Total
Male	20	29	14	63
Female	13	29	27	69
Total	33	58	41	132

Table 13.2 *Economic Status & Age of Respondents*

Economic status: Age	Well-off	Poor	Destitute	Total
16–25	9	11	4	24
26–35	9	27	5	41
36–45	3	15	3	21
46–55	8	8	1	17
56–	2	2		4
Total	31	63	13	107

The group is also mixed in terms of class, with a large portion of well-off people, even though the majority are poor. This classification is relative and subjective in that we told the research assistants to use their own judgement, taking into account the prevailing economic and cultural context. Their judgements have led to a classification of a small group of people who are almost destitute, a large group of poor people who are representative of the general population of Tanzania (Helena from our introduction was included in this group), and a significant group of people with an economic status above the average for the general Tanzanian population. Women tended to be among the 'poor'. Nine of the 13 classified as destitute were women and 61 per cent of the poor category were women. It is no wonder, then, that with this mix of people we find an equally varied response in terms of why people joined the group.

Why do people join?

Nkwera claimed that the main reason people joined his ministry, after responding to the call of the Blessed Mother, was for the counselling people received through direct private revelations, the homilies of the services and private counselling sessions. Non-followers of the ministry and especially church officials claimed that most of the *wanamaombi* were people with problems, especially psychological problems, looking for a source of identity and belonging.

Wanamaombi themselves indicated that there were four main reasons they joined. The first, cited by 33.3 per cent of respondents, was that people joined 'to praise and worship God by praying together in enjoyable liturgies'. Second, 17.6 per cent claimed they originally joined due to personal or health problems. Third, 17.5 per cent indicated that they joined primarily to 'gain eternal life'. Finally, 11.4 per cent said they joined 'to be helped materially'. These findings were confirmed by another question that allowed people to list four reasons for joining. Interestingly, 'personal and health problems' was significant only as a first reason and insignificant as a second, third or fourth reason – indicating that there is a significant minority of followers who joined the group originally because of personal or health problems, but most did not view this as a reason for their joining at all. Instead, the vast majority of people expressed more spiritual reasons, describing their original attraction to the group and their continuing participation as related to the liturgies themselves as lively and enjoyable means of praising and worshipping God.

These responses varied by gender and class: 67 per cent of the respondents claiming 'personal and health problems' to be their main reason for joining the ministry were women; and 63 percent of those indicating 'to praise and worship' were men. Furthermore, within the 'personal problem' category the more highly educated tended to talk about personal problems while the less educated spoke more of health problems. This division was further supported by the fact that 55 per cent of those categorized as 'destitute' mentioned health problems as their main reason, and 33 per cent of those who called themselves 'housewives' also said that 'health problems' were their main reasons for joining the ministry.

This pattern was confirmed by findings from subsequent life histories of poorer members of the movement and focus group discussions. Excerpts follow from four life histories which show the variety of problems facing the poor and their testimony to the help they have received by belonging to the group.

Elenora

My name is Elenora; I am 25, and my husband, who is slightly older, is James. We were married in the church and we are both *wanamaombi*. I was the first to join the group. For years, I was bothered by pains throughout my body to the point that I couldn't even do normal kitchen chores. I went to a number of traditional doctors who did nothing for me. One day on my way to see a traditional healer, the pain was so severe, I had to sit down on the side of the road, and I began crying. A man came by and asked me what was wrong and suggested that we pray together three Our Fathers, three Hail Marys and three Glory be to the Fathers. Then he advised me that instead of going to the traditional healers I should go to see Fr Nkwera.

I began to attend regularly and when Father was consulted about my problems, he told me that I had a lack of faith, and that God was reminding me not to forget God in my life. Also, that either I or my friend or relative needed to change our behaviour, and my suffering was meant as an invitation to do this. Therefore, she would suffer for a period, but if she had faith she would recover. I became very committed to the group and began to experience relief from my suffering; later I recovered.

The Tanzanian Postal Service was pressured into laying off a number of workers by the World Bank. James, my husband, was one of them. I convinced him to come with me to the prayer services, and he did. Fr Nkwera prayed over him and called him to pray for himself, which he did. He was later rehired by the Postal Service.

Nuru

I am a Muslim woman named Nuru who was the firstborn in my family. After my father died, my mother was inherited by my uncle. My problems really began when I decided to move in with a man who was much older than myself and had six children of his own. After two years, I still had not conceived, and I began to seek medical help. First, I went to government clinics and hospitals, and after they failed to help me, I started visiting traditional doctors. In those visits it was revealed that my mother-in-law and her friend, a neighbour, had put a 'spell' over me and were trying to kill me. I went from traditional doctor to traditional doctor, but instead of getting better, I only got worse. I was acting like someone possessed and started talking strange languages.

Then, one day, my friend came and told me about Fr Nkwera. At first I was hesitant to go because I didn't want to associate with Christians, but later, with a lot of encouragement from my friend, I went to the services. The services are given free, and Fr Nkwera showed he had the power to chase away evil spirits. After only two sessions my problems started to disappear. Even though I have not conceived, my insanity has stopped. Also, my husband has now passed away.

I would like to become a Christian, but right now my mother is sick and she would be upset if she heard I had changed my religion. I believe in the Blessed Mother and I believe that it is through her prayers that I have been healed.

Flora

My name is Flora. I have been very sick from the time I lived in Moshi. My diseases were not able to be cured in hospitals. Then I tried going to traditional healers, but once again I received no relief. In 1981, I moved to Dar es Salaam and my condition continued to worsen until one of my neighbours told me that there was a Catholic priest who cures sicknesses like mine without any charge, and this was when I decided to go to him.

The day I went, there was a long line waiting to see him. When the person in front of me entered to see Father, I started to shake all over. Then, when I went in, Father looked at me just as I fell down and went unconscious. When I regained consciousness, my sister told me that I was filled with devils that started talking with Father, and as he prayed over me, they began to leave me one after the other. Father then told me to continue to attend the prayer services.

From that time on, my condition has steadily improved. I have regained my health, and these days I am eating like I used to before I became sick. I have gained weight and people who knew me when I was sick are surprised to see how healthy I am. From 1981, I have been a *mwanamaombi* and I will not stop.

Daniel

I am Daniel and I joined this group a few years back. I was in a bus accident and broke my leg. For a long time the bone refused to join together, and I began getting sicker and sicker. Then one day one of my fellow workers told me that I should go to see the Servant of God. When I went, I was cured, and I thank God that I was able to be healed both bodily and spiritually.

Certain patterns emerge from these stories concerning the poor within this group. First, most of them are women. The men who were classified as poor or destitute turned out to be mainly students who were introduced to the group either by their parents or friends. In fact, people are generally introduced to the group by other *wanamaombi*. A variety of problems, such as sicknesses, injuries, unemployment and marital strife appear open to being solved by being a *mwanamaombi*. None of these problems are viewed by people as existing within a vacuum. They are seen as connected to how one lives one's life, to evil spirits, to people's control of these spirits, or to the behaviour of relatives or friends. This is very similar to a general African understanding of sickness and death. Even James's unemployment is seen as the result of other forces in his life rather than the redundancy policies of the government, World Bank or IMF. Through prayers and participation in the services of the MFHM, his problem was solved. With physical and emotional ailments, another pattern emerged that was confirmed by the survey. People tended first to seek treatment in hospitals that follow a germ theory programme of treatment. When people did not find relief there, they then went to traditional healers, and finally to Nkwera.

A major point made in all the interviews was that Fr Nkwera did not charge. The MFHM is a free service. Traditional healers end up being quite expensive for most people. Furthermore, during the late 1970s and early 1980s, there was almost a total collapse of government-provided health services. And since the mid-1980s, again under pressure from the IMF and World Bank, the government of Tanzania has been involved in a steady privatization of social services and the implementation of 'cost sharing' policies in government social service provision. For some of the poor, these policies may have taken health services out of the realm of possibility. Thus, even though it may not be the major reason for joining, the MFHM is one of the few free services to which they can turn. While Fr Nkwera may present the healing centre as another medical facility similar to clinics, hospitals and health centres, however, very few of the people – no matter whether rich or poor, women or men, highly educated or having minimal education – saw the centre as their only medical option: 67.7 per cent of the respondents said that they combined prayer, the Marian Centre and other medical facilities to treat themselves or sick relatives.

In terms of those who saw prayer as their only medical option, almost all of them identified the special holy water as the single most effective element of the rituals and sacramentals used in the ministry. This water is used to bless oneself, to cook, to sprinkle on the home and to drink, in addition to its uses in the rituals of the vigil.

How are the poor helped?

When asked how the poor were helped, the vast majority of respondents listed the following as the major assistance that the poor received:

1 Charity in the form of clothing, housing, money and jobs.
2 Being prayed for.
3 Counselling and comfort received from prayer, their leaders and the community.
4 Being strengthened in their faith and perseverance.

Examples from people's life stories illustrate a number of cases where people have been helped by the ministry. One widow, who had been evicted from government housing after her husband's death, received housing. Another widow was found a job, and an unemployed woman was hired in the business firm of another *mwanamaombi*. Of the destitute group, 70 per cent acknowledged that they had been helped materially by other *wanamaombi*, but, interestingly, none of them indicated 'knowing that they are not alone' as help they received by joining the ministry.

Focus group discussions also showed that the destitute and poor did not view their poverty in terms of broader structural dimensions. Rather, they saw it as a real, but not a hopeless situation. They stressed that the only way to escape this situation was to work hard. They also said that Father stressed in his homilies and teachings that each person had to live by her own hard work and that she should only pursue legal ways of making a living. Some cited the Bible as recommending that only those who work should eat. Working together or organized cooperation in improving each other's lives is not an explicit part of this group's ideology, but, in fact, they do help each other in various ways as the story of Helena indicates. We also observed that a great deal of help is provided at the time of funerals and in the neighbourhoods through the visiting of the sick.

The second major finding was how deep the faith of the followers of this ministry is in terms of the efficacy of prayer. While many respondents did not cite the strengthening of faith as assistance they had received, the vast majority said that God responds to prayers in a real and pragmatic way, and that the major help the poor receive results from prayer. These findings were supported by a related question concerning how their faith had changed: 30 per cent of the respondents felt that the major change was that they had grown in their love of prayer and worship. Since most of the followers interviewed experienced real help in their lives through the prayers of the ministry, it is very difficult to see why they would give up their participation in the group simply because of the bishops' decree. A person who has been sick for years, and has experienced no relief except through the prayers of MFHM, is unlikely to turn her back on the movement.

Focus group discussions confirmed that the biggest benefit received by the poor in the group was through prayer. People were helped tremendously by being prayed over by the 'Servant of God', by one of his assistants or by their fellow *wanamaombi*. It is normal practice for a *mwanamaombi* to ask other *wanamaombi* to gather and pray for him or her, while most said that little material help was actually available because the vast majority of the members are poor. It would thus appear that 'transformative action on behalf of justice for the poor' is not a major part of the explicit beliefs of this group. Rather, members tend to emphasize charity and prayer as the major benefit received by the poor who belong to it. Both of these are traditional Catholic values, and this group's responses are probably not that different from those of the general Catholic population of Tanzania. They may not be as unpolitical, however, as they claim.

The Church Militant and the War with Satan

One of the central features of the *wanamaombi* belief system is a return to an emphasis on the Church Militant. The church is seen as being involved in a war on earth. The competing sides are the forces of darkness, centred on Satan, and the forces of light, centred around Christ through the Blessed Mother, Mary. The *wanamaombi* do not see this as a war of impersonal forces, but rather as a war between personalized forces who work through people. Not only does Mary speak to her seers, therefore, but the devil also speaks through people and can even disguise itself to sound like Mary. War with Satan was emphasized by research assistants evaluating the difficulties they encountered in doing their research:

> This group is like an army. No one will speak to you until Father gives his approval. They are very conscious of security and very sceptical about the motives of people who are asking questions about them. They are more security minded than the Tanzanian Army.

The war with the forces of darkness is carried out in all spheres of life, including the church itself. In the conflict with the local hierarchy, *wanamaombi* claim that many church officials are being used by Satan to destroy the church. They also see many political leaders as instruments of the devil, and, whenever there were indications of religious unrest in Tanzania, they viewed these as signs of the devil's work. Followers of the ministry were asked to name the four major signs of the devil. The major sign, named by 60 per cent of the respondents, was war. Others included, in order of importance: fornication, violence, new and strange illnesses, disrespect by children, witchcraft, religious strife, denying of God, accidents and famine. Women were the most prominent (83 per cent) in selecting violence and new illnesses, such as AIDS. The poor were also strongly represented (92 per cent) in selecting these two. Domestic violence was also mentioned frequently. When asked how one can fight against the devil, *wanamaombi* again stressed prayer, mostly in the form of rosaries, novenas and special services. Fasting, being humble, making sacrifices and doing good works followed in that order.

This heavy stress on the work of the devil and evil spirits has led many church officials to conclude that the ministry is more African than it is Catholic. Citing Nkwera's own testimony and that of other leaders, however, members claim that their cosmology is traditional Roman Catholic – and, as such, it has many points of contact with African culture. But Nkwera has emphatically preached against such traditional practices as honouring the ancestors and other traditional rituals as satanic. From his point of view, there is a clear distinction between what he and his followers believe and African culture; nor is what he is doing an example of inculturation.

Studies of African independent churches note that in the main European Christianity has abandoned its explanatory character for the emotional and relational dimension, leaving explanation to science.[15] The attractiveness of independent churches, they say, results from Africans' attempts to understand the world around them and their marginal position in that world; the devil, demons and evil spirits form a crucial part of their explanation of worldly events. Fr Nkwera, the 'Disposer of Demons', offers the same explanation that Roman Catholicism offered before it abandoned that function to science.[16]

Action Aimed at Social Transformation: *Wanamaombi* and Politics

Nationalism

Tanzania is the second-poorest country in the world economy, according to certain World Bank economic indicators, marginal almost to the point of being insignificant.[17] It has no strategic value for the dominant powers in the world. It has no major crop or mineral base with which it can earn foreign exchange. It has a minimal industrial sector and is therefore heavily dependent on imports for consumer goods. Thus, from the perspective of the world system, Tanzania is poor, insignificant and marginal, a fact that is reinforced daily by the mass media.

In opposition to this view, Nkwera gives voice to the cries of Tanzanians, claiming that their nation is a 'Chosen Nation'. It is a nation that is central to salvation history in that it was dedicated to the Queen of Peace and put under her protection by Pope John XXIII on its independence day, 9 December 1961. It is the Blessed Mother herself who has agreed to care for Tanzania and to purify it. A major part of the services of the group is dedicated to praying for Tanzania. Within those services is a special prayer rededicating Tanzania to the Blessed Mother. Much of Nkwera's writing and preaching is directed towards dispelling the idea of Africa being the lost continent, and he highlights Tanzania as the 'Star of Africa and Mountain of Peace' as well as the liberator of Southern Africa.[18] Much of the praise given to Tanzania is implicitly directed at President Nyerere as Father of the Nation.

All this is indicative of Nkwera's own background as a civil servant during the Nyerere years and his own political understanding as it was shaped by his experiences under the ideology of TANU/CCM. For Tanzanians who lived under colonial rule and witnessed the peaceful transition to independence, Nkwera's nationalism is very appealing and resonates with their own position. They know the scorn that they have had to bear of being a colony and of being African. For them, the devastation of poverty was not primarily economic but cultural. In the struggle against the insignificant and marginal status of Tanzania, Nkwera proposes that it is unique as a 'Chosen Nation', and that Tanzanians as a 'Chosen People' have a special role to play in carrying out God's will as communicated by the Blessed Mother.

The force of his preaching is indicated by the response of all the respondents who were included in the survey, case studies and focus groups. Everyone, without exception, expressed their belief that Tanzania has been dedicated to the Blessed Mother and is under her special protection. Some even clarified why this was so. The celebrations for the independence of Tanzania began on the eve of Independence Day, 8 December 1961 – the evening of the feast of the Immaculate Conception of the Blessed Mother – and, at midnight, independence was announced. They explained that they were reminded of this by Nkwera and his assistants, but emphasized that it was not Nkwera who actually dedicated the country to Mary. As one said:

> The news that Tanzania is under the special protection of the Blessed Mother has been given to us by the 'Servant of God' and his assistants. But more importantly the devils and evil spirits themselves have been forced to confirm this during the prayer services when the power of God, Mary and the angels force them into submission and they begin to tell the truth through people. Tanzania is our hardest battleground because it is a Chosen Nation under God's special protection.

Another indicated the peace that Tanzania has experienced as a sign of the fact that Tanzania is under Mary's protection:

> This country was dedicated to Mary twice. Once at the time of Independence and then later when Pope John Paul II visited and rededicated it to our Blessed Mother. A clear sign that our country is under Mary's protection is the fact that we have never experienced any disaster or turmoil like our neighbouring countries of Uganda, Kenya, Ethiopia, Somalia and the Sudan. The presence of people like Idi Amin are clear signs of the devil, and Tanzania's ability to dispose of him was proof that Tanzania is under Mary's protection.

Many others affirmed the fact that the peace experienced by Tanzania is the clear sign that Mary is protecting it.

Prophetic voice

Together with nationalism, Nkwera also provides a strong prophetic voice against both the church and the government. He forcefully proclaims *nchi imeoza* ('The country is rotten') and claims that 99 per cent of church and government leaders are also rotten. Most government leaders, he says, are unsatisfactory and respect neither God nor human rights. Corruption, misuse of public property, adultery, witchcraft and a lack of justice characterize government leadership. A major problem, says Nkwera, is that both government and church leaders do not want to listen to the truth. They only listen to lies, and they themselves spread lies and witness to lies as being the truth. The nation is rotten because most leaders are rotten, and the few good leaders who remain are abused, shunned, publicly mistreated or discredited.[19]

Mosques are also called to conversion in Nkwera's writing and preaching. Instead of preaching the word of God, Muslim leaders are accused of advocating murder as well as spreading lies and becoming rotten. Because of this, he says, neither church, mosque nor government is able to defend the rights of people and speak out on behalf of justice. Followers themselves stressed that they are constantly reminded of the abuses and corruption of leaders. As one said:

> Corruption and bribery are not good things and even the government has outlawed them. We are counselled to live by legal means. Even though economic conditions are very bad, we should not look to illegal means to make our living. These include bribery, misuse of public property, stealing by use of a pen and irresponsibility. We should live by an income that is legal according to the laws of the land and the laws of God.

The Elections of October 1995

Augustine Mrema emerged as a significant figure in the transition to multi-party governance. As Minister of Home Affairs, he had become popular as a defender of the oppressed, the weak and the marginal. Gradually his popularity began to worry many of the old guard in CCM. Seen as a reformer and potential presidential candidate by people at the grassroots, CCM leaders portrayed him as a dictator who acted as policeman, judge and jury. Finally, he broke with CCM and became the presidential candidate of the opposition party, NCCR.

Mrema's personal war against corruption and the lack of justice in Tanzania thus seemed very much in accord with Nkwera's own emphasis on the need for reform. Mrema once asked that he be remembered in the prayer services of the *wanamaombi*, and from that time on he was mentioned publicly in the prayers of the faithful. The prayer was usually worded: 'Let us pray for Minister Mrema and national security.' The phrase 'national security' was emphasized in the context of the devil's use of religion to disrupt Tanzania. Nkwera had once foretold a Muslim demonstration against butchers who were selling pork. The demonstration subsequently took place and resulted in a certain amount of damage. Mrema was then called upon to restore order, and his actions remained controversial throughout the presidential campaign. Thus, the prayers for him and for 'national security' were aimed against all those forces who were used by the devil to disrupt Tanzania's security. By implication, this meant that Mrema was not a part of those satanic forces.

Nkwera did not publicly declare his support for any candidate during the elections, however, and when CCM announced their candidate was Ben Mkapa, also a Catholic and a former student of Julius Nyerere, one influential member of the group remarked:

> Now it doesn't really matter who people vote for because we have both the top candidates [Mrema was also a Catholic]. If CCM had nominated Kikwete [a Muslim], then there would have been a struggle, and Mrema would have had all our votes.

As the elections of October 1995 approached, *wanamaombi* responded by initiating a special weekly prayer service to pray for the elections, for Tanzania and for peace and security. But, in a private revelation after the elections, the Blessed Mother critically evaluated them, noting three basic evils of the elections:

1 Witchcraft: leadership was not sought by depending on God; instead, many candidates actually went to witchdoctors and performed sacrifices of many types to gain election.
2 Bribery: while the government claims to be bankrupt, hospitals have no medicine and people are suffering and even dying, a tremendous amount of money was used to buy votes by the ruling party.
3 Lies: falsehoods were spread about certain candidates and people were frightened by falsehoods about violence and how multi-parties would turn Tanzania into another Rwanda.

Nkwera was thus led to question: how can the same people who came to office by corruption do away with corruption? How can the same people who were brought to office by lies do away with lies? How can a nation be led by justice when the leadership did not come to office in a just way? As the Blessed Mother says:

> Until now, the hearts of many of her children are burdened and saddened by the lack of justice that was followed during the elections; they have despaired and see no chance for change in the near future.[20]

Nkwera continues to stress that what is left is to continue to pray for Tanzania for God alone can conquer the work of the devil.

Conclusion

Our study has shown that different followers are attracted to the MFHM for a variety of reasons. Tanzania has been marked over the years by a high degree of regional differentiation. Two regions which are considered the richest are Kagera, especially the Bukoba area, and Kilimanjaro. These two regions were highly receptive to Christian missionary efforts and the education that accompanied those efforts. Thus many of the longest-serving, best-educated and wealthiest Tanzanians come from these regions. As such, these people make up a large portion of the better-off Catholic followers of the MFHM, and they were attracted to it by the traditional Catholic piety that was so much a part of their earlier socialization into Christianity.

The poor and the destitute followers of the ministry, by contrast, are more attracted by their need to attain help for long-standing problems. Most of these are women and widows who came to the group through an invitation from a follower, and many of them testified to the fact that their problems were solved through 'prayer'. More pragmatically, a number of them received material help from better-off followers of the ministry. In terms of their poverty, the group has a strong belief in the power of hard work. They stressed that the only way to solve their economic problems was to work hard and live by the sweat of their own labour. There is no conscious effort to organize people to help one another as a group to attack their poverty, and members see their poverty as a real but not a hopeless situation.

Followers of the ministry see the world as a battleground between the forces of the devil and the forces of God through Mary. All the evil in the world, whether it affects rich or poor, individuals or whole nations, results from the workings of the devil. As a country under the special protection of Mary, Tanzania has enjoyed decades of peace and tranquillity. According to the ministry, however, the devil is still at work in Tanzania, as demonstrated by the pervasive corruption and abuse of both government and religious leaders during the elections of 1995. The primary way of fighting the devil is through prayer. By the prayers of the ministry, people are cured, demons are expelled, problems are solved and the devil is repelled. Followers are called upon to dedicate their lives to God, centring all aspects of their lives around the ministry in the war with evil in all its forms.

While general beliefs in the powers of spiritual forces are common across Africa, all the specific beliefs and rituals of the ministry are based emphatically on traditional Catholic rites and beliefs. The ministry sees itself as a devotional group firmly within the Roman Catholic Church. They also see themselves as a reform movement calling the church back to its foundations, but they have no intention of breaking away. Rather, they see their present estrangement from the official church hierarchy as another sign of the devil's presence in the church. They are convinced that eventually, through the intervention of the Vatican, the ministry will be recognized and their suspensions will be removed.

In conclusion, it can be said that this group is truly a 'popular' move-ment in all the senses of the term described earlier. While it has struggled to maintain its status as an 'official' popular group within the Catholic Church, however, church officials have reacted strongly to the ministry and appear to be committed to alienating the group from the church in order to protect the role of the hierarchy in matters of teaching and authority. A possible result of this conflict will be to transform the MFHM into a 'popular' popular movement, outside and against the official Catholic Church establishment.

While clearly a 'popular' movement, however, the ministry as clearly aligns itself within Roman Catholic tradition. All of its rituals, beliefs and prayers have been generated by that tradition. While open to people of other faiths and denominations, the ministry is clearly perceived by its followers and by outsiders as Catholic – and all interviewees indicated that its leaders and followers are determined to remain within the church and have no desire to become an 'independent' church.

Notes

1 World Bank, *World Development Report, 1995* (Oxford, 1995).
2 Brian Cooksey, 'Who's poor in Tanzania?', in M.S.D. Bagachwa (ed.), *Poverty Alleviation in Tanzania* (Dar es Salaam, 1994), 59.
3 Tanzania Gender Networking Programme, *Gender Profile of Tanzania* (Dar es Salaam, 1993), 98.
4 See Gwinyai H. Muzorewa, *The Origins and Development of African Theology* (Maryknoll, 1995), 38–41.
5 See Joseph Healey and Donald Sybertz, *Towards an African Narrative Theology* (Nairobi, 1996), 291–336.
6 Ron Kassimir, Chapter 12 above, 255.
7 Jason Kalemera, *Huduma za Maombezi in its Historical Perspective* (Dar es Salaam, 1993), 13.
8 *Ibid.*, 35–6.
9 Based on Kalemera, *Huduma za Maombezi*.
10 *Ibid.*, 47–9.
11 *Ibid.*, 36–7.
12 Focus Group Discussion, July 1996. Participants were poor women.
13 Focus Group Discussion, July 1996. Participants were poor men.
14 The sample was drawn from the 2,000 plus followers who attend the monthly vigil and who were willing to be interviewed after it. We also observed the services, collected individual life histories, and conducted focus group discussions with select groups of *wanamaombi*.
15 Muzorewa, *Origins and Development of African Theology*.
16 Br Paul Davis, *Fr. Nkwera Disposer of Demons*, (Dar es Salaam: private printing, 1994).
17 World Bank, *World Development Report 1995*.
18 Fr F. V. Nkwera, *Kanisa, Serikali, Msikiti na Uchaguzi Mkuu Tanzania, 1995* (Dar es Salaam, 1996), 2–13.
19 *Ibid.*, 24–7.
20 *Ibid.*, 44–5.

Fourteen

Contending
for the Faith
Spiritual Revival
& the Fellowship Church
in Tanzania

JOSIAH R. MLAHAGWA

For four days early in January 1997, the bishops and pastors of the Evangelical Lutheran Church in Tanzania gathered for an unprecedented conference at the foot of the Uluguru Mountains in Morogoro. The subject of revival in the church featured conspicuously on the agenda and in the deliberations of the assembly. At the end of the conference the leaders of the most populous among the non-Catholic Christian denominations in the country unanimously recognized spiritual revival as the spinal cord of the church.[1] Henceforth they resolved that they were going to be more actively involved in the promotion, direction and momentum of the revival movement, and they expressed their resolve to work closely with the revival fellowships in their respective churches.[2]

The Lutheran conference symbolized in a significant way the spirit of revival currently sweeping the country in a defining moment in the history of the Christian faith in Tanzania. The changes taking place in Tanzanian Christendom are multifaceted, but they can be reduced to two basic dimensions: the tangible quantitative aspects of church growth and the qualitative formation of the church body. Each of these aspects has its own dynamics, and both dimensions define the spiritual revival movement in general, while the growth of the fellowships could be construed as the fulcrum of the movement.

The quantitative aspect of revival in Tanzania is very conspicuous. Almost every evangelical church in the city of Dar es Salaam, for example, has an expansion programme or is in the process of executing one. New church structures are being built and old buildings are being remodelled so as to accommodate more churchgoers. Churches unable to enlarge their buildings cater for increased churchgoers by launching more worship services. It is not uncommon for churches to conduct three services every Sunday, each service attended by different people. There is also a noticeable increase in mid-week activities. While previously people went to church only on hearing the gong on Sunday morning, church premises now are bustling with group activities throughout the week.

The qualitative dimensions of revival are even more interesting. Hardly a week passes without one seeing or hearing about a seminar, a crusade meeting or a denominational evangelical rally taking place somewhere in the city. Many of the meetings attract huge crowds of people. Common to such meetings is fiery preaching followed by a call to repentance, when people are invited to come forward, repent and invite Jesus as Lord and Saviour into their lives so that they can become born-again Christians. Another important aspect is the open prayers conducted by the preachers, aimed at casting away demons from people and delivering them from their ailments and other problems. Undoubtedly, the crowds are attracted to these meetings by the hope of being healed or delivered from their social problems, just as much as they are drawn by the Gospel message and the popularity of the principal speaker.

Those who come forward as new converts to the Christian faith, together with older converts who now express their willingness to accept Jesus Christ as their personal Lord and Saviour, are advised by the leaders of the crusades to join the fellowships that operate in areas close to their homes. In previous times, such born-again Christians often joined Pentecostal charismatic churches, whose members consider themselves as authentic Christians in contrast to the nominal believers in mainstream denominational churches. Although not all who are registered during evangelical meetings as born-again Christians continue to be faithful members of their own church or fellowship, the fellowships have continued to swell with new members who express renewed commitment to the Christian faith.

Our main objective in this chapter is to examine the dynamics of the revival movement and the quantitative and qualitative transformation of the Christian faith in Tanzania. In most evangelical churches and increasingly in other Protestant churches as well, there is a growing trend towards the development of fellowships as organizations virtually independent of the pastored churches. Although usually situated on the same premises as the pastored churches, fellowships operate on quite distinct organizational and spiritual premises. It is our task to analyse the internal dimensions of the fellowship church, its relations with the denominational hierarchy, and how both these aspects contribute to the transformation of Tanzanians' expression of Christianity.

Revival: a Brief History

A detailed historical analysis of the revival movement in Tanzania will not be attempted here.[3] It is sufficient to note that the history of revival in Tanzania has been influenced or shaped by three factors: the East African setting of the revival movement in general, the crucial role of individuals in its success or problems, and the non-denominational character of the phenomenon.

The current revival in Tanzania is a revised version of the East African Revival movement of the post-Second World War period, when the Great Lakes region was caught in a spiritual awakening that had far-reaching effects. Uganda took the lead in that revival.[4] Prominent individuals like William Nagenda and Festo Kivengere became the first group of modern-day, born-again Christians with a passion for winning souls for Christ. As lay evangelists they were determined to propagate the Gospel message beyond the borders of their country.

In the late 1940s, Kivengere moved to Tanganyika and took a teaching post at Alliance Secondary School, Dodoma. This school had been built by the Anglican Church Missionary Society; it was run in alliance with the Moravians and the Africa Inland Mission, and it recruited staff and students from a wide area within and outside Tanganyika.[5] In addition to teaching, Kivengere became a renowned evangelist and proved to be invaluable to the Anglican Church. Kivengere eventually returned to Uganda and became one of the most prominent Anglican bishops in East Africa, with strong connections beyond the African region.

From Dodoma, the message of salvation fanned out to other parts of the country. While Kivengere was busy in central Tanganyika, Brother Matovu was propagating the Good News around Lake Tanganyika. In Kasulu, Matovu met Omari, a junior worker in a local dispensary, received the message and became a born-again convert, abandoning Islam. Baptized as Yohana Omari, he established a number of churches in Kasulu and Kigoma and ended up becoming the first bishop of the newly formed Anglican Diocese of Morogoro, carved from the huge Diocese of Central Tanganyika. After his death in 1964, the Morogoro Diocese was headed by Graceford Chitemo, another dynamic born-again teacher-turned-pastor and product of the early revival movement.[6]

While the revival had started with non-clergy taking the lead, a number of these charismatic lay preachers were soon ordained as pastors and some of them ended up heading dioceses, as the cases of Kivengere and Omari show. The involvement of pastors was much more noticeable in Bukoba, where the revival had gained a strong foothold earlier than in central Tanganyika. The Bukoba revival was a chapter of the Rwandan spiritual awakening of the 1940s and 1950s.[7] Bishop Josiah Kibira, Pastor Kasimbazi and Brother Mushumbuzi were revivalists who played a role in sustaining the movement for a long time beyond the borders of that region. In Mwanza, the spirit of the revival penetrated the Africa Inland Church with the conversion of Moses Kulola, who went on to become one of the most celebrated charismatic preachers in Tanzania. In Kilimanjaro, Lutherans were not spared the fire of revival. Emmanuel Lazaro became the backbone of spiritual awakening in the area. As was the case with Bukoba, these latter leaders were pastors in their denominations when they joined the revival movement and then became pastor-evangelists preaching to a wider audience throughout the country.

By 1970 the revival movement was a force to reckon with in the country. It had been started by lay Christians taking the initiative in its promotion and sustenance, but gradually the mantle of leadership passed to the clergy, or lay preachers turned pastors. This transformation had a dual effect on the movement. First, it brought a qualitative change in the way people related to their Christian faith. They became more committed believers under born-again charismatic pastors and leaders. Bible studies and Christian fellowships raised their level of understanding of the scriptures and testimonies edified many of them.

But this progress was also a potential source of schism. The problem surfaced when leaders of the mainline churches urged the rank and file of the saved to adhere to the rules and traditions of their own denominations. Most mainline churches were still solidly anchored in the traditional missionary doctrines, which did not subscribe to a belief or promotion of the manifestations of the most visible gifts of the Spirit, such as speaking in tongues, prophetic utterances and healing. Frustrated by such rigidity and increasing control of the revival movement by conservative clergy, a number of born-again believers left their denominational churches to join new Pentecostal churches that were rapidly springing up, while others followed the Kenyan example of establishing their own independent churches.[8]

The establishment or consolidation of the charismatic churches thus coincided with and was given momentum by the overall revival movement. Evidence of this is seen in the impact of Moses Kulola and Emmanuel Lazaro, who defected from the Africa Inland and Lutheran churches respectively to establish the Assemblies of God in Tanzania. Under such leadership, the charismatic churches drew numerous individuals from the mainline denominations. It often appeared that the foremost Christians were defecting from the traditional Protestant establishments as well as from the Catholic Church to the new charismatic churches. This was a cause for worry in traditional church circles, and there was a growing feeling of animosity or even hatred towards the charismatics. Conversely, the new charismatics fell into the temptation of assuming that only they were saved, while those who remained in mainline churches were lost. Thus the common task of evangelizing the populace was giving way to denominational strife as mainline church leaders accused the charismatics of a systematic poaching campaign, while the latter fell into a doctrinal distortion that speaking in tongues and baptism by immersion (*maji mengi*) were prerequisites for salvation.[9]

The hatred between the two camps grew to such magnitude that the Protestant churches teamed with the Catholic Church to pass a delimitation treaty, summarized in the following terms:

1 A believer from any of the Pentecostal churches should not be allowed

to preach in any of the Protestant and Catholic churches.
2 No member of their churches (Protestant or Catholic) should be allowed to preach in any of the Pentecostal churches.
3 Should a member from their churches cross over to a Pentecostal church, that member should consider himself or herself as a defector and thus forfeit all benefits and help from the Protestant or Catholic Community.

In passing such a resolution, church leaders were retracing the animosity and hatred their European mentors had expressed earlier against other denominations.[10]

  With this resolution, which apparently is still on the books today, the Protestant leaders aimed at containing the development of the revival movement. Their immediate motive, however, was to prevent what they considered as the undue influence of Pentecostalism in the Protestant churches.[11] The charismatics had appropriated the gifts of the spirit, and the Protestants had erroneously regarded those gifts as exclusively Pentecostal in a denominational sense and not in a doctrinal Biblical sense, leading them to reject the gifts. For the Protestant leaders, this meant that all those who professed to be born-again believers but opted to remain in their denominational churches were required to conform to missionary Protestant doctrines, regulations and traditions, as defined and interpreted by the church hierarchies.

  In such a critical environment, some of the major gains achieved in the initial thrust of the revival movement within the churches were lost. It was not uncommon to see leading members of the clergy showing open hostility to those who proclaimed they were saved. The majority of pastors, however, tended to steer a middle course, contending that they were shepherds of the whole flock, saved and unsaved. And others continued to preach the old establishment doctrine that all those who had converted to the Christian religion through baptism and confirmation were on their way to heaven, irrespective of whether they openly professed salvation or not.

Crusade Evangelism

The two decades from the mid-1970s have witnessed three further developments associated with the revival movement. The first has been the rise of a ministry based on the operational principles of the first New Testament church, as shown in the Book of Acts, especially the first four chapters. Edmund John, a lay Anglican in Dar es Salaam, received a visitation from God and was instructed to tell people to repent and prepare for the imminent return of the Lord Jesus Christ. John took his calling seriously, and he soon emerged as a powerful lay preacher with a healing touch. His base was the Anglican church, but the revival movement that arose from his work became an inter-denominational ministry that took the name of the House-to-House Angelical and Prayer Ministry (popularly known as HUMANN, from the Swahili name of the ministry, Huduma ya Uinjilisti na Maombi Nyumba kwa Nyumba).

The Anglican Church leadership in Dar es Salaam tried to restrict John by giving him a church to pastor, but he was not easily contained. For three years in the early 1970s, Edmund John became a household name, especially in Anglican circles, as he moved in and out of Dar es Salaam preaching the house-to-house message. He was endowed with special healing powers and powers to cast out demons, while prayer and fasting became his greatest source of strength. He would spend days in prayer and fasting, sometimes completely cut off from the world surrounding him, before a major assignment, and he would often go without meals during his campaigns. His was a powerful ministry, filled with signs and wonders confirming the Word, but it rested almost entirely on a lone individual. John overstretched himself, and he died prematurely.[12]

After the death of its founder, the House-to-House Ministry tried to separate itself from Anglican influence by acquiring separate government registration and convening its fellowship meetings on neutral ground rather than on Anglican Church premises or in the house of the leader, as had been the case hitherto. Official registration demanded that the ministry have an organizational structure, and, by the late 1980s, the ministry was organizing annual Big Harvest crusades in Dar es Salaam sponsored by local chapters in and outside the city.

The second major development that has affected the revival movement in Tanzania over the past couple of decades is the split that has emerged within the charismatic church, centred around a conflict between the two leading personalities in the Tanzanian Assemblies of God Church, Bishop Emmanual Lazaro and his deputy Moses Kulola. The conflict between these two proved to be so devastating that it not only paralysed their ministries, adversely affecting the revival movement in general, but also led to a rupture in the church and intervention by the state. Kulola and his followers succeeded in establishing a new denomination, called the Evangelical Assemblies of God of Tanzania. In the course of the battle, fought largely on personal grounds, testimony has been tarnished, wounds are still being nursed and the damage to the revival spirit has been significant.

The third and most important development with regard to the revival movement has been the birth of an organization specifically geared toward conducting evangelical crusades in the country. In 1986, a group of born-again Christians organized a non-denominational crusade at the Mnazi Mmoja grounds in Dar es Salaam. It was a great success, not only because of the large turn-out but also because of its broad, non-denominational organization. For the first time, believers, pastors and non-pastors from charismatic and mainline denominations were able to sit down and plan a crusade that attracted multitudes of Christians and non-Christians to listen to an unadulterated non-denominational gospel message. The Lord honoured this spirit of cooperation by saving hundreds of people and delivering multitudes from disease and demonic bondage. The meeting was held in November, and henceforth the organization that ensued came to be called the Big November Crusade. After that first success, subsequent crusades were held at the larger and more central Jangwani grounds.

Ever since it was launched over a decade ago, the Big November Crusade has grown by leaps and bounds. It is an officially registered inter-denominational body. Its mission field has expanded from Dar es Salaam to all 20 regions of mainland Tanzania, and recently the ministry has embarked on evangelizing Zanzibar. Speakers in the crusades are renowned international preachers drawn from Africa, Europe and North America. The major annual crusades in Dar es Salaam and regional centres usually take two weeks, and several hundred thousands of people attend these meetings for their duration. Functionaries in attendance continue to be drawn from churches across the board; the only prerequisite to serve as an usher, as an intercessor or in the deliverance ministry is a profession of salvation and proof that one belongs to a recognized fellow-ship of born-again believers. Among the mainline Protestant denomina-tions in Dar es Salaam, the Lutheran Church has the largest number of adherents. The unreserved support by the Lutheran leaders, especially Bishop Elinaza Sendoro and his assistant Yohana Marko, has been a tremendous boost to the Big November Crusade efforts in Dar es Salaam and hence to the revival movement in general.

Everywhere a crusade is held under the auspices of the Big November Crusade, the same principles of teamwork and cooperation of all born-again believers in the area are duplicated and emphasized. Usually organizational work is taken up by the local team of the New Life Crusade ministry, whose branches have spread to almost all the major churches in all the regions.

Apart from its organizational aspects, the Big November Crusade has drawn its strength and unity from a doctrinal standpoint that is non-denominational and biblical. The ministry's 12-point doctrinal statement reads as follows:

We cooperate with all the churches which believe that:

1 The Bible is the inspired Word of God and God's revelation to man.
2 God is one, truly alive, and has revealed Himself to mankind in the Trinity: God the Father, the Son, and the Holy Spirit.
3 Jesus Christ is the Son of God and Saviour of the world.
4 Man needs to be saved by being born again.
5 All believers are required and have a right to be filled with the Holy Spirit.
6 Jesus Christ heals diseases and performs miracles even today for He has never changed.
7 Believers are commanded to live only sanctified life by separating themselves from sinful worldly living.

8 The church is the body of Christ and every believer is an integral important part of that body, the church.
9 One day Christ will return to pick up His church – the rapture of the church.
10 There will be dominion rule of Christ for a millennium together with His saints – the church.
11 There is the last judgement whereby all sinners will be judged according to their evil deeds.
12 There will be a new heaven and a new earth where the saints will rest with God for ever and ever.[13]

There is nothing in this doctrinal statement of belief that divides those who subscribe to the spirit of the Big November Crusade. The ministry has painstakingly avoided sowing seeds of discord among Christians, such as advocating particular modes of baptism or speaking in tongues. There are, of course, a few leaders, particularly among the Pentecostal churches, who are not happy about the Big November Crusade for not giving weight to speaking in tongues or baptism by immersion, and these leaders occasionally discourage their followers from attending BNC meetings.

Apart from the work performed by the Big November Crusade, there are several other groups and individuals associated with the development of spiritual revival in Tanzania. Preachers such as Christopher Mwakasege, Emmanual Mbwambo and Kakobe are becoming household names in the revival movement. While Mbwambo and Kakobe have established their own ministries and churches, Mwakasege has opted to operate within the established denominations, especially the Lutheran church to which he belongs, together with ministries such as the Big November Crusade and New Life Crusade. He has emerged as one of the most charismatic preachers and teachers in the country, attracting huge crowds to his meetings. The secret of Mwakasege's success does not lie only in his charismatic character, but in his inter-denominational approach to his ministry and his ability to work closely with the established order. His insistence that born-again Christians remain in their denominations has endeared him to Protestant church leaders, who are now less worried with his unadulterated evangelism.[14]

Other ministries and organizations involved in revival work include the African Evangelistic Enterprise (AEE), whose East and Central African zone was formerly headed by the famous Festo Kivengere and, after his death, by Bishop Graceford Chitemo.[15] The AEE has become famous for its crusade theme 'Back to God', and it has directed its efforts to the training of youth evangelists, who are helped to lead independent, self-reliant lives. The Tanzanian Fellowship of Evangelical Students (TAFES) and the Campus Crusade for Christ (best known as the Life Ministry) have also had a significant impact on the youth.

303

Fellowship Structure and Functioning

We have already noted that one of the main features of the revival movement is the existence of fellowships in almost every Protestant church, especially in urban centres such as Dar es Salaam. We have also observed that most fellowships are conducted within the premises of the churches, but are virtually independent of church authority. In the non-Catholic and non-charismatic churches where the fellowships are a feature, each revival group or branch has its own leadership, recognized by the pastor but not controlled by him, consisting of a chairman and his assistant, a secretary and a deputy secretary, a treasurer and members of the executive committee, including the heads of the youth, choir, women and evangelism departments. The leaders of the fellowship control their own funds, obtained through offerings during meetings. Some individuals also tithe 10 per cent of their income exclusively to the fellowship, while others apportion it between their church and the fellowship.

Fellowship worship meetings usually take a charismatic form. There is no reading or singing of a liturgy, in contrast with the churches to which most of the members belong, but rather spontaneous choruses of praise and worship, testimonies, preaching of the Word and prayers. Occasionally, the sick are called forward and a selected group pray for them and cast out demonic forces from individuals who manifest such problems.

The affinity of members to their fellowship is usually stronger than that to the church in which they are registered. And the stronger and more popular the leadership of the fellowship is, the more committed are its members. Most fellowships endeavour to cater for the non-spiritual needs of their members as well. Members of the fellowship visit their sick colleagues in hospitals and homes, pray for them and provide them with material support such as food, clothing or money. Should one be bereaved, brethren offer services of consolation. The same cooperation is extended when a member of the fellowship marries or has a child. It is becoming normal for young people preparing for marriage to expect considerable financial, material and non-material help from their fellowship. In an environment where churches are growing more populous and impersonal, it is edifying and beneficial to belong to a fellowship. In the fellowship one is not lost in the crowd, nor is one just a pebble on the beach. The tangible and intangible benefits are substantial, just as they are in the Marian Faith Healing Ministry discussed by Comoro and Sivalon previously.

Problems and Prospects

The achievements of the fellowships are linked dialectically to the problems confronting the revival movement in Tanzania. A number of these problems have already been mentioned. Many pastors have viewed the existence of the fellowships in their churches as a threat to their authority.[16] A strong fellowship, numerically and organizationally, tends to erode the power of the pastor as members become increasingly committed to their fellowship. In cases where fellowships have become detached from the church leadership and grown larger with the passage of time, a problem of arrogance has emerged on the part of fellowship leaders. An example of such a problem occurred in 1996 in Magomeni, where the leader of a large inter-denominational fellowship that had met in a Lutheran church enticed many people to defect from the church and launched his own church composed mainly of members of the fellowship.

Most fellowships are torn between adherence to tradition, on one hand, and to the manifestations of the Holy Spirit, on the other.[17] As the ministrations of the Holy Spirit start affecting the fellowship in a more significant way, the saved tend to see the church establishment as superfluous, especially when a leading pastor does not show a strong affinity with the fellowship spirit.

The impact of the fellowships and the revival movement in general is conspicuous everywhere in the country. Few dispute that the quality of Christianity has improved tremendously over the past decades. All denominations, including a few Catholic Church leaders, have accepted the movement as being central to Christianity.[18] In contrast to a couple of decades ago, few pastors are willing to jeopardize their credibility by preaching against the salvation experience. One might pay lip-service to salvation or make little mention of it in sermons, but it is increasingly risky to attack born-again believers openly. The time when born-again Christians were unceremoniously thrown out of their churches is long past. Despite continued adherence to their liturgical traditions, ordinary church services are becoming livelier as the gospel message is disseminated to the congregations.[19] Gradually and steadily, fellowship Christians are playing a significant role in bringing revival inside their own churches as they become more involved in preaching and other areas of services.

The recent Lutheran Conference in Morogoro is an omen of what is expected as we approach the next century. There is a growing seriousness as well as renewed dedication to the spirit of revival. The spirit of cooperation within and between fellowships is symbolic of a real sifting of the body of Christ as denominational boundaries are demolished gradually, or at least rendered anachronistic in the face of a growing unity of purpose and spirit of the believers in Christ Jesus.

Notes

* This chapter has been made possible by the provision of vital research notes by my friend Godred Lema, who has served on the Executive Board of the Big November Crusade since its inception in 1986 and has also served on the Executive Board of the New Life Crusade Ministry.
1 About a quarter of non-Catholic practising Christians in Tanzania belong to the Lutheran Church.
2 Information supplied by Rev. Aligawesa, a delegate to the Morogoro conference.
3 The Tanzanian variant of revival is not as well documented as it is in other parts of Eastern Africa. See, for example, David Barrett *et al.* (eds), *Kenya Churches Handbook* (Kisumu, 1973).
4 For the Ugandan revival movement see, for example, Catherine Robins, '*Tukutendereza:* a study of social change and withdrawal in the Balokole revival of Uganda' (PhD, Columbia, 1975); Kevin Ward, '*Tukutendereza Yesu:* the Balokole revival movement in Uganda', in Z. Nthamburi (ed.), *From Mission to Church* (Nairobi, 1991), 113–44.
5 Other schools that were run jointly by the Anglican Church and other missionary establishments included Rungwe Teachers Training Centre, Musoma Secondary School and Kigoma Secondary School.
6 When Chitemo was Headmaster of Mgugu Middle School in the mid-1950s, about half of the school's boys declared themselves born-again Christians.
7 For the Rwandan revival and its influence in East Africa, see George Mambo, 'The Revival Fellowship (Brethren) in Kenya', in Barrett, *Kenya Churches Handbook*, 215–23.
8 Mambo, 'Revival Fellowship in Kenya'.
9 This was accompanied by an exercise with the new converts aimed at grounding them in the new Pentecostal doctrine and strengthening their loyalty to the Pentecostal movement.
10 See, for example, the resolutions of the Vatican Councils outlined in Richard P. McBrien, *Church: The Continuing Quest* (New York, 1970), 7–9.
11 An example of continued mistrust occurred in 1966 when a Dodoma Lutheran bishop blocked arrangements to have a Pentecostal bishop open a seminar in the Lutheran cathedral organized by the inter-denominational New Life Crusade.
12 Edmund John's story and ministry can be found, in brief, in Joseph Namata, *Edmund John: Man of God* (Dodoma, 1980).
13 The points outlining the BNC's doctrinal beliefs are translated from the Ministry's four-page pamphlet titled *Get Acquainted with the Big November Crusade Ministry* (Dar es Salaam, nd).
14 Interview with Christopher Mwakasege, 15 November 1996, Dar es Salaam.
15 After serving as Zonal Team Leader for Eastern and Central Africa, Bishop Chitemo has retired, but he still preaches widely and serves as adviser to the AEE.
16 Interview with Pastor Musomba, Secretary General, Christian Council of Tanzania, 15 October 1996.
17 For further intellectual insights on the subject of the Holy Spirit, see John C. Cooper, *Radical Christianity and its Sources* (Philadelphia, 1968), 88–9; Alasdair Heron, *A Century of Protestant Theology* (Philadelphia, 1980).
18 There are at least three Roman Catholic churches in Dar es Salaam that conduct charismatic revival fellowships on their premises, and Catholic born-again Christians are an integral part of the revival movement in Morogoro.
19 Interview with Pastor Msomba, 25 October 1996.

VII

Christianity
&
Society

One of the initial sparks for this project was Spear's attempt to understand popular discourses in bars, markets and bus stalls, where Christian images inflect the speech of Christians and non-Christians alike. As in nineteenth-century British novels, biblical images and metaphors continually infuse common speech. Christianity is no longer an exotic transplant in Africa today, but is deeply embedded in everyday thoughts and expressions. As many of our studies show, local and Christian 'traditions' are now so intertwined that we can no longer separate them analytically or see them as discrete entities. African worlds are still 'enchanted', but now their spiritual universe embraces both African and Christian forms.[1]

The previous studies in this book have focused largely on religious and social institutions as Africans encountered Christian missions and adopted the faith for themselves. But mission Christianity was only a part of people's lives, which also included 'traditional' beliefs and social practices, colonial politics and new forms of labour. How did people reconcile the new ideas introduced by the missions and other colonial institutions with their own concepts and beliefs? Maddox notes some of the ways in which Fr Stephen Mlundi 'domesticated' Catholicism in the context of his own continuing allegiance to Gogo values and practices. Similarly, Giblin here shows in intimate detail how Christianity was only one factor among many that transformed the lives of individuals and which, in turn, they used to under-stand and come to terms with those changes. His is a nuanced, carefully contextualized view that warns us against facile generalizations about wholesale transformations brought about by Christianity in Africa while at the same time revealing how deeply Christianity has become incorporated within African 'tradition'.[2]

Notes

1 Karen Fields, *Revival and Rebellion in Colonial Central Africa*. (Princeton, 1985); Peter Geschiere, *The Modernity of Witchcraft* (Charlottesville, 1997).
2 Further examples of the deeply embedded nature of Christian ideas and practices in contemporary African thought were presented to our workshops in the context of contemporary politics in Kenya (by Michael Schatzberg), Rwanda (Timothy Longman) and southern Sudan (Sharon Hutchinson) to demonstrate how Christian ideas of justice, rights and behaviour inform contemporary political discourse.

Fifteen

Family Life, Indigenous Culture
& Christianity in Colonial Njombe

JAMES GIBLIN

Preceding chapters have focused on Christian communities and institutions, such as Fipa society, the Leipzig Mission Society and the Marian Faith Healing Ministry. By contrast, this chapter concentrates on individuals and on social changes which are often considered part of 'Christianization'. In so doing, I draw heavily upon the experiences of several Tanzanians for whom Christianity has been an important part – though only one part – of their lives. The purpose of this approach is to emphasize that, if studies of African Christianity wish to appreciate the rich diversity of Christian experience in Africa, they must be attuned to African voices and to the variety of social and personal contexts in which Africans have encountered Christianity.

Unfortunately, some ways of thinking about African Christianity hinder appreciation of the diversity of African Christian experience. This is particularly true of work such as that of the Comaroffs, which describes Christianization as a passage from a state where something is missing to a state where the missing element (be it literacy, consciousness of self-identity or awareness of linear history) is achieved.[1] Such an approach produces a reductionist viewpoint for at least two reasons. First, it confuses the apparent absence of certain aspects of culture, particularly intangible aspects such as self-awareness with the shortcomings of sources. The resulting failure to leave room for lacunae in fragmentary evidence impoverishes our understanding of precolonial culture. At the same time, this approach suggests that the process of obtaining literacy, self-awareness or the capacity for narrative dominates the experience of Christianization. When we begin to listen to the voices of Christians, however, we may find that these matters were not very important in their experience.

One of the most eloquent examples of this approach grew out of research in the same Southern Highlands region of Tanzania from which the material in this chapter comes. Study of Nyakyusa communities over several decades persuaded the anthropologist Monica Wilson that Christianity had fostered a degree of self-awareness which, particularly for women, had been impossible in what she regarded as the highly parochial and communal world of the precolonial Nyakyusa.[2] She made little allowance, however, for the possibility that scarcity of historical evidence may have caused the precolonial Nyakyusa to seem featureless and lacking in individuality. Moreover, her view of Christianization as a process through which the individual personality is liberated from the constraint of communal tradition may have concealed a much more complicated intertwining of opportunity and dilemma which, as we shall see, resulted elsewhere from the encounter with Christianity.

While Christianity introduced various opportunities, including the possibility of achieving a novel and fulfilling form of spirituality, it also posed intense and highly personal moral dilemmas for individuals who sought to reconcile Christian teachings with older concepts of moral responsibility. The anxiety caused by these dilemmas and the resulting feelings of inadequacy and moral failure, which contrast strongly with ideas of 'accommodation' and 'resolution' often found in the literature, testify to the spiritual and moral complexity of lives in which non-Christian norms retained great moral force. The idea of liberatory Christianity, like other stories of Christianization as evolution or progress, underestimates the diversity and moral complexity of non-Christian culture. This is why our understanding of African Christianity can benefit not only from studying Christian communities, institutions and doctrines, but also from contemplating the untidy confusion of conflicting responsibilities and unreconciled feelings which mark at least one kind of Christian experience.

The Context of Christian Lives in Njombe: Labour Migration, Colonial Politics and Family

The Christians whose lives are discussed here come from the southern Tanzanian district of Njombe. Njombe was part of a vast arc of territory in western and southern Tanzania which provided migrant labour to the colonial economy. From the 1920s to the early 1960s, at least a quarter of its men were usually absent as migrant labourers. They worked for periods ranging from several months to many years in various distant regions of European-controlled export production, though their primary destination was the sisal plantations of northeastern Tanzania. After the Second World War, however, as motor transport (and even air travel) became common, migrants from Njombe travelled much further, not only to the Copperbelt in northern Zambia, but also to European tobacco farms in Zimbabwe and the gold mines of the South African Witwatersrand.

The emergence of Njombe as a labour reserve has been traced in an unpublished dissertation by James D. Graham. Predominantly Bena-speaking men from Njombe first travelled to sisal plantations during 1906–9, when tax collecting became more thorough following the suppression of the Maji Maji Rebellion. The flow of migrants declined during the First World War and its aftermath, but, by 1926, 20 per cent of Njombe's adult males were working outside the district.[3] The proportion of men absent from their homes as migrants appears to have remained in the range of 20 to 30 per cent through the 1930s, even though the Depression led sisal producers to reduce their workforce drastically and more than halve wages.

As the 1930s wore on, however, jobs became available in other regions. These places included nearby Mufindi, where European settlers started growing tea in the early 1930s; the adjoining Iringa District, where European farmers already depended upon Njombe for 70 per cent of their migrant labour force in 1929;[4] and Chunya, where a gold rush about 200 miles from Njombe attracted thousands of panners and miners despite horrendous living conditions. In 1933, very soon after the beginning of the gold rush, 12,000 labourers had already found work in the mining centre of Lupa, where 7,700 men from Njombe were working in 1938.[5] 'Practically all the able-bodied natives who own no cattle have gone to such places as Mufindi, Iringa, and Kilosa [a sisal-growing area of central Tanzania] in search of work,' reported Njombe's assistant district officer in 1933. 'Those who go so far afield as the [sisal estates of the] coast usually stay away from their homes for at least two years; the others return at about this time for the planting season.'[6]

The proportion of men absent increased dramatically during the Second World War, when the demand for plantation labour, combined with conscription for military and labour service, severely taxed Tanzania's labour resources. An investigation undertaken by Njombe's district officer in 1943 found that only about a third of adult male villagers were at home. After the war, the proportion of men performing migrant labour outside Njombe District returned to the pre-war level of 20 to 30 per cent.

Labour migration produced striking gender imbalance in the communities of Njombe. In 1957, the ratio of men to women aged sixteen years or more was only 569/1,000. In some sub-chiefdoms, moreover, the ratio of adult men to women was as low as 439/1,000 (Lupalilo), 484/1,000 (Imalinyi) and 505/1,000 (Luwumbu and Mdandu).[7] Such imbalances had by the late 1950s existed for several decades, and they persisted into the 1970s in some parts of Njombe. Nevertheless, while the overwhelming majority of migrants were men, labour outside the district was also sought by women and children, including girls as well as boys.

Njombe's marginal position within the colonial economy as a labour reserve was an important impetus to the adoption of Christianity. Marcia Wright has argued that the absence of opportunities to enter the colonial economy created widespread enthusiasm for missionary education and patronage.[8] Indeed, the first European missionaries to work among the Bena, members of the Berlin Mission Society, moved into northern

Njombe from the nearby mountains of Ukinga only after a delegation from Njombe persuaded reluctant missionaries to extend their activities onto the Bena plateau. In 1898 and 1899, the Berlin Lutherans established important stations at Kidugala and Ilembula, and, by the outbreak of the Maji-Maji war, they had extended their work into eastern Ubena. According to Wright, Ilembula rapidly developed into a 'small chiefdom' which witnessed 'a general transfer of faith'. The Lutherans relied heavily on Bena evangelists to extend their influence. By 1931, the Lutherans employed some 52 African teachers in an extensive system of 'bush schools',[9] and in 1934 they ordained eight African ministers. Their reliance on African evangelists and ministers led to the emergence of a modernizing Christian elite, which had begun claiming ecclesiastical autonomy by the 1930s. Nevertheless, adoption of Christianity proceeded very gradually. Many older Lutherans in northern Njombe today are first-generation converts who were raised in non-Christian households.

Christianity, colonialism, labour migration and the absence of many men all contributed to inspiring debate about family life and domestic relations.[10] This discussion reflected both a keen interest among women and equally sharp anxieties on the part of men about their relations with women and younger men. Such debate was already going on in the 1930s, when the anthropologists A. T. and G. M. Culwick discovered that Bena-speaking communities of the Ulanga Valley could not agree about how to define 'clan' and 'family'.[11] Such disagreement had surely been encouraged by the institution of Indirect Rule a decade earlier, for, in seeking to place chiefly powers in the hands of representatives of the clans which had held precolonial political authority, British administrators provided a compelling reason to place great significance on clan identities, to develop both inclusive and exclusive conceptions of the clan, and to devise ways of claiming affiliation with chiefly clans.

By the 1950s, however, the emergence of nationalism prompted the chiefs to modify their position, even though they continued to regard family relations as a fundamental basis of their authority.[12] Whereas in the 1920s and 1930s chiefs had portrayed themselves as the leaders of sizeable clans that traditionally had dominated other clans, by the 1950s, as nationalists began to stress the need for broad unity in the struggle against colonialism, the Bena paramount, Joseph Mbeyela, argued that overemphasis on clan identities sowed division within the Bena tribe. Mbeyela also recognized that nationalism would eventually undermine the authority of tribal chiefs such as himself. Consequently, he sought to foster a progressive tribal unity that, by achieving improved education, health care and opportunities to earn money within Njombe, would lessen the appeal of nationalism. He also believed, however, that tribal unity could only be attained once labour migration no longer drained young men and women away from Njombe. His antagonism to labour migration thus led Mbeyela to favour changes in marital and family life that would reduce pressure to seek plantation and mine employment and allow men to find contentment by remaining at home in stable marriages.

Together with other political activists, Mbeyela proposed changes which would both decrease labour migration and increase family stability as well as 'tribal cohesion'. He sought to reduce bridewealth. He proposed modifying the sanctions against adulterers to deter behaviour rather than recognizing control by husbands over the sexuality of wives: fines levied on adulterers would be paid to the government rather than to kin of an individual whose spouse had been caught in adultery. And he wished to grant women who had been abandoned by long-absent migrants the right to divorce and to refuse marriage to brothers-in-law. These and related issues dominated the deliberations of the 'tribal' and district councils which supplanted Indirect Rule during the 1950s. Councillors in Njombe discussed polygyny; the inflation of bridewealth; the apparent increase in divorce, adultery and desertion of husbands; and the abandonment of wives by migrant workers who refused to come home.

Although these councils were composed entirely of men, their motivations were much broader than simply protecting male prerogatives. As fathers, they were concerned that their daughters were being trapped in bad marriages by inflated bridewealth which few fathers could repay in settlement of a divorce. As brothers, they worried that widowed or abandoned sisters were being forced into unwanted marriages with brothers-in-law. Like Mbeyela himself, the councillors placed enormous weight on the education of Njombe's children, and they constantly urged parents to send their daughters as well as their sons to school.

Underlying all these questions was the more fundamental issue of how to define one's family. For example, many thought that bridewealth inflation, which forced men into labour migration, was caused by the claims of an excessively large number of kin to shares in bridewealth. The solution, they asserted, was to narrow the circle of relatives who participated in sharing bridewealth. Likewise, matters of divorce, marriage to brothers-in-law and custody of children all led back to the question of whether marriage was simply a relationship between spouses or was also a union between two families.

It would be easy to see this debate over family and marital relations as a predictable aspect of the creation of a Christian culture. Indeed, there was a good deal of truth in this view, for some of the political leaders involved in this debate came from the mission communities at Ilembula and elsewhere. Moreover, this debate was in fact part of a long-term process that over the next several decades would lead to the increasing acceptance of what might be considered ideal Christian marriages − voluntary, companionable unions between monogamous spouses committed to educating their children, who looked to churches and hospitals as the proper places for sex education and care of reproductive health. Nevertheless, an interpretation which regards these debates and changes as merely part of 'Christianization' misses their complexity.

For, while councillors and other participants in public debates might sometimes base their arguments for change on explicitly Christian grounds (for example, that forced marriage to brothers-in-law violated Christian norms), they did this only rarely. The unwillingness to invoke Christian teachings stemmed partly from recognition of Njombe's pluralism, for those who wished to promote change knew that they must find ways of appealing to their non-Christian neighbours. More fundamentally, however, the debate itself was as much a response to the political, social and moral problems created by the economy of labour migration as it was to Christianity. While Christianity shaped thinking about these problems, moreover, so too did non-Christian norms and ideals. Thus when councillors declared that inflation of bridewealth was enslaving women, for example, they were acting not merely upon the teachings of missionaries and evangelists, but, even more importantly, out of concern over their increasing inability to provide the assistance to their daughters in troubled marriages that had been expected of their own fathers and grandfathers.

Chief Mbeyela's position epitomized the complexity of the considerations and influences that lay behind the interest in family and marital change. Mbeyela obviously had a personal interest in fending off nationalism, or at least in establishing a place for chiefs within the nationalist movement. At the same time, however, he regarded himself as the heir of a tradition of Bena chiefship which thrust upon him responsibility for guiding his people out of the impoverishing trap of labour migration. Thus, while these considerations may have led him to adopt positions on family and marriage that were being advocated by the Christian churches, his views were certainly not derived primarily from Christianity. In some respects, in fact, Mbeyela was antagonistic to Christians. He encouraged *matambiko* (the propitiation of ancestors) and made the woods where his family venerated their ancestors the most important *matambiko* site in Njombe. Indeed, his position in the debate over family life during the 1950s shows that the emergence of a new kind of Christian marriage and family was the consequence not merely of Christian teaching, but also of much wider concerns, including labour migration and pre-Christian norms of moral responsibility.

Christianity, New Colonial Knowledge and Non-Christian Morality

The complex circumstances described in the preceding section are reflected in the stories that men and women from Njombe tell about their own lives. The following sections draw upon their accounts to show how their experience with Christianity was influenced by a wider social context. The aspects of this context that appear most prominently in their stories are the economy of labour migration, the intense desire for education and literacy and the continuing force of non-Christian morality.[13]

Both during and after the colonial period, residents of Njombe commonly attributed their marginal position in the colonial economy to their lack of education and they often describe the colonial period as a learning experience. In 1992, for example, a businessman in the town of Makambako told me that Njombe's people had been drawn into migrant labour 'because at first they didn't know any other way of achieving progress, but later they learned alternative ways of making money at home'. In the same year, the chairman of Palangawanu village, explaining why Indian traders rather than small African shopkeepers such as himself had obtained the lion's share of business profits in the colonial period, said: 'they were well educated in business, that's why they would give you only a small share of the profit ... but we could use only our raw intelligence without any education, that's why we were taken advantage of for many years'.

This deeply ingrained sense that they had been marginalized by their ignorance of the wider world helps explain why Christians often describe their conversion as part of a wider learning experience. They became Christians not merely to obtain schooling and literacy, however, but also because the Christian faith itself became a cherished part of a broader body of new knowledge. As a gateway to wider knowledge and understanding, Christianity was perhaps even more important for women than for men, because women lacked men's opportunities to travel and work in distant places. Thus 'Mary', a former employee of the Lutheran hospital and now a leader of the Assemblies of God congregation, described her conversion in this way:

> I was born at Ulunda, the same place where I was married. While I was there, people came to preach stories of Jesus. Well, for me, [their stories] struck me in the heart [*zikanichoma moyo*], so I said farewell to my father and mother. I said, 'I want to go to Ilembula and become a Christian.' But we were then living in nations [*tulikuwa mataifa*, meaning that they were pagans], so my father forbade me to go. Well, I ran away. There were relatives of mine here [at Ilembula], and they wanted me to know God and to be a Christian. Well, they took me in and I lived here. I was still a small child and I went to a 'bush school' where I learned to read and write. When I returned home to my father's place I could read! He was delighted. 'So you know how to read!' he said. Then a letter came from someplace for my father, and he said, 'Come here, come here and read the letter.' And I replied, 'Well, didn't you forbid me to go and be saved?' 'You've done well,' he replied. So I read the letter for him and he was happy.

In the case of Pastor L.M., it was his youthful experience as a plantation worker that impressed him with the importance of literacy. His desire to learn reading and writing led him to Christianity in the early 1950s and eventually into a career as a Lutheran evangelist and minister. He first perceived his illiteracy as a handicap while working as a teenager with literate men on sisal plantations in Tanga: 'When we got our wages we had to sign for them. I had to make a thumbprint while others were signing their names – this is what convinced me to get an education.' After returning home, he enrolled in adult education classes, learned to read and write, and eventually discovered the Bible:

> I decided to be baptized after reading the Word of God. After reading the Word of God I began to believe that indeed there is a God who created me, goodness, he created me!... God breathed life into me and I began to breathe, it wasn't something else [breathing], it was I, myself!... So in this way I listened and learned, until I myself decided that I had to be baptized.

Like Mary, L.M. found in his reading of Christian texts a powerful reaffirmation of his faith and his individuality. Having made the decision to become a Christian, he set about refashioning his life as a Christian, though initially he went through a prolonged period when his faith in the power of God increased only very gradually:

> At first, before my faith had matured, I slept in fear not knowing what would happen to me at night. If I had nightmares or if I slept badly because something got twisted around my neck, I thought it must be witchcraft. Later, after learning the Word of God and learning about progressive things [*kujifunza kimaendeleo*], well then I knew it was just a dream. If some kind of power is coming to harm me, well, God would be with me. Later, when I fell ill, I realized I should go to the hospital where I was treated and cured; that's when I realized that the hospital could really help me to get better. But at first, before I truly accepted Faith, I experienced fear in my life, even though I was a Christian.... After I learned all this, I continued to teach people that even though the power of the devil exists, the devil's power can do you no harm if you depend on God.

Of course, many people around him, including his father, remained outside the Christian community. Thus, when he began preaching the Gospel, he encountered considerable resistance and scepticism. He also found that he had to justify his actions in accordance with his father's non-Christian conception of moral behaviour, though he did so by combining Christian concepts with ideas that were more familiar to his father. The main issue that came between them was whether his marriage would be monogamous:

> My father told me I should marry a second wife, but I thought this would cause me a lot of trouble, because with two wives I would have to divide my attention between them. How could I be thinking about them both at the same time, thinking of this one and thinking of that one, there would be only one of me and they would start fighting over me. And if they were fighting over me, they might eventually hurt me [use evil powers against him]. So I told my father, 'I want only one wife, the one whom you've already helped me to marry'. But he said, 'No, you must

take a second wife because if you do, you'll have many children. You'll get two children with this one, and three with that one, even if one wife has only one child, the other will still have children. But if you marry only one wife, maybe her child will die and she'll have no more.'

So I thought hard about the Word of God, and I told my father, 'God is the one who gives children, if God wants me to have five children, I'll have five children. You know, father, if I have two wives I'll just be adding graves,' that's what I told father. 'I'll be adding graves because rather than death occurring in another house, it will happen in my house. I mean, if a woman was married by someone else and she had a child who died, the death would happen in his house, but if I married her, the child would die in my house. So I will marry only one wife.'

My father accepted this, but he was not happy about it. Now, I married in the same year and after only nine months my wife had a child. My father was happy, oh yes. Now I waited two years, because we allowed children to breast-feed for two years, but at the end of the third year I had a second child, and both were sons! Now father was really happy, and until the day he died, he had faith in me.

Pastor L.M. thus invoked both his belief that God would provide sufficient children and his apprehension that polygyny would introduce jealousy and witchcraft into his household to defend monogamy against a father who believed that his son had a responsibility for taking at least two wives. It was only L.M.'s success in fulfilling his father's expectations for many children, however, that finally healed the rift between father and son and reconciled the father to his son's Christian monogamy. Indeed, the pastor commenced his life story by describing the educational attainments of each of his nine children, of whom he himself is immensely proud.

Although Christians such as L.M. have found comfort in a personal relationship with their Creator and credit their faith with having allowed them to raise large families, in other men and women the sense of responsibility for having children has produced intense feelings of anxiety, guilt and failure. This has happened particularly when they have found that polygyny and various practices and beliefs which their families have long associated with success in child-bearing could not be reconciled with their Christianity. One such woman is V.K., a practising Catholic now in her fifties and mother of two surviving sons, one of whom became a monk. When she spoke with us in 1994, she described a deeply troubling relationship with Christianity. Her Christianity has been closely connected with the joys and sorrows of motherhood, which she described at length:

All together I had six boys, but they died and they died until only two remained. It was a terrible hardship, and I had a lot of pain in my neck [during childbirth], but you know how men are [how they want sons].... Yes, my sons died, and they were so beautiful, people would never think they were my children, they just wouldn't believe it.

When we visited her, V.K. chose to unburden herself of a shameful secret, though she would reveal it only by speaking privately to the only woman among her visitors. After she had been married, she explained, her mothers-in-law (for her father-in-law had at least two wives) introduced her to a practice of which she is now terribly ashamed:

> My mother-in-law came and taught me this – to go to the river with a boy like this [gesturing to her son, who was sitting some distance away], go into the woods and do this [and here words seemed to fail her, but she gestured to show that she meant pulling and kneading her son's penis to stretch it and make it erect].

And why must she do this? As a mother, it was her responsibility to ensure that her son would have many children, and, besides, knowing that she had done so should give her great joy. After the treatment had been completed,

> when you are carrying the son on your back you'll know when the penis stiffens, well that's when you're very, very happy, you say to yourself, 'I've saved myself, I've saved myself' [from the blame that would be borne by a mother whose son could not have children].

Yet making sure that her son's penis would be strong was not the worst of it, because when people gathered at camps in the woods to be instructed about these things,

> People insult each other, they say the most filthy things, they talk about things that you could never say openly, this family is cursed, you've never seen anything like it, by God [and here she spits on the ground] … the worst thing is what's said in this kind of group, they talk about penises and vaginas and fucking and how big penises and vaginas are, they actually talk about them by name!

V.K. feels compelled to participate in these matters, both because she doesn't want to risk harming her sons' ability to have children, and because these practices are traditional in her husband's patrilineage. Yet her own brother knows nothing about her involvement in them, and she is horrified by the suggestion that she would teach such things to her daughters, whose children, of course, will belong to different patrilineages. Yet there is no doubt that taking part in these things makes her feel dirty and deeply ashamed:

> Truly our family is not good, it's really bad. Sometimes you just want to be alone. During the farming season if you are invited to take part in communal farming, you put it off and wind up not going at all because you are scared, I mean, if you go and the time comes to do these things, and then you leave suddenly, people will be shocked, they'll say 'what's wrong with her?'… if they did these things out in the open people would say, '*Jamani*, are those people crazy?'

Nevertheless, V.K. remains a Catholic, and as she ages she is thinking more and more that her involvement in these practices may cost her salvation:

Now we old folks are going to get out of these things.... I don't want this business any more, I'm getting out ... [of] all these dirty things that we do in my husband's clan ... we've really been led astray [*tumechezewa*], I don't know with God how it will be.... It's utterly shameful, shameful, but what can you do with old people like us, it's totally shameful.

Christianity, Non-Christian Culture and Individual Autonomy

The experience of a woman troubled by familiar practices and beliefs concerning sexuality and childbirth may perhaps suggest that Monica Wilson and others have been correct in saying that indigenous, non-Christian culture is less likely than Christianity to encourage individual initiative. Nevertheless, when we discover, as we shall see in the following paragraphs, that women have used non-Christian moral concepts to assert independence from men and defend their autonomy, we are led to ask whether Wilson did not exaggerate the influence exerted by the 'yeast of the Gospel' in stimulating innovation and individuality.[14]

The capacity of non-Christian Bena culture to provide women with grounds for defending individual autonomy is shown in particular by their ways of avoiding a great danger during the era of labour migration – unwanted marriages with brothers-in-law. One woman who avoided such a marriage, M.K., is an elderly resident of Njombe who since the death of her husband in the late 1950s has guarded her independence. Having worked with her husband to build one of the first substantial African businesses in Njombe, M.K. acquired considerable influence in the clan of her husband and children. After his death, M.K. raised and educated their children, one of whom numbers among the most prominent citizens in national affairs to have come from Njombe. M.K. places great weight on her responsibilities, so much so that when we visited her, accompanied by two of her daughters, she fashioned her life's story into a series of lessons for her daughters about the duties of a proper Bena woman. Nevertheless, she also explained how she violated 'traditional' expectations by refusing to be married to her brother-in-law after the death of her husband:

I refused. I said [to him], 'No, I can't. You can find me right here if you want to look after your [brother's] children.' I said the children I already had were enough. These children will look after me. One of my co-wives married my brother-in-law, but because he was full of problems and complications she later left him. Yes, I refused. I didn't want to get together with any man because you never know what kind of man is marrying you. Sometimes these new husbands can say, 'Look at your children, they are eating up all my food.'

Her reasons for rejecting her brother-in-law were quite clear. Because her children inherited a substantial estate from their father, and because she was confident that she could rely upon their support, she had no need of another spouse. Not only that, but she also understood the resentments that could develop when a man was made responsible for his deceased brother's children. Most of all, she was simply unwilling to risk losing the independence that she had enjoyed even during her years of marriage.

M.K. has been a practising Muslim since early in her life, and Christian ideals of marriage played little part in her refusal to be married by her brother-in-law. Instead, she made her decision after estimating the qualities of her brother-in-law and the prospects of her children. In so doing, she relied on moral and practical criteria that had probably served women in similar circumstances long before the coming of Christianity.

One sees a similar kind of judgement being made by Mary, the devout Christian from Ilembula whose conversion to Christianity and schooling we have already discussed. Even though she had been exposed since childhood to Christian education, Mary invoked similar considerations in explaining why she twice rejected offers of marriage by brothers-in-law. Mary has been an adventurous individual throughout her life. While still a young girl, she ignored the objections of her father and became a Christian. As a young woman in the 1950s, at a time when long-distance travel by women was dangerous and nearly impossible, Mary disguised herself as a boy and travelled via the buses and rest camps of the male plantation workers until she reached Tanga. Later, she abandoned her lifelong affiliation with Lutheranism and joined the Assemblies of God. But, in her estimation, her greatest moral crises came when she rejected two brothers-in-law who wished to marry her. Yet, in explaining her decisions in these cases, she did not invoke Christian teachings about polygyny and the sinfulness of wife inheritance. Instead, she described the weaknesses and faults of both men, and thus explained, in terms readily understood by non-Christians as well as her fellow Christians, why she rejected marriage to two very undesirable husbands.

She first rejected the husband of her sister, who wished to make her his second wife, because he was, in her view, a poor husband. Indeed, her elaborate portrayal of his many inadequacies seems to have been intended to persuade men who disapprove neither of polygyny nor of marriage to brothers-in-law that this man would not make a good husband. Her brother-in-law, she says, had a ferocious temper, yet was given to self-pity. He was improvident and cruel, yet was easily deceived by his wife and sister-in-law even though he intimidated his male employees. Having fended off her sister's husband, Mary married some years later, only to be harassed by a brother of her husband, who was then absent and working in Tanga:

> I think my husband was bewitched because other men lusted for me when I was young. So they made him stay away for many years. His older brother would come to tempt me:
> 'Your husband has disappeared there [in Tanga]. He won't return.

You have a lot of problems by yourself. Come to my place, I'll marry you and you can live with me.'

'Hey,' I replied, 'you want me to cause a dispute among the two of you [*niwachonganishe*]? You say I should leave your younger brother's house and come to you? Won't you quarrel with him?'

'I don't care if we quarrel,' he said. 'Just come and live at my place.'

'No, that's not the way I am.'

'My God, if you were a cow, I'd say, "My younger brother is unable to tend these cattle. Let's take in his wife and care for her."'

'Even so, I'm going to wait for your younger brother until he returns. I can't move into your house.'

I think this is the one who harmed him, who ruined his intelligence so that we would separate and I would no longer be married to him. But I feared that I would provoke a quarrel between brothers. My husband later died as a result of running with women. He got an incurable illness.

Like many women in Bena culture, Mary confronted the likelihood that she would be married into a polygynous household, and, like many women, she sought to avoid it. As a devout Christian, she might simply have taken the position that it violated Christian precepts. Lutheranism has long struggled against polygyny in Njombe. Certainly Mary might have been expected to assume that the simplest way to explain the rejection of her brothers-in-law to an American would have been to say that polygyny is unchristian. After all, an American would understand that Christianity opposes polygyny. Besides, Mary is familiar with such arguments and employs them elsewhere in her life's story.

Yet this is not how she told her story. Its carefully constructed fore-shadowing of events and mention of incidents whose significance would only be revealed later show that it was rehearsed. Mary told it to us as she had told it many times before (for she was not inclined to stifle her grievances) to courts, government officials, doctors and missionaries. Her main intention in constructing her life's story was not to have it understood by an American, but rather to persuade Bena-speaking men who approve of and practise polygyny. Indeed, Mary explained her rejection of her brothers-in-law in much the same way that Christian preachers in Njombe avoid talk of immorality and Christianity when dealing with polygyny, appealing instead to a mature man's sense of obligation by stressing that under modern conditions a polygynist cannot provide adequately for multiple wives and many children. Likewise, Mary's explanation said nothing about Christianity or about the immorality of polygyny. Instead, she made the kind of arguments that women had probably used long before the appearance of Christianity to avoid becoming a second or third wife. In the case of her sister's husband, she elaborately described his inadequacies, while, in the case of her husband's brother, she stressed the importance of avoiding discord among brothers.

Although this morality was highly gendered, Mary nevertheless drew from it justification for rejecting unwanted marriage with her brothers-in-law. Thus, Bena culture provided women with ways of resisting polygynous marriages, even if they did not wish to invoke Christian teachings. By assessing the attainments and characters of men and making arguments about the importance of maintaining good relations among kin, women like Mary could avoid both invoking Christian norms, which not everyone accepted, and also condemning their polygynous fathers, uncles and neighbours for immorality.

Conclusion

As colonial Njombe became a predominantly Christian region, marital and family life became the subjects of vigorous debate. In local government councils and in private settings, residents of Njombe struggled with how to define families, establish proper amounts of bridewealth, and best teach their young about sexuality and care of reproductive health. They considered, among other issues, whether widows ought to be married by brothers-in-law, whether women should have the right to seek divorce and retain custody of their children, and whether men should have multiple spouses. While such issues might be thought to have arisen inevitably in the course of Christianization, Bena men and women regarded them as problems caused by the economy of labour migration. It was this system which, by inflating bridewealth and necessitating long-term separations of spouses, forced them to contemplate changes in domestic relationships.

New ideas about family and marriage were only one part of the unfamiliar knowledge sought by the people of colonial Njombe. They believed that they needed many kinds of new knowledge and experience to prosper within the colonial economy. Political leaders like Chief Mbeyela spoke incessantly about the need to eradicate *ujinga* – ignorance – by building schools, increasing literacy and creating opportunities to engage in skilled crafts and business. Christianity was a crucial source of new knowledge, not simply because its evangelists spread literacy as well as new ideas about health care, hygiene and the place of Africans in a wider world, but also because it provided novel ways of thinking about moral purpose, an individual's relationship with Creation and the prospect of eternal salvation. Indeed, part of the reason why converts experienced Christianization as a deep spiritual and moral struggle was because they took the substance of their Christian faith very seriously. The other reason why the encounter with Christianity involved struggle, however, was that non-Christian concepts of morality, evil and spiritual power remained compelling. Rather than renouncing indigenous concepts of morality, men and women struggled, not always successfully, to reconcile them with Christian beliefs. As they did so, they found in them ways of justifying the changes that they were making in their lives as they became Christians and entered the colonial economy.

Notes

1 Jean and John Comaroff, *Of Revelation and Revolution*, vol. I (Chicago, 1991).
2 Monica Wilson, *For Men and Elders* (London, 1977), especially 23, 27 and 171–5. See also Godfrey and Monica Wilson, *The Analysis of Social Change* (Cambridge, 1945) and Monica Wilson, *Religion and the Transformation of Society* (Cambridge, 1971). Conceptions of Christianization which contrast Western individuality with African communalism remain current. Lamin Sanneh has recently written that 'the Christian Scriptures' brought about in Africa 'the kind of intellectual revolution that in the West produced the idea of the primacy of conscience, and thus of the free individual as the linchpin of redemption and social emancipation. In Africa, by contrast, it produced a fresh narrative cultural sensibility set in the context of family, tribe and nation.' Lamin Sanneh, *Encountering the West* (Maryknoll, NY, 1993), 86–7.
3 James D. Graham, 'Changing patterns of wage labor in Tanzania: a history of the relations between African labor and European capitalism in Njombe District' (PhD, Northwestern, 1968), 35 and 60–1.
4 *Ibid.*, 60.
5 *Ibid.*, 114–17.
6 Assistant District Officer (Njombe), 'Safari Report' (27 November 1933), Tanzania National Archives [hereafter TNA] 178/1/4.
7 Census of 1957 in TNA 576/P.2/2/v.
8 Marcia Wright, *German Missions in Tanganyika, 1891–1941* (Oxford, 1971).
9 This colonial term remains in Njombe the usual English translation of '*shule ya kienyeji*', which literally means 'native school'.
10 The extent to which these influences actually changed patterns of marriage and inheritance is uncertain, however, because we have little evidence of them from either the precolonial or colonial periods.
11 A. T. and G. M. Culwick, *Ubena of the Rivers* (London, 1935), 179–89.
12 The following paragraphs are based primarily on records of tribal and district council meetings found in TNA 465/L.5/9 and 178/G. 37, and on an interview with Joseph Mbeyela (Mdandu, 29 June 1994).
13 The remaining pages of this essay are based upon interviews in Njombe District in 1992 and 1994. To preserve their confidentiality, the names of interviewees and other details are withheld. The interviews were conducted together by myself and Blandina Kaduma Giblin.
14 Monica Wilson, *Communal Rituals of the Nyakyusa* (London, 1959), 219–20.

Bibliography

'African Brotherhood Church', *Ecumenical Review*, 24 (1972), 145–9.

Ajayi, J. F. A., *Christian Missions in Nigeria, 1841–1891*. London: Longman, 1965.

Allen, Tim, 'Understanding Alice: Uganda's Holy Spirit movement in context', *Africa*, 61 (1991), 370–99.

Anderson, Benedict R. O'G., *Imagined Communities*, 2nd edition. New York: Verso, 1991.

Anderson, David M. and Douglas H. Johnson (eds), *Revealing Prophets*. London: James Currey, 1995.

Ariarajah, Wesley, *Gospel and Culture*. Geneva: WCC Publications, 1994.

Badone, Ellen (ed.), *Religious Orthodoxy and Popular Faith in European Society*. Princeton: Princeton University Press, 1990.

Baeta, C. G., *Prophetism in Ghana*. London: SCM, 1962.

Baroin, Catherine, 'Religious conflict in 1990–1993 among the Rwa: secession in a Lutheran diocese in northern Tanzania', *African Affairs*, 95 (1996), 529–54.

Barrett, David B., *Schism and Renewal in Africa*. Nairobi: Oxford University Press, 1968.

Barrett, David B. *et al.* (eds), *Kenya Churches Handbook*. Kisumu: Evangel Publishing House, 1973.

Bax, Mart, 'Religious regimes and state-formation: toward a research perspective' and 'Marian apparitions in Medjugorje: rivalling religious regimes and state-formation in Yugoslavia', in Eric R. Wolf (eds), *Religious Regimes*, 7–27, 29–53. Albany: SUNY, 1991.

Beattie, John, 'Sorcery in Bunyoro', in J. Middleton and E.H. Winter (eds), *Witchcraft and Sorcery in East Africa*, 27–55. London: Routledge and Kegan Paul, 1963.

Beattie, John, 'Spirit mediumship in Bunyoro', in J. Beattie & J. Middleton (eds), *Spirit Mediumship and Society in Africa*, 159–170. London: Routledge and Kegan Paul, 1969.

Bediako, Kwame, *Christianity in Africa: The Renewal of a Non-Western Religion*. Maryknoll: Orbis, 1995.

Behrend, Heike, 'Is Alice Lakwena a Witch? The Holy Spirit movement and its fight against evil in the north', in H.B. Hansen and M. Twaddle (eds), *Changing Uganda*, 162–77. London: James Currey, 1991.

Behrend, Heike, 'The Holy Spirit movement and the forces of nature in the north of Uganda 1985–1987', in H.B. Hansen and M. Twaddle (eds), *Religion and Politics in East Africa*, 59–71. London: James Currey, 1995.

Beidelman, T. O., *Colonial Evangelism*. Bloomington: Indiana University Press, 1982.

Bell, Marion L., *Crusade in the City*. Lewisburg: Bucknell University Press, 1977.

Berger, Iris, *Religion and Resistance: East African Kingdoms in the Precolonial Period*. Tervuren: Musée Royal de l'Afrique Centrale, 1981.

Berman, Bruce and John Lonsdale, *Unhappy Valley*, 2 vols. London: James Currey, 1992.

Bertsch, F., *Notes on the History of Karema Diocese*. No place or publisher, 1964.

Bowie, Fiona, Deborah Kirkwood and Shirley Ardener (eds), *Women and Missions*. Providence: Berg, 1993.

Bredekamp, H. and R. Ross (eds), *Missions and Christianity in South African History*. Johannesburg: Witwatersrand University Press, 1995.

Brenner, Louis (ed.), *Muslim Identity and Social Change in Sub-Saharan Africa*. Bloomington: Indiana University Press, 1993.

Brierley, Jean and Thomas Spear, 'Mutesa, the missionaries, and Christian conversion in Buganda', *International Journal of African Historical Studies*, 21 (1988), 601–18.

Buijtenhuijs, R., *Essays on Mau Mau*. Leiden: African Studies Centre, 1982.

Burbridge, O. L., *Taki: Soldier, Evangelist, Translator*. London: African Inland Press, nd.

Burns, Gene, *The Frontiers of Catholicism: The Politics of Ideology in a Liberal World*. Berkeley: University of California Press, 1994.

Byabazaire, Deogratias M., *The Contribution of the Christian Churches to the Development of Western Uganda 1894–1974*. Frankfurt: Peter Lang, 1979.

Byaruhanga-Akiika, A. B. T., *Religion in Bunyoro*. Nairobi: Kenya Literature Bureau, 1982.

Bibliography

Cabral, Amilcar, *Return to the Source*. New York: Monthly Review Press, 1979.

Cashmore, J. H. R., 'Studies in district administration in the East African Protectorate, 1895–1918', PhD, Cambridge University, 1965.

Catholic Bishops of Uganda, *Celebrating Our Ancestors in the Faith*. Kisubi: Marianum Press, 1984.

Catholic Directory of Tanzania. Tabora: Tanganyika Mission Press, 1988.

Chegge, John, 'Hadithi ya Kanisa ya Roho Mtakatifu', unpublished manuscript, Nyahururu, nd.

Clough, Marshall S., *Fighting Two Sides*. Niwot, CO: University Press of Colorado, 1990.

Coldham, Geraldine E. (compiler), *A Bibliography of Scriptures in African Languages*. London: British and Foreign Bible Society, 1966.

Coleman, John A., '*Raison d'église*: organizational imperatives of the church in the political order', in J. K. Hadden and A. Shupe (eds), *Secularization and Fundamentalism Reconsidered*, III:252–75. New York: Paragon House, 1989.

Comaroff, John and Jean, *Of Revelation and Revolution*, Vol. I. Chicago: University of Chicago Press, 1993.

Comaroff, John and Jean (eds), *Modernity and its Malcontents*. Chicago: University of Chicago Press, 1993.

Cooksey, Brian, 'Who's poor in Tanzania?' in M. S. D. Bagachwa (ed.) *Poverty Alleviation in Tanzania*. Dar es Salaam: University of Dar es Salaam Press, 1994.

Cooper, John C., *Radical Christianity and its Sources*. Philadelphia: Westminster Press, 1968.

Corfield, F. D., *Historical Survey of the Origins and Growth of Mau Mau*. London: HMSO, 1960.

Coupland, Reginald, *The Exploitation of East Africa*. London: Faber, 1939.

Culwick, A. T. and G. M., *Ubena of the Rivers*. London: Allen and Unwin, 1935.

Davis, Br Paul, *Fr. Nkwera Disposer of Demons*. Dar es Salaam: private printing, 1994.

Depelchin, Jacques, *Silences in African History*, forthcoming.

Devisch, Rene, 'Frenzy, violence, and ethical renewal in Kinshasa', *Public Culture*, 7/3 (1995), 593–629.

Dirven, Peter, 'The Legio Maria: the dynamics of a breakaway church among the Luo of East Africa', MissD, Pontificia Universitas Gregoriana, 1970.

Donovan, Vincent J., *Christianity Rediscovered: an Epistle from the Masai*. Notre Dame: Fides/Claretian, 1978.

Douglas, Mary, *Purity and Danger*. New York: Praeger, 1966.

Dundas, Charles, *Kilimanjaro and Its People*. London: Frank Cass, 1968.

Fadiman, Jeffrey A., *When We Began, There Were Witchmen*. Berkeley: University of California Press, 1993.

Feierman, Steven, *Peasant Intellectuals*. Madison: University of Wisconsin Press, 1990.

Feierman, Steven, 'Africa in history: the end of universal narratives', in Gyan Prakash (ed.), *After Colonialism*, 40–65. Princeton: Princeton University Press, 1995.

Fields, Karen, *Revival and Rebellion in Colonial Central Africa*. Princeton: Princeton University Press, 1985.

Fleisch, Paul, *Hundert Jahre Lutherischer Mission*. Leipzig: Verlag der Evangelisch-Lutherischen Mission, 1936.

Fraser, Donald, *The Future of Africa*. London: Young People's Missionary Movement, 1911.

Fukiau kia Bunseki, *Nkongo ye Nza Yakunzungidila: Cosmogonie Kongo*. Kinshasa: Office National de la recherche et de développement, 1969.

Fukiau kia Bunseki, *The African Book Without Title*. Cambridge, 1980.

Fukiau kia Bunseki, 'Mukuku Matatu', unpublished MS, 1983.

Fukiau kia Bunseki, *Self-Healing Power and Therapy*. New York: Vantage, 1991.

Fukiau kia Bunseki, 'Ntangu-Tandu-Kolo: the Bantu-Kongo concept of time', in J. K. Adjaye (ed.), *Time in the Black Experience*, 17–34. Westport: Greenwood, 1994.

Galaty, John, 'Being "Maasai"; being "people of cattle": ethnic shifters in East Africa', *American Ethnologist*, 9 (1982), 1–20.

Garvey, Brian, 'The development of the White Fathers' mission among the Bemba-speaking peoples, 1891–1964', PhD, University of London, 1974.

Geschiere, Peter, *The Modernity of Witchcraft*. Charlottesville: University of Virginia Press, 1997.

Gifford, Paul, *African Christianity: Its Public Role*. London: Hurst, 1998.

Githieya, Francis K., 'The new people of God: the Christian community in the African Orthodox Church (Karing'a) and the Arathi (Gikuyu Spirit Churches)', PhD, Emory University, 1992.

Githieya, Francis K., *The Freedom of the Spirit: African Indigenous Churches in Kenya*. Atlanta: Scholar's

Press, 1997.

Gossett, Thomas F., *Race: The History of an Idea in America*. Dallas: Southern Methodist University Press, 1963.

Gould, David, *Bureaucratic Corruption and Underdevelopment in the Third World*. New York: Pergamon, 1980.

Graham, James D., 'Changing patterns of wage labor in Tanzania: a history of the relations between African labor and European capitalism in Njombe District', PhD, Northwestern University, 1968.

Gramsci, Antonio, *Selections from the Prison Notebooks*, Quintin Hoare and Geoffrey Nowell Smith (ed. and trans.). New York: International, 1971.

Gratton, John, 'The relationship of the Africa Inland Mission and its national church in Kenya between 1895 and 1971', PhD, New York University, 1974.

Gray, Richard, *Black Christians and White Missionaries*. New Haven: Yale University Press, 1990.

Gutmann, Bruno D., *Das Seelenleben der Dschagga-Neger*. Leipzig: Negger, 1909.

Gutmann, Bruno D., *Christusleib und Nachstenschaft*. Feuchtwangen: Frantenverlag Sommer und Schoor, 1931.

Gutmann, Bruno D., *Die Stammeslehren der Dschagga*, Vol. II, Munich: Beck, 1935.

Haar, Gerrie Ter, *Spirit of Africa*. Trenton: Africa World Press, 1992.

Hansen, Holger Bernt, *Mission, Church and State in a Colonial Setting: Uganda 1890–1925*. London: Heinemann, 1984.

Hansen, Holger Bernt and Michael Twaddle (eds), *Religion and Politics in East Africa*. London: James Currey, 1995.

Hastings, Adrian, *A History of African Christianity, 1950–1975*. Cambridge: Cambridge University Press, 1979.

Hastings, Adrian, *African Catholicism: Essays in Discovery*. London: SCM Press, 1989.

Hastings, Adrian, *The Church in Africa, 1450–1950*. Oxford: Clarendon, 1994.

Healey, Joseph and Donald Sybertz, *Towards an African Narrative Theology*. Nairobi: Pauline Publications, 1996.

Hefner, Robert, 'Introduction', in R. Hefner (ed.), *Conversion to Christianity*, 3–44. Berkeley: University of California Press, 1993.

Heremans, Roger, *Les Etablissements de l'Association Africaine au Lac Tanganika et les Pères Blancs: Mpala et Karema, 1877–1885*. Tervuren: Musée Royal de l'Afrique Centrale, 1966.

Heremans, Roger, *Education dans les missions des Pères Blancs en Afrique Centrale*. Brussels: Éditions Nauwelaerts, 1983.

Heron, Alisdair, *A Century of Protestant Theology*. Philadelphia: Westminster Press, 1980.

Hill, Christopher, *The English Bible and the Seventeenth Century Revolution*. London: Penguin, 1993.

Hillman, Eugene, 'Missionary approaches to African cultures today,' *African Ecclesiastical Review*, 22 (1980), 342–56.

Hillman, Eugene, *Toward an African Christianity*, New York: Paulist Press, 1993.

Hodgson, Dorothy, 'The politics of gender, ethnicity and "development": images, interventions and the reconfiguration of Maasai identities', PhD, University of Michigan, 1995.

Hodgson, Dorothy, 'Engendered encounters: men of the church and the "church of women" in Maasailand, Tanzania, 1950–1993', Workshop on African Expressions of Christianity, Madison, 1994.

Hoehler-Fatton, Cynthia, *Women of Fire and Spirit*. New York: Oxford University Press, 1996.

Hoover, Sandra, 'Social stratification in Toro: a study in social change', PhD, Indiana University, 1978.

Iliffe, John, *A Modern History of Tanganyika*. Cambridge: Cambridge University Press, 1979.

Ingham, John M., *Mary, Michael and Lucifer: Folk Catholicism in Central Mexico*. Austin: University of Texas Press, 1986.

Isichei, Elizabeth, *A History of Christianity in Africa*. Grand Rapids: Eerdmans, 1995.

Jackson, Robert H. and Edward Castillo, *Indians, Franciscans, and Spanish Colonization*. Albuquerque: University of New Mexico Press, 1995.

James, Wendy, *The Listening Ebony*. Oxford: Clarendon, 1988.

James, Wendy and Douglas Johnson (eds), *Vernacular Christianity* (Journal of the Anthropological Society of Oxford Occasional Publication No 9) Oxford: JASO, 1988.

Johnson, Douglas, *Nuer Prophets*. Oxford: Oxford University Press, 1994.

Johnston, H. H., *The Kilima-Njaro Expedition*. London: K. Paul, Trench, 1886.

Kaaya, B., 'The planting of Christianity in Meru: its conflicts and similarities with the traditional culture of the Wameru', Fieldwork Report, Diploma in Theology, Makerere

Bibliography

University, 1978.

Kahimbaara, John Akiiki, 'Some traditional beliefs of the Batooro', *Occasional Research Papers in African Traditional Religion and Philosophy*, 29 (1974), 1–43.

Kalemera, Jason, *Huduma za Maombezi in its Historical Perspective*. Dar es Salaam: private printing, 1993.

'Kanisa la Kiinjili la Kilutheir la Tanzania', Arusha, 1996.

Kanogo, Tabitha, *Squatters and the Roots of Mau Mau*. London: James Currey, 1987.

Kaplan, Steven, 'The Africanization of missionary Christianity', *Journal of Religion in Africa*, 16 (1986), 166–86.

Karamaga, Andre, 'Problems and promises of Africa', in Margaret S. Larom (ed.), *Claiming the Promise*, 21–31. New York: Friendship, 1994.

Kassimir, Ronald, 'Complex martyrs: symbols of Catholic Church formation and political differentiation in Uganda', *African Affairs*, 90 (1991), 357–82.

Kassimir, Ronald, 'The social power of religious organization: the Catholic Church in Uganda 1955–1991', PhD, University of Chicago, 1996.

Kassimir, Ronald, 'Ambiguous institution: the Catholic Church and the reconstruction of Uganda', in L. Villalón and P. Huxtable (eds), *The African State at a Critical Juncture: Between Disintegration and Reconfiguration*. Boulder. Lynne Reinner, 1998.

Kenya Land Commission, *Evidence and Memoranda*, 4 vols. London: HMSO, 1934.

Kibicho, Samuel G., 'The interaction of the traditional Kikuyu concept of God with the biblical concept', *Cahiers des Religions Africaines*, 2 (1968), 223–38.

Kibicho, Samuel, 'The Kikuyu conception of God: its continuity into the Christian era', PhD, Vanderbilt University, 1972.

Kieran, John, 'The Holy Ghost Fathers in East Africa, 1863–1911', PhD, University of London, 1966.

Kimambo, I. N., *Three Decades of Historical Research at Dar es Salaam*. Dar es Salaam: University of Dar es Salaam Press, 1993.

King, Kenneth J., 'A biography of Molonket Olokorinya Ole Sempele', in K. King and A. I. Salim (eds), *Kenya Historical Biographies*, 3–28. Nairobi: East African Publishing House, 1971.

King, Kenneth J., 'The Maasai and the protest phenomenon, 1900–1960', *Journal of African History*, 12 (1971), 117–37.

Kiragu, D. M., *Kiria Giatumire Independent Igie* (Independent Church Origins). Nairobi: Regal Press, nd.

Kitching, Gavin, *Class and Economic Change in Kenya*. New Haven: Yale, 1980.

Kituyi, Mukhisa, *Becoming Kenyans*. Nairobi: ACTS, 1990.

Knox, Elizabeth, *Signal on the Mountain*. Canberra: Acron Press, 1991.

Kongola, Ernest, *Historia mfupi ya Mbeya ya 'Wevunjiliza' toka 1688 mpaka 1986: 'Mbukwa Muhindi wa Cimambi'*. Dodoma: np, 1986.

Kongola, Ernest, *Ybile ya almasi ya Dayosisi ya Central Tanganyika*. Dodoma: np, 1987.

Kselman, Thomas, 'Ambiguity and assumption in the concept of popular religion', in Daniel H. Levine (ed.), *Religion and Political Conflict in Latin America*, 24–41. Chapel Hill: University of North Carolina Press, 1986.

Lamprey, Richard and Richard Waller, 'The Loita-Mara region in historical times', in P. Robertshaw (ed.), *Early Pastoralists in South-Western Kenya*, 16–35. Nairobi: British Institute in Eastern Africa, 1990.

Landau, Paul, *The Realm of the Word*. Portsmouth: Heinemann, 1995.

Larsson, Birgitta, *Conversion to Greater Freedom?* (Acta Universitatis Upsaliensis. Studia historica Upsaliensia, 162). Uppsala: Almqvist and Wiksell, 1991.

Launay, Robert, *Beyond the Stream*. Berkeley: University of California Press, 1992.

Lazarus, Sylvain, *Anthropologie du nom*. Paris: Editions du Seuil, 1996.

Lechaptois, Mgr, *Aux Rives du Tanganyika*. Alger: Imprimerie des Pères Blancs, 1932.

Legum, Colin and Geoffrey Mmari (eds), *Mwalimu*. London: James Currey, 1995.

Lema, A. A., 'The impact of the Leipzig Lutheran Mission on the peoples of Kilimanjaro, 1893–1920', PhD, University of Dar es Salaam, 1975.

Lemenye, Justin, 'The life of Justin', H. Fosbrooke (ed.), *Tanganyika Notes and Records*, 41 (1955), 31–57, 42 (1956), 19–30.

Levi, Giovanni, *Inheriting Power*. Chicago: University of Chicago Press, 1988.

Levine, Daniel H., 'Popular groups, popular culture and popular religion', *Comparative Studies in Society and History*, 32 (1990), 718–64.

Levine, Daniel H., *Popular Voices in Latin American Catholicism*. Princeton: Princeton University

Bibliography

Press, 1992.

Levtzion, Nehemia (ed.), *Conversion to Islam*. New York: Holmes and Meier, 1979.

Lienhardt, Godfrey, 'The Dinka and Catholicism', in J. Davis (ed.), *Religious Organization and Religious Experience*, 81–95. London: Academic, 1982.

Linden, Ian, *Church and Revolution in Rwanda*. Manchester: Manchester University Press, 1977.

Linden, Ian and Jane, 'John Chilembwe and the New Jerusalem', *Journal of African History*, 12 (1971), 629–51.

Longman, Timothy, 'Christianity and crisis in Rwanda', PhD, University of Wisconsin, 1995.

Lonsdale, John. 'Mau Maus of the mind: making Mau Mau and remaking Kenya', *Journal of African History*, 31 (1990), 393–422.

Lonsdale, John, '"Listen while I read": the orality of Christian literacy in the young Kenyatta's making of the Kikuyu', in L. de la Gorgendiere, K. King and S. Vaughan (eds), *Ethnicity in Africa*, 17–53. Edinburgh: Centre of African Studies, 1996.

Lonsdale, John, 'Jomo, God and the Modern World', African Studies Association, 1997.

Low, D. A., *Religion and Society in Buganda, 1875–1900*. Kampala: East African Institute of Social Research, 1955.

Low, D. A., *Buganda in Modern History*, London: Weidenfield and Nicolson, 1971.

Low, D. A. and J. M. Lonsdale, 'Introduction: towards the new order, 1945–1963', in D. A. Low and A. Smith (eds), *History of East Africa*, III:1–63. Oxford: Oxford University Press, 1976.

McBrien, Richard P., *Church: The Continuing Quest*. New York: Newman Press, 1970.

MacGaffey, Wyatt, *Religion and Society in Central Africa*. Chicago: University of Chicago Press, 1986.

McIntosh, B. G., 'The Scottish mission in Kenya, 1891–1923', PhD, Edinburgh University, 1969.

McLoughlin, William G., *Revivals, Awakenings and Reform*. Chicago: University of Chicago Press, 1978.

MacPherson, Robert, *The Presbyterian Church in Kenya*. Nairobi: Presbyterian Church in East Africa, 1970.

Maddox, Gregory, '"Leave, Wagogo! You have no food!": famine and survival in Ugogo, Central Tanzania 1916–1961', PhD, Northwestern University, 1988.

Maddox, Gregory, '*Mtunya*: famine in Central Tanzania, 1917–1920', *Journal of African History*, 31 (1990), 181–98.

Magesa, Laurenti, 'The expatriate worker in Africa', *African Ecclesiastical Review*, 36 (1994), 92–103.

Magesa, Laurenti, 'Authentic African Christianity', *African Ecclesiastical Review*, 37 (1995), 209–20.

Malishi, Lukas, *A History of the Catholic Church in Tanzania*. Peramiho: Tanzania Episcopal Conference, 1990.

Mamdani, Mahmood, *Citizen and Subject*. Princeton: Princeton University Press, 1996.

Mandao, Martha and C. Omari, *Hayati Askofu Stefano Ruben Moshi*. Moshi, 1994.

Masquelier, Adeline, 'Identity, alterity and ambiguity in a Nigerian community: competing definitions of "true" Islam', in R. Werbner and T. O. Ranger (eds), *Postcolonial Identities in Africa*, 222–44. London: Zed Books, 1996.

Matovu, Nathan B., *Mityana Bishops*. No place, publisher or date.

Mbise, A. S., 'The evangelist: Matayo Leveriya Kaaya', in John Iliffe (ed.), *Modern Tanzanians*, 27–41. Nairobi: East African Publishing House, 1973.

Mbiti, John S., *African Religions and Philosophy*. London: Heinemann, 1969.

Mbiti, John S., *Bible and Theology in African Christianity*. Nairobi: Oxford University Press, 1986.

Mbiti, John S., *Introduction to African Religion*, 2nd edition. Portsmouth: Heinemann, 1991.

Meyer, Birgit, '"If you are a devil, you are a witch, and if you are a witch, you are a devil": the integration of "pagan" ideas into the conceptual universe of Ewe Christians in south-eastern Ghana', *Journal of Religion in Africa*, 22 (1992), 98–132.

Middleton, John, 'Kenya: Administration and changes in African life', in V. Harlow and E. M. Chilver (eds), *History of East Africa*, II:362–73. Oxford: Oxford University Press, 1965.

Mnyampala, Mathais E., *The Gogo: History, Customs, and Traditions*, Gregory H. Maddox (ed. and trans.). Armonk, NY: M. E. Sharpe, 1995.

Moore, Sally Falk, 'Post-socialist micro-politics: Kilimanjaro, 1993', *Africa*, 96 (1996), 587–606.

Moore, Sally Falk and Paul Puritt, *The Chagga and Meru of Tanzania*. London: International African Institute, 1977.

Bibliography

Mpaayei, J. G., *Inkuti Pukunot oolMaasai*. Oxford: Oxford University Press, 1954.

Mudimbe, V. Y., *The Invention of Africa*. Bloomington: Indiana University Press, 1988.

Muller, Emil, *Madschame, die ältest Leipzinger Station am Kilimanjaro*. Leipzig: Verlag der Evangelisch-Lutherischen Mission, 1936.

Munro, J. Forbes, *Colonial Rule and the Kamba*. Oxford: Clarendon, 1975.

Murphee, Marshall, *Christianity and the Shona*. London: Athlone, 1969.

Murray, Jocelyn, 'Production of Christian literature', in David B. Barrett, *et al.* (eds), *Kenya Churches Handbook*, 93–9. Kisumu: Evangel Publishing House, 1973.

Murray, Jocelyn, 'The Kikuyu circumcision controversy', PhD, University of California at Los Angeles, 1974.

Murray, Jocelyn, 'The Kikuyu spirit churches', *Journal of Religion in Africa*, 5 (1974), 198–234.

Museveni, Yoweri, *What is Africa's Problem?* Kampala: NRM Publications, 1992.

Mutambirwa, Jane, 'African religious traditions', in Margaret S. Larom (ed.), *Claiming the Promise*, 88–96. New York: Friendship Press, 1994.

Muzorewa, Gwinyai H., *The Origins and Development of African Theology*. Maryknoll: Orbis Books, 1995.

Namata, Joseph, *Edmund John: Man of God*. Dodoma: Central Tanganyika Press, 1980.

Nasari, C. T. S., 'The history of the Lutheran Church among the Meru (Warwa) of Tanzania', BD, Lutheran Theological College Makumira, 1980.

Neckebrouck, Valeer, *Le Onzième Cmmandement* (Nouvelle Review de Science Missionaire, Supplementa, Vol. 27). Immensee: Nouvelle Review de Science Missionaire, 1978.

Neckebrouck, Valeer, *Le Peuple affligé*. Immensee: Neue Zeitschrift für Missionswissenschaft, 1983.

Ne Muanda Nsemi, *L'Histoire du Congo Central*. Kinshasa: Editions Mpolo Ngimbi, 1990.

Ne Muanda Nsemi, *Le Kikongo et la science*. Kinshasa: Editions Mpolo Ngimbi, 1991.

Ne Muanda Nsemi, *La Spécificité de la religion Kongo*. Kinshasa: Editions Mpolo Ngimbi, 1992.

Ne Muanda Nsemi, *Le Kikongo et la science nucléaire*. Kinshasa: Editions Mpolo Ngimbi, 1994.

Ne Muanda Nsemi, *Le Kikongo et l'enseignement*. Kinshasa: Editions Mpolo Ngimbi, 1994.

Ne Muanda Nsemi, *Makaba 118*. Kinshasa: Editions Mpolo Ngimbi, 1995.

Ne Muanda Nsemi, *Soba Ngindu*. Kinshasa: Editions Mpolo Ngimbi, 1995.

Ne Muanda Nsemi, *Mayala*, 5 vols. Kinshasa: Editions Mpolo Ngimbi, 1995–6.

Ne Muanda Nsemi, *Connaître Bundu dia Kongo*. Kinshasa: Editions Mpolo Ngimbi, 1996.

Ne Muanda Nsemi, *Le Problème Hutu et Tutsi*. Kinshasa: Editions Mpolo Ngimbi, 1996.

Ne Muanda Nsemi, *Les Africains sans papiers*. Kinshasa: Editions Mpolo Ngimbi, 1996.

Ne Muanda Nsemi, *Les Frontières coloniales*. Kinshasa: Editions Mpolo Ngimbi, 1996.

Newman, Jeremy R., *Ukamba Members Association*. Nairobi: Transafrica Publishers, 1974.

Ngugi wa Thiong'o, *Devil on the Cross*. Portsmouth: Heinemann, 1982.

Ngugi wa Thiong'o, *Matigari*. Portsmouth: Heinemann, 1987.

Niwagila, Wilson, 'From the catacomb to a self-governing church', thesis, University of Hamburg, 1988.

Nkashama, Pius Ngandu, *Eglises nouvelles et mouvements religieux*. Paris: L'Harmattan, 1990.

Nkashama, Pius Ngandu, *L'Eglise des Prophètes Africains*. Paris: L'Harmattan, 1991.

Nkwera, Fr F. V., *Kanisa, Serikali, Msikiti na Uchaguzi Mkuu Tanzania 1995*. Dar es Salaam: Marian Faith Healing Ministry, 1996.

Nolan, F., 'Christianity in Unyamwezi', PhD, University of Cambridge, 1976.

Nyamiti, Charles, *Christ as Our Ancestor*. Gweru: Mambo Press, 1984.

Nyamiti, Charles, 'Uganda martyrs: ancestors to all mankind', *African Christian Studies*, 2 (1986), 41–66.

Oliver, Roland, *The Missionary Factor in East Africa*. London: Longman, 1952.

Omari, C. K., 'Episcopacy: a sociological trend in the Lutheran Church in Tanzania', *Africa Theological Journal*, 16 (1987), 4–12.

Omari, C. K., 'The management of tribal and religious diversity in Tanzania', in G. V. Mmari and C. Legum (eds), *Mwalimu*, 23–31. London: James Currey, 1995.

Oosthuizen, G. C., *Post-Christianity in Africa*. London: C. Hurst, 1968.

Ossola, R., *1919–1969: The Consolata Missionaries in the Diocese of Iringa and at Tosamaganga*. Iringa: Diocese of Iringa, 1969.

Parratt, John, *Reinventing Christianity*. Grand Rapids: Eerdmans, 1995.

Paton, David (ed.), *Breaking Barriers, Nairobi 1975*. Grand Rapids: Eerdmans, 1976.

Peel, J. D. Y., 'The cultural work of Yoruba ethnogenesis', in E. Tonkin, M. Chapman and M. McDonald (eds), *History and Ethnicity*, 198–215. London: Routledge, 1989.

329

Bibliography

Peel, J. D. Y., 'For who hath despised the day of small things? Missionary narratives and historical anthropology', *Comparative Studies in Society and History*, 37 (1995), 581–607.

Peires, J. B., 'The central beliefs of the Xhosa cattle-killing', *Journal of African History*, 28 (1987), 43–63.

Pels, Peter, *Critical Matters: Interactions between Missionaries and Waluguru in Colonial Tanganyika*. Amsterdam: School of Social Research, 1993.

Perrin Jassy, Marie-France, *Basic Community in the African Church*. Maryknoll: Orbis, 1973.

Perrot, Marie-Dominique, 'The "cultural dimension of development": a new gadget', *EADI Journal*, special edition, forthcoming.

Petersen, Kirsten Holst (ed.), *Religion, Development, and African Identity*. Uppsala: Scandinavian Institute for African Studies, 1987.

Philp, H. R. A., *A New Day in Kenya*. London: World Dominion, 1936.

Pirouet, Louise, *Black Evangelists*. London: Collins, 1978.

Priest, D. T., *Doing Theology with the Maasai*. Pasadena, 1990.

Purritt, Paul, 'The Meru of Tanzania: a study of their social and political organisation', PhD, University of Illinois, 1970.

Ranger, T. O., *The African Churches in Tanzania* (Historical Association of Tanzania Paper, No. 5). Nairobi: East African Publishing House, 1969.

Ranger, T. O., 'The death of Chaminuka: spirit mediums, nationalism, and the guerilla war in Zimbabwe', *African Affairs*, 81 (1982), 349–69.

Ranger, T. O., 'Protestant missions in Africa: the dialectic of conversion in the American Methodist Episcopal Church in eastern Zimbabwe, 1900–1950', in T. D. Blakely *et al.* (eds), *Religion in Africa*, 275–313. London: James Currey, 1994.

Ranger, T. O., *Are We Not Also Men?* London: James Currey, 1995.

Ranger, T. O. and I. N. Kimambo (eds), *The Historical Study of African Religion*. London: Heinemann, 1972.

Ranger, T.O. and John Weller (eds), *Themes in the Christian History of Central Africa*. London: Heinemann, 1975.

Rasmussen, Ane Marie Bak, *A History of the Quaker Movement in Africa*. London: British Academic Press, 1995.

Rasmussen, Ane Marie Bak, *Modern African Spirituality*. London: British Academic Press, 1996.

Raum, Otto F., *Chaga Childhood*. Oxford: Oxford University Press, 1940.

Rawcliffe, D. H., *The Struggle for Kenya*. London: Victor Gollancz, 1954.

Ray, Benjamin C., *African Religions*. Englewood Cliffs: Prentice Hall, 1976.

Ray, Benjamin C., *Myth, Ritual and Kingship in Buganda*. New York: Oxford University Press, 1991.

Richardson, Kenneth, *Garden of Miracles*. London: Africa Inland Press, 1968.

Rigby, Peter, *Cattle and Kinship among the Gogo*. Ithaca: Cornell University Press, 1967.

Rigby, Peter, *Persistent Pastoralists*. London: Zed Books, 1985.

Robert, R. P. J. M., *Croyances et coutumes magico-religieuses de Wafipa païens*. Tabora: Tanganyika Mission Press, 1949.

Robins, Catherine, '*Tukutendereza*: a study of social change and withdrawal in the Balokole revival of Uganda', PhD, Columbia University, 1975.

Rosberg, Carl and John Nottingham, *The Myth of 'Mau Mau'*. New York: Praeger, 1966.

Rowe, John A., 'The purge of Christians at Mwanga's court', *Journal of African History*, 5 (1964), 55–72.

Rowe, John A., 'Revolution in Buganda, 1856–1900. Part One: The reign of Kabaka Mukabya Mutesa, 1856–1884', PhD, University of Wisconsin, 1966.

Rweyemamu, S. and T. Msambure, *The Catholic Church in Tanzania*. Peramiho: Benedictine Publications, 1989.

Sabean, David W., *Power in the Blood*. Cambridge: Cambridge University Press, 1984.

Sahlberg, Carl-Erik, *From Krapf to Rugambwa: A Church History of Tanzania*. Nairobi: Evangel Publishing House, 1986.

Sandford, G.R., *An Administrative and Political History of the Masai Reserve*. London: Waterlow, 1919.

Sandgren, David, *Christianity and the Kikuyu*. New York: Peter Lang, 1989.

Sangree, Walter, *Age, Prayer and Politics in Tiriki, Kenya*. London: Oxford University Press, 1966.

Sankan, S.S., *The Maasai*. Nairobi: East African Literature Bureau, nd.

Sanneh, Lamin, *West African Christianity*. Maryknoll: Orbis, 1983.

Sanneh, Lamin, *Translating the Message*. Maryknoll: Orbis, 1989.

Sanneh, Lamin, *Encountering the West*. Maryknoll: Orbis, 1993.

Bibliography

Schwartz, Nancy, 'World without end', PhD, Princeton University, 1989.

Scott, James, *Domination and the Arts of Resistance*. New Haven: Yale University Press, 1990.

Shaffer, R. T., *Road to Kilimanjaro*. Grand Rapids: Four Corners Press, 1985.

Shorter, Aylward, *African Christian Theology – Adaptation or Incarnation?* Maryknoll: Orbis, 1977.

Smythe, Kathleen R., 'Fipa childhood: White Father's missionaries and social change in Nkansi District, 1910–1980', PhD, University of Wisconsin, Madison, 1997.

Sorrenson, M. P. K., *Origins of European Settlement in Kenya*. Nairobi: Oxford University Press, 1968.

Spear, Thomas (ed.), *Evangelisch-Lutherisches Missionsblatt*. Madison: African Studies Program, 1995.

Spear, Thomas, *Mountain Farmers*. Oxford: James Currey, 1997.

Spear, Thomas and Richard Waller (eds), *Being Maasai*. London: James Currey, 1993.

Spencer, Paul, *The Maasai of Matapato*. Bloomington: Indiana University Press, 1988.

Ssemeju, Charles, 'Categories of Catholics', in J. M. Waliggo and M. D. Byabazaire (eds), *Rethinking the Mission of the Church in Africa*, 63–72. Kisubi: Marianum Press, 1989.

Stauffacher, G., *Faster Beats the Drum*. Kijobe: Kesho, 1977.

Stevens, Leslie, 'Religious change in a Haya village, Tanzania', *Journal of Religion in Africa*, 21 (1991), 2–25.

Stewart, James, *Dawn in the Dark Continent*. Edinburgh: Oliphant, Anderson and Ferrier, 1903.

Stock, Eugene, *The History of the Church Missionary Society*, 4 vols. London: Church Missionary Society, 1899–1916.

Strayer, Robert, *The Making of Mission Communities in East Africa*. London: Heinemann, 1978.

Sumbawanga Diocese, *History of Sumbawanga Diocese 1885–1985*. Peramiho: Peramiho Printing Press, 1985.

Sundkler, Bengt, *Bantu Prophets in South Africa*. London: Lutterworth, 1948.

Sundkler, Bengt, *Zulu Zion and Some Swazi Zionists*. Oxford: Oxford University Press, 1976.

Sundkler, Bengt, *Bara Bukoba*. London: Hurst, 1980.

Swantz, Lloyd W., 'The Zaramo of Tanzania: an ethnographic study', MA, Syracuse University, 1965.

Swantz, Lloyd W., 'The role of the medicine man among the Zaramo of Dar es Salaam', PhD, University of Dar es Salaam, 1974.

Swantz, Marja-Liisa, *Ritual and Symbol in Transitional Zaramo Society*. Uppsala: Almquist and Wikells, 1970.

Tambila, Anselm, 'A history of the Rukwa region (Tanzania) *c.*1870–1940: aspects of economic and social change from pre-colonial to colonial times', PhD, University of Hamburg, 1981.

Tanzania Gender Networking Programme, *Gender Profile of Tanzania*. Dar es Salaam: TGNP, 1993.

Taylor, John V., *The Growth of the Church in Buganda*. London: SCM, 1958.

Temu, A. J., *British Protestant Missions*. London: Longman, 1972.

The New Delhi Report: The Third Assembly of the WCC (London, 1962).

Tibemanya, John, 'Dark side of Masaka cult revealed', *New Vision*. 23 October 1991.

Tignor, Robert L., *The Colonial Transformation of Kenya*. Princeton: Princeton University Press, 1976.

Trimingham, J. S., *Islam in East Africa*. Oxford: Clarendon, 1964.

Tucker, A. R., *Eighteen Years in Uganda and East Africa*, 2 vols. London: Edward Arnold, 1908.

Turner, Harold W., *Religious Innovation in Africa*. Boston: G. K. Hall, 1979.

Twaddle, Michael, 'The emergence of politico-religious groupings in late-nineteenth century Uganda', *Journal of African History*, 29 (1988), 81–92.

Uganda Catholic Secretariat, *The Catholic Directory of Uganda*. Kisubi: Marianum Press, 1992.

Vail, Leroy and Landeg White, *Power and the Praise Poem*. Charlottesville: University of Virginia Press, 1991.

Vansina, Jan, *Paths in the Rainforests*. Madison: University of Wisconsin Press, 1990.

Van Zwanenberg, R. M. A. with Anne King, *An Economic History of Kenya and Uganda, 1800–1970*. London: Macmillan, 1975.

Von Sicard, S., *The Lutheran Church on the Coast of Tanzania, 1887–1914*. Uppsala: Almquist and Wiksells, 1970.

Von Sicard, S., 'The Lutheran Church on the coast of Tanzania, the war years, 1914–1920', *The African Theological Journal*, 15 (1986), 91–102.

Waliggo, John M., 'The Catholic Church in the Buddu Province of Buganda, 1879–1925', D Phil, Cambridge University, 1976.

331

Bibliography

Waliggo, John M., 'Ganda traditional religion and Catholicism in Buganda, 1948–1975', in Edward Fashole-Luke *et al.* (eds), *Christianity in Independent Africa*, 413–25. Bloomington: Indiana University Press, 1978.

Waliggo, John M., *et al.* (eds), *Inculturation: Its Meaning and Urgency*. Kampala: St Paul Publications, 1986.

Waller, Richard, '*Emutai*: crisis and response in Maasailand, 1883–1902', in D. Johnson and D. Anderson (eds), *The Ecology of Survival*, 94–101. Boulder: Westview, 1988.

Waller, Richard, 'Pastoral poverty in historical perspective', in D. Anderson and V. Broche-Due (eds), *The Poor are Not Us: Poverty and Pastoralism in East Africa*, James Currey, forthcoming.

Waller, Richard and Neal Sobania, 'Pastoralism in historical perspective', in E. Fratkin, K. A. Glavin and E. A. Roth (eds), *African Pastoralist Systems*, 48–55. Boulder: Westview, 1994.

Walls, Andrew, 'The Anabaptists of Africa: the challenge of the African Independent Churches', *Occasional Bulletin of Missionary Research*, 3 (April 1979), 48–51.

Wamba-dia-Wamba, Ernest, 'Democracy, multipartism and emancipative politics in Africa: the case of Zaire', *Africa Development*, 18 (1993), 95–118.

Wamba-dia-Wamba, Ernest, 'Africa in search of a new mode of politics', in U. Himmelstrand, K. Kinyanjui and E. Mburugu (eds), *African Perspectives on Development*, 249–61. New York: St Martins, 1994.

Ward, Kevin, 'The development of Protestant Christianity in Kenya', PhD, Cambridge University, 1976.

Ward, Kevin, '*Tukutendereza Yesu*: the Balokole revival movement in Uganda', in Z. Nthamburi (ed.), *From Mission to Church*, 113–44. Nairobi: Uzimba, 1991.

Warneck, John, 'Studies of African religions (book review)', *The International Review of Missions*, 2 (1913).

Warren, Max, *Revival*. London: SCM Press, 1954.

Weber, Max, *Economy and Society*, Vol. II, Guenther Roth and Claus Wittich (eds). Berkeley: University of California Press, 1978.

Welbourn, F. B., *East African Rebels*. London: SCM, 1961.

Welbourn, F. B., *East African Christian*. London: Oxford University Press, 1965.

Welbourn, F. B., *Religion and Politics in Uganda 1952–1962*. Nairobi: East African Publishing House, 1965.

Welbourn, F. B. and B. A. Ogot, *A Place to Feel at Home*. London: Oxford University Press, 1966.

Were, Gideon, 'Politics, religion and nationalism in Western Kenya' in B. A. Ogot (ed.), *Politics and Nationalism in Kenya*, 85–104. Nairobi: East African Publishing House, 1972.

Westervelt, J. H., *On Safari for God*. Kijobe: np, nd.

White, Louise, 'Vampire priests in Central Africa: African debates about labor and religion in colonial northern Zambia', *Comparative Studies in Society and History*, 35 (1993), 746–72.

White, Paul, *Doctor of Tanganyika*. Sydney: G. M. Dash, 1943.

Willis, Roy, 'Changes in mystical concepts and practices among Fipa', *Ethnology*, 7 (1968), 139–57.

Willis, Roy, *A State in the Making*. Bloomington: Indiana University Press, 1981.

Wilson, Godfrey and Monica, *The Analysis of Social Change*. Cambridge: Cambridge University Press, 1945.

Wilson, Monica, *Communal Rituals of the Nyakyusa*. London: Oxford University Press for International African Institute, 1959.

Wilson, Monica, *Religion and Transformation of Society*. Cambridge: Cambridge University Press, 1971.

Wilson, Monica, *For Men and Elders*. London: International African Institute, 1977.

Wilson, Stephen (ed.), *Saints and Their Cults*. Cambridge: Cambridge University Press, 1983.

Wipper, Audrey, *Rural Rebels*. Nairobi: Oxford University Press, 1977.

Wolf, Eric R. (ed.), *Religious Regimes and State Formation*. Albany: State University of New York Press, 1991.

World Bank, *World Development Report 1995*. Oxford: Oxford University Press, 1995.

Wright, Marcia, *German Missions in Tanganyika 1891–1941*. Oxford: Clarendon, 1971.

Wright, Marcia. *Strategies of Slaves and Women*. New York: Lilian Barber, 1993.

Wrigley, C. C., 'The Christian Revolution in Uganda', *Comparative Studies in Society and History*, 2 (1959), 33–48.

Index

Index

Kamba Brotherhood Church 229
Kamba language 172-3, 177
Kamba people 38, 167-70, 172-93; culture
  180, 184-5
Kambangwa 72
Kamenzya, Elijah 176, 182
Kangundo 172, 175-84, 188
Kapere, Mwene 131-2
Kapuufi, Mwene 131
Karema 130, 135
Kasaija, Lawrence 261-2
Kasimbazi, Pastor 298
Kassimir, Ron 277-8
Kassuku, Daniel 68-9
Kate 131-5, 141-2
Kate, Yoswa 13
Kathithymaa 187-8
Katigondo 266
Katoosa 260-1
Katumi 219
Kawule, George 263
Keekonyukie section 98
Kenya 1-2, 7, 10, 12, 15-19, 33, 85, 110,
  167, 185-6, 229, 232, 246; Emergency
  192
Kenya National Archives 183
Kerarapon 86
Kiambu 232
Kiatu, Mwene 131-2
Kibasila, Chief 70-2
Kibelengi, Marta 135-6
Kibira, Bishop Josiah 18, 298
Kibira, Mugo 238
Kibo 48, 50
Kibosho 159
Kibwezi 86
Kidugala 312
Kidunda 72
Kifipa language 130, 134
Kigamboni 77
Kijabe 87-8, 90, 93, 102-3
Kijabe Bible School 109
Kikongo language 217, 222, 226
Kikuyu Central Association 15, 105, 240
Kikuyu Independent Schools Association
  187
Kikuyu language 233, 241
Kikuyu people 2, 10, 14-15, 82n, 98, 104,
  108, 172, 186, 231-42
Kikuyuland 96-7, 102-3
Kilgoris 96-7
Kiliku, Simion 177, 181-2, 186
Kilimanjaro 37, 41-2, 52, 54-5, 80, 82n,
  86, 155, 198-9, 204, 206-7, 294, 298
Kilosa 311
Kimbangu, Simon 216-17, 219, 221-3, 226
Kimbanguism 32, 215
Kimosi 219
Kimpa, Vita 217, 219, 221
Kinampanda Teachers' College 77-8
Kingoyi 216

kinship 235
Kipalapala 159-60
kipande 98
Kirando 130-1, 133, 140, 142
Kirilo, Japhet 200
Kirore 15
Kirumbi, Andrea 77, 80
Kisangire 70, 72
Kisarawe 64-5, 68-9, 71-7
Kitonga 72
Kitui 188
Kivati, John 186-7, 190-2
Kivengere, Festo 298, 303
Kivukoni 279
Kiwanuka, Bishop 13
Klamroth, Rev. Martin 69, 71-2
Kniess, Rev. 70
Kolelo 70-1
Kolowa, Rev. Shebastian 202
Kondoa 154-5
Kongo Church 168, 213, 215-27
Kongo Kalunga 222
Kongo people *see* Bakongo people
Krelle, Rev. Hermann 70, 72-3, 75
Kulale, Chief 92, 95-6
Kulola, Moses 298-9, 301
Kupfernagel, Rev. J. 70
Kuyioni, Peter 104, 106
Kweka, Bishop 200-2
Kyoyo, J. M. 189-91
Kyumbe 66

'L. M.', Pastor 315-17
labour, migrant 310-15, 319, 322
Laikipia 88, 90-2, 96
Lakwena, Alice 250, 253
land 95
languages 5-6, 29-30, 69, 196, 214-15 *see
  also* name of language
Larsson, Brigitta 151-2
Lassit 92, 95, 97, 106
Latin America 250, 255-7
Lavigerie, Mgr 131
Lazaro, Bishop Emmanuel 298-9, 301
leaders *see mndewa*
Lechaptois, Mgr 135
Lefebvre, Archbishop 250
Legion of Mary 245, 251, 256-61
Leipzig Missionary Society 37, 41, 52-5,
  58, 60, 197, 309
Lema, A. A. 37
Lemenye, Justin 87, 113-14n
Life Ministry *see* Campus Crusade for
  Christ
Lingala people 215
living dead 45-6, 50-1, 54, 59
Livingstone, David 4
Loitokitok 92, 94-7
Lord's Resistance Army 250, 253
Lubeladio 219
Ludwig, Fr 155

Luganda language 12, 18
Lukela, Samuel Yesaya 78
Lukewille, Fr 141
Luo people 2, 15-16
Lupa 311
Lusinde, Job 157, 159
Lusinde, Petro 158
Luther, Martin 209-10
Lutheran Bible School 78
Lutheran Theological Seminary 78
Lutherans 5, 17, 37, 52-4, 58, 60, 63-4, 73, 78, 127, 168, 196-7, 200, 207-10, 296, 298, 315, 320-1
Luwero Triangle 269n
Lwanga, St Charles 272n
Luyia people 2, 16-17
Luyimo, Nichi 202

'M. K.' 319-20
Maa language 105
Maasai Association 108
Maasai Moves 88, 93-4
Maasai people 38, 83-126; Educated Maasai Group 108
Maasai Reserves 88-91, 96, 98
Maasailand 37, 83-126
Maass, Rev. Bernhard 65, 67
Machakos 171-4, 178, 183-4, 187-8, 190
Maddox, Gregory H. 307
Magambo, Bishop Serapio 258-9
Magessa, Adelphina 279
Magomeni 305
Maji Maji Rebellion 31, 37, 70-1, 74, 311-12
Makaba see Makongo
Makambako 315
Mako, Chief 96
Makoko 219
Makongo 215, 217-19, 225-6
Makumira 199-200, 202
Malecela, John 202-4
Malecela, Yohana 29, 158
Mama Yemo Hospital 216
Mamboya 151
Maneromango 63-82
Mangaya, Samuel 187-8
Mango, Alfayo Odongo 15-16
Marangu Teachers' College 75, 77-8
Marian Faith Healing Ministry 246-7, 275-95, 304, 309
Mariani ole Kitela 90
Marko, Rev. Yohana 69, 80, 302
marriage 104, 106, 138, 178-9, 185, 304, 313-14, 316, 319-22
martyrs 12, 19, 245-6, 250, 257, 259-62, 264
Marxism 214, 226
'Mary' 315, 320-2
Maryknolls 5
Masaka 13, 250
Masenha 158

Masikonte, Chief 89, 91-2, 95
Matovu, Br 298
Matsoua, André 219
Matsouaism 215
Matai Muanda 219
Mau Mau 15, 31, 170, 186-8
Mazengo 158, 161
Mbanza Kongo 218
Mbeyela, Joseph 312-14, 322
Mbiti, John 34, 41, 44-5
Mbitini 189
Mbole, Philip 181
Mbooni 172-3, 175-82, 184-5
Mbumba 222
Mbusu, Elijah 176-7, 181
Mwambo, Emmanual 303
McGregor (missionary) 86, 90
medical services 77, 241, 287
medicine men *see waganga*
Meeting of the Lord God of All Forces *see* Holy Quaternity Movement
Mengo Church Council 12
Mengwa 71-2
Meru Cooperative Union 199
Meru, Mount 197-8, 202-7
Meru people 168, 196-208
Meru Social Development Trust 199-201, 206
Mexico 256
Mfumbo, Vincent 261-2
mfumu (fig tree) 48
Mhalaka 72
Mihayo, Archbishop Mark 278
Mijikenda people 21n
Mika 68
Milingo, Archbishop Emmanuel 274n
Mill Hill Fathers 5
millenarianism 232, 239-40
Minimbegu (*akida*) 70-1
miracles 250
Misokia, Anton 73-4
Mission Coordination Committee 78
missionaries 4-9, 20, 25, 27-32, 53, 110-11, 127, 214, 229, 246, 307; Kenya 14-15, 170, 233, 241; Tanzania 35, 37, 43, 52-61, 63-80, 294, 311-12; Uganda 1, 12, 249, 251-8 *see also* name of organization
Mitaboni 184, 186-7
Mkapa, Ben 293
Mkubwa, Salehe 67
Mkumbalu, Yosia 73, 77-80
Mlahagwa 247
Mlundi, Fr Stephen 128, 150-66, 307
mmasya see diviners
mndewa (leaders) 66
Mnyampala, Mathais E. 156, 158, 161, 165n
Mobutu, Sese Seko 215, 224
Moi, Daniel Arap 19
Molonket ole Sempele 87-9, *88*, 92-3, 96, 100-1